INTEGRITY
AND MORAL RELATIVISM

PHILOSOPHY OF HISTORY AND CULTURE

VOLUME 10

TUTA SUB AEGIDE PALLAS · 1683 ·

INTEGRITY AND MORAL RELATIVISM

BY

SAMUEL FLEISCHACKER

E.J. BRILL
LEIDEN • NEW YORK • KÖLN
1992

The paper in this book meets the guidelines for permanence and durability of the Committee on Production Guidelines for Book Longevity of the Council on Library Resources.

Library of Congress Cataloging-in-Publication Data

Fleischacker, Samuel.
Integrity and moral relativism / by Samuel Fleischacker.
p. cm.—(Philosophy of history and culture, ISSN 0922-6001; v. 10)
Includes bibliographical references and index.
ISBN 9004095268
1. Ethical relativism. 2. Integrity. I. Title. II. Series.
BJ1031.F57 1992
171'.7—dc20 91-43930
CIP

ISSN 0922-6001
ISBN 90 04 09526 8

PRINTED IN THE NETHERLANDS

for my parents

ACKNOWLEDGEMENTS

I would like to thank Sarah Buss, Ernest Davies, and above all Karsten Harries for their detailed comments on drafts of this work. I have also learned a great deal from discussions with them, and with Daniel Klerman, Thomas Brockelman, and Laurance Rosenzweig. Ethan Zuckerman and Bernie Kluger have give me invaluable assistance in preparing the manuscript, as has my wife, Amy Reichert, who has also provided patience and moral support well beyond the point at which I deserved it. The preparation of the manuscript has been financially supported by a fund at Williams College, and the writing of it was supported, at an earlier stage, by a generous grant from the Charlotte W. Newcombe Foundation.

S.W.F.

Williamstown
October, 1991

CONTENTS

CHAPTER ONE

CONSEQUENCES OF RELATIVISM

Like jeans and health foods, ethical relativism has in recent years begun to shed its countercultural appearance and enter the establishment. While cognitive relativism withdraws increasingly to the fringes of the academic world, ethical relativism, fitted out with a new, less threatening image, is gaining wide respectability. Versions of this new relativism can be found in major articles by Philippa Foot and Gilbert Harman,[1] but it appears most lucidly and explicitly in the recent work of Bernard Williams. As set out in "The Truth in Relativism" and chapter nine of his new book, *Ethics and the Limits of Philosophy*,[2] this descendant of the Protagorean doctrine is meant to fit in unproblematically with those of our pretheoretical moral intuitions that incline us towards some kind of absolutism. Unlike the popular cultural relativism associated with the politics of the 1960s and with certain schools of anthropology, Williams' account allows us to chastise our neighbors, teach our children that ours is the best way to live, and criticize even those with different values from our own.

Let us first look at the traditional problems posed by popular relativism and then examine Williams' response to them. By "popular relativism" I refer to a position that holds, roughly, that ethical norms and claims are right or wrong only in relation to the standards of particular groups, and that there is nothing to choose between the standards of different groups. In the self-contradictory form that Williams once characterized, and refuted, as "vulgar relativism,"[3] the position goes on to say that the good is defined by what each group calls "good"; more mildly, the position may simply refuse meaning to any judgment a member of one group makes about the values of other societies.[4]

Although relativization of values to cultural groups is probably the most common form of popular relativism, I want to begin by looking at a position yet more extreme than this. "Egoistic relativism," as I shall provisionally call it, holds that what is good for me is what *I* feel, or have been brought up to think, is good. The egoistic relativist goes on to demand that I neither make nor act

---

1 Philippa Foot, "Are Moral Considerations Overriding?" and (especially) "Morality as a System of Hypothetical Imperatives," in (Foot, 1978). Gilbert Harman, "Moral Relativism Defended," *Philosophical Review* 84, re-printed in (Meiland & Krausz, 1982).

2 "The Truth in Relativism," in (Williams, 1981), and (Williams, 1985).

3 (Williams, 1972), chapter 3.

4 My actions may reveal an implicit judgment that I do not state explicitly, of which I may not even be fully aware. Thus the extreme relativist demands not only that I avoid condemning or praising other people in words, but that I carefully scrutinize my behavior to make sure I am not treating anyone with a warmth or coldness arising from a specifically moral response to that person's actions or beliefs.

on judgments on the value of anyone's behavior other than my own, and indeed may even refuse to allow me to evaluate my own actions and possibilities for action in terms of anything except my desires and aversions. As a claim about what I *have reason* to do, this position is even more difficult to make sense of than Williams' "vulgar relativism"; as an attempt to place an absolute value on every person's refraining from trying to influence any other person's actions, it represents an implausible, but widespread, interpretation of the virtue our culture calls "tolerance."

I do not know whether any major philosopher has ever held quite this position, but its general popularity is unquestionable. Traces of it can perhaps be found in Nietzsche and the post-war Sartre, in Kierkegaard's and Wittgenstein's quietism, in the noncognitivism of Ayer and Stevenson, and in the voluntarism of such contemporary writers as Philippa Foot and Harry Frankfurt,[5] but none of these thinkers deserves to be saddled with its extreme indifference to the social component of ethics. On the other hand, the most fundamental problem with this position has nothing to do with its asocial tendencies, and resurfaces again and again in its more sophisticated kin. This problem concerns the fact that the agent cannot regard any values entirely dependent on her[6] emotions and desires as guides for her actions, hence *as* values at all. When I am told that my desires determine what I consider good and bad, important and unimportant, I respond that my desires continually change, that I feel I have some control over those changes, and that when deliberating over action I therefore want to consider not just what possible actions might be better than other actions *given* my desires, but what changes in my desires might be better than other changes. If my desires themselves determine what is better and worse for me, however, it makes no sense to speak of changing my desires for the better. But in that case whatever whimsical and arbitrary events lead me to change my desires also lead me to change my values, and I can never be sure that my current values are any guide to what I will consider good in the future. Nor will an appeal to deeply-seated or long-term desires help much here,[7] since it is up to me what I desire to count as my desires (else the motivation behind the position we are considering falls away), and I can just as well opt at any moment to identify with my short-term desires as with my long-term ones. Values thus drop out as an independent term in the deliberative process.

---

[5] See (Frankfurt, 1982), and Foot, *op. cit.*

[6] I shall be alternating, chapter by chapter, between using male and female impersonal pronouns. I am not entirely happy about this as a stylistic device, but then I am torn between feeling that the whole issue of "non-sexist language" is primarily an easy distraction from the important problems of women in today's society and being aware that ignoring the issue, now that it has been raised, does make half one's audience feel excluded. (I owe the suggestion of this particular compromise to Liz Shanks, Haverford Class of 1989.)

[7] But see chapter three, where "interests"–a socially constituted and in part cognitive version of my long-term desires–will indeed help guide my decisions.

In addition, and relatedly, even if we could draw a significant distinction between, say, will and mere desire, as the voluntarist seems to do, those who root values in what we happen to want put far too much trust in our ability to take what we happen to want seriously. Among the things we often and perhaps generally happen to want is to feel that we are doing something important. Values are supposed to be guides to what we consider important, guides that prevent all options for choice from blurring into that equivalence of pointlessness in which even freedom would be empty, since there would be no reason to prefer our free choice—or what our free choice would direct us to—over a random toss of a coin or someone else's choices for us. We want our desires to be guided *by* values, to be directed to what, if anything, is actually important; otherwise we consider them mere whims. Deciding to act on them then seems itself a mere whim, as does deciding not to act on them, or deciding to change them. Sabina Lovibond describes this situation excellently:

> But there is a difficulty with [the] rehabilitation of [volition,] in so far as it involves thinking of the latter as logically isolated from that part of our mental life which is regulated by external reality. The difficulty is that 'subjective' dispositions, thus represented, are liable to flag when too much attention is fixed upon them. The part they are expected to play is embarrassingly naïve—as if we were asked to relive the experience of some early childhood birthday party, where we were expected to gurgle enthusiastically over our presents, but under the benign scrutiny of a band of adult spectators, were awkwardly unable to mount the required show of glee (for even a child can grasp the fact that he is only a child, and that although the scrutiny of the adults is benign, there is also condescension in it)...If value is constituted by our desires, simply as such, ...what difference does it make...what we choose? And what is to prevent us from lapsing into an inert condition in which no choice seems worth making?[8]

Any conception of ethics that fails to give us satisfactory reasons for why we should want one thing rather than another, and in particular the conception we have hitherto been describing as egoistic relativism, we will henceforth call, with a polemical eye on its enervating effect on our will, "ethics on a whim."

Let us now look at a milder version of this extreme relativism: consider the position of one who, without making any claims about the ground of value or the status of desire, merely refuses to see any role for argument or discussion in ethics. She attempts never to "impose her values on others," and she regards any attempt at suasion as imposition. Call this position "quietism." What undermines it is instructive, and can provide a fruitful starting-point for our examination of how relativism tends to misconstrue the ethics of social interaction. It will, in the first place, be virtually impossible for the quietist to participate in political projects or to raise children. (Why impose her values on them more than on anyone else? And how can she resist or block the

---

8 (Lovibond, 1983), pp. 8-9.

attempts of others—her friends, her spouse, her neighbors—to educate them in values contrary to her own?) Friendship will be difficult, if only in that she will have trouble succoring people who turn to her for support in emotional crises, since she will be unable to give them any kind of advice. In addition, whenever people around her want to do something of which she strongly disapproves, she will have to simply withdraw. Often, this will be a matter of only minor and temporary inconvenience, but sometimes people close to her may embark on a project she dislikes that promises to take up a large chunk of their lives (starting a movement to keep the neighborhood segregated, marrying a Nazi, running a porn shop, joining a fundamentalist church), thereby forcing her to withdraw from association with them in almost all respects and permanently. And the mere constant possibility that she will need to withdraw will make close relationships, including marriage, virtually impossible.

Now even the quietist may well value social contacts, both for themselves and for the things that can only be brought about through them. The very project of getting people, including her own children, to adopt individualistic and quietistic attitudes requires educational and political support from a larger society.[9] Of course, as a consistent quietist, she may not have such a project, but she will want at least to limit her own dependence on force in the pursuit of her needs and desires. To do that, she will have to find some non-coercive way of preventing people from continually blocking the fulfillment of her projects, and she will have to ensure that her mental health does not deteriorate to the point at which she cannot control her own actions. But argument and persuasion are the primary alternatives to coercion, while a certain amount of friendship and respect from others is usually essential to sanity. Hence the mere attempt to pursue one's own values will almost inevitably require a degree of social interaction that is incompatible with quietism.

Writers like Foot and Hare combine their emotivism with a call for a band of "volunteers...to fight for liberty and justice and against inhumanity and oppression."[10] This, however, immediately raises a problem which none of them, as far as I know, has ever dealt with adequately: Intrinsic to a group's sharing values at all are practices that exclude potential members from the group and that reject or sanction actual members who fail to live up to its norms. Why this is so we shall see in detail shortly. But if there is no rationale explaining, at least *to* the members of the group, why just these virtues are required to

[9] Cf. Margaret Mead, on trying to duplicate what she took to be the Samoan way of life: "The individual American parents, who believe in a practice like the Samoan, and permit their children to see adult human bodies and gain a wider experience of the functioning of the human body than is commonly permitted in our civilization, are building upon sand. For the child, as soon as it leaves the protecting circle of its home, is blocked by an attitude which regards such experience in children as ugly and unnatural. As likely as not, the attempt of the individual parents will have done the child more harm than good, for the necessary supporting social attitude is lacking." ([Mead, 1943], p.177).

[10] Foot, "Morality as a System...," p. 167. On Hare, see (Lovibond, 1983), pp.4-5.

belong in good standing, and why just these members fall short, the group will not be able to remain a group of volunteers, a group held together by a commitment to values rather than by force. On the other hand, the possibility of such a rationale would violate the emotivist grounds on which voluntarism is based.

This dilemma comes out sharply in Lovibond's discussion of voluntarism:

> ...Hare thinks that we can deal with ["fanatics"] by challenging them to *try* to put their principles into practice in their own lives. The "sting" attaching to this challenge is that even if, as Hare maintains, the individual is logically free to want *anything*...still he will not always be free to act upon his chosen principles, because if they are too pernicious, the rest of "us" will prevent him. So there is, after all, a practical limit to the individualism of Hare's moral world—a limit imposed by the militant commitment of ordinary people to their own intersubjective, or consensual, morality.[11]

On reading this, we want to ask Hare what gives us "ordinary people"—that "rest of us" who possess desires to behave decently—the right to impose a way of living on people who do not at any level want to live that way, to behave toward the so-called "delinquents" or "fanatics" in a way *we ourselves regard as indecent*. What gives us the right in our own eyes, let alone in theirs?—although it is of course because we define our own rights in terms of what we can get others to accept that the question even arises.

But now we might ask whether we need condemnatory practices at all. The voluntarist may well not lament the passing of possibilities of condemnation, since the motivation behind her position may well be to provide grounds for a sweeping program of toleration. However, condemnation, intimately intertwined with praise, advice, and ethical dialogue, turns out to be essential to the maintenance of any social commitment to values. In "Freedom and Resentment," PF Strawson includes condemnatory practices as primary elements of what he calls the "reactive attitudes," of which he says, "being involved in inter-personal relationships as we normally understand them precisely is being exposed to the range of reactive attitudes and feelings." Reactive attitudes are not merely a *technique* for preserving ourselves our interpersonal relationships; they are part of what it *is* to want and to maintain human company: "our practices do not merely exploit our natures, they express them."[12]

In terms of our "band of volunteers," we can deepen this account of what we might call the phenomenology of our moral sentiments. A group devoted to a particular project must exclude and censure some people out of more than

11 (Lovibond, 1983), pp.4-5, 101-2.

12 "Freedom and Resentment," in (Strawson, 1974), pp. 11, 25.

the psychological needs of its members.[13] For one thing, some members and potential members may threaten to destroy the group effort—either by harming other members, physically or psychologically, or by performing their role so misguidedly or lackadaisacally as to nullify others' accomplishments, or by behaving so repellently in general as to keep potential members away from the group and drive current members out of it. Then, members need a standard for what constitutes good membership in the group—a representation of how to live according to the group's values or how to contribute to its goal—and such standards frequently require pointing to specific acts of specific people as exemplars. "*That's* what you're supposed to do! *That's* what you're not supposed to do!" will usually clarify a standard more accurately than any set of general rules. Finally, much as we do not like to think about this fact, we just do not have "world enough and time" to care for all the other people around us who would like our attention.[14] There are too many people and projects in the world for any individual to give them all as much love or interest or effort as they demand. This does not mean that each of us is besieged by thousands of people wanting our personal love or friendship, but most people must make selections even here, and we all face large groups—churches, schools, political movements, cultural centers, etc.—each of which would like us to devote much or all of our energies in its cause. The members of the band of volunteers, like everyone else, must make use of certain condemnatory reactive attitudes, both towards outsiders and towards each other, in order to clear their way for the people and projects to which they do want to devote themselves, and to create a hierarchy of values and interests that will allow them to give as many of the others as possible a decent hearing. Williams details the relevant attitudes wonderfully, as "dislike, resentment or contempt, or such minor revelations of the ethical life as the sense that someone is creepy," and points out, correctly and importantly, that if we try to drive these attitudes out because we cannot justify them morally, they will only withdraw "into a grumbling retreat, planning impersonation and revenge."[15]

---

[13] On the two senses in which group projects require standards of excellence, compare Alasdair MacIntyre: "...consider what would be involved...in founding a community to achieve a common project, to bring about some good recognised as their shared good by all those engaging in the project. As modern examples of such a project we might consider the founding and carrying forward of a school, a hospital or an art gallery; in the ancient world the characteristic examples would have been those of a religious cult or of an expedition or of a city. Those who participated in such a project would need to develop two quite different types of evaluative practice. On the one hand they would need to value–to praise as excellences–those qualities of mind and character which would contribute to the realisation of their common good or goods....They would also need however to identify certain types of action as the doing or the production of harm of such an order that they destroy the bonds of community in such a way as to render the doing or achieving of good impossible in some respect or at least for some time. Examples of such offences would characteristically be the taking of innocent life, theft and perjury and betrayal." (MacIntyre, 1981), pp.141-2.

[14] "Jealousy...is founded on our fear that there will not be enough time, indeed that there is more love than can be put into time." (Bloom, 1973a), p.88.

[15] (Williams, 1985), p.38.

But if we can give no moral reason, no rationale, for our application of the reactive attitudes, our groups will fall apart. Without a known, public standard of condemnation, which members can assent to, measure themselves by, and administer jointly, either the group will give up on condemnation altogether and allow its efforts to fall into chaos, or a fairly small[16] subset of its members will come to pass critical judgment unilaterally, establishing a rule by force that could itself destroy the group physically or pervert its ends, and will in any case end the voluntarism that both gives the group its appeal and defines it as an expression of a commitment to values. As Strawson says about the recommendation that we take a purely pragmatic ("objective") attitude towards offenders against the principles of our society, "...it would be hard to make *this* division in our natures. If to all offenders, then to all mankind. Moreover, to whom could this recommendation be, in any real sense, addressed? Only to the powerful, the authorities. So abysses seem to open."[17]

Can we now get our ethics away from individual desires altogether, by turning to cultural relativism? As it happens, rooting our ethical claims in cultural norms merely defers the conflict with the phenomenology of our ordinary ethical lives that we have already noted in quietism and voluntarism. Converting to other groups comes to play the role of changing desires or violating group standards in threatening our ability to take our cultural norms seriously. Once we have no grounds on which to judge the differing practices of members of other groups, we are inclined to doubt the value of our own practices. If my own society condemns action x, while another group performs x with every sign of pleasure and approval, I will want to ask, "if they can do it, why can't I?"[18] Of course, I may sometimes be told that doing x in their context is quite different from doing x around here (as polygamy in a society that accepts it openly is quite different from marrying two people who have grown up expecting to marry monogamously), but often this is not the case, and even if it is I may just restate my question as, "why may I not go there and do x, or duplicate their context, as best I can, over here?" The force of these questions is not so much that I actually want to do x as that I want to be able to give myself reasons for why I don't go over to the other group whenever I feel like it. I know, after all, of cases of ethically acceptable conversion, even partial conversion—why may I not "convert" to another society whenever I find one

16 Necessarily small, else the problems of maintaining energy, discipline, and shared standards will simply reappear in the subset.

17 Strawson, p.21.

18 I may also feel, upon seeing another group disapprove of my society's action y, "if they don't like it, what business do I have accepting it?" This seems to happen less often, but consider, for instance, the tendency of Western vegetarian groups to appeal to Hindu or Buddhist practices as evidence that they are not advocating "unnatural" human behavior (the same would go, I suppose, for homosexual appeals to the practices of ancient Greece, or other societies in which homosexuality was an accepted part of life). The point, in any case, is general: we tend to assume human universality at least insofar as we seek outside limits to what we should and should not do.

of my neighborhood's standards getting in my way? We can try to set limits to the justifiability of such piecemeal and temporary conversions, but those limits will again depend on our own cultural norms, and the would-be (piecemeal) convert can always claim to be simply following the milder strictures on conversion of her new group. And if I may make temporary and piecemeal conversions, or if I may convert completely to another way of life for no reason whatsoever, it seems hard to find a sense in which I am really attached to my own ethical standards. They seem more like accidental, conditioned responses, commitment to which I can maintain or drop on a whim.

Tied to this problem is, again, a difficulty in sharing my values with my children, and with others near and dear to me. If I have no confidence in my own grip on my ethical beliefs, I may well feel I have little basis on which to tell my children what to consider good and bad, right and wrong. Revealing my unease about this is likely to mar my child-rearing considerably, while pretending confidence seems hypocritical. Then, attempts to raise children on several religions at once have tended to produce confused children, and raising them on a smorgasbord of ethical systems is likely to have the same effect. Of course, ethical systems may not resemble religions in this respect, and even if they do, mental health may be simply one of the provincial fetishes I should not impose on my children... But in fact raising healthy and decent children is probably one of the more important goals of my own life, and I will face a real conflict here between my relativism and the values to which it is meant to apply.

Moving beyond my children and those close to me, I also want some grip on the values of my neighbors in order to rebuke, advise, and discuss ethical matters with them. It would seem that by appealing to shared cultural norms I should have this grip, but sharing ethical views remains difficult when my partner in conversation can always opt out by claiming that she has recently or intends shortly to convert (piecemeal or wholesale) to the standards of another group. I think I am justifiably accusing a friend of callousness by eating meat only to discover that she has left the Hindu faith in which we both were raised to sign up on a whaling ship, and I feel my grounds for rebuking her have been cut out from under me.

Finally, I may well want to be able to judge societies different from my own in certain situations. Sometimes I may want to condemn, and even encourage interference with, a practice I think people should never perform whatever their society thinks; institutionalized torture and racial degradation come to mind. Sometimes the fact that some other people has a particularly wonderful practice may be a reason I want to appeal to in encouraging my own society to adopt that practice. Here I *need* the possibility that we can "go over" to other forms of life, that people's culturally induced values can slip away—theirs in the first case, ours in the second—although that possibility challenges the trustworthiness of values with no basis other than cultural inducement.

Williams' position is not supposed to have any of these threatening implications. Beginning from a strongly "absolutist" view of knowledge in general, Williams sets out several non-relativist conditions for there to be any meaningful relativism at all. The most important of these is that we have "a form of thought not relativized to our own [system of belief]...for thinking about other [systems] which may be of concern to us, and to express those concerns," that there be a set of agreed beliefs, descriptions, etc. which can at least determine the "locus of exclusivity" between two groups.[19] Then he draws two distinctions: between real and unreal options for an individual in a given group, and between real and notional confrontations between groups. A system S_2 is a real option for an adherent of S_1 if she can adopt S_2 without losing her "hold on reality," or "engaging in extensive self-deception, falling into paranoia, and such things," and if she could also live through and later acknowledge her transition to S_2 "sanely," in the light of "as much rationality as is available on a given type of issue."[20] A "real confrontation" between any systems S_1 and S_2 is one in which "there is [a person or] group for whom each of S_1 and S_2 is a real option," and in any real confrontation we use a "vocabulary of appraisal—'true-false,' 'right-wrong,' 'acceptable-unacceptable,' etc." to help us decide which system we will adopt or stick with and why.[21] Now, for "*some* types of S_1" relativism arises whenever two Ss are only in notional confrontation. "There is so little to [the] use [of terms like 'true,' 'right,' etc. in these cases,] so little of what gives content to the appraisals in the context of real confrontation, that we can say that for a reflective person the question of appraisal does not genuinely arise...."[22] We can recognize that systems in purely notional confrontation with us are "related to our concerns too distantly for our judgments to have any grip on them."[23] In "The Truth in Relativism," Williams claims that this relativism in fact applies to everything about distant ethical outlooks; in "Relativism and Reflection," he allows us to make some significant judgments about particular ethical concepts "even when the outlook of the society in which they lived is not in real confrontation with ours"[24] but says that we cannot make such judgments about the outlook as a whole.

Williams tries, with these ideas, to save most of the phenomena of ordinary moral discourse in the face of relativism. In the first place, he insists that we can intelligibly and legitimately continue to make ethical evaluations of others. Having ethical dispositions, he says, "involve[s] a disposition to assess others"; ethical qualities and views indeed "structure one's reactions to others."[25] We can even be said to "*have reason* to encourage people to have [such]

---

19 "Truth in Relativism," (Williams, 1981), p.142, 135, 137.

20 *ibid*, p.139.

21 *ibid*, pp. 138, 141.

22 *ibid*, p.141.

23 *ibid*, p.142.

24 (Williams, 1985), p.162.

25 *ibid*, p.37.

dispositions—e.g. in virtue of possessing them ourselves."[26] On the other hand, we can *use* reason as part of our encouragement and rebuke only when talking to people who at some level share our values, since the only reasons a person has for action are "internal reasons"—reasons belonging to or easily derived from her own desires and projects.[27] In general we will therefore probably want to limit our attempts to guide others in their actions to those cases in which we can appeal to what Williams now calls an "appropriate deliberative projection"[28] of the other person's internal reasons. But this does not constitute a serious restriction on our ethical discourse, since "the aim of such discourse is not to deal with someone who probably will not listen to it, but to reassure, strengthen and give insight to those who will."[29]

In raising our children, moreover, we need not be bound by the limitations of rational argument. Whether or not we can rationally demonstrate the value of our practices, "it is a mark of our having ethical values that we aim to reproduce them." Hence, "to our immediate successors, our children at least, we have reason to try to transmit more" than the mere practices surrounding rational deliberation itself.[30] Williams also hints that we can supplement rational argument in maintaining our values even among the adults in our societies. We need to ground our practices in "confidence," he says, a social and psychological phenomenon bolstered by certain "kinds of institutions, upbringing and public discourse"—and featuring rational argument, but only insofar as it can affect social states, which, as Williams himself shows,[31] is not all that far. Again, when discussing "blame," Williams describes non-rational "practices of encouragement and discouragement, acceptance and rejection, which work on desire and character," as "forms of persuasion" that one should "distinguish in spirit from force and constraint."[32]

Moving now beyond the bounds of our own ethical community, Williams again finds that relativism need no longer pose dangers for us. Outside of our community, we meet other ways of life that may or may not be real options for us. But if they are real options for us, there exists, by definition, some language of appraisal by which we can give reasons showing why we prefer not to go over to them, while if they are not real options for us, we need not worry about evaluating them, since they cannot possibly threaten our attachment to our own way of life. In addition, Williams tells us specifically that we cannot go over to any society that has a lower level of reflective consciousness than we (in the West) have. Whether this is because less

---

26 "Internal and External Reasons," (Williams, 1981), p.113
27 *ibid*, pp.104-5
28 Lecture at Yale University, Spring, 1986
29 (Williams, 1985), p.26
30 (Williams, 1985), p.173. See also "Internal and External Reasons," p.113.
31 "Internal and External...," *passim*, (Williams, 1985), chapter 2, Postscript, and pp.167-9
32 (Williams, 1985), p.194

reflective societies are not a real option for us, or because "to try to suppress reflection...can lead to nothing but disaster,"[33] he does not make quite clear, but in any case we can rule out our adopting any of the traditional ways of life that pose the most dramatic contrasts to the Western set of values. We are thus left to evaluate only the relatively minor differences we may have with our fellow (secular) Westerners (over sexual mores, perhaps, or the relative value of competition and cooperation in the marketplace), with whom we already share the vast majority of our ethical language in any case.

With this account of what I can say to others on ethical matters, it seems I should not lack reasons to prevent my own values from just "slipping away" from me. I know, after all, 1) that whatever value system I hold, it must fit into some social group, structuring my reactions to others and their reactions to me, 2) that it does not matter if my particular values have been handed down to me in not entirely rational ways, since it is impossible for anyone to pass down values by rational argument alone, while it is natural, and indeed essential to having values, for each generation to try to pass them down to the next, 3) that the answer to "if they can do it, why can't I?" is, in most problematic cases, that their way of life is not a real option for me, and 4) that whatever value system I come to hold, it must make room for the high level of reflection I have when I begin asking questions about values in the first place. Points 1 and 2 guide me toward whatever ethical system I have been raised in; points 3 and 4 guide me towards a North American or Western European way of life in particular.

Thus Williams has a program for combining the attractive notion of toleration for what lies beyond your ken, which he rightly sees as the heart of "vulgar relativism," with a hierarchical set of evaluative judgments and responses to sceptical questions that replaces objectivism in giving us confidence in our own ethical standards. If these judgments and responses satisfactorily met our intuitions about ethics, I would have little to do in this book. As it is, I think he lets himself off the challenge of relativism too easily.

To begin with, the notion that we may comfortably propagate our values even where we fail of rational argument for them is highly suspect. Ordinarily, and not just under the influence of Kant,[34] we regard alternatives to rational discussion as coercive to some degree or other, while we feel justified in using coercive means only against someone whom we believe is not currently listening to rational argument, but whom, if she *would* listen,we could persuade of the wrongness of her acts. Thus we punish the burglar forcefully, while believing that we can give her justifications for protecting property. We yell at or spank importunate children, believing that they will someday understand

---

33 *ibid*, p.168

34 According to Williams it is "morality," the Kantian system which "we would be better off without," that "leaves us, as the only contrast to rational blame, forms of persuasion it refuses to distinguish in spirit from force and constraint." (Williams, 1985), pp. 174 and 194

the value of decorum. When we discover the poverty of our reasons for a value, we tend to become less inclined to want to impose it on others. Imposing values we cannot justify seems an infringement on another person's, or another society's, right to choose for her—or itself. As for Williams' hints that we ought to make room for "forms of persuasion" between argument and coercion, we should remember that we condemn (with reason, if ethical judgments ever have reason) exhortative speeches that, because they cannot appeal to decent argument, try to bypass our critical faculties and rouse us to their cause by playing on our emotions—as "dangerous propaganda," when delivered by journalists and powerful political figures, or "empty rhetoric," when delivered by parsons and powerless political figures. We do not want to make room for persuasion independent of argument, because we do not want to be swayed at all where we cannot thoughtfully resist such suasion.

Williams tries to stop the argument that we should cease to pass our values on to our children by saying that reproducing one's values is part of having them at all, that it is "natural," and that it is part of the conception of "well-being," which is something we wish for our children. That reproducing one's values is part of having them seems just untrue. I may believe that my life has not been particularly good, or that everyone should choose for herself, and as a consequence not value passing my way of life on to others. Perhaps I will then want to pass on only my tolerance or quietism itself, although I need not want even that, and I certainly will not want to pass on any other specific values. Yet, in that I make my own choices according to them, they remain no less values for me. Indeed, we here in the West do tend to believe that traditionalism causes dangerous prejudices and foolish superstitions to persist from generation to generation, and therefore value having our children taught to question and reject some of the very things we teach them. The general rule that "we have reason to encourage people to have [our] dispositions...in virtue of possessing them ourselves" has important exceptions. And since neither it nor any other general principle can tell us where these exceptions lie, we always have reason to doubt its application to any one of our specific values.

That passing on values is "natural," on the other hand, does not seem a sufficient reason for its being right. Williams says that "the formation of ethical dispositions is a natural process in human beings,"[35] and implies, later in the same passage, that raising one's children to these dispositions is a similarly natural process. Here, as when he looks forward to a possible naturalistic account of human well-being,[36] and, especially, when he speaks of the "reproduction" of values, Williams echoes JL Mackie, who held that values,

[35] "[E]ven if there have been contented hierarchies [in the past], any charm they have for us is going to rest on their having been innocent and not having understood their own nature. This cannot be recreated, since measures would have to be taken to stop people raising questions that are, by now, there to be raised." (Williams, 1985), p.164.

[36] *ibid*, pp.152-5.

like genes and organisms, were biological facts that reproduced themselves in an evolutionary pattern.[37] But these natural facts, if such they are, do not provide a reason why we *should* do anything. We are not obliged to follow any path evolution has taken.

That our ethical values constitute part of what we mean by "happiness" or "well-being" seems true to some extent, yet still not sufficient for passing them on. For one thing, we do not know that what makes us happy will make our children happy; for another, we may well value something like decency, religious devotion, or simply "radically free choice" (whatever we may think that is) above happiness. Before Williams' naturalism can get a grip on us, we would have to fix a definition for "well-being," and explain why we should value it.

Turning now to the issue of ethical discourse within and without our community, it is not clear that Williams has in fact satisfactorily supplied a basis for encouragement, rebuke, and advice. Let us follow a possible ethical conversation some distance. Suppose that I am talking to Jones, who I have long known to share the values of my own ethical community. He tells me, however, that he has just demoted a woman at his firm because he believes she belongs in the kitchen. Because I value women's participation in the public world, because I have an interest in establishing that value in our shared community, and because I am concerned for him (which entails my being concerned for his self-respect, his decency, the possibility of my remaining friends with him, and the possibility of his retaining other friendships, especially with women), I try to rebuke him. I therefore draw out a deliberative projection of his interests—of, say, his long-standing commitment to equal opportunity for all members of our society—that I have every reason to consider appropriate. He responds that he has just converted to an extremely fundamentalist brand of Islam, and now redefines his commitments in its light. I am thus wrong to assume that I have correctly projected his interests.

What should my response be?

1) Bypassing the issue of whether such a conversion is a real option for him, or assuming that it is, I can note that a conversion to fundamentalist Islam properly involves going to live in a fundamentalist Islamic community. If he did move into a community of this kind, I would have nothing more to say, since my vocabulary of appraisal loses its grip on that way of life as a whole. As it is, I question his sincerity. He responds by pointing out that just as there can be American Jews and Hindus, there can be American Muslims. I must admit the truth of this, but then ask what other Muslim practices he follows. He says, "None," but remarks that that merely makes him a "bad" or "lazy" Muslim, of which there are many. I ask what ceremony of conversion he has gone through, what steps he has taken to join the community. He tells me that

---

[37] *ibid*, pp. 48, 171.

he does not believe in ceremonies, but has converted in his heart, "in the eyes of God." In fact, he is a fundamentalist Muslim primarily, or solely, with regard to his views on women. Is that so strange? he asks. Do you not know many other members of religious communities who adhere only very selectively to the beliefs and practices of their religion? After all, external practices and rituals are not the heart of any religion, and he is, if not a typical adherent of this religion, at least someone who is trying to live in what he considers its spirit (which he may identify with its views on women). In at least some respects, another community has persuaded him to adopt its values. Such things have been known to happen to sincere and decent people. Jones can even claim that he has become a Muslim "at heart" for this particular case alone (to *this* case, he wants to say, the Muslim view applies); after demoting this woman, he may intend to revert to his old beliefs and practices. Regrets over conversion, even hasty regret and hasty re-conversion, have also been known to happen to sincere and decent people.

I stress in this example that at each step Jones takes to insulate his particular "change" from my rebuke, he can appeal to cases of rational and decent people doing what look like very similar things. When we bring up any of the usual criteria by which we judge something as a religious conversion—observance of certain rituals, undergoing a conversion ceremony, joining a community, accepting a whole set of beliefs, making a permanent rather than a transitory commitment—Jones can point out that other members of the group to which he is converting, as well as other people whom we could comfortably recognize as converts, violate each of these conditions, that we ourselves like to say that ethical, and particularly religious, beliefs are ultimately an "internal" matter rather than a matter of external trappings. We may feel frustrated with these arguments because we feel that Jones, unlike the people he cites as models, is being facetious, insincere in his dismissal of our criteria in the name of something "internal," but we have at this point no account of what facetiousness and insincerity *are*, much less grounds on which to condemn them. As long as we remain committed (as pretty much all Western ethical thinkers have been since Kant), to the view that for human beings to have an ethics they must view their actions and the values according to which they plan them as ultimately the responsibility of a self, we are stuck when we come to someone like Jones: we can neither deny his right to appeal to an "internal" standard beyond social conventions nor tell him what that standard ought to consist in. Of course, we can claim that Jones has simply lost his grip on the reality of what constitutes "conversion" and "sincerity," but, in the first place, the criteria for the use of those terms are themselves heavily laden with our values and if Jones wants, even temporarily, to opt out of those values, he can deny their application to him, and, in the second place, he can admit he is acting in "bad faith" but say, "What of it? What is so bad about bad faith?" If we cannot answer that, we can never block this mode of evading rebuke. The value of or need for good faith, as either a part or a consequence of an account of the self, is thus crucial for an appropriate deliberative projection, and we will return to it once we look at the other possible response to Jones' "conversion."

2) I can, either immediately or after going through the above dialogue, deny that conversion to Islam represents a real option for Jones. Even if he is much more sincere than I have portrayed him so far, Jones may have to engage in "extensive self-deception" or lose his "hold on reality" to convert to fundamentalist Islam. This approach raises serious difficulties, however, since surely not every actual conversion has such dire consequences. Like many actual converts, Jones can simply deny the gravity of self-deception or claim that what we call "self-deception" his mullahs call "discovering truth for the first time," and even that what we call "reality" his mullahs call "illusion" or "lies." Williams thinks we can refute these claims by the fact of scientific realism, proven by convergence.[38] I do not accept this method of proof, but will deal with that issue later. For the moment, let us put the weight on self-deception: what is so bad about (what we call) self-deception? As self-deception is one mode of bad faith, this brings us to the same point at which we left our first response.

Sincerity, consistency with one's own interests, has long been one of the few things Williams believes ethics can demand of a person. As early as his "Critique of Utilitarianism," he described integrity as central to any ethical life, defining that concept in terms of having one's actions and decisions "flow from the projects and attitudes with which [one] is most closely identified."[39] The emphasis here belongs on the word "projects,"[40] and the use of a Sartrian term foreshadows Williams' later stress on anchoring one's choices solely in "internal reasons," on the ways that reflection destroys ethical knowledge by revealing new ethical possibilities,[41] and on the need to avoid self-deception. But Sartre, unlike Williams, sees integrity as itself a form of "bad faith," hence bad faith as "an immediate, permanent threat to every project of the human being."[42] Rather than positing human consciousness as a constant drift between facticity and transcendence, as something that has interests and goals at one moment only to be able to deny them the next,[43] Williams talks as if I have a fixed self, insisting that "my projects, purposes, and needs [are not]... considerations *for* me. I must deliberate *from* what I am."[44] Of course, I may deliberate my way to new projects or the jettisoning of old ones—"practical reasoning is a heuristic process, and an imaginative one, and there are no fixed

---

38 (Williams, 1985), chapter 8.
39 "Critique of Utilitarianism," in (Smart & Williams, 1973), p.117. Henceforth: CU.
40 *ibid*, pp.110-1.
41 (Williams, 1985), pp.145-7.
42 (Sartre, 1977), pp.106-7, 116.
43 *ibid*, pp.98, 106.
44 (Williams, 1985), p.200.

boundaries on the continuum from rational thought to inspiration and conversion"[45]—but I must start from my present commitments and work outwards. I may never, therefore, justifiably adopt a new project that seriously and fundamentally conflicts with one of my current projects, without at the same time working my way to a change of attitude towards that current project. By definition, no "appropriate deliberative projection" of my interests could lead me to an "annihila[tion] of what [I] posit within one and the same act."[46]

It is supposed to follow from this that I can never renounce deliberation or rationality itself. "There is no route back from reflectiveness," says Williams.[47] He admits that many things can in fact lead to the reduction of reflectiveness, but claims that these would not be a "route," a "way in which we can consciously take ourselves back from it."[48] By contrasting "things" reducing our reflection to our performing the reduction ourselves, he presumably means that *as* agents, as consciously deliberating beings, we cannot choose to reduce our reflectiveness, which would follow from his position on violating one's own projects if we add that as deliberators we are always at least committed to the project of deliberating. This would also make sense of Williams' belief that "we cannot consistently leave out the reflective consciousness itself" in what we transmit to the future, even though on the whole "we should not try to seal determinate values into future society."[49]

But *why* can we not deliberately set out on a course of bad faith, a course that violates our current projects? I want to approach this question by introducing another, somewhat more plausible, imaginary dialogue. Again the imagined interlocutor is Muslim, this time highly appropriately since Williams singles out contemporary "Islamic forces" as perpetrators of failed attempts to reverse practices of reflectiveness.[50] This time, however, the interlocutor has a basis in reality: she comes from VS Naipaul's book *Among the Believers*. Explaining how he decided to make a journey through four countries undergoing a revival of fundamentalist Islam, Naipaul describes an Iranian woman who appeared on Connecticut television "with her head covered to tell us that Islam protected women and gave them dignity":

> Fourteen hundred years ago in Arabia, she said, girl children were buried alive; it was Islam that put a stop to that. Well, we didn't all live in Arabia (not even the woman with the covered head); and many things had happened since the seventh century. Did women—especially someone as fierce as the woman addressing us—still need the special protection that Islam gave them? Did they still need the veil? Did they need to be banned from public life and from appearing on television?

---

45 "Internal and External Reasons," (Williams, 1981), p.110.
46 (Sartre, 1977) p.87.
47 (Williams, 1985), p.163.
48 *ibid*, pp.163-4.
49 *ibid*, p.173.
50 *ibid*, p.165.

> ...An American or non-Islamic education had given the woman with the *chador* her competence and authority. Now she appeared to be questioning the value of the kind of person she had become; she was denying some of her own gifts.[51]

Suppose we were able to speak to this woman, and ask her, picking up on one of Naipaul's internal questions, whether she was not acting in bad faith, in appearing on American television to praise a revolution that banned women from television. Perhaps at first she would deny the charge, but let us say she eventually admits to being torn between the reflectiveness her education has given her and the less reflective life-style she is trying to live now. She might add, "Aware of my debt to my education and of the struggle within me, I have consciously chosen to try to suppress my reflectiveness, to reduce my ties to my education, to develop dispositions of humility, obedience, and submissiveness. I hope eventually, by these means, to get rid of the conflict I now feel. Then I will not appear on television. Then I may also live with my people in Iran." If we ask her how she intends to accomplish this, she may tell us that she is making herself practice all the external observances of Islam, she is training herself not to answer back, or skeptically question, anything that a religious leader tells her, and she is throwing herself into such projects as raising a family or furthering her political causes so as not to have much time to sit and think during her transition period. By dint of these exercises, she is developing new habits of thought and behavior, and, she reminds us, Aristotle showed long ago that habits are the key to establishing a mode of practice.

Now, if we have just been reading Williams, we may be tempted to say that this is not a *route* back from reflectiveness. Although she can "consciously embark on a course to reduce reflection," we may tell her, "[she] cannot consciously pursue that course, and if [she is] successful, [she] will have had to forget it."[52] It seems to me, however, that she can reasonably wonder what kind of objection this is at all. She does not particularly *want* to pursue a course consciously, if that means pursuing a course of thought, and she probably does not mind in the least if she eventually forgets how she got to be a contented Muslim, or what she was before—that is indeed her goal. Williams' objection is unclear. How can it have force against someone who does not already regard reflectiveness as an all-important value? And what does he mean here by a conscious pursuit of a goal? *Of course*, the woman cannot "consciously pursue" her attempt to forget her education if that means constantly remembering what she is trying to forget. But she can consciously decide to perform this or that ritual act, this or that household chore, and she probably is even often aware of her long-term goal of eliminating her internal conflict by these means. That is about as conscious an approach as we ever adopt to a goal that requires a lot of physical activity. Williams seems transfixed by the picture of someone trying

---

51 (Naipaul, 1981), pp.12-13.

52 (Williams, 1985), p.164.

to get rid of an unpleasant or annoying thought by mental exercises. But while the boy who wants to stop thinking about his forthcoming visit to the dentist will not succeed by mental exercises alone, he can get it out of his head by going for a swim. And if he chooses to go for a swim *in order* to stop thinking about the dentist, this is as much a consciously chosen route to his goal as any action in the situation could be.

To all this, one might respond that I have not given Williams' main argument at all. In the passage I have cited he may even be admitting that "in the individual case" a route away from reflection exists, although we cannot consciously pursue it; he wants to stress only that "in the social case there will be people who do not want to pursue it, and they will try not to let the others forget it."[53] If we try to suppress their questions and resistance, we will "produce results that are ludicrous on a small scale and hideous on a larger one." Similarly, he says later on that trying to suppress reflection "can lead to nothing but disaster," or at least involves "sacrificing other goods."[54] The problem with the woman in chador's bad faith, on this view, is not that it is impossible, but that it is dangerous.

If this is Williams' argument, however, it is worse than the other one. Admittedly, Khomeini's Iran is not everybody's money, but to show that its violence was wrong rather than a necessary evil requires an argument establishing both that those it suppressed had a right to their dissent and that the goods it purchased by suppressing such rights were not worth the trouble. Nor is it clear that all reactionary politics need employ violence, at least over the long haul: a state might simply re-educate its people so that they do not have the wherewithal or inclination to raise questions about its religious teachings. (Are the questions then still "there to be raised," as Williams would say?)[55] This need entail nothing more violent than the disbanding of certain schools.

Indeed, the woman in chador can provide an ethical defense for her attempt to reduce her own reflectiveness in terms even we might consider compelling. "What do you gain by your reflectiveness and the institutions that uphold it?" she might ask. "Despair of having any purpose in life, a science unrestrained by moral considerations, and in consequence a violent youth culture, broken marriages, and nuclear weapons. With such a record, who are you to complain of the violence in my tradition? And what with your televisions, and your mind-deadening jobs on assembly lines and at computer terminals, you have dubious claim even to intellectual advantages over us, at least as far as the bulk of your

---

53 *ibid*, p.164.

54 *ibid*, pp. 168, 170.

55 "[E]ven if there have been contented hierarchies [in the past], any charm they have for us is going to rest on their having been innocent and not having understood their own nature. This cannot be recreated, since measures would have to be taken to stop people raising questions that are, by now, there to be raised." (Williams, 1985), p.164.

society is concerned. Finally, while bad faith would seem to me in any case a small price to pay to get away from the horrors of your civilization, were the price not so small you still could not reasonably complain to me about it. As Sartre has pointed out, bad faith is an intrinsic feature of your own culture, even when you are being reflective. Is not the whole project of integrity itself in bad faith? It thrives on the supposition that one cannot, or at least cannot reasonably, make radical changes in one's character, abandon one's own deeply held projects. Yet I myself am living proof to the contrary. Thus my position: given the choice between bad faith in pursuit of what you call free thought and bad faith in pursuit of Islamic tradition, I have chosen the latter, hoping one day to reconcile myself enough with that tradition to be able to give it all my heart and all my soul."

If we are to answer this woman, we will have to say much more than that what she has chosen is not a real option for her. I hope, indeed, to have shaken our confidence by now in what constitutes a real option. Williams himself does not clarify the matter much. As examples of unreal options, he mentions attempting to live the life of a Bronze age chief or a medieval samurai today. "There is no way of living them," he says, "...no way of taking on those outlooks."[56] But why is there no way? We are not dealing with physical impossibility here. One could set up a community where people dressed, ate, talked, worked, etc. in as close a manner as possible to that of the medieval samurai. Nor are we dealing with psychological impossibility: the community could surely train its members, and especially the children of its members, to read only the literature the samurai knew, to hold samurai values dear, to speak and write only on issues that concerned samurai. Williams, referring to efforts of this kind as "utopian projects among a small band of enthusiasts," says that they would not reproduce "*that* life."[57] I understand the emphasis on "that" as implying that living the life of a medieval samurai entails a *logical* impossibility of some kind. A samurai, after all, had various beliefs and expectations—beliefs about the time he was living in, about his own history, about people who were not samurai or not Japanese, expectations about people's regard for him and his role in their lives—that no contemporary could have without being psychotic. Hence a contemporary of ours must either lack many samurai beliefs and expectations or be psychotic, in either case failing to resemble the average samurai in important respects.

This only proves the impossibility of reproducing samurai society, however, if the "important respects" are essential to the definition of a samurai, which is not at all evident. The original samurai were not, after all, a monolithic group—why should contemporary samurai not differ from them in some important beliefs? They were also seriously deluded in many ways, about the

---

56 *ibid*, p.161.
57 *ibid*, p.161.

ultimate nature of the world around them, if nothing else—why should contemporary samurai not be deluded about their relationship to the world around them? And even if we do grant Williams that a contemporary band of enthusiasts will not reproduce "*that* life," still their attempt to do so, while involving the false belief that they are successful, is itself certainly possible. Williams claims that "re-enacting [such an existence] in the context of modern industrial life would involve a vast social illusion,"[58] but what makes that so bad? Many societies are based on illusion, and adopting illusion willingly is no more difficult than ceasing to reflect, which we have discussed above. Whatever one might say about being an actual samurai, being a samurai in foolishness or bad faith is clearly one of our options.

We thus need something stronger than insincerity or danger to rule a way of life out of bounds for us. Here we confront the fundamental problem with Williams' refusal to supply a solid grounding—"an Archimedean point"[59]—to ethics. He is, I believe, right that there is no such grounding to be found in the places philosophers have traditionally looked. Theories of human nature are indeed no longer enough to give ethical dispositions precedence over "other cultural and personal aspirations,"[60] while an account of the workings of practical reason cannot ever justify specific ethical choices.[61] But moving from these failures to an avowal of nonobjectivity in ethics will make it well-nigh impossible to stop even the worst threats of relativism.

Nonobjectivity alone "does not imply any relativistic attitude," as Williams rightly points out.[62] We can continue to hold our values and reject those of others, since on the nonobjectivist account there is no more reason against such an attitude than for it, or for any other one. Williams himself acknowledges, however, that there would be "something blank and unresponsive," something "remarkably inadequate," in such an attitude,[63] and I think we can say more.

First, however, we need to clarify what we mean by "nonobjectivity." Literally, of course, to call a claim or set of claims "nonobjective" means that it does not describe any object. Thus all emotions, desires and tastes may be called "subjective" rather than "objective" because they are largely (though not exclusively) due to pre-dispositions on the part of the subject. Emotions caused by physiological states but directed at people or external events may be called "nonobjective" because directed to the *wrong* object. And fictions of one sort or another may be called "nonobjective" because the objects they describe do not exist (again, they may still be, in part, about other objects that do exist). To say that a scientific claim is not objective is to compare it to fictions or

58 *ibid*, p.161.

59 *ibid*, p.29.

60 *ibid*, p.52.

61 *ibid*, chapter 4 (especially pp. 64 and 69). See also Hegel's criticisms of Kant in the Phenomenology of Spirit and Philosophy of Right.

62 *ibid*, p.159. See also chapter 3 of (Williams, 1972).

63 (Williams, 1985), pp. 159, 160.

misguided emotions, in that the objects it purports to describe do not exist as such, but to call an ethical claim nonobjective has quite a different force, since ethical claims, we want to say, do not *purport* to describe objects at all. Now, "objectivity" belongs, in the philosopher's vocabulary of favorable appraisal, together with "knowledge," since knowledge, in Kant's canonical formulation, is the correspondence of thought to object.[64] As there are no objects for ethics, it would seem there can be no ethical knowledge. So says noncognitivism, which Williams' position closely resembles. But Kant himself thought that there could be objective ethical claims, insofar as those claims could appear necessarily true.[65] He did not believe that there are objects in ethics—on his account of "object," there could be no such thing—so here objectivity must mean something else. Presumably, it remains simply the opposite of "subjectivity," which in this context refers to whatever is *peculiar to* the individual subject. Thus to find what is objectively right or good, the subject must determine a principle, or determine a maxim on the basis of a principle, that does not depend on her emotions, tastes, desires or circumstances. This minimal sense of objectivity fits nicely what we have sought in our attempt to make ethical claims sufficiently independent of the subject who holds them that others can try to guide her, correct her, change her mind, etc. and she can accept the possibility that such judgments might be better advised than her own. In that case she could be right or wrong in her ethical beliefs; she could have reasonable or unreasonable grounds for them; they could be true or false. This is the sense of "objectivity" I will use in adopting ethical cognitivism.

For the purposes of the fallacious argument that derives relativism from nonobjectivity, however, the latter may be taken primarily as shorthand for the discovery that what we thought made ethics objective does not do so, for the denial of the traditional arguments that people have accepted as reasonable grounds for their values. The inference from nonobjectivity to relativism proceeds, I suggest, by pointing out that although the one does not follow with any strict logical or empirical necessity from the other, it is hard to see what *could* ground our values once the traditional bases have failed. If divine imperatives, theories of human nature, and the implications of pure practical reason will not (no longer?) suffice as a ground, then it seems we have no reason for maintaining our values at all. Of course, there might be other grounds, but what? Intuitionism has rightly been hooted off the stage, and for reasons that should frighten away many other potential candidates: the ever-increasing evidence that intelligent and rational people maintain and have maintained radically different ethical principles, and that they adhere to those principles for reasons much like those we give for our own practices. What rational

---

[64] (Kant, 1965), p.156 (B137).

[65] See, for instance, (Kant,1964), pp. 68-9, 80-1, footnote on 88, 95-6 (Royal Prussian Academy edition 400-1, 412-4, note on 421, 427-8. The pagination from this edition will be given along with citations from a translation.)

argument could possibly justify any one of these systems over another, and what argument that failed to make such a selection could possibly be relevant to our own actual ethical choices? I do not pose this question purely rhetorically, since I do not see any way to rule out the possibility of such an argument, but I also do not see how we might even start looking for it. And given the likelihood that there is no such argument, it is not unreasonable for a person who considers ethics nonobjective to draw the worst consequences of what we have been calling "extreme relativism," or "ethics on a whim."

Now, Williams thinks he does supply an alternative to the traditional arguments for objectivism in a version of voluntarism bolstered with appeals to the importance of reflection and the danger of "bad faith." We have shown the inadequacy of these principles as proofs that changing one's ethical standards radically or whimfully need involve impossibility or insanity, but suppose we simply view them as normative appeals, drawing us to our values as a whole on the strength of a pre-supposed commitment to a certain special subset of them. Could we not accept our ethical system as a whole on the basis of the value we ourselves place on "being true to ourselves" (sincerity, intellectual honesty), on social patterns that allow us the greatest possibility of unrestricted reflection, on expressing and releasing, rather than repressing, our natural inclinations? Perhaps, although our ethics is voluntarist, the call to arms springs from values we hold so strongly that we do not in the least want to resist it.

Perhaps, but I doubt it. If ethical dispositions in general no longer take obvious precedence over "other cultural and personal aspirations," good faith and reflectiveness specifically can claim no such extraordinary status. When saying "You [or I] shouldn't do that, because God forbids it, because it's unnatural, or because it's irrational" no longer has much impact, saying "You [or I] shouldn't do that because you would be in bad faith, or destructive of your future possibilities for reflection" will not have any more impact. And saying, as some pure voluntarists might, "You shouldn't do that because you don't really want to do that" is, in most important cases, empty or ridiculous. One of the chief causes for the demise of the traditional sources of ethical objectivity was the weakness of their appeal,[66] but the replacements offered for them are weaker than they ever were.

It should now be clear that at the heart of my difficulties with Williams' program lie the problems of noncognitivism. Williams does not describe

---

66 Consider the way God's commands, to Kant, nature, to GE Moore, and practical reason, to Hegel, seem primarily, both at first glance and after argument, simply irrelevant to ethics, (rather than false, incoherent, dangerous, etc.). Williams' accounts of Aristotle and Kant, in chapters 3 and 4 of (Williams, 1985), also stress the fact that it is unclear why the agent should care about living up to her true nature, on the one hand, or the demands of practical reason, on the other. Compare also Foot and Frankfurt, op. cit. in notes 1 and 5.

himself as a noncognitivist, probably because he sees the possibility of "an intelligible form of ethical objectivity,"[67] but, as he goes on to say in the very sentence from which this phrase is taken, he does not believe there is any "convincing argument" that our ethical thought actually possesses such objectivity. He also evinces considerable sympathy for the positions of JL Mackie, as we have already seen, and for the writings of RM Hare,[68] perhaps the two leading spokesmen for noncognitivism in recent years. In addition, he approaches noncognitivism in his claim that we can have significant ethical discourse only with our fellow ethical "volunteers" and in his appeal, through the notion of "confidence," to something like a socialized version of the moral sentiments. But most important for our purposes is the stark contrast he draws between ethical and scientific discourse and the use he makes of that contrast to support his flat assertion that "ethical realism is false."[69]

This book starts from the position that what Williams calls ethical realism is not only true but the best, or even the only, alternative to "ethics on a whim." Philippa Foot points out that Williams makes no distinction between ethical realism and ethical cognitivism,[70] and like her I prefer to speak of cognitivism than realism, so as to allow for knowledge in ethics without being committed to any sort of ethical "objects" that might exist entirely independently of human beings and their wills. Cognitivism demands only that we be able to call ethical sentences "true" or "false," and "truth" is much less bound to the possibility of perception than are most uses of the word "reality." What it does require I hope to show more fully over the course of the next five chapters, but as a first stab at defining the term, let me endorse the four "truisms" by which David Wiggins characterizes "regular truth":

> (1) the compatibility of every regular truth with every other regular truth, (2) the answerability of regular truth to evidenced argument which will under favourable conditions converge upon agreement, and (3) the independence of regular truth both from our will and from our own limited means of recognizing the presence or absence of the property in a statement. (2) and (3) together suggest the truism (4) that every regular truth is true in virtue of something.[71]

One thing missing here is the fact that truth is action-guiding, which will become increasingly important in the next few chapters, but Wiggins' account deals beautifully with the issue of correspondence. Truism (3) suggests that any statement claiming truth must have some possibility of corresponding or

---

67 "Ethics and the Fabric of the World," in (Honderich, 1985), p.208.

68 (Williams, 1985), pp. 124ff and 135ff. (But note, on p.135, that Williams prefers, for important reasons, the phrase "the ethical" for what Hare and others have standardly called "the prescriptive" or "the evaluative." As we shall see in chapters 4 and 5, this only brings his position into sharper contrast with the one I want to defend.)

69 "Truth in Relativism," (Williams, 1981), p.143. See also "Ethics and the Fabric of the World," p.210.

70 Foot, "Moral Realism and Moral Dilemma," p.268, in (Gowans, 1987).

failing to correspond with something outside of itself and its speaker's intentions and beliefs, but it in no way requires correspondence with any kind of *object*. To be ethically true, therefore, a statement could accord with a standard, a series of other judgments, or the speaker's "entrenched desires" as opposed to ephemeral whims. Chapters three and four will consider what kinds of separation between the subject and her ethical beliefs might allow for such possibilities of fitting and failing to fit.

But I do not want to become entangled in the contemporary academic debate over whether one should view ethics from a cognitivist standpoint at all. Although I hope to make clearer just what "truth" might mean in ethics, I will not be greatly concerned to defend ethical cognitivism as an important or coherent position. That has already been superbly done in Sabina Lovibond's recent book *Realism and Imagination in Ethics*. I shall address instead what seems to me the most serious weakness of her book: its excessive universalism. I want to open her position to a greater acknowledgement of both the fact and the dangers of radical human difference, to build cultural pluralism into the cultural foundation she provides for ethical discourse.

A few words only, therefore, on the advantages of cognitivism. Above all, attributing truth or falsehood to something is considerably stronger than saying it is good or bad, right or wrong, attractive or repellent, a real or unreal, sane or insane option. For Williams, calling a view false ends discussion over whether one should adopt it or not. "Relativism is rejected" for science, he says, even where confrontations of scientific views are purely notional, because "there is something to be said in appraisal of [such outdated scientific beliefs as] phlogiston theory, that it is false." Trying to live "the life of a convinced phlogiston theorist in contemporary academia" is not merely "as incoherent an enterprise as trying to live the life of a Teutonic Knight in 1930's Nuremberg"; phlogiston theory does not constitute a real option precisely because "it cannot be squared with a lot that we know to be true."[72] Knowing something to be true thus has an independence of societal standards and practices, for Williams, in a way that evaluating something does not.

We should note at least in passing that this view of truth is by no means obvious. We do in fact want to know the truth, but that need not be so. We could want to live amidst lies, illusions, fictions. Of course even to live amidst falsehood, one needs some truths, but one may not need many, and one certainly does not need them always and in all respects. Moreover, if our contemporary academic world lacks phlogiston theorists, it contains creationists,[73] revisionist

---

71 (Wiggins, 1976), p.357.

72 (Williams, 1985), pp.161-2.

73 Steven Jay Gould reports that Dr. Leonard Bailey, who performed the transplant of a baboon heart into Baby Fae, gave his fundamentalist beliefs as a reason for ignoring the arguments of those who had recommended chimpanzees because they are evolutionarily closer to us. (Storrs Lectures at Yale Law School, 1986).

historians of the Hitler and Stalin eras, and racist geneticists, many of whom are quite sane and some of whom are even respected. In such cases, falsehood seems not to constitute even a sufficient condition for turning a set of beliefs into a notional option. What force it does have is not at all clear.

Yet we will allow Williams the use of truth as a trump card among terms of appraisal, although we will not separate it so entirely from social practices. Whether "truth" is merely our highest term of praise, or whether it describes something that determines all our thought including our terms of praise, whether the creationist thinks her beliefs true or knows the truth but wants to live in illusion, whether we can always, or ever, irrefutably prove true what we consider true and whether that matters or not, to call something true takes precedence over any other appraisal. Truth is an essential guide; we inevitably see ourselves, and translate others, as aiming at it. If I can satisfactorily show how "true" and "false" can be applied to ethical statements, I shall have gone a great distance towards meeting the challenge of whimful relativism.

For Lovibond, anything we can reasonably make assertions about, anything we can talk about in the indicative mood, we can reasonably call true or false, real or illusory.

> ...[T]he only legitimate role for the idea of 'reality' is that in which it is coordinated with...the metaphysically neutral role of 'talking about something'...It follows that 'reference to an objective reality' cannot be intelligibly be set up as a target which some propositions—or rather, some utterances couched in the indicative mood—may hit, while others fall short. If something has the grammatical form of a proposition, then it *is* a proposition: philosophical considerations cannot discredit the way in which we classify linguistic entities for other, non-philosophical, purposes.[74]

But we have non-philosophical purposes for and practices of couching ethical utterances as well as scientific ones in the indicative mood, of arguing about ethical questions just as we argue over science. If Lovibond is right, we have no reason to discard such practices, and "moral reasoning... can be restored to parity with scientific reasoning on the strength of its answerability to similarly public canons of evidence."[75]

Whether she is right or not depends on the success of her consensus account of objectivity, which in turn is grounded in what she calls the "homogeneity" of language. Basing herself on the later Wittgenstein, she argues for "a homogeneous or 'seamless' conception of language,...a conception free from invidious comparisons between different regions of discourse."[76] Such distinctions would only make sense if the objectivity of our judgments depended on some kind of "independent verification," like that the empiricist seeks in

---

74 (Lovibond, 1983), pp.25-6.
75 *ibid*, p.43.
76 *ibid*, p.25.

the "'hard data' supplied by the senses," but there is no and cannot be any mode of verification independent of human involvement.[77] We have no "access to any distinction between those of our beliefs which are *actually true*, and those which are merely *held true by us*. No such distinction can survive our conscious recognition that some human authority has to *decide* the claim of any proposition to be regarded as true—and, accordingly, that the objective validity of an assertion or argument is always at the same time something of which human beings ... are subjectively persuaded."[78] It follows that objective truth cannot be separated from the canons of evidence that establish it, and indeed, while we cannot say that "objectivity *means* intersubjectivity..., there is nothing else for it to *be*."[79] "Objectivity (sound judgment) and rationality (sound reasoning)" must be "grounded in *consensus*," in "conformity to the consensual norms of valid reasoning which happen to apply within the appropriate field."[80] This is the case whether we are speaking of scientific rationality or the reasoning and debate characteristic of ethical practice and reflection. The "homogeneous conception of the relation between language and the world can be understood, by comparison with the [ethical noncognitivist's] view, either as a levelling-up of evaluative discourse *vis-à-vis* scientific discourse, or as a levelling-down of the latter relative to the former."[81]

Some will see in this approach a danger of the kind of scientific (cognitive) relativism associated with Kuhn, Feyerabend, and especially their popular followers. I will say a little to allay such fears in the fourth chapter, but, as I have already mentioned, I am not primarily interested in arguing for the cognitivist position. Not only do I believe that Lovibond does so adequately, but there is a limit to how far those who accept the position can defend it, given its own ultimate[82] appeal to consensus as the ground for rational belief and justification. I want to focus instead on the *kind* of consensus to which Lovibond appeals. That "a shared form of life...is constitutive of rationality itself," she says, entails Davidson's position that it is incoherent to suppose that "different linguistic communities might operate with different and mutually

---

77 *ibid*, p.38.

78 *ibid*, p.37.

79 *ibid*, p.42.

80 *ibid*, pp. 40, 45.

81 *ibid*, p.42.

82 "Ultimate," because it does not require that we immediately appeal to consensus on any issue: we never say a philosophical or scientific or ethical claim is true simply because people agree to it. On the other hand, realizing that one's final ground is in fact consensus, even if that consensus cannot itself feature as an argument, means that after one has put her best argumentative foot forward, she does not necessarily feel either that one or the other party has been convinced or that there remains anything for either party to say. ("You say 'That is red,' but how is it decided if you are right? Doesn't human agreement decide? - But do I appeal to this agreement in my judgments of colour?...Our language-game only works, of course, when a certain agreement prevails, but the concept of agreement does not enter into the language-game. If agreement were universal we should be quite unacquainted with the concept of it." (Wittgenstein, 1967). Compare also (Lovibond, 1983), p.42.

incommensurable, 'conceptual schemes.'"[83] Since we can construe others' words and behavior as rational, as making sense at all, only if they share our form of life—the form of life in which (what we call?) rationality is constituted—we must assume general agreement in beliefs and desires with any group we try to interpret. Lovibond quotes Williams' reading of the Wittgensteinian "we," according to which not only all humanity, but all "language-using creatures" belong to the "we," all the apparent alternatives to it, apparent outsiders to our shared rationality, being mere thought experiments and not "actual groups of human beings whose activities we might want to understand...."[84]

The consensus, then, is a universal consensus, in which we must assume that others are believers of those truths and lovers of that good that are true and good "by our own lights."[85] But this will not work. Whether or not our scientific thought allows room for incommensurability, we cannot easily wipe away ethical incommensurability. There simply does not exist either evidence or argument to show that ethical differences among peoples are merely illusory, or insignificant next to a deeper ethical agreement, or the result of mass delusions. That ethical discourse is highly culturally specific, that "the consensual norms of valid reasoning" within ethics differ irreducibly across cultures seems irrefutable. To quote Lovibond's mentor, Wittgenstein: "How did we *learn* the meaning of [the word] 'good'...? From what sort of examples? in what language-games?"[86] For Wittgenstein, the general terms we use in aesthetics and ethics are hopelessly vague, like a mixture of colors so blurred that any and no sharp outline will define them,[87] and they can receive meaning only from the specific examples with which and language-games in which we learn them. But every culture has its own such examples and ethical practices, often quite different from and unacceptable to, those of other cultures. As philosophers and international lawyers, a society may try to speak a universal language, but in teaching ethics to its children it draws on a very provincial literature indeed. And as long as the meaning of our language(s) of value

---

[83] *ibid*, p.40.

[84] "Wittgenstein and Idealism," (in (Williams, 1981)), p.159. See also (Lear, 1982). Since I disagree both with this reading of Wittgenstein and with the considerations that motivate it (see chapters 2 and 4, especially), I should point out that my own use of "we," in general, is meant primarily to voice a local, if sometimes large group: that of my presumed readers, or, in some cases, of what I might roughly characterize as "Westerners," or at least "believers in the Western scientific method." This characterization has to be rough both because we do not yet have enough theoretical material to clarify it further, and because, as I show in chapter 7, the term "culture" is essentially vague, and culures can only be picked out in a general fashion. Ultimately the reader will have to decide for herself whether she belongs to the "we" I delineate. I might add that I shall try to avoid using "we" for my voice as the writer, even if this sometimes leads to an awkward reliance on the first person singular.

[85] Donald Davidson, "Mental Events," (Davidson, 1980), p.222.

[86] (Wittgenstein, 1958), I §77. Henceforth: PI.

[87] *ibid*. Cf. also (Wittgenstein, 1970), pp.1-2, and (Hallett, 1977), p.157.

depends on something so irremediably specific, we will not be able to define a general conception of value justifiable to all human groups. In a creditable attempt to develop Davidson's intriguing hint that his theory of interpretation can be applied to ethics, David Cooper has recently argued that we need to share some of the general aims of another group's practices in order to interpret those practices as concerning ethics at all.[88] But even if we grant this point, we can still differ with another group over so many, and such extremely important, specifics to which the general aims we share do not reach, that what we assume we have in common will not help us at all.

Williams fully recognizes this cultural variation, as we have amply seen, and he does not mean to extend the universality of the Wittgensteinian "we" to ethics, (indeed, his argument about that "we" has been used to buttress ethical noncognitivism).[89] Lovibond wants to make no such distinctions in her use of Wittgenstein, but she does not naively embrace ethical universalism either. Declaring that "moral discourse is an area where the reach of intellectual authority [i.e., the ground for intellectual dispute] is relatively short,"[90] she points out that her metaphysical stance of moral cognitivism does not commit her to denying phenomenological differences between ethics and science or mathematics. Later, she acknowledges that there is a difficulty in saying "what degree of historical specificity is supposed to attach to the 'shared form of life,'"—but then, for political reasons, warns against interpreting the phrase too narrowly.[91] She also allows for the existence of a wide range of moral dissent and difference,[92] and insists that it is not a philosophical matter "to commend any specific *policy* towards groups or individuals whose practices diverge from our own."[93] Yet all these claims, themselves problematic as we shall see later on (chapter eight), leave the issue of *justifiable* moral difference vague, and ultimately Lovibond explicitly declares herself a universalist. We need to seek an immanent realization of the "absolute conception of reality," she says, such that "the individual or local perspectives of all human beings would be able to find harmonious expression"—a realization of "a form of life which [is] in agreement, as the Hegelian idiom would have it, with 'universal reason.'"[94]

This project, it seems to me, sets us in pursuit of a chimera. Human difference is too deeply rooted for such a universal form of life, and the very attempt to reach it would violate our (local) ethical commitment to respecting other people's projects as much as possible. If Williams provides too easy an answer to relativism, Lovibond does not take the question seriously enough.

---

88 (Cooper, 1978).
89 By Jonathan Lear in (Lear, 1983). See also (Williams, 1985), pp. 97-99, 102-4.
90 (Lovibond, 1983), pp.67-8.
91 *ibid*, pp. 97, 99.
92 *ibid*, pp. 170-2, 211-3.
93 *ibid*, p.212, cf. pp.173-5.
94 *ibid*, pp.218-9.

Yet her position can stand a richer acceptance of cultural differences. Instead of moving to universalism, I suggest that we not see difference as a threat to cognitivism. That is, after all, only another capitulation to the noncognitivists' invidious comparison between ethics and science. Of course, we cannot affirm as true a set of statements that contain a contradiction—which is to say, we cannot take up a cognitivist stance towards such a set of statements—but a realm of discourse is not a mere set of statements, and recognizing disagreement within such a realm is not the same as affirming a contradiction. When we take a cognitivist view of a realm of discourse, we mean that the sentences uttered in that realm are capable of truth or falsehood, not that they are all true. Hence we can accept the fact that disagreements, even incommensurable (irresolvable) disagreements, will appear in a given realm without denying the possibility of knowledge in that realm. Now, this thesis at least appears to be in tension with Davidson's conception of language and denial that there are any incommensurable differences. I thus turn next to the task of laying the groundwork for a culturally specific version of ethical cognitivism by making room for incommensurable disagreements within Davidson's views.

CHAPTER TWO

NOTES ON THE GRAMMAR OF THE WORD "MISTAKE"

How far can we accommodate disagreement and still make sense of truth? Given that I believe x, can I regard someone who believes not x as anything other than in error? Well, there are some areas where we easily make room for such differences. I have no trouble believing "olives are horrible" while allowing others to believe "olives are wonderful." Of course, we can index these two sentences to their speakers ("olives are (taste) horrible *to me*"), so that they do not conflict, but even when judgments of taste and desire do conflict—"I don't see how anyone could like that movie"/"I don't see how anyone could *dislike* that movie"—we rarely feel inclined to say that one of the two judges must be wrong. But this model of tolerant disagreement is not very interesting, if only because we tend to say that there is no matter of truth about taste and desire. We therefore face great danger in attempting to assimilate a set of disagreements over truth (cognitive disagreements) to disagreements about desire: the very success of such an assimilation might well vitiate cognitivism for the subject matter concerned.

For all that, I do want to bring certain cognitive disagreements down to something much like a matter of differing desires. My strategy will be to show that this is possible for science, taking that as a paradigm of a subject where cognitivism makes sense, and drawing the possibility of cognitivist ethical difference *a fortiori*. Such a strategy must take great care not to draw any easy linkage between scientific claims and the desires of particular scientists or audiences for science, as that would make nonsense of scientific truth. Avoiding this danger will require a refinement of what to count as "desire."

In addition, when we disagree with someone over a matter of fact, and we are quite sure our opinion on the matter is correct, we generally say one of two things: either 1) there has been a failure of communication—we have failed to translate the other's words accurately or he has failed to translate ours, or 2) the other has made a mistake. In either case, we need not assume there is any significant difference between us, for in the first case we can hold that if we did understand each other properly we would agree, while in the second case, it belongs to the definition of a mistake that we attribute to the other a failure of information, perception, calculation, or inference, which, if pointed out to him, we believe he would correct—and thus come to agree with us. Now, what happens when we meet someone with quite different standards for what should count as information, perception, calculation or inference, someone from another culture, say? Some influential schools of anthropology—the so-called

"Intellectualists" from James Frazer on—have held that all disagreements with members of other cultures can be put down to error, that other cultures think pretty much the way we think except that they don't do it as well (and a sociological account of their intellectual authorities explains why they maintain their errors), while other schools of anthropologists—the so-called "Symbolists" and "Fideists"—hold that other cultures are doing something quite different from us, something we are failing to translate properly, when they seem to be making gross errors. Philosophers concerned with truth and interpretation often seem to assume, somewhere in the back of their minds, that these modes of explanation will cover all cultural disagreement. If that assumption fails, we may need to add to our ways of explaining disagreement a category such as "incommensurability," naming failures of understanding that cannot be put down to translation, and beliefs reasonable enough to be recognizable as beliefs while contradicting our beliefs irrefutably.

An investigation of mistakes may therefore begin to tell us something about the variety of meanings we can give "disagreement" and "truth."

1. In his "Remarks on Frazer's Golden Bough" and "Lectures on Religious Belief," Wittgenstein explicitly announces the attitude I will want to take up:

> *Remarks on Frazer*:
>
> Frazer's account of the magical and religious notions of men is unsatisfactory: it makes these notions appear as *mistakes*.
>
> Was Augustine mistaken, then, when he called on God on every page of the *Confessions*?
>
> Well—one might say—if he was not mistaken, then the Buddhist holy man, or some other, whose religion expresses quite different notions, surely was. But *none* of them was making a mistake except where he was putting forward a theory.
>
> It may happen, as it often does today, that someone will give up a practice when he has seen that something on which it depended is an error. But this happens only in cases where you can make a man change his way of doing things simply by calling attention to his error. This is not how it is in connexion with the religious practices of a people; and what we have here is *not* an error.
>
> A religious symbol does not rest on any *opinion*.
>
> And error belongs only with opinion.
>
> Baptism as washing.—There is a mistake only if magic is presented as science.
>
> If the adoption of a child is carried out by the mother pulling the child from beneath her clothes, then it is crazy to think there is an *error* in this and that she believes she has borne the child.[1]

---

1 (Wittgenstein, 1979), pp. 1e, 2e, 3e, 4e.

Lectures on Religious Belief:

> If you compare it with anything in Science which we call evidence, you can't credit that anyone could soberly argue: "Well, I had this dream...therefore...Last Judgment." You might say: "For a blunder, that's too big." If you suddenly wrote numbers down on the blackboard, and then said: "Now, I'm going to add," and then said: "2 and 21 is 13," etc. I'd say: "This is no blunder."
>
> There are cases where I'd say he's mad, or he's making fun. Then there might be cases where I look for an entirely different interpretation altogether. In order to see what the explanation is I should have to see the sum, to see in what way it is done, what he makes follow from it, what are the different circumstances under which he does it, etc.[2]

Some things are "too big" to be mistakes, and two alternatives to that category are "madness" and "making fun." What other alternatives there might be, what the "entirely different interpretation" might lead us to, Wittgenstein leaves unclear. To some extent he remedies this unclarity in *On Certainty*,[3] with a set of detailed explorations into the concept of error. "What we call 'a mistake,'" he says, "plays a quite special part in our language games" (OC 196). We cannot admit the possibility of mistake over the question, for instance, of whether the earth has existed during the last hundred years, even though the existence of the earth over the past hundred years is an ordinary empirical fact. Allowing for doubt about certain ordinary empirical facts, however, would so overthrow the structures by which we learn empirical facts at all that we could not carry out the practice of "correction" that is supposed to go with the attribution of a "mistake":

> OC 138: ...There are [no] historical investigations...into whether the earth has existed during the last hundred years. Of course many of us have information about this period from our parents and grandparents; but mayn't they be wrong?— "Nonsense!" one will say. "How should all these people be wrong?"—But is that an argument? Is it not simply the rejection of an idea? And perhaps the determination of a concept? For if I speak of a possible mistake here, this changes the role of "mistake" and "truth" in our lives.

For similar reasons, we cannot use the word "mistake" of one who wrongly reports his sex, or whether he has just had lunch, or, in general, "who keeps on making mistakes where we regard a mistake as ruled out, and in fact never encounter one[...] E.g. he says he lives in such and such a place, is so and so old, comes from such and such a city, and he speaks with the same certainty (giving all the tokens of it) as I do, but he is wrong." (OC 67) The kinds of circumstance that identify the practice of attributing error and correcting it are missing here, as (relatedly) is the confidence that we share any set of judgments,

---

2 (Wittgenstein, 1970), pp.61-2.

3 (Wittgenstein, 1977). References to this work will henceforth be incorporated into the text by "OC" and section number.

or attitude towards truth, with such a person. But who is the "we"? In §156 Wittgenstein remarks that "[i]n order to make a mistake, a man must already judge in conformity with *mankind*," but in §§ 106, 239, 262, and 336 he suggests that entire groups of people not only might but do exist who disagree with judgments he elsewhere takes as examples of places "where we regard a mistake as ruled out." Clearly he believes that even some sort of local "we" must consider certain statements neither true nor simply in error.

On the other hand, Wittgenstein acknowledges that *sometimes* people can make simply erroneous judgments even about whether they have just had lunch: "I might, for example, have dropped off immediately after the meal without knowing it and have slept for an hour, and now believe I had just eaten." (OC 659). But it is important that such situations only happen *sometimes*,[4] and that there are easy empirical criteria by which to pick them out. Sometimes we can call a remark too big to be a mistake a "slip of the tongue," a mis-use of words, a "momentary confusion," but for all these modes of explanation there are empirical criteria, and we twist their use, and thus their meaning, if we drag them into play where those criteria are missing. Wittgenstein insists on this point:

> 624: "Can you be mistaken about this colour's being called 'green' in English?" My answer to this can only be "No."...
>
> 625: But does this mean that it is unthinkable that the word "green" should have been produced here by a slip of the tongue or a momentary confusion? Don't we know of such cases? —One can also say to someone "Mightn't you perhaps have made a slip?" That amounts to: "Think about it again." —
>
> But these rules of caution only make sense if they come to an end somewhere....

We should keep this warning in mind when Wittgenstein talks about "mental disturbance."[5] A person may surely make remarks too large to be blunders without having any of the physiological symptoms of mental illness. Wittgenstein seems quite aware of this, using the phrase "mental disturbance" in §71 with a somewhat ironic tone ("If my friend were to imagine one day that he had been living for a long time past in such and such a place, etc. etc., I should not call this a *mistake*, but rather a mental disturbance, perhaps a transient one"). Referring to one of his strange tribes' arithmetical practices, he quotes Frege as saying that in such cases "we have a hitherto unknown kind of insanity," but adds that "[Frege] never said what this 'insanity' would really be like." And we surely do not want to call Augustine, or the Buddhist, or the practitioner of baptism, or the tribal woman in the *Remarks on Frazer* and

---

4 "...The language-game that operates with people's names can certainly exist even if I am mistaken about my name, —but it does presuppose that it is nonsensical to say that the majority of people are mistaken about their names" (OC 628).

5 See, for instance, OC 71-5, 155-6, 257, 420, 467, and 659.

Lectures on Religious Belief "mad" any more than "mistaken." If we do, we will simply empty the term "mad" of meaning. A person must have a certain history of bodily conditions, behavior, beliefs, etc. to be mad, and we must look at a long list of specific conditions in order to decide whether to call someone "mad" or to look for "an entirely different interpretation" ("I should have to see the sum, to see in what way it is done, what he makes follow from it, what are the different circumstances under which he does it, etc."). The point here is that both ordinary *and* extra-ordinary attributions and explanations of error have empirical conditions and limitations. Precisely because categories such as "error," "slip of the tongue," and "mental disturbance" have roles to play in our lives beyond that of explaining unusual remarks, we can justify using them only by a pattern of behavior into which the remark might fit, and not by the utterance of the remark alone. Explanations of error are situated in empirical contexts, rather than mere appeals to the way a statement fits or fails to fit "the facts." It follows that we must maintain a sense that all such explanations may fail, and should beware of theories trying to rule out that possibility.

2. Let us now look at an examination of an actual mistake. In 1983, the anthropologist Derek Freeman published an exhaustive refutation of Margaret Mead's classic study, *Coming of Age in Samoa*.[6] Freeman cited evidence from dozens of other works on Samoa, primary sources such as police records, Samoan informants and literature, and his own experiments and observations, to show that Mead's picture of Samoan adolescents as non-competitive, peaceful and sexually easy-going was not only false but practically the opposite of the truth. Before and after presenting all this alternative evidence on Samoa, he spent many pages on historical and biographical information about the circumstances of Mead's research and its reception—about Mead's own qualities as a researcher at the time (young, little trained as yet in anthropology, and unacquainted with the Samoan language), her teacher Franz Boas' scientific and political concerns, and how useful Mead's results were for Boas, in the light of those concerns.

My question is, why so much sweat? If one makes a mistake simply by getting the facts wrong, surely Freeman could have convincingly demonstrated Mead's mistakes with his contrary evidence alone. Why do we need information about Mead's limitations or the historical context of her work? Of course, Mead has a very famous and well regarded name, but what difference does that make to the facts? Well, if it makes no difference to the facts, it does make a difference to the reception of the facts. The evidence to which Freeman appeals has been quite well-known for some time—indeed, since long before Mead's study—yet *Coming of Age in Samoa* remains widely respected, even among

---

6 (Freeman, 1978). As will become clear, I am more concerned with how he sets out to refute Mead than with which one of them is in fact correct.

people who have themselves researched Samoa and confirmed Freeman's picture of that society. Mead's authority, clearly, is one of the facts with which anthropological observers feel they have to reckon, even when it runs beyond the facts upon which they suppose it to be based. Even in this most clear-cut case of an observational error, other observations are not enough to refute the error.

Freeman takes Mead's own error as a demonstration of how the limbic system of the human brain may attach "strong affective feelings of conviction" to a deeply held belief (here, in cultural determinism) regardless of contrary evidence.[7] Can such an analysis be extended to the whole community of scientists that accepted Mead's work for so long? If so, we must wonder whether that community, Freeman himself, or we the readers, might not be suffering under the influence of a similar affect in accepting his refutation (this time tending us toward compromises between biological and cultural modes of explanation).

This problem brings out the excellence of Freeman's book as well as threatening it, for he is well aware, as we have seen, of the need to explain the mistaker in order to justify to a community that something is a mistake. He cannot simply present contrary evidence; he must show why we should believe him rather than Mead and those who have accepted her work. To do this, he limits the role that affect might play in his own study by 1) letting us know that his own deeply held beliefs were originally identical to Mead's,[8] 2) quoting other writers and sources for support (which Mead does not do), and 3) making clear that Mead's Samoan research was an exception to, rather than typical of, the work of great scientists. He also details the intellectual struggles of the time to show how very necessary a study like Mead's was to Boas and his followers when it appeared, and implies that this is why Boas here, but not characteristically, failed to check Mead's account with the earlier literature on Samoa or send someone to replicate her investigations.[9] We can regard Mead's study as an exceptional case, and need not fear that anthropological thought in general, Freeman's thought in particular, or the bulk of our own thought, is similarly distorted by affective factors. Hence Freeman allows us to retain a background against which to evaluate the disagreement between him and Mead.

It is the need to retain this background, however, that has protected Mead's work in the past, and not a mass delusion produced by the limbic system of the brain. Freeman's analysis, so convincing when it comes to Mead and Boas, does not adequately account for the acceptance of Mead's error by the wider community. Freeman finds more perplexing than he should, for instance, the fact that Eleanor Gerber, a 1970s scholar whom he regards as a fine

---

[7] *ibid*, p.292.
[8] *ibid*, pp.xiii-xiv.
[9] *ibid*, p.291.

ethnographer, would interpret her own researches on Samoa so as to preserve Mead's findings.[10] "Could any myth," he asks,"have acquired, within the confines of a scientific discipline and during the second half of the twentieth century, a greater potency?"[11] But Gerber need not be simply capitulating to a "myth", in the sense of an ungrounded belief unworthy of science and the scientific age, a superstition to which one clings for purely emotional reasons. She may be aligning her evidence to meet the standards of her community and its authorities, and if so, she is doing that not because the actions of the limbic system are psychologically constitutive of belief, but because reliance on one's community and its authorities is and must be *logically* constitutive of belief.

Here I come to the crux of my interest in this case. We take what other people say as authoritative, more authoritative, sometimes, than the testimony of our own observations, because in general they represent a body of observations themselves. Margaret Mead gathered in her lifetime a certain amount of information, about Samoa specifically, as well as about anthropology, science, and human nature in general, to which Gerber, and Freeman, do not have access. We cannot have access to everything everyone else knows, so we must regard others as in part extensions of our own information-gathering apparatus. That another scientist (sincerely, and in his capacity as a scientist) says something is *prima facie* evidence for its truth, else no scientist could proceed beyond the limitations of his own experience. Dependence on authority in this way, furthermore, is not merely an empirical consequence of the shortness of human lives, but a necessary condition for any knowledge. The context against which we judge any particular claim is heavily informed by beliefs we take to be true on authority. This must be so, or we could not even have a language in which to discuss truths. If I do not accept quite a lot of claims about mountains on authority, I will never learn so much as what a mountain is (what to call "a mountain").[12] The same holds for most words, most principles, most theories. If each of us tried to investigate the world entirely on his own, he would find himself not only without enough information to make reasonable generalizations, but without any security even about his own sense-impressions (about which ones to trust and which not, about whether he remembers them correctly or not, about which ones belong with which objects or other impressions, etc.) *After* we adopt a picture of the world on authority, we can

10 By deciding that her Samoan informants must be "rewriting...history" when they contradict Mead: p.108.

11 *ibid.*

12 "I am told, for example, that someone climbed this mountain many years ago. Do I always enquire into the reliability of the teller of this story, and whether the mountain did exist years ago? A child learns there are reliable and unreliable informants much later than it learns facts which are told it. It doesn't learn *at all* that that mountain has existed for a long time: that is, the question whether it is so doesn't arise at all. It swallows this consequence down, so to speak, together with *what* it learns." (OC 143).

change some of it, perhaps any part of it, but only with much of it remaining intact to serve as a basis on which to evaluate the change (cf. Neurath's boat). Wittgenstein eloquently describes this relationship to authority in *On Certainty*:

> 160. The child learns by believing the adult. Doubt comes *after* belief. [Cf. 170: I believe what people transmit to me in a certain manner. In this way I believe geographical, chemical, historical facts etc. That is how I *learn* the sciences. Of course, learning is based on believing.]
>
> 161. I learned an enormous amount and accepted it on human authority, and then I found some things confirmed or disconfirmed by my own experience.
>
> 162. In general I take as true what is found in text-books, of geography for example. Why? I say: All these facts have been confirmed a hundred times over. But how do I know that? What is my evidence for it? I have a world-picture. Is it true or false? Above all, it is the substratum of all my enquiring and asserting...
>
> 94. But I did not get my picture of the world by satisfying myself of its correctness; nor do I have it because I am satisfied of its correctness. No: it is the inherited background against which I distinguish between true and false.
>
> 105. All testing, all confirmation and disconfirmation of a hypothesis takes place already within a system. And this system is not a more or less arbitrary and doubtful point of departure for all our arguments: no, it belongs to the essence of what we call an argument. The system is not so much the point of departure, as the element in which arguments have their life.

Now, communities must rely on structures of authority to keep their picture of the world enough in one piece that they can pass it down and make sense of corrections to it. For this purpose, certain experiences, thinkers, and reporters of experiences come to be taken as more important than others, as paradigms, to use Kuhn's word, against which new claims are usually measured. Margaret Mead's book was one such paradigm, and Mead herself one such respected authority. To attack her, then, shakes the foundations of the entire field of anthropology. "If even Mead can fail so badly," people may think, "how much else that we believe—including the evidence on which we accept her critics—might be wrong?" Thus Gerber could well have had good *reasons*, not merely a strong inclination, to shy away from contradicting Mead. Such a contradiction would be *prima facie* evidence, even in her own eyes, against the import of her own work.

When we come to adjudicating Freeman v. Mead as a community, we opt for Freeman, if we do, only with difficulty. The issue throws us back on ourselves as individuals—for a while, at least, there is no clear authority on the matter—and we must for once use our individual judgments to choose which scholars and opinions we are to take as authoritative, rather than using authorities to form and revise our individual judgments. When *I* try to weigh

Mead against Freeman, I find internal evidence in Mead's book for her intelligence (she writes beautifully, infers accurate conclusions from the observations she reports, and pulls out interesting implications I would not have come up with myself)[13] and scrupulousness (she admits her limitations and the possibility of her own error, and she is more careful with statistics than is Freeman).[14] On the other hand, Freeman presents a huge mass of contrary evidence, some of it excellent (that is, up to *my* standards for excellent evidence), satisfactorily exonerates himself from the kind of charges he levels against Mead's conditions of research, and, most importantly, satisfactorily explains how Mead could have come to make her errors. Previously, people had suggested that Mead had been lied to by the children who spoke to her, but by itself this suggestion does not ring true. Intelligent anthropologists do not get so easily and completely fooled. Together with what Freeman tells us, however—about Mead's limited anthropological background at the time, limited knowledge of Samoan, accommodation with an American family rather than in a Samoan home—the suggestion that she was taken in by teasing children looks more plausible. (That is: I can imagine making such a mistake myself, however smart I might be. And this begins to tell us what counts as a satisfactory explanation of a mistake.) I thus come up with an opinion on Freeman's work based on my own standards for intelligence, scrupulousness, evidence, explanation, and error, all of which are heavily dependent on beliefs I have adopted from authorities that include Mead, all of which I have adopted as unquestioningly as those who have learned anthropology by reading Mead.

Even if I ultimately opt for Freeman, therefore, I know that *I* (never mind Freeman) do not have significantly more or more convincing grounds for my judgment of Mead than she had for her judgment of Samoa, hence that for me, as for any similarly situated reader of Freeman, the refutation of her mistake is not and cannot be so complete as to rule out all possible doubt on the matter. That is not to say that Mead's account is only dubiously mistaken, but that a claim does not have to be irrefutably shown false for us to accept it as a mistake. Mead's work remains a piece of the evidence on Samoa, even if we consider it mistaken, simply because an intelligent observer wrote it and it was accepted by her community. She remains an authority, if an overridden authority—which

---

13 Consider, for instance, her subtle and imaginative discussion of work/play distinctions: (Mead, 1943), pp.181-5.

14 On p.206 Mead writes, about her own study, "As there were only sixty-eight girls between the ages of nine and twenty, quantitative statements are practically useless for obvious reasons." She goes on, in this appendix (2) and in appendix 5, to lay out her methodology, with its advantages and disadvantages, very carefully. By contrast, Freeman leaps to statistical conclusions from samples half this size and smaller. (For instance: "If we assume, conservatively, on the basis of Mead's reports, that among the twenty-five adolescents she studied there was *one* delinquent act per annum, this is equivalent to a rate of forty such acts per thousand." (257) Or: "[According to a] detailed analysis of fifteen cases of surreptitious rape,...[s]ome 75 percent of assaults took place late at night." (247) See also pp. 238, 248, 260.)

means that at some point in the future she could turn out to be right after all. This is not likely, but nor was the enormous error of her work likely.

We see clearly here that we cannot simply appeal to empirical evidence in the settling of controversies. No fact is ever demonstrated once and for all; no empirical evidence ever settles a question all by itself. If we accept such evidence as the demonstration of a fact, we do so on the basis of standards we have adopted on authority, we do so on the basis of trusting and having trusted *persons* as sources of truth, and we do so *as* persons, each with a limited life, limited knowledge, and interests that guide and blind our thought.

3. Four "catch-all" categories for truth and error, four explanations obscuring the empirical use of the word "mistake" run as follows:

i) *Stupidity*: Even respectable thinkers evade deeper analysis of differences between people by supposing that those who disagree with us insistently may just be "stupid." W. Newton-Smith casually remarks that "if we are to have an interesting case [of a radically different way of reasoning] we have to set aside situations in which this happens through stupidity or carelessness."[15] In a list of possible explanations for remarks that appear ordinarily or extraordinarily erroneous, Steven Lukes includes "extreme stupidity" along with such things as "non-standard perceptual conditions,...some abnormal physical or physiological condition of the believer... mental derangement, [or] a religious trance."[16] In situations of radical disagreement, however, what counts as "stupidity" comes itself into question. The word is peculiarly liable to casual application as a catch-all category for everyone we fail to understand, yet its proper use belongs in highly specific contexts. No one opinion marks a person as stupid. Even saying someone is stupid "today" or "on this matter" means more than that they present an incorrect opinion (they argue for it badly, perhaps, or act in a silly or immature manner about it). People are stupid if they cannot learn, if they refuse to learn, if they adopt opinions without being able to give reasons for them, if they never say things that surprise us, if they have difficulty finding their way in new situations. While we do call some things "stupid opinions," we mean by this that they are opinions generally held in a stupid manner, not that there is something stupid about the opinions themselves. Thus if someone generally intelligent presents a "stupid opinion" with an intelligent demeanor, we cannot immediately dismiss it as we would do ordinarily.

ii) *Desires*: We may decide that someone clings to his mistaken belief in the face of all our evidence to the contrary out of a desire that the belief be true which overwhelms his capacity to evaluate evidence rationally. Classically,

[15] W. Newton-Smith, "Relativism and the Possibility of Interpretation," in (Hollis & Lukes, 1982), p.108. I will henceforth refer to this collection as "RR."

[16] Steven Lukes, "Relativism in its Place," RR, p.294.

this category functions as part of some psychoanalytic mode of explanation. We might say, for instance, that so-and-so hates his mother in spite of all his avowals to the contrary, but has such a strong aversion to admitting this to himself that he cannot face any evidence for it, investing his intellectual energies instead in inventing ingenious alternative explanations of all such evidence. Even people not terribly "neurotic" may fear their own or others' cruelty sufficiently to re-interpret the compliments and insults they receive and disperse, or may desire comfort, security, or an abatement of the fear of death sufficiently to maintain beliefs in astrology, I Ching, cults or religions, for which they can (otherwise?) provide no grounds. I will not detail this category too much here, since I will return to it in comment 6, below, and chapter three, but we need to remind ourselves at this point that it, too, requires empirical conditions for its application. When we say that Jones clings to belief x because his desires overwhelm his judgment, we usually have evidence for that claim of the kind, "He's very touchy about x" or "He's usually so articulate, but he doesn't defend x at all well" or "He gets pale, nervous, upset when you bring up his desires about x." We also know that people can hide such evidence very cleverly, so we sometimes attribute blinding desires to anyone who holds an unreasonable belief, especially when we think either "He should know better" or "He usually doesn't think much, believing instead what he wants to believe." On the other hand, the ubiquity of blinding desires, and the cleverness of people at hiding them, must not lead us into using desires as a catch-all explanation for error. It remains an empirical explanation of *some* beliefs, applying only to people who avoid reflecting on a subject more than they usually do, or more than most of us usually do, as a result of desires that we can recognize both as desires and as capable of overcoming someone sufficiently to cut off his judgment.

iii) *The Expressive Theory of Religion (Fideism)*: This is taken to be one of Wittgenstein's own explanations, indeed what he was pointing to with the phrase "an entirely different interpretation" in the *Remarks on Frazer*. Especially as developed by such Wittgensteinians as Peter Winch and D.Z. Phillips, Fideism sees "all religious life as the expression of [a] commitment to communion with the Spiritual Being,"[17] recommending that we regard super-mistakes—such as the remarks of St. Augustine, the Buddhist and the baptist—as poetic expressions of religious commitment rather than statements of any kind of fact. Since they are not statements of fact, they are not in error, even large error; it was merely our mistake to translate them as statements about the world.

Even if we ignore, for the moment, the fact that not all strange claims are meant to be religious (unless we extend the meaning of "religion" so far that it becomes empty), this theory will not work for all strictly religious language.

---

17 Robin Horton, "Tradition and Modernity Revisited," RR, p.208.

Wittgenstein has been strongly criticized for his excessive reliance on Fideism to account for how religious people behave. It is simply not the case that, in connection with religious practices, "you [never] make a man change his way of doing things...by calling attention to his error[s]"[18]—as anthropologists have amply shown with regard to the effect of Western science on African religious rituals. Nor need we go so far for evidence: Wittgenstein calls religious claims erroneous when put forth as "a [scientific] theory,"[19] yet himself admits that some (purportedly?) religious people do think of their religion as such a theory. More people than he would imagine, I suspect; and in any case he has no means of proving these people either less religious or more comprehensible than their Fideist brethren.

To call incomprehensible remarks "religious expression" also requires empirical evidence, although such evidence may be harder to interpret than evidence for other ways of categorization. But if our supposed religious believers do not connect their belief with anything we could recognize (note, again, the necessary appeal to our own standards) as a God or gods, an afterlife, some kind of supernatural reward and punishment, or at least a set of mysterious rituals, we can hardly call it religious.

iv) *The Sociological Explanation*: We know of many cases in which social dynamics make it difficult or impossible for people to learn, to understand, or to acknowledge truths. In traditional societies with very strict hierarchies, for instance, certain figures and the traditions for which they speak may both control the means of education and have such personal authority that others dare not even try to think out certain things for themselves, for fear of human or divine punishment. Only the "priests" are here able to think through the beliefs they pass down, and each one of them may avoid doing so, for fear of the others, or, indeed, of the indoctrinated people.

Again, we have a temptingly "catch-all" mode of explanation. The power structures we are discussing can be found in some form in almost any society: having authorities, as we have seen in considering Freeman and Mead, is essential to the very formation of a community's beliefs. As we move toward modern Western societies, it may become easier to challenge the authorities, and the punishment for unacceptable dissent may take the relatively mild forms of ridicule or exclusion from the academic world, but there remain authorities and punishment nonetheless. We can therefore claim, whenever we find a sane, wide-awake and intelligent person holding a belief we think too wrong to be a mistake, that he holds it only because he has been indoctrinated in it by the power structures of his society.

Yet this mode of explanation also has empirical limitations. If we generalize it to all beliefs, as Marxists tend to do, it either contradicts itself (by calling

---

18 (Wittgenstein, 1979), p.2e.

19 *ibid*, p.4e, and (Wittgenstein, 1970), pp.57-59.

itself false) or ceases to pick out falsehood from truth (by allowing that socially conditioned beliefs may yet be true). I have described a rather crude version of the sociological explanation, using words like "priests," "punishments" and "indoctrination" in order to highlight the very specific conditions on this category. When we say that a priest holds a belief out of fear of divine punishment, that is not yet a sociological explanation, for it presupposes a belief in divine punishment whose social source(s) we have not traced. Of those who are indoctrinated, we can say that they fear their indoctrinators, but who do the indoctrinators fear? The category we are using demands that we find evidence of coercion by or fear of other human beings, and we have not done that so far. Indeed, if we want to call the child-rearing process in the society "indoctrination" at all, with all the coercive connotations of that word, we must see the so-called "indoctrinators" actually employ not education—discussion, argumentation, the encouragement of reflective belief—but some mindless, Pavlovian method of inducing behavior. We of course appeal in this to what "we, around here" mean by "education" and "behavior," but that is the only basis we, around here, have for constructing explanations.

It follows that the appeal to sociological terms and theories depends on certain specific kinds of observations. Most obviously, in a society whose beliefs we want to dismiss as socially induced, we expect to see a fairly strong intellectual hierarchy, some set of powerful figures, and/or a prevalence of superstitious fears. Where intellectual hierarchies are weak and fluid, as they are in the West, where people revere few, if any, of their neighbors, where no-one fidgets, changes the subject, or grows pale and unhappy when we bring up beliefs we want to attribute to the influence of a power structure, there sociological reductions should begin to lose their foothold. Similarly, such theories work best where there is a lot of "parroting" behavior—where people repeat what they have learned practically word for word, rather than constructing imaginative and eloquent arguments for their beliefs. Finally, we expect that when we take indoctrinated people away from their society and teach them our science, mathematics, history, and general ways of reasoning, most of them will "see the error of their ways" and agree with us. And if they do decide to return to their old home and practice their old rituals, we expect that they will do so out of certain desires—a fondness for the comforts of home or so—and not because they disagree with us on any factual matter. Should many members of some society continue to cling to their *beliefs* in the face of our offering of "enlightenment", we would have good *prima facie* reason to back off our attempts to explain those beliefs sociologically. At what point we must entirely give up those attempts no philosopher can say. I merely point out that this category gives us an empirical, not a transcendentally grounded, license to mop up the difficult intellectual disagreements we have with other societies, and as such fails when no good empirical reason supports it.

It is worth noting that the popularity of this particular category has historical roots in a science that viewed the members of all non-Western cultures as quite literally stupider than we are, for either racial or environmental reasons. The notion that non-Westerners are genetically less intelligent than Westerners flourished until at least the 1920s,[20] competing from the Enlightenment until the middle of our own century only with the notion that oppressive social structures preventing free questioning constitute the main reason why religion and other superstitions survive. Under the first of these hypotheses, every member of an alien society is necessarily unintelligent, hence not puzzling or challenging to us. Under the second hypothesis, the beliefs of Augustine, the Buddhist and the baptist turn out to be large mistakes after all, which should vanish, with all their kin, under the light of reason and scientific method that modern Western culture can provide. Given that we have by now both found good reason to consider members of other cultures very intelligent, and discovered that even Western religions do not vanish after exposure to Enlightenment, the catch-all use of the sociological mode of explanation should itself be regarded as something of a superstition that has outlasted, for social reasons, the life of its grounds.

4. I have gone through these categories so exhaustively because I want to stress the fact that the explanations enabling us to classify something as a mistake, being empirical and rooted in ordinary conditions rather than transcendentally justified, may run out, and indeed run out together. Certainly we have a great variety of techniques to deal with statements violently at odds with what we normally consider true. We can say the speaker is mad, or sleepy, or ignorant of the language, or making fun of us, or expressing a (comprehensible) religious commitment, or parroting his society's authorities, or... That the person could be saying just what he seems to be saying although he is intelligent enough to realize, if we do, that he must be in error, seems a possibility we need not confront, given how many and how varied our techniques are for avoiding such confrontation. I suspect that when philosophers who dislike the very notion of incommensurability are presented with evidence for its value, they think of the mere number and flexibility of these techniques and assume that one of them will surely take care of the troublesome evidence. But while profuse, our strategies for explaining challenges to what we consider true are not infinite, nor are they sufficient to turn every strange remark into an error by another name.

Let me now clarify what I mean by a "mistake" and a "super-mistake." I cannot give a scientific theory of mistakes here, because the category I am defining is constitutive of what we mean by "truth" and "error," hence what we mean by "science." Instead, I am suggesting definitions that I hope will

---

[20] See (Freeman, 1978), chapters 1-3, and (Gould, 1981).

elicit general agreement from those who use the terms. And indeed the paradigm use of the word "mistake" itself depends crucially on the actual or at least expected agreement of the mistaken one that he is in error. Paradigmatically, you make a mistake when you misperceive something (perceive something you (would) agree you normally would perceive differently), reason wrongly or miscalculate (perform a calculation or draw an inference you (would) agree comes out other than you thought), or rely on misinformation or ignorance (rely on factual claims you (would) agree are incorrect, or on inferences for which you (would) agree you need facts that you did not know). Somewhat more broadly, we can take a remark of yours as a mistake when and only when we can reasonably expect to be able to persuade you that it is an error. A super-mistake, therefore, is paradigmatically an error so large that we think, "if you believe *that*, you probably don't share enough of our modes of evidence for us to persuade you of anything." Sometimes we can attribute this to your simply lacking capacities that we can reasonably suppose (*must* suppose, if we are to distinguish thinking from chaos at all) you would rather possess if you had a choice in the matter. This is a tremendously weak and vague counterfactual that will not survive very close examination, but it will do us no harm to allow it to support our categories of "madness," "neurological breakdown," "sociological determination," etc. for the purposes of this argument. Even with this counterfactual, after all, there are times when we cannot reasonably apply any of our normal categories of breakdown to you, cannot attribute our inability to persuade you to anything wrong with you. At such times, we begin to find appealing the category we might want to call "incommensurable disagreement," a category in which our grip on the "erroneous" or "false" quality of the remarks and beliefs in question weakens dramatically.

It weakens, given the consensus view of truth. If we could tie truth simply to correspondence with a transcendental object, all mistakes would just be statements that failed to mesh with the facts. Then we would call all who disagree with us "mistaken," even when we could neither persuade them nor dismiss them as insane, stupid or confused—whenever we guessed that their beliefs, rather than ours, failed to mesh with the transcendental facts. Now, the response of the consensus view to this Kantian approach is to deny not the reality of the transcendental object, or the truth of transcendental laws, but their *usefulness* to us in any real debate over truth. If the statements we use for empirical evidence are true only by virtue of according with some set of "transcendental facts" or following from some set of transcendental laws, then we, who have no access to such facts or laws except via other non-transcendental statements we use in argument and persuasion, are always only guessing at the truth—even when we accept this very hypothetical—and that makes the words "guess" and "true" lose their meaning. But if we limit or waive our right to appeal to anything beyond our consensus, what we mean by calling a statement "true" comes to have much to do with whether the speaker can persuade us of it, and what we mean by calling a statement "mistaken" has much to do with whether we can persuade the speaker otherwise. This leaves us with little to say about the truth or error of statements made by someone significantly outside our consensus about modes of evidence. Our consensus itself makes room, as we have seen, for many categories of error, but each of those categories can fail to apply, and there is no reason to suppose that they could not all fail to apply together. To stretch these categories to cover all aberrant cases would distort the ordinary meaning of such notions as "madness," "disturbance," "social conditioning," which get their role in our lives out of our sense that some, but not all, of our fellow human beings would like to share what we consider the true view of the world but are unable to. Such categories have their meaning within the context of our normal use of "truth" and "error," and cannot be used in turn to supply those terms with an absolute or transcendental definition.

On the other hand, we should note that none of this means we have to call the positions of someone outside our consensus *not* erroneous, nor that we must revise our law of excluded middle and call it neither true not false. We may simply refuse to call it anything. We do not know what to call it; we do not understand it well enough to call it anything. After all, our use of the terms "true" and "false" does not have to do *only* with whether we can persuade the speaker or are persuaded by him. Indeed, it is part of our very consensus that "objectivity" and "truth" do not *mean* consensus, even if we recognize that our use of them must depend on one. We are forced, in a way that will become clearer later in chapter four, to move constantly back and forth between what we might call an "inside" and an "outside" view of truth, according to which, on the one hand, we do not have the slightest idea what it would be to accept something as true except on the kinds of grounds we normally accept as such, while on the other hand, we do not want to define the truth thus testified for *by* the grounds and consensus about grounds that supply the testimony. The question remains, then, how "truth" and "falsehood" can possibly apply to views or modes of evidence beyond our consensus. Worse, given the link Davidson has rightly shown between our language for truth and our language for understanding, how can we possibly say we understand such views at all? How can we even count them as "views" and "modes of evidence"? But if we are to make any sense at all of the word "consensus" in the consensus view of truth, we must understand it in terms of empirical conditions, which means that we must, and I believe we can, give some meaning to the notion that we can understand—and thus find, in some respect, "possibly true"—ways of thinking and arguing beyond our consensus.

5. I want to indicate, at this point, what range of beliefs could qualify as belonging significantly outside our consensus, as the locus of "radical" or

"incommensurable" disagreement. I have used the phrase "modes of evidence" to suggest that such a disagreement must not concern mere individual facts, on the one hand, nor methods of logical inference, on the other. In particular, I want to avoid defending Peter Winch's notorious and unfortunate suggestion, that "Criteria of logic...arise out of, and are only intelligible in the context of, ways of living or modes of social life."[21] Much of the debate over conceptual relativism has focussed on whether it makes sense to suppose that different cultural groups might have different logics. Donald Davidson, for example, is concerned first and foremost to show that we must read "the logical structure of first-order quantification theory (plus identity)" into any language we want to translate, and Jonathan Lear, in his Davidsonian reading of Wittgenstein, argues against the suggestion that there might be groups with radically different ways of thinking from ours primarily on the grounds that we cannot imagine (make sense of imagining) a group that disagreed with us over such things as *modus ponens*.[22] That logic might "arise out of" social structures is indeed a self-defeating and barely intelligible suggestion, but "logic" does not embrace everything interesting about the way we think or ascertain truth. Importantly, Wittgenstein himself rarely talks about logical principles (never, as far as I know, about *modus ponens*), and when he does bring up either a logical or a mathematical law, he always speculates only about how its *application* might differ from one group to another, making clear that while its application defines most of what interests us about it, there remains a sense (an "architectural" sense, perhaps, such that the way we define the law forms "a kind of ornamental coping")[23] in which we must regard the law as universal and necessary.[24] Hence, he would have no truck with Winch's implication that our laws of logic might themselves be contingent, or the conclusion Winch draws that "one cannot apply criteria of logic to modes of social life as such," although he might agree with the more cautious suggestion that criteria of logic are "only intelligible in the context of" forms of social life.

I want to stay away from criteria of logic altogether, while stressing that logic alone can never settle an argument over a particular, non-logical truth we care about. No logic can determine the relevance of an argument to a given question,[25] and every argument can be construed as an enthymeme by someone who disagrees with its conclusion and wishes to construct a logical proof of the opposite. Just as differences over manners and custom are uninteresting, too small for incommensurability, "differences" over logic (and perhaps mathematics) are too large. They will indeed never occur, but precisely because

---

21 (Winch, 1958), p. 100.

22 (Lear, 1982), especially p. 389.

23 PI 217. See also OC 211.

24 See, for instance, (Wittgenstein, 1964), pp. 50, 89-90, 225-7. Henceforth: RFM.

25 See Ronald de Sousa's discussion of the so-called "frame problem" in (de Sousa, 1987), and de Sousa, "The Rationality of Emotions," in (Rorty, 1980), pp. 135-6.

they could never make a difference. As Lear has shown, we cannot imagine a group that differed with us over principles of logic, but I suggest that that is because we *define* logic as the field of those principles of method we cannot imagine being otherwise. Insofar as we can imagine differences that we might want to describe as differences in reasoning or method of thought, we must imagine that those differences entail something substantive, some different conclusion about how the world is or might be, some difference over fact. In this way, all differences that can interest us come down to differences over modes of presenting empirical evidence. Even an apparent disagreement over *modus ponens* or the law of non-contradiction will either boil down to a disagreement over modes of evidence or make no sense at all as a difference. We might say: the very scope of a disagreement over logic or mathematics will necessarily render it vacuous. Only a difference over matters of fact can have the scope necessary to constitute an incommensurable difference between groups while remaining intelligible as a difference.

But all this entails making considerably more precise what "modes of evidence" might mean. As I use it, the phrase should correspond to much of what Wittgenstein means by a "world-picture," what Cavell means by "routes of interest and feeling," what Lear calls "perceptions of salience, feelings of naturalness, etc."[26] "Modes of evidence" are ways that one statement may be used to support another. Wittgenstein gives the example of one society supporting statements about the future by appealing to utterances of an oracle, while another appeals to observations gathered by physicists. This familiar illustration covers up the multiplicity of such modes, and the question of choosing one out of several alternative modes of evidence is not as remote as we might imagine. In the first place, there are several different interpretations of the familiar illustration itself. Do we mean by "oracle" a high priest who throws dice to determine yes/no answers to specific questions (as was the case, apparently, with the Biblical Urim and Thummim)?[27] Or a hidden person at a certain shrine who actually answers yes or no to specific questions, like the Delphic Oracle? Or an astrologer, pastor, guru, etc. who gives detailed instructions to visitors on how to run their lives, possibly after examining astronomical facts or a sacred text?

A second level of multiplicity enters when we consider the different ways, within our own culture, in which we support scientific, aesthetic, ethical, and religious statements. When evaluating a work of art, the feeling of pleasure it gives me or fails to give me can form a reasonable touchstone for any judgment; when making an ethical decision, any feelings of pleasure arising from one or another alternative may be a consideration, but should not be paramount; when

---

[26] (Lear, 1982), p. 385, and Cavell, "The Availability of Wittgenstein's Later Philosophy," in (Pitcher, 1968), pp. 160-1.

[27] (Cody, 1969), pp. 14, 25.

doing science, feelings of pleasure about a theory should be quite irrelevant. Similar distinctions hold for the value of the opinions of others, of the testimony of my senses, of fitting my reasons for my conclusions in with a tradition of reasons for similar conclusions, and so forth.

This second level of multiplicity raises questions about how we know when one mode or another is appropriate to a given argument. Usually we have no problem simply "telling" when we are discussing art, ethics, science, etc., but the question can become difficult—as when, for example, we come to the study of the human being. Should we regard other human beings, for the purpose of understanding them, from an aesthetic point-of-view,[28] an ethical one, or a scientific one? And if this is a difficult question, then so is the one about how to regard modes of evidence used by other human groups, for different modes of evidence are constituted by and help to constitute much of what we consider important about other human beings: their views, ethical decisions, aesthetic sensibilities.

If the application of modes of evidence seems problematic just in the case of the human sciences, we can make it a more general difficulty by looking at the multiplicity even within the kinds of evidence acceptable to what we have so far labelled simply "physics" and "science." In the first place, the well-known distinctions between statistical and experimental evidence have long played a role in arguments among scientists themselves. Whether one can ever or always be reduced to the other has brought into doubt, on the one hand, the status of such fields as economics, geology, biology and medicine as sciences at all, on the other, the claims intrinsic to physics and chemistry that their laws constitute a universal, inviolable and full explanation of the phenomena to which they apply.

Then, consider the relation of "hard scientific" to common-sensical evidence. When we want to know whether there is a mailbox on the corner, we are not even tempted to call the physicist or conduct an experiment; we "just go and check." Ultimately, we use similar, although not exactly the same, methods for determining what and where most of the ordinary objects of our world are, how best to use them, and in what way we can best preserve our health and happiness when around them. Now suppose we want to adjudicate between the common-sensical and the physico-chemical approaches to truth. Common-sense recognizes the value of the hard sciences, of course, and the hard sciences could presumably find a necessary role for something corresponding to common-sense in the history of the physico-chemical

28 There are hints of such a suggestion in the writings of Gadamer and Cavell: consider Gadamer's crucial analysis of "play," and use of Kant's *Critique of Judgment* (which, admittedly, he criticizes for removing judgment from the ethical realm), and Cavell's increasing tendency to use the analysis and experience of drama and film as an entry into ethical questions: (Gadamer 1975: 10-153). Stanley Cavell, "The Avoidance of Love," in (Cavell, 1969). See also (Cavell, 1979), part IV.

structures we call "human beings." But if they differ widely on some particular matter, which method of proving and defining should we prefer? From the point-of-view of common-sense, the hard sciences are useful only insofar as they enhance our (common-sensical) ability to find our way around our world: if what they determine to be "medicine," for instance, just doesn't give us what we ordinarily consider longer and healthier life, we have to regard their proofs and experiments on the matter to be wrong. Moreover, as this very example implies, the hard sciences *depend* on common-sense insofar as human beings pursue them. When we want to know a water level or temperature in an experiment, we "just go and check." It makes no sense to devise yet another experiment to examine our perceptions, or yet a better machine to replace them, because at some point that further experiment or machine will also depend on our ordinary perceptions. On the other hand, the hard scientist can show that common-sense itself is merely a neurological system, explicable down to the level of the interaction of the molecules that make up the relevant nerves, with a place in a certain physico-chemical structure. Should this system evince views that conflict significantly with the conclusions of hard science, it would simply be malfunctioning, and this can be shown in a description of the structure to which it belongs. No claims about the dependence of hard science on common-sense itself need shake this argument, since the scientist can hold that at most such claims only point to a limitation in what we can know of science, and make no difference to what actually happens at a physico-chemical level.

Because unsettleable arguments like this exist, there will be no final answer to the question of where to apply which mode of evidence. If no logic determines relevance, different people may apply different kinds of factual evidence to the same issue, and some will appeal to aesthetic, ethical, political or religious concerns where others would appeal to science. Arguments about which mode is appropriate in a particular case tend only to lead to further, often more radical, differences in approach. And from this, irresolvable disagreements over truth arise: reasonable people may recognize others as reasoning, all right, but reasoning in a different mode, and they need have no reason to give their mode priority in the situation over the mode of the others.

> OC 609. Supposing we met people who did not regard [the propositions of physics] as a telling reason. Now, how do we imagine this? Instead of the physicist, they consult an oracle. (And for that reason we consider them primitive.) Is it wrong for them to consult an oracle and be guided by it?—If we call this "wrong" aren't we using our language-game as a base from which to *combat* theirs?

> OC 610. And are we right or wrong to combat it? Of course there are all sorts of slogans which will be used to support our proceedings.

> OC 611. Where two principles really do meet which cannot be reconciled

with one another, then each man declares the other a fool and a heretic.

> OC 612. I said I would 'combat' the other man,—but wouldn't I give him *reasons*? Certainly; but how far do they go? At the end of reasons comes *persuasion*....

6. I would now like to work through an example of a disagreement we might come to see as incommensurable, and try to see what account we might give of that incommensurability.

Consider first Jones, who insists that cigarette-smoking is good for one's health. Jones smokes, of course, and draws on his own experience for evidence. I counter this evidence with data from scientific experiments on the subject, and an argument begins. At this point, we have what looks like an ordinary error, on one side or the other, with agreed-on evidence, and modes of evidence, available for settling the matter. But Jones, trying to wriggle out of a losing battle of data, starts raising wider and wider questions about the very nature of the evidence I present. First he accuses me of ignorance or lying, which is reasonable enough, or casts aspersions upon the scientists I quote, which is also reasonable. Then, when I find other sources that confirm my data and praise my scientists, he suggests that all contemporary work in biochemistry and medicine is hogwash, and when I point to the empirical successes of these fields, he questions the trustworthiness of empirical evidence, or the scientific method, in general. At this point, without having said anything literally senseless, Jones has moved beyond the realm in which I can persuade him on this matter. Neither I nor anyone listening to us, however, should have any trouble in continuing to regard him as simply mistaken. Even if he is not mad, not making fun, not tripping over his tongue, we recognize that the desire to continue smoking can override a person's commitment to rational argument and we do not take him seriously. In any case, as long as he denies all socially accepted canons of argument we will not consider him reasonable enough to have a claim on the truth. If rationality is tied to a consensus about modes of argument, a person must appeal to some society's argumentative canons (albeit ones *we* (around here) can accept as canons, of a society, and concerning argument) for us to consider him reasonable when we consider his position unreasonable. With a member of a quite different society, therefore, we might take an attitude like Jones' more seriously. ("It would strike me as ridiculous to want to doubt the existence of Napoleon; but if someone doubted the existence of the earth 150 years ago, perhaps I should be more willing to listen, for now he is doubting our whole system of evidence." (OC 185))

Consider now Awali, raised in a community very unlike our own, both in interests and in beliefs about the world. Awali is well-educated in both his own society and ours—he is a tribal leader who has gone to Oxford, let us say—but even after coming down from Oxford, he believes in a complicated afterlife in which one will do best if one guides one's actions on earth according to the dictates of a certain oracle. On this oracle's recommendation, Awali also believes that cigarette-smoking is healthy (along with playing with cobras). Can we regard him as making a mistake?

We can dismiss some of our categories for mistakes and non-mistakes very quickly. Awali is not misperceiving anything, miscalculating, or drawing badly reasoned conclusions. He need not be, and I shall assume he is not, making fun of us, sleepy or otherwise temporarily confused, insane or generally stupid (on other subjects he thinks imaginatively and well, by our lights). His English is excellent and he is well acquainted with our science and literature.

Furthermore, we cannot reasonably take up a "Fideist" attitude toward his beliefs. We may regard his belief in the oracle, and even his belief in an afterlife (properly interpreted) as expressing some kind of commitment to a spiritual being, but not his beliefs about cigarette-smoking and rattlesnakes. Yet we cannot siphon the latter off from the former, since he derives claims about cigarette-smoking from claims about the oracle.

The sociological explanation of Awali's beliefs will probably evade strict refutation, but it may well be unsatisfying. Presumably we will find that Awali's religion has been handed down from generation to generation in a hierarchical community, but, as we have seen, to make this into a reason for considering the community's beliefs *wrong* we need to show 1) that the individual believers—in this case, Awali—hold their beliefs *because and only because* they have been indoctrinated by their community (they have not, for instance, seriously questioned them and reflected on them), and 2) that the authorities in the community who originally passed on the beliefs were lying, making a mistake, or falling into a recognizable category of super-mistake. In this case, we will probably neither be able to determine what the original sources of Awali's religion thought and did, nor give an account of how we suppose they erred that will satisfy Awali. In addition, I am assuming Awali to be an Oxford graduate in order to suggest that he retains or returns to his old beliefs after learning what we believe, receiving what we consider enlightenment, and getting a chance to perceive his old authorities in a sociological light, and to criticize and question what may once have been dogma for him. We may suppose that he shows evidence of having done this thoroughly, of having reflected and reflectively decided to keep his old beliefs. Then, although we may still assume that he has been molded by his society, we have no reason to continue assuming that that molding interferes with his thought any more than our own molding interferes with our thought. We cannot now use the sociological explanation to establish a distinction in the power of our respective abilities to think; we cannot use it as a lever that raises us closer to truth, lowers him towards error.

This leaves us with the category of desires. Now, it is tempting to attribute all strange claims that resist other explanations to the influence of desires. In the first place, a few extremely familiar desires—notably, the desire for security, or to conform with others, the desire for perversity, or to stand out from others, and the desire to survive death—can explain almost any human behavior. The urge towards perversity alone, by definition, can lie behind anything otherwise inexplicable. In the second place, desires can be hidden and disguised very easily, so neither a lack of evidence nor the existence of contrary evidence need count against an attribution of desire. On the other hand, we know that desires normally come in certain degrees and certain hierarchies (the desire to conform, for instance, normally takes precedence over the desire to stand out, since one normally wants to stand out among friends and admirers, not among strangers), and are normally expressed in some actions rather than others. If the category of desires is not to become useless as a mode of explanation, we need to limit our employment of it as a ground for attributing error to conditions like these. If a person speaks to us seriously and humbly, does not usually try to stand out much from his peers, insists that he believes what he says on the grounds he has given us, accepts reproof and considers his remarks carefully, we have reason not to attribute his beliefs to an urge for perversity.

In Awali's case we are likely to want to see his beliefs as rooted either in a desire for the comfort and security of home or in the fear of death. Even if he stays among us (consulting his oracle by mail or on short visits), we may say that he clings to the old beliefs to retain some sense of home about him, yet perhaps we would withdraw this explanation if he seems really debonair about his alienation, if he is close enough to his society not to need its beliefs, if the beliefs get in the way of much that he wants to do, or if those back home no longer regard the religion as particularly important. The fear of death, on the other hand, given its overwhelming importance even among ourselves, we are likely to attribute to him in the face of almost any evidence.

I want to focus on this fear of death, because it will bring out the significance and limits of the explanation by desire. Suppose Awali displays behavior strongly indicating that his fear of death is not pathological, not overwhelming, not obstructing his thought. He does not get angry or upset when we discuss the subject. When we suggest that it may underlie his religion, he responds intelligently. He may still fear death, but we cannot suppose that he does so more than we do, and, as with the sociological explanation, this puts an obstacle in the way of using his fear to dismiss his beliefs. At least in our capacity as scientists, we think we do not allow our fear of death to dictate what entities or systems we should posit, so why should Awali's fears work differently? After all, we would all most satisfactorily meet our fear by discovering something that would actually enable us to overcome either death or the fear of it, and we do this project a disservice if we allow the fear itself to fool us or misdirect our researches. Thus a worshipper will sacrifice to his gods just as much because he *believes* that practice will bring him a good afterlife as because he *wants* a good afterlife. Even the person who adopts a religion on a Pascal wager must have some independent cognitive commitment to the religion, since the wager will work only if there is some reason to opt for a particular one of the many conflicting systems that promise salvation.

In general, I think we try to assimilate beliefs like Awali's to error by claiming that such speakers are violating, out of a psychological need, a principle we consider essential to any search for knowledge: Occam's Razor. Rather than stripping away all assumptions not required to account for the available "evidence," they are positing unnecessary principles or entities in the world so as to make room for what they want to exist in the midst of what does. But in the circumstances I have described we would no longer be able to describe our differences with someone like Awali in this manner. Instead, this example shows us that Occam's Razor does not work as a simple, universal principle enabling anyone to purify cognition of all desires and interests; it works only *given* certain interests (those that lie behind the ontology we initially accept in any investigation) and its use is itself interested. I will elaborate the argument for this claim in the next chapter, noting at the moment only that if it can be made good, our difference with Awali will at root be one of interests: we will not understand why Awali has the interests that he does.

This turns out to be the only way we can make sense of the notion of understanding that we have an incommensurable disagreement with someone. If we do not understand what they say, after all, that leaves us open to assume that they think much like us—believe true what we believe true and make the kinds of mistakes we expect to make—and then if they disagree with us in beliefs, one of us must simply be making some kind of error. For disagreement between us to transcend error yet not get large enough as to cast doubt on our translations of what they say, we look to interests and desires, where we know that people can differ significantly. We must assume *general* community of desires and interests, however, in order to interpret other people. To translate "chair" or "house," we have to assume that a speaker shares with us desires for rest, shelter and warmth; to attribute a vocabulary for plants and animals to people, we must assume desires to organize the world in certain ways that facilitate prediction and control; to translate any language at all we need to assume that the people we are translating want to communicate with each other, and indeed want to communicate in specific ways much like our own (such that poets and priests need not always make themselves clear, while technicians must be both clear and precise and salesmen clear but not precise). Even Awali's desires have to be quite familiar to us if we are to describe what we find perplexing about him. To know that he guides his life by his oracle, we must recognize many of the kinds of problems for which he consults the oracle, and to do that, we must attribute to him the desires similar to our own. Only if he appears to dislike illness and seek cures for it can we say that he seeks "health," for instance. And if he never seems to seek health we will begin to doubt that we know what he means by "health."

It is indeed not clear what might constitute failing to recognize another's desires. Gabriel Garcia Marquez describes a girl who enjoys eating dirt,[29] which seems on the face of it quite a strange desire, but we do not take it on its face. Instead, we place it in a context of other desires or facts that bring it closer to our own experience. Marquez himself suggests that the taste for dirt was acquired in an unusually poverty-stricken childhood, and connects it with a more general desire to revolt against the conventions of civilization. He might well not have supplied such an explanation, but had he not, we would have allowed the oddity precisely because the account is a novel, perhaps assuming that a creature desiring to eat dirt shares a human physiology with us only in fantasy.

What we fail to understand about Awali is therefore not what desires he has, but why his desires come in this rather than another order. Why, that is, does he reflectively allow his interest in overcoming death to take precedence over his interest in enjoying the life he has, or his interest in the security and order which his society provides to take precedence over the risk and freedom which our society provides? Here we can comfortably say, "I understand *that* Awali has this hierarchy of interests, but I don't understand *why* he does." And yes, "I don't understand why you (or how you can possibly) find security, perversity, risk, magic, love so important" does bear a certain resemblance to "I don't understand how you can possibly like olives," in that desires are involved and I feel that I recognize the relevant desire even though I don't share it, but not all desires have the same form, and the ones I am now attributing to Awali, unlike desires about olives, leave room for discussion. I will reserve the word "interests" for this kind of motivation for action, and note that while we may not dispute *de gustibus*, we do, vigorously and to the point of irresolvability, dispute about interests. For this reason, and considering that interests underlie all discussion, they do not vitiate objectivity as desires do. Why this is so, how interests and desires differ, and why interests must underlie all discussion, are the topics of the next chapter.

---

[29] (Marquez, 1978), p.42.

CHAPTER THREE

DESIRES AND INTERESTS

> What interests us would not interest *them*. Here different concepts would no longer be unimaginable. In fact, this is the only way in which *essentially* different concepts are imaginable. (Wittgenstein, *Zettel §388*)

> To every faculty of the mind an interest can be ascribed, i.e., a principle which contains the condition under which alone its exercise is advanced. (Kant, *Critique of Practical Reason*)

> [E]ven the ...[rational] will can *take an interest* in something without therefore *acting from interest*. The first expression signifies *practical* interest in the action; the second *pathological* interest in the object of the action. (Kant, *Groundwork*)

> An interest is that in virtue of which reason becomes practical—that is, becomes a cause determining the will. Hence only of a rational being do we say that he takes an interest in something: non-rational creatures merely feel sensuous impulses. (Kant, *Groundwork*)[1]

With these quotations, and these thinkers, as my guide, I have adopted the term "interest" for something weightier and more "world-guided" than mere "desires" (what Kant here calls "pathological interests"). In what follows, I want to argue that facts without desires are blind, desires without facts are empty, that the two make sense only in the complex I am now calling an "interest."

BLIND FACTS, AND DESIRES THAT SEE

I approach my subject indirectly, via a discussion of skepticism. I agree with Thomas Nagel[2] that skepticism is both irrefutable and inescapable, but would add that most interesting skepticism boils down to scepticism about induction. The radical skeptic about material objects, the external world, or the justification for knowledge, with all her evil demons and mad scientists, will presumably behave towards chairs, tables, etc. just as we do, at least if we are to translate anything she says; it is thus unclear what her doubts amount to, and whether they are in fact doubts. Skeptical (like incommensurable) positions only threaten us when they affect predictions about the future. Nothing about our world will change if we think we are brains in a vat unless we infer from that that the scientist programming our brains might radically change the program.

---

1 (Kant, 1956), p.124 (119), (Kant, 1964), pp.81 (413), 128 (460).

2 (Nagel, 1979), p.19, footnote 1.

Nor does it matter if we disbelieve in material objects unless we begin to fear that the illusions we have of them might disappear. Even someone who said the world was created 150 years ago would bother us not when she called our geology and history mythological, but when she refused to accept inferences about the present world drawn from that geology and history.

Skepticism about induction, however, may itself take nonsensical forms. We must avoid speaking of a principle of induction that some believe and others doubt, since in the first place we could not formulate any *principle*, divorced from such specific elements of the contexts in which we make inductions as what Goodman calls "entrenched predicates,"[3] to use as a separate step when drawing inductive inferences, and in the second place we could not translate anyone, and certainly not recognize anyone as "making predictions," who did not generally rely on what I will call our inductive *practices*.[4] Even the person who goes to the oracle expects her home, clothes, and food to behave roughly the way they did yesterday, or she could have no home, clothes or food, and she goes to the oracle, if not because it has actually helped her in the past, at least because she believes that the reality on behalf of which it speaks has not changed. Though this be induction, it is not our induction; the visitor to the oracle does not rely on induction in the way we do. She may, for instance, assert that the events of this world have no bearing on the nature of the afterlife and refuse to draw inferences from past experience when a question pertains to the afterlife, or she may assert that this world will undergo a radical change at a certain time and refuse to draw inferences from past experience about facts taking place in that time. And unlike Goodman's "grue," the predicates on the basis of which she makes these claims may well be entrenched in the language she speaks.

Now, what kind of answer can we give the skeptic who presents such a case as the motivation for her doubts—a person who comes into conflict with our inductive practices only in certain well-defined instances, when she turns to an oracle instead of relying on sensory evidence? Our best bet, I suggest, is to use a combination of Reichenbach's pragmatic approach to induction with Braithwaite and Black's predictionist one,[5] declaring that on a secondary level of justification our mode of prediction has pragmatic grounds, since it has worked better on the whole than any other mode. The straight predictionist approach makes the mistake of claiming the secondary level of induction as a *proof* (albeit an inductive one) of the value of the primary level—for which reason it gets into all kinds of subtle and not so subtle problems with

3 (Goodman, 1978), p.128.

4 Compare Keith Campbell's argument in "One Form of Scepticism About Induction": "...the general, unrestricted denial of the propriety of induction cannot be coherently made[, although] scepticism concerning particular inductive procedures is proper and doubtless often warranted." In (Swinburne, 1974), p.148.

5 Braithwaite, "The Predictionist Justification of Induction," and Max Black's part of the exchange, "Self-Supporting Inductive Arguments," also in (Swinburne, 1974).

circularity[6]—while Reichenbach wisely insists that on the secondary level we look for different kinds of reason than we do on the primary one, that we seek grounds to *bet on* familiar induction rather than to prove its adequacy. On the other hand, I prefer to use inductive evidence as the basis for this bet than Reichenbach's own arguments, because I do not believe he shows the uniformity of nature to be a necessary condition for all prediction. Reichenbach tells us that we have better reason to place our bets on our familiar inductive practices than on any alternative mode of prediction, because if there are any uniformities in nature at all, our familiar inductions will be able to pick them up at least as well as any alternative. Suppose a "clairvoyant" turns out to make consistently correct predictions. Then those predictions themselves will constitute a series with a limit to the frequency of the predicted qualities, a regularity in the world over which we can make scientific inductions. Indeed, says Reichenbach, we would only come to rely on the clairvoyant at all if we could "test" her by checking her predictions against other inductions.[7]

But all this assumes that we want to use the alternative mode of prediction recurrently, as a regular *method* comparable to the way we use our familiar inductions, rather than that we might one time, or under a few special circumstances, break away from our familiar inductions for a sudden appeal to oracles or prophets. Certainly, a regular use of an oracle pre-supposes a limited frequency which our familiar inductions will ultimately be best suited to pick up. The use of an oracle on any one specific occasion, however, may pre-suppose precisely the opposite: that here, for some reason, the practices we *normally* endorse will break down, that a super-natural structure or being is displaying its super-natural status precisely by overruling what is otherwise the natural order. And the reason for appealing to the oracle in such a case may have nothing to do with prior success. We might choose the person because of her ethical qualities or charisma, because she occupies a social role hallowed by tradition, or because we simply have a strong affection or love for her. (Compare the conditions Maimonides gives for regarding someone as a prophet: "Not every one showing a sign or token is on that account to be accepted as a prophet. Only if a man, by reason of his wisdom and conduct wherein he stands preeminent among his contemporaries, is already recognized as worthy of the prophetic gift, and his life, in its sanctity and renunciation, is favourable to the prophetic calling,—then, when he shows a sign or token and asserts that God had sent him, is it one's duty to listen to his message, as it is said, 'Unto him ye shall hearken' [Deut.18:15].")[8] The assumption that we choose the oracle

---

6 See Peter Achinstein's part of the exchange, "Self-Supporting Inductive Arguments," in (Swinburne, 1974).

7 (Reichenbach, 1938), pp.353-4.

8 (Maimonides, 1981), p.43b.

because of her prior success already builds in a subtle prejudice in favor of scientific induction.[9]

Of course, if the oracle only works on sudden and special occasion, we shall never know when to appeal to it—we can never prove in advance that it will work *here*. But Reichenbach concedes that we do not know or prove scientific induction to be successful. We seek reasons to place our trust in it, rather than to be assured of its truth. He tells us we have such reasons because "it corresponds to a procedure the applicability of which is the necessary condition of the possibility of predictions," but if, as I have maintained, it is the necessary condition only of *most* predictions, and of any exceptionless *method* of prediction, this reason fails to establish adequately that one should not trust a seer chosen on ethical, mystical, or traditional grounds in specific, exceptional cases.

Now it still remains up to the challenger of our familiar inductive practices to justify the claim that there are or might be breaks in the uniformities we see around us, and we might quite plausibly point out that those making such claims in the past have generally, if not universally, been wrong. Since the challenger as she has now been constructed must in general accept our inductions, this appeal to the failure of oracles in the past should have some purchase on her, even if an appeal to the necessity of our mode of induction does not. Given the sensory evidence on which we and the challenger agree, there is reason to think that if any method of inductive inference will work in the future, ours will, and there is no reason to think that any other inductive practice will work better. We can add, concerning other practices, that there is (as far as any of us knows) no more going for any one of them than for thousands of others—against the oracle in question we could put up astrologers, psychics, readers of entrails, priests of one religion or another...—all of which may even boast some successes here and there.

But the visitor to the oracle might reasonably respond that we read the record of success and failure all wrong. If we take into account the value of her way of thought for having a good afterlife (or a good time in the eschatological period about to descend on us), we will see that she has in fact made the more successful predictions. To this we can only answer that we do not take theories about afterlives and eschatology into account, citing in our defense, perhaps, Occam's Razor. This raises yet more difficulties, however, for we can use the razor only when there is no *reason* to adopt an additional assumption, and that is precisely what our interlocutor denies. We come here to the weakness of all attempts to defend our familiar inductive practices: they work only if we have independent reason to restrict our generalizations to the "sensory evidence" that we believe is available to all human beings. We must assume

---

9 As does Reichenbach's very choice of a "clairvoyant"–one who "clear"ly "sees" the future–rather than an oracle (one who *hears* divine wisdom) or a prophet (one who *interprets* a divine ethical or historical law).

that there have been and will be no special revelations, by which some but not all of us might come to have knowledge of radical changes in or exceptions to what we normally consider the course of nature.

I suggest that we do make this assumption, but on the basis of certain rather specific *interests*, intrinsic to the definition of Western science. These are 1) the interest in manipulating physical objects to increase our pleasure and life-expectancies to their greatest possible limit, and 2) the interest in treating human beings in as egalitarian a way as possible. The latter demands that we see knowledge as accessible, in principle at least, to all human beings, that we disallow the separation off of certain individuals as special seers. As Arthur Lovejoy has pointed out, it is part of the Enlightenment conception of the human being (which in many respects, especially when it comes to evaluating the project of science, the overwhelming majority of us still share) that "anything of which the intelligibility, verifiability, or actual affirmation is limited to men of a special age, race, temperament, tradition or condition is [in and of itself] without truth or value, or at all events without importance to a reasonable man."[10] It follows that we must deny the existence of any ghost, spirit, deity, etc. that cannot be sensed by everyone and is not required to explain what can be sensed by everyone. And interest 1) defines what counts as the relevant sphere to which we want to apply our egalitarian "sensory evidence": hallucinations, mirages, afterimages, and the visions of the mad do not count, since predictions on the basis of them do not tend to enhance anyone's pleasure or life-expectancy.

The simple justification for such a move is that the rationality of a bet depends on the nature of the stakes as well as the odds of winning and losing, and in our Reichenbachian bet on a way of knowledge, our egalitarian, humanistic interests set the stakes. But such an account is somewhat too simple. For one thing our two central interests need not always cohere. If the way to pleasure and long-life is specially revealed to Hindu Brahmins, we will miss something we want to know if we put our interest in egalitarian knowing above everything they say. Nor is it by any means clear that we want to abandon interest in an afterlife or eschatological world, should there be any such, or that the interest in pleasure can adequately encompass our concerns for human relationships or for such institutions as art. Hence, if we indeed practice a science that makes a Reichenbachian bet on ordinary induction out of trust in these two interests, we can no longer be sure that what we call "science" adequately satisfies what we want from what we call "knowledge."

My response to this depends on two points: 1) that interests are not mere wishes or desires, mere products of our will, our subjective life, our fantasy;

---

10 (Lovejoy, 1948), p.80. See also pp. 82-85, and 172, and (Lovejoy, 1964), pp. 7-10, 288-93. What Lovejoy calls "uniformitarianism" is very similar to the interest I refer to as "egalitarianism" or "egalitarian knowledge."

and 2) that we have no choice but to rely on them. To begin with the latter: Imagine that we had all the facts in the world, or all the facts pertaining to a particular subject matter. We may take a positivist reading of "facts" here, not because the positivists are right, but because they more than anyone tried to keep human desires out of cognition, so if they fail, everyone else should pretty much come along *a fortiori*. We therefore have a collection of pure phenomena, sense-data, or what have you, which we want to put in some order. How do we decide what kind of order we seek, and which phenomena are more relevant than which others to that order?[11] How do we decide to regard one set of perceptions as excessively biased by the emotional state of the perceiver, another as atypical or eccentric? How do we decide not to count hallucinations, mirages, and afterimages? The obvious answer might be that we look for the method that has had the most success in predicting the recurrence of the phenomena it studies—measuring "success" purely numerically—but this is quite unsatisfactory. In the first place, why seek numerical superiority? We may answer that that gives us our best bet at secure prediction of the future, but precisely whether we want security is in question here. Or we might say that the greater our success at prediction the closer we come to describing all of reality, but we have no right to such a definition of "reality." The mystic and the gambler may reasonably prefer to reserve the term for the riskier (because less well anticipated) world they believe in.

In the second place, what exactly do we want to predict? The simplest, least "biased," rule we might accept would commit us to trying to predict the recurrence of the very same sensations we use as evidence—of the particular hallucinatory and real images, of the particular appearances of "red," "solid," "chair," "smoky-taste," etc. in whose presence we have been in the past. But it is ridiculous to think that this is what we want when we try to predict sensations. We seek rather to predict the recurrence of certain general *types and combinations* of sensations, and different methods of prediction will have widely different measures of success depending on how the sensations are grouped. (They will thus be quite literally "incommensurable"—without a common measure.)

That interests direct the way we carve up the world is a point Wittgenstein frequently uses to counterbalance the apparent arbitrariness of his language-games:

> *Remarks on the Foundations of Mathematics I*, 18. Thus even in a game I am inclined to distinguish between essential and inessential. The game, I should like to say, does not just have rules; it has a point.

---

[11] Compare, again, de Sousa on the "frame problem" (de Sousa, 1987) and his argument that, since "[n]o logic determines salience," it must be "emotions [that] ask the questions which judgment answers with beliefs." In (Rorty, 1980), pp.135-6.

RFM I 23 The game is supposed to be defined by the rules! So if a rule of the game prescribes that the kings are to be taken for choosing by lot before the game starts then that belongs essentially to the game. What objection might be made to this?—That one does not see the point of this rule.

RFM VII 15 "But a contradiction in mathematics is incompatible with its application.

If it is consistently applied, i.e. applied to produce arbitrary results, it makes the application of mathematics into a farce, or some kind of superfluous ceremony. Its effect is e.g. that of non-rigid rulers which permit various results of measuring by being expanded and contracted." But was measuring by pacing not measuring at all? And if people worked with rulers made of dough, would that of itself have to be called wrong?

Couldn't reasons be easily imagined, on account of which a certain elasticity in rulers might be desirable?

"But isn't it right to manufacture rulers out of ever harder, more unalterable material?" Certainly it is right; if that is what one wants!

"Then are you in favor of contradiction?" Not at all; any more than of soft rulers.

PI 69 Is it only other people whom we cannot tell exactly what a game is?—But this is not ignorance. We do not know the boundaries because none have been drawn. ...[W]e can draw a boundary—*for a special purpose*. Does it take that to make the concept usable? Not at all! (*Except for that special purpose.*) [Italics mine. Compare also §14.]

Using Wittgenstein, we can also expand the realm in which interests matter, from the formation of empirical concepts to the use of such words as "sense-data," "objectivity," "knowledge," and "truth." We have already asked why we should consider successful prediction a mark of knowledge; now we might ask why we are interested in getting a view independent of desire at all (why can I not simply believe in precisely (what we call) my fantasies?), why we care about sense-data (instead of "visions," "creations," "Ideals,"...), why we want to avoid (what we call) madness and its so-called illusions. For Wittgenstein, there is no transcendental answer to these questions. His critique of rules in the *Investigations* makes the notion of a foundational principle for knowledge impossible. No sentence can possibly guide our practices, whether for seeking knowledge or for anything else, independently of other practices that give it its meaning. No sentence has meaning unless it plays a role in a practice, and that entails that it have a clear possibility of being false. In consequence, "if the words 'language,' 'experience,' 'world' have a use, it must be as humble a one as that of the words 'table,' 'lamp,' 'door.'" (*PI* 97) We have therefore no position outside our interests (practices) from which to criticize interested knowledge.

Indeed, we can make sense of "facts" only from the perspective of a hierarchy of desires. "Bare," "raw" facts do not tell us how they should be ordered or why they matter. They do not really say enough to make them facts at all. ("But how does experience *teach* us, then? *We* may derive [our way of judging] from experience, but experience does not teach us to derive anything from experience." (*OC* 130)) "Pure" sensations, if that is even what we want (we still haven't shown what's wrong with visions, revealed laws, etc. as basic data), do not tell us that they are well- or badly-made, good or poor examples of, chairs, trees, or blue, although we need paradigm examples of these categories to use them at all, and we need these categories to make the kinds of predictions we want to make. We determine good chairs or good examples of trees by the role we want those objects to play in our lives, and we determine what categories to use at all, and how to place objects in them, by the kind of knowledge we seek in general, and the ends for which we seek it. Hence facts without desires are blind—so blind indeed that, like Kant's intuitions without concepts, the very word we use to describe them (even the pronoun "them") does not alone pick out any set, has by itself no clear reference. What we normally mean by "facts" is actually something highly informed by desires, as what we mean by the word "intuitions" is actually something highly conceptualized. This is not so terrible, even for those who think they want to get all human input out of cognition, because desires, far from being a mere human projection onto the world, also depend on facts.

Desires Track Facts

Desires have long been regarded with suspicion. From Plato at least through Kant, philosophers have held that the project of reflection requires the bracketing of desires; they have moreover often held that the *purpose* of reflection involves the elimination of some or all desires. Freedom they define against desire, and freedom is built into the very definition of reflection.

Both Plato and Kant warn against identifying ourselves with our desires—the former puts them in the lowest part of our soul, the latter in our empirical (apparent), rather than essential, nature. The motivation behind their positions is the insight that at any moment at which we reflect on our choices we realize that we could do something other than what we desire to do, that we could, indeed, have other desires. Therefore we *are* not the desire in question, but the free being who has the desire. It follows that if we believe something that a desire but not our free self would have us believe, the belief cannot be a result of reflection, and we represent it to ourselves falsely if we take it as a product

12 "Inclinations themselves, as sources of needs, are so far from having an absolute value to make them desirable for their own sake that it must rather be the universal wish of every rational being to be wholly free of them." (Kant, 1964), pp. 95-6 (428). Paton notes that this line may show the influence of Plato's *Phaedo* (p.138).

of reflection. Desires thus bind us, prevent us from thinking, or obstruct the process of thought with distortions and irrelevancies.[12]

I want to adopt neither the transcendentalism of Plato and Kant nor their belief in an entirely desireless condition of thought, but there remains great truth in their positions. As an empirical matter, it is simply true that desires, especially when strong, can distract us, that they are often short-term, hence bad guides to our life-long interests in the world, and that they often feel alien to our thought or real natures, hence open to and deserving of suspension when we reflect. To expand these themes:

1) Loneliness, starvation, anxiety, or sexual need can breed desires that severely interfere with our ability to think. The discomfort of leaving these desires unsatisfied may lead us to abandon reflective projects with hasty and shoddy solutions, to make decisions we would otherwise regard as unwise, to assent to beliefs the mere avowal of which will help us attain our ends (pretend to political views that make us sexually attractive, or steel our consciences against theft by murmuring Marxist slogans to ourselves), or to ignore evidence and beliefs that would make us desist from our desired course of action.

2) Because these desires, and many others, fade in time whether satisfied or unsatisfied, it can be a mistake to satisfy them at the cost of other, longer-term projects. One brief love-affair now may bar my way to other love-affairs that will matter more to me in the future; one theft now may bar my way to access to money in the future, or may ruin a self-respect that matters more to me than what I wind up stealing. Similarly, we might not mind adopting the views to which our short-term desires lead us, were it not that those beliefs might interfere with the information we need for our longer-term projects. We do not want to lie to ourselves to satisfy one desire, if that lie obstructs our satisfaction of other, later or more important, desires. Given, in addition, that most of us have some desire to exist eternally, whether as individuals in some kind of afterlife, or in the form of passing something down to future generations, we must take into account not only desires that persist over or guide a life-time, but what we desire for, and expect to be desired by, our children, and what we might come to desire should we have the time to be exposed to every possible object of desire. Since we are not identical with any particular desire or set of desires, it is clear that over this longest haul we cannot justify allowing any self-deception dictated by a particular desire to remain unchallenged.

3) When we commit ourselves to what we call "freedom," we express a desire to be able to adopt or relinquish any other desire. We can elucidate freedom as the sense that we are capable of any desire and bound to none. In seeking it we show that we have a desire for at least a glimpse of the nature of the world independent of our desires, for, that is, desireless knowledge. That this desire itself may be nothing more than a fantasy, or at least an unattainable ideal, does not prevent us from having it, although we may need to soften or suspend its demands.

These reflections bring us to the heart of the problem with desire: namely, that we don't *want* to live purely in our fantasies. We *might* have wanted to—at least we might have wanted to restrict what we know to that minimum necessary to give us objects about which to fantasize—and we do sometimes not mind spending a while dreaming, or even deluding ourselves in order to enhance a present pleasure. But on the whole, and especially when we consider ourselves as somehow or potentially eternal, we want to let the world break in on our thoughts, to negotiate with that interference in spite of the pain it may cause, to adapt our thoughts to the world rather than the world to our thoughts. As a result, desires track facts.

I use Nozick's term "track" to draw a deliberate parallel with what he says about beliefs. While our desires may often fail to match the world as it is, we want them to have some possibility of fulfillment, and we revise them when this possibility becomes remote. I do not desire to desire a love-affair with someone non-existent, someone I will never know, or someone who will never fall in love with me—unless I also desire to languish sentimentally, in which case the real object of my concern (my own dissatisfaction) *will* exist—and should I become aware that I have such a desire I will try to eliminate it. Indeed, awareness of the real state of affairs may itself mitigate the desire. Then, I sometimes try to match my desires to the options open to me, taking an interest in my father's business, say, if that seems my best shot at a career. Even in these cases, however, the relation between desires and the facts is not direct, proceeding instead by aiming the desire in what one guesses is a possible direction and then making a series of revisions in response to the impingement of one's errors on one's attempts to fulfill the desire.

This view of desires finds support in recent work on emotions. Emotions and desires are of course not identical—although Patricia Greenspan suggests that desire may be a form of emotion[13]—and the assimilation of moods, emotions, desires and tastes is a crude over-simplification of our affective life, but for present purposes this matters little, since emotions are if anything yet more arbitrary and "subjective" than desires, so if even they can be made out to have cognitive qualities, the same can surely be said of desires. Now, in "Emotions and Choice," Robert Solomon drew a strong comparison between emotions and judgments, a position which he has since somewhat qualified but still holds sufficiently to consider emotions part of the rational strategies we use to get around the world.[14] Ronald de Sousa gives emotions much the same role in cognition that we attributed to desires in section A above, calling them "determinate patterns of salience among objects of attention, lines of inquiry and inferential strategies."[15] "No logic determines...what to attend to, what to

---

[13] Patricia Greenspan, in (Rorty, 1980), p.245, note 10.

[14] See the version of "Emotions and Choice" in (Rorty, 1980).

[15] de Sousa, in (Rorty, 1980), p.137.

inquire about," he says, and he suggests that "emotions ask the questions which judgment answers with beliefs." They are like Kuhnian paradigms, in that "they are what we see the world 'in terms of.'"[16] De Sousa sets up "appropriateness" as a canon by which to evaluate their success as a part of our rationality, and traces the appropriateness of each particular emotion to its relationship with the paradigm situations that evoke it; these paradigm situations then constitute the (paradigm) object of the emotion. Both de Sousa and Amélie Rorty use a modified version of Davidson's principle of charity to ground claims for the rationality of emotions: we cannot interpret someone as having a particular emotion at all unless we can see how an appropriate object might have evoked it. "Might have evoked it," for Rorty gives wide scope to the psychoanalyst to understand emotions as irrational or misdirected by limiting the application of the principle of charity to the "*formation* of a person's intentional system," and allowing that, once directed to a specific kind of object in childhood, emotions may remain intractable to evidence against the appropriateness of the object evoking them.[17] For all these qualifications, however, we find here good methodological and empirical reasons to attribute a certain objectivity even to the affective aspects of the human mind.

INTERESTS

With facts chasing desires and desires chasing facts—in a circle not unrelated to the hermeneutic one—we may locate truth in some kind of equilibrium between the two. To change metaphors, we may better make out the ultimate direction of the vectors representing "fact" and "desire" by looking at their resultant. This brings us to interests.

Interests are in the first place long-term desires. They represent projects like the attainment or maintenance of a job or marriage, the commitment to a religion or a political cause, in contrast to immediate wishes (which, parallel to these interests, might be for money, sexual satisfaction, a feeling of closeness with a deity, or the alleviation of a neighbor's immediate suffering). They are desires that have survived the moods and emotions of a moment or a day, that need not be continuously "felt" or "experienced" throughout the period in which a person may be said to have them. I may desire a good job for several years without maintaining any particular feeling of yearning or anxiety over that time, or even over the periods in which I think about good jobs (unlike, say, a child's wish for a particular toy, or an adolescent's for a particular love-object). I need not find that my thought about jobs is being blocked by feelings, nor that I am unable to suspend my desire enough to consider whether it is worth having. It lacks the distracting, antireflective qualities described earlier, and I may therefore suppose that I have had at least a real possibility of thinking about

16 *ibid*, pp.136,138.
17 Amélie Rorty, "Explaining Emotions," in (Rorty, 1980), p.104.

its chances of fulfillment and adjusting it to some extent to reality. It has presumably survived the test of fact as well as the test of competition with other (short- and long-term) desires. For this reason, it has a cognitive as well as an affective stance toward reality built into it, and it is much more likely than more ephemeral desires to reflect the projects with which we want to identify our true selves.

Furthermore, interests almost necessarily have a social component. To survive the struggle with facts, they must be tested against the consensus of the individual's society about what is and is not attainable, and to survive the struggle with other desires they usually wind up being heavily informed by what the individual's society considers a wise project to pursue over time. We learn what interests to hold much as de Sousa tells us we learn "the vocabulary of emotion":

> by association with *paradigm scenarios*, drawn first from our daily life as small children, later reinforced by the stories and fairy tales to which we are exposed, and, later still, supplemented and refined by literature and art... An essential part of education consists in identifying [certain paradigm situations and their characteristic] responses, giving the child a name for [these responses] in the context of the scenario, and thus teaching it that it is experiencing a particular emotion.[18]

This social molding of our affective life, moreover, is something that the individual, on reflection, ought not object to, for it is rational to try to have desires one can share, to some degree, with one's neighbors. Since I want as much aid from my society as possible in fulfilling my desires, I naturally try to have desires that my society can help me fulfill. I also need to bring my desires into some harmony, and I look to people around me for examples of how that can be done. Finally, I want my desires to be those I consider proper for and worthy of a human being—I have a strong if not overriding desire for self-respect—and I develop a conception of what to consider proper and worthy, once again, by looking at the people around me that I respect. For all these reasons, my interests will probably come to resemble those of my neighbors, and be guided or checked by much the same facts and feelings.

We must take care to distinguish what I am defining as interests from such related ideas as Harry Frankfurt's second-order desires.[19] While both make room for and require greater reflection than first-order desires do, and interests are likely to incorporate some second-order desires (my interest in maintaining a high-level job may well demand that I cultivate a second-order desire to desire spending my time on business matters), interests are primarily directed at external objects rather than other desires. They also need not be *felt* at all,

---

18 de Sousa, in (Rorty, 1980), p.142.

19 See (Frankfurt, 1971).

unlike second-order desires, which paradigmatically—as in Frankfurt's example of the desire not to desire a drug—are felt as acutely as any first-order desire. We might call them "established desires"—desires given roots, by their connection to facts, by their place at the foundation of other desires, and by their social grounding—but these features only bring out how importantly unlike ordinary desires they are. Although I began by using the term, it may be best not to describe interests as a kind of desire at all. The two function quite differently, and it is, I believe, the confusion between them that has given interests a bad name.

As an example of an interest, consider egalitarian knowledge, mentioned above in the discussion of induction. In the West, particularly since the eighteenth century (but with deep roots in the Jewish and especially the Christian tradition), we both want people to have equal access to knowledge and believe that they do in fact have such access. Of course, this claim needs refinement: people are not in fact, and we do not say people are, equally perceptive or intelligent. Instead we say that people have roughly and in principle the same capacities for perception and intelligence. We all have the same faculties; some of us are simply able to use them more effectively than others, and on the whole the less intelligent and perceptive can see the work of their more capable siblings as an extension of what they can do themselves. This contrasts sharply with the notion, present in some form in any culture that sets certain people off as seers, prophets, witches or what-have-you, that some of us possess special powers to perceive events or truths in principle inaccessible to others. Views of this kind often provide grounds for tremendous differences in power between those with and those without the special insight, and the desire component of our interest in human equality can perhaps best be defined as a dislike of such hierarchical—and potentially tyrannical—power-structures.

Egalitarianism provides an excellent example of an interest because we can so easily see both the looseness of fit between the desires and the facts, and their general support for one another. On the one hand, people are not in fact equal in intellectual capacity and some people in fact have experiences entirely unknown to others (epileptic visions, mystical ecstasies, hallucinations, extreme or life-long passions). We must de-emphasize the former and explain the latter within a theory of knowledge based on readily accessible experience, in which they become symptoms of physiological disturbance, if we want to keep the facts in accordance with our desires. On the other hand, it is partly the tremendous success of egalitarian knowledge in explaining facts—success both in terms of manipulating physical objects and in meeting our intuitions about other people and other societies—that keeps us from desiring to give anyone an exalted role in our cognitive projects.

If we are not to regard a given interest as a transcendental presupposition in our thought quite independent of the ordinary desires and beliefs it is meant to explain, we must have falsifiability conditions for our claims about it—we must be able to imagine how we could *not* hold it. In the case of egalitarian knowledge, we might not value it if either the facts changed significantly, such that, for instance, a hierarchical society had much greater success than we in predicting and controlling physical objects, or we came to desire a hierarchical society, in order, say, to provide us with the greater sense of security that comes of placing one's decisions in someone else's hands. A change in the facts, a hitherto unthought-of inference, or a change of desires can all lead us to re-define our interests.

Or rather: to re-define the priority of our interests. Our interests can change because there is a potential for conflict between them. Each interest constitutes a large part of the evidence against which we weigh the others, such that we hold to egalitarian knowledge partly because of its success in manipulating physical objects while we attend to physical objects partly because they make up the realm to which we can most easily assume equal access (as opposed to realms of abstract ideas, on the one hand, and ghosts, etc. on the other). For the methodological reasons elaborated by Davidson, we can probably not assume the existence of radically alien interests, hence not of interests suddenly coming to be or disappearing. Instead, interests ascend or descend in priority over one another. In the contemporary West, the interest in human equality and manipulation of this worldly objects has taken precedence over the interest in eternal life and human authority, and we may understand those who have a different ordering of interests as reasonable but can never settle fundamental disagreements with them. This applies primarily to the members of a different society, since interests are first and foremost socially entrenched, not individual, transformations of desires, but even within a society individuals may value, say, security and risk, or this-worldly pleasure and concern about death, differently enough to have significantly different attitudes towards, and accept to significantly different degrees, rival claims to knowledge being considered by their society. Hence, "*Very* intelligent and well-educated people believe in the story of creation in the Bible, while others hold it as proven false, and the grounds of the latter are well known to the former." (*OC* 336)

One thing must be added to make this a working model for incommensurability: that the differences we have with those who place their interests in a different order are not mere glorified arguments over taste. Despite the fact that we see Awali's belief in the oracle as irrefutable, we consider him in some sense *wrong*. Not wrong in the sense of (simply) failing to mesh with the facts, nor wrong in the sense that we could "in principle" convince him otherwise to his own satisfaction, but wrong in the sense that *we would like to coax him* into other interests. Interests can change if either our facts or our desires change. To change someone else's interests, therefore, we either present her with new facts, or, by dint of force or appealing rhetoric, induce her to adopt other desires. We normally disapprove of (have an interest in not using) both of the latter means, but on occasion we recognize a legitimate role for rhetoric, and that is what I refer to by "coaxing." Now, unlike desires, which we are inclined to hold and release, and let others hold and release, without much argument, we tend to see a certain set of interests as the proper guide for a minimally decent and/or sensible human life. Indeed, one way we might define interests is by the desires that remain, as reasonable and irremovable, when we try to strip away all our desires in the pursuit of objectivity. They may be irremovable because otherwise the facts turn into a chaotic blur, or they may be irremovable because, given that we must have some desires, we do not want to get rid of just *these*, but at any rate they determine our conception of how to think and how to act.

Given the foundational role that interests play, we are not inclined to accept a dissent from our fundamental interests as merely a difference in desire, whether we are conversing about the best way to live or about the best way to understand the world (say, with Awali). Rather, we feel inclined, at least when arguing with them and called upon to defend ourselves,[20] to coax the dissenters towards our interests. I therefore put forward the following as a rough translation for the different meanings of "true" and "false" in the context of commensurable and incommensurable disagreements: 1) X says that P, I am talking to X in front of a crowd with whom I essentially agree, and X either essentially agrees with me or is stupid, mad, etc. Then, "P is false" means "X has made a mistake and I can show that in principle to her and in actuality to you [the crowd]." 2) Y says that P, the crowd remains the same, but Y disagrees with us incommensurably. Then, "P is false" means "I can show you [the crowd] that Y is wrong. I cannot show Y, given her beliefs and interests, but I want to—and don't you feel we should?—coax her." These definitions depend crucially on there being an audience to the dialogue, both to give force to the "in principle" in 1), and to distinguish between my desires (what "I want to" do) and our interests (subjected to the scrutiny of what we "feel we should" do).

Again, de Sousa's discussion of emotions strongly parallels what I have said about interests. He too talks of "hierarchies—some temporary, just for the purposes of an occasion of deliberation, and some more permanent—among our wants and values"; he asserts that "the hierarchies and orders of precedence among emotions are, in a given culture, fixed to a great extent"; and he shows that arguments between people with different hierarchies of paradigm scenarios

---

20 We may often in fact *not* want to coax the others into agreeing with us, but that is not of importance to my point here, which is that if we do want to reach agreement in circumstances like these, we will not be able to regard the other's position as possibly correct, or their interests as "just as good" as ours. Deciding on when to strive for agreement and when to let disagreement stand is an ethical matter (see chapter eight), but when we do opt for agreement, it becomes important that we consider our views "true," even if they depend on interests and a debate over them must eventually turn into "coaxing" or "seduction."

will be "virtually impossible to resolve."[21] The propounder of an argument intended to change someone else's emotional reaction to a situation will see the situation in the light of a certain scenario, the mere allusion to which "is sufficient for a vivid evocation of its power." The hearer of such an argument, on the other hand, may see the situation with an entirely different paradigm scenario in mind, and not find salient, not find worthy of emotional and hence cognitive attention, the features of the situation that demand attention for the propounder. From outside the propounder's scenario, "[this] demand often appears literally meaningless, even mad."[22]

And to bridge such incommensurable gaps, to overcome emotional differences that literally fail of any common measure, de Sousa suggests that we try to "seduce" people. He hastens to define "seduction" as "induc[ing] a specific emotion," and describes it as "what Plato both practised as 'dialectic' and condemned as 'rhetoric,'"[23] but he surely does not mean us to ignore the disreputable aura of the word entirely (as I do not with the word "coax"). He diminishes that aura considerably, however, by comparing seduction to the techniques used in aesthetic argument (embracing the analogy to arguments over taste from which I have somewhat shied away, but with a Kantian ring that makes clear the taste in question is constituted, at least in part, by reflection). Here,

> as Arnold Isenberg has shown,...the point of reasons...is not to lead to an inference but to lead to a perception. Similarly, a writer, actor, or film-maker who wants an audience to share a certain emotion will have to show the situation and the characters 'in a certain light'.

The "real seducer, the successful emotional persuader," de Sousa remarks,

> will not simply be content with pointing to features of her own scenario that seem salient to her. Instead, she will point to features that have already captured the imagination of the "mark." The vulgar lovers' argument says, "Come into my play: let me audition you for this part." But the real seducer says, "I come to you from your own play. Look: here is your part."[24]

Another word for what I have been calling "coaxing" or "seducing" might be "conversion," especially as Bernard Williams uses that term: "In the limiting case of incommensurable exclusivity [between groups],...[t]here will be little room...for anything except conversion."[25] I noted in chapter one that Williams

---

21 de Sousa, in (Rorty, 1980), p.147.

22 *ibid*, and (de Sousa, 1987), p.xviii. See also the example of a "lovers' argument" on pp.265-74.

23 *ibid*, p.258.

24 *ibid*, pp.257-8.

25 "Truth in Relativism," (Williams, 1981), p.139. Cf. also "Internal and External Reasons," (*ibid*), p.110 ¶ 2.

tries to broaden the range between argument and coercion with "forms of persuasion" that he "distinguish[es] in spirit from force and constraint";[26] perhaps he means to include "conversion" here. Wittgenstein uses both "conversion" and "persuasion" for similar purposes:

> *OC* 92. ...Men have believed that they could make rain; why should not a king be brought up in the belief that the world began with him? And if Moore and this king were to meet and discuss, could Moore really prove his belief to be the right one? I do not say that Moore could not convert the king to his view, but it would be a conversion of a special kind; the king would be brought to look at the world in a different way...
>
> *OC* 262. I can imagine a man who had grown up in quite special circumstances and been taught that the earth came into being 50 years ago, and therefore believed this. We might instruct him: the earth has long...etc.—We should be trying to give him our picture of the world.
>
> This would happen through a kind of *persuasion.*
>
> *OC* 612. ...At the end of reasons comes *persuasion.* (Think what happens when missionaries convert natives.)

We have hints here of how ethical conversations might take place even across widely differing cultures, and how those conversations might aim at truth even if they depend crucially on the interests of the parties involved. I will return to these hints when I come to the ethical questions about evaluating whole ethical systems and, quite literally, converting from one to another.

---

[26] (Williams, 1985), p.47.

CHAPTER FOUR

WORLD-PICTURES AND THE ETHICAL PERSPECTIVE

World-Pictures

1. In tying beliefs to the way we act, in speaking of interests as socially established desires, in refusing to establish any desires or beliefs as foundations and seeing them all rather as supporting each other, I approach Wittgenstein's notion of a "world-picture." Elaborating what he says on this subject will help put together the discussion so far, balance the emphasis on interests as an affective construct, and clarify the notion of different uses for the word "truth."

We never have an incommensurable disagreement with someone over one sentence alone. To ring a change on Donald Davidson's thesis that false beliefs must hang together with many other true beliefs to be clearly beliefs at all: they must also hang together with many other false beliefs to be more than mere errors. From people who say that the earth is flat we expect also to hear statements to the effect that the earth has edges over which one could fall, or forms the infinite bottom half of a universe the top half of which is the heavens; we expect to see certain fears and hopes about travel and/or astronomical phenomena that we would not share; we expect to see behavior shaped by these claims and emotional responses. If they do not accept our scientific evidence on astronomical matters, we expect to see a wider array yet of alien practices. Simply denying our claims and justifications may only signify failing to understand them; true rejection requires not only that one not accept our evidence for astronomy, but that one not accept any empirical evidence on this subject at all (and rely instead, perhaps, on a text, an oracle, or a sign), that one refuse to make, perhaps even to use, the predictions and technological creations we draw from our assumptions and observations, to share the attitudes towards thought and the goals for human life that we uphold.

Through incommensurable differences, we perceive the contingency of our own social consensus about what beliefs are true and what untrue, the limits that define it *as* a consensus. These differences show up not over grand methodological principles, but over specific, contingent claims. According to this conception of thought, however, what we believe is always more accurately and fully characterized by a set of more or less specific, contingent claims than by overarching principles of method. As Wittgenstein explains them, our claims to truth take the following form:

> *On Certainty* 94-5: ...I did not get my picture of the world by satisfying myself of its correctness; nor do I have it because I am satisfied of its correctness. No: it is the inherited background against which I distinguish between true and false.

OC 162: In general I take as true what is found in text-books, of geography for example. Why? I say: All these facts have been confirmed a hundred times over. But how do I know that? What is my evidence for it? I have a world-picture. Is it true or false? Above all it is the substratum of all my enquiring and asserting...

OC 167: It is clear that our empirical propositions do not all have the same status, since one can lay down such a proposition and turn it from an empirical proposition into a norm of description. Lavoisier makes experiments with substances in his laboratory and now he concludes that this and that takes place when there is burning. He does not say that it might happen otherwise another time. He has got hold of a definite world-picture—not of course one that he invented: he learned it as a child. I say world-picture and not hypothesis, because it is the matter-of-course foundation for his research and as such goes unmentioned.

OC 233: If a child asked me whether the earth was already there before my birth, I should answer him that the earth did not begin only with my birth, but that it existed long, long before. And I should have the feeling of saying something funny. Rather as if the child had asked if such and such a mountain were higher than a tall house that it had seen. In answering the question I should have to be imparting a picture of the world to the person who asked it...

OC 209, 211: The existence of the earth is rather part of the whole *picture* which forms the starting-point of belief for [us]...Now it gives our way of looking at things, and our researches, their form. Perhaps it was once disputed. But perhaps, for unthinkable ages, it has belonged to the *scaffolding* of our thoughts. (Every human being has parents.) [In connection with the parenthetical remark, see 239: "I believe that every human being has two parents; but Catholics believe that Jesus only had a human mother. And other people might believe that there are human beings with no parents..."]

OC 132: Men have judged that a king can make rain; *we* say this contradicts all experience. Today they judge that aeroplanes and the radio etc. are means for the closer contact of peoples and the spread of culture.

2. Once interests are defined as composed of both beliefs and desires, shaped by social institutions, and passed down from parents to children in ritualistic ways that often acquire meaning only after their formal syntax has been learned, a hierarchy of interests becomes more or less a synonym for a "world-picture." The various components of interests can thus give us alternative ways of describing the interlocking that takes the place of foundational beliefs in Wittgenstein's account of the way thought works. I would like briefly to spell out some of these alternatives.

Since I have already spoken of the way beliefs are tied to desires, and of how they are interwoven with each other, I begin here with the role of social institutions. In OC 239 Wittgenstein alludes to the influence of the Catholic church in shaping a specific world-picture, and in OC 132 he implies that some of our contemporary judgments serve the interests of various technological industries (implies, indeed, that these judgments are not unlike the means by which kings of other ages and places convinced people to respect their power). That certain institutions in every society propagate beliefs suiting their interests is of course a tiresomely familiar fact, after a century and a half of Marxist theories, but it need not be as baleful as its most dogmatic proponents have suggested. For institutions, like desires, need not be mere manifestations of a "blind will." Clifford Geertz has recently described orthodox Marxism as having "too anemic" a psychology and "too muscular" a sociology. On the one hand, it narrows human motivations to an oscillation between "consciously recognized personal advantage" and complete determinacy by social forces the individual neither controls nor understands, while on the other hand it views society "as a clash of interests thinly disguised as a clash of principles," instead of taking into account the role that principles can play in shaping the social forces that supposedly determine them.[1] The Catholic church and the technological industries mentioned earlier are presumably run by individuals who desire more than either their own survival or the survival of their institution, and who pursue even the good of the institution by directing its policies in accordance with beliefs generally taken to be factual in the wider society. The institution can itself be described both as having "desires" beyond its own survival (the church presumably seeks salvation for its adherents, as well as world peace and the glorification of God, while industries seek at least the material well-being of their owners) and as adjusting its "desires" to its "beliefs" about what it can and cannot accomplish. Finally, institutions exist within societies for the same reason that societies themselves exist: because it is impossible for human beings to define, let alone pursue, any ends beyond the desires they have as infants without the possibilities opened up by communication with others like themselves. Individuals want and need institutions to inform and challenge their beliefs and desires, just as institutions need individuals to give them purpose (desire), maintain and adapt their policies (actions), and propagate or reform their principles (beliefs). Of course institutions can and do use their power beyond its legitimate or reasonable limits, but in itself that power is essential to the structure of human thought and activity, not subversive of them.

One can say something similar about the approach to world-pictures I adumbrated above by suggesting that the meaning of rote formulas passed down from parents to children may only supervene on their syntax. People we might loosely describe as "structuralists" can find in some of Wittgenstein's remarks support for a view that we learn primarily by parroting certain structures uttered or presented by adults, the meaning of which we only grasp once we have the ability to translate each structure in terms of the others, and to apply it at the

---

1 (Geertz, 1973), pp.202-3.

appropriate moments in our common practices.[2] We repeat and play with complex utterances like "feed the kitty" or "I can't function in the morning without my coffee"[3] and only later, after we can use many other complex utterances, do we learn how the parts of any of them properly work. This makes language and thought rather like music (a comparison Wittgenstein frequently makes—see, for instance, PI 341, 527), in which only repetition and context turn a set of notes into a theme rather than a bridge passage, a chaotic outburst, or a collection of bits of other themes, in which one can only makes sense of any specific element in terms of an entire language of other elements. Such an approach to thought is appealing because it finesses questions about foundational principles, or about the relative priority of belief and desire. It also accounts well for the apparent irrationality with which beliefs and desires tend to survive both their grounds and their causes. People continue to mouth some utterances ("superstitions") and perform some actions ("rituals") long after the appropriate reasons for them have disappeared. We could therefore see world-pictures as the enshrinement of certain abstract structures, emphasizing the formal rather than the representational features of the word "picture."

But again, we cannot even make sense of such an approach without allowing for a distinction between meaningful and meaningless strings of phonemes, between at least potentially rational beliefs or desires and those that have outrun their grounds, or between useful and destructive cases of "parroting." After all, the tendency of children and converts to memorize and play with structures before learning what they mean is a necessary part of their coming to share in our communication at all, and the repetition of slogans and rituals is sometimes a healthy way for a society to maintain at least the shell of its ethos or religion in a period of severe challenge, while those adults who restrict their thinking to what they know by rote, and those traditions that persist once the way of life supporting them has entirely collapsed or disappeared, we rightly regard as unhealthy. These considerations indicate that abstract structures, like desires and institutions, make sense as a way of explaining the thought and practices of a society only when taken as interwoven with the factors they sometimes underlie.

Finally, world-pictures can be interpreted in terms of the environmental events to which they respond. Those who regard themselves as "naturalists," or who want to apply some version of evolution to every development of the human mind, have used Wittgenstein's rare references to "forms of life" to show that he would be sympathetic to such an interpretation. Again, there is

---

2 For example, OC 95, (quoted above, in section 1 of this chapter), or OC 160, 167, 209, or 233.

3 See Hanna Pitkin's discussion of a three-and-a- half year-old telling her parents, "I can't function in the morning without my blanket," in (Pitkin, 1972), p.57.

something to this, both as a useful account of thought and as a reading of Wittgenstein, but we also have to recognize that our beliefs and desires, practices and institutions shape what we take to be "nature" as much as it shapes them.

The point, by now, should be clear. For certain purposes, we may take up an idealist, psychological, sociological, structuralist or naturalist (Hegelian, Freudian, Marxist, Levi-Straussian, Darwinian) stance towards world-pictures, but it makes no sense to *reduce* them to any one of these perspectives rather than another. Neither beliefs, nor desires, nor social institutions or forces, nor abstract structures, nor biological events can claim to be the true foundation of all the rest of these factors. The virtue of Wittgenstein's account is that he keeps all such modes of explanation in play, without favoring any one above the others. Indeed, the ugly and odd term "world-picture" helps him in this, for it simultaneously alludes to all the different approaches ("pictures" are schemata of beliefs (representations), but also ways of satisfying our aesthetic desires, things bought by patrons and museums, formal compositions, and expressions of a natural human tendency; the "world" is something we either construct or react to, depending on whether one opposes it to "earth" and "chaos" or "mind" and "idea") and stands uncomfortably outside the normal jargon of each of them. I use it here to show the complexity of what I have called "interests," and to indicate the many ways in which hierarchies of interests may come to differ, but I would rather stress Wittgenstein's own favorite way of characterizing his "pictures": as *ways of judging*.

3. Judgement (*phronesis*), according to Aristotle, is a faculty concerned, like perception, with the particular, and learned only by experience and example.[4] According to Kant, determinant judgment is the application of a rule to a particular, while reflective judgment, an indefinite process without a clear end, seeks the specific rules we might want to apply.[5] For the later Wittgenstein, who argued that rules can only be defined in terms of the way that they do apply, every determinant judgment would appear to entail a new reflective one and vice versa. And in *On Certainty*, where he uses the term "world-picture" most often, he also spends more time than in any other work on the notion of judgment.[6]

Judgment is the meeting-place of the general and the specific. Judgments always concern particulars, but they always place them, if only by describing them at all, into general categories. It follows that a general characterization of what it is to judge would seem to be a misguided project. In the first place,

---

4 Aristotle, *Nicomachean Ethics*, Book VI, 1141b14-21, 1142a13-19, 1142a24-31, in (Aristotle, 1941).

5 (Kant, 1951), introduction §§ IV and V.

6 OC 66, 124, 126,128-32, 137, 140, 149, 150, 156, 232, 308, 419-20, 490, 492-4, 519, 603, 606, 614, 645.

those who do not already know how to apply generalities to particular cases will not know how to apply the characterization of judgment either (we might call this "the epistemological problem"), and in the second place, such a project pre-supposes, before encountering each particular, that it can be adequately accounted for in general terms (and if the first is epistemological, this is the metaphysical problem). Yet surely judgment can be learned, with or without an explicit characterization of its nature. For we know, from daily life and from the practice of common law, that there are good and bad judges, and that one can learn to judge well, at least from practice and an acquaintance with many different specific cases.

The kind of knowledge we need for our daily decisions always comes down to a judgment or set of judgments. Hence Aristotle's remark that the philosopher lacking in *phronesis* will be renowned, like Anaxagoras or Thales, for not knowing how to get around in daily life (1141^{b}4-8). We can characterize our knowledge in general as a set of judgments, and when we do, we emphasize the interrelation of knowledge with our needs and decisions, our interests and environment. If we add to this that we learn judgment from practice and knowledge of other judgments, we may infer that we need someone to point out judgments to us, and what to count as a good or bad judgment. Hence we need authorities, perhaps parents or teachers, to show us how to judge, and such authorities will surely pass down a mode of judgment highly influenced by a certain set of institutions. World-pictures can therefore be described as ways of judging, and I prefer this description of them because the specificity of judgment removes all temptation to see it as foundational in the way beliefs, desires, structures, or institutions might be. There is nothing "absolute" about a judgment: its very form reeks of limitation, finitude, "situatedness." It betrays on its face its need to be interwoven with other judgments; it cannot help revealing its helplessness, as it were, as well as its birth in particular situations, in the mouth of particular speakers, and in the service of particular actions. "Nixon was a terrible president." "The sponge cake tastes better if you make it with six eggs." "This is a daisy." In each case, there is an explicit reference to a particular and an explicit or implicit use of an evaluative term: even when we place "this" into the daisy category, we must do so against an implied standard of comparison (think of where the "this" has been damaged, or is not obviously a daisy). To know what the particular is, one needs much other knowledge, general and particular. To understand the comparison one needs a sense of how the standard works, of what it is for, and of how it has worked in other specific cases. For both these reasons, judgment is *necessarily* not self-sufficient. Judging seems to be an epistemological stopgap, a measure we take in particular situations to clarify and delimit our knowledge because we need whatever knowledge we have available to pursue particular actions—although it were best, we might think, that a being should not act at all until it has all the knowledge there is, or at least all that it could possible need. Every judgment involves a risk—of being wrong, or making a wrong decision. Judgments cannot appear, as foundational principles, desires, and social forces do, to offer the safety of being unquestionable ("self-evident") or inevitable.

Wittgenstein is fascinated by our ability to judge without being able to say in general what constitutes good judgment. "My judgments themselves characterize the way I judge," he says, or, more unsatisfyingly yet, "*This is* judging." (OC 149, 128) If you want to know whether something is a good judgment, don't look to foundational principles but to other judgments ("*Terrible* president?! He had a good foreign policy.") If you want to know the foundations of all our thought, look to our network of judgments, "our game of judging" (OC 131): "I am not more certain of the meaning of my words than I am of certain judgments. Can I doubt that this colour is called 'blue'?" (OC 126) And: "If language is to be a means of communication there must be agreement not only in definitions but also (queer as this may sound) in judgments. This seems to abolish logic, but does not do so." (PI 242) So what happens if, accepting finally how important judgments are, you insist that you need to know, in general, how to judge, to learn what judgment *is*? Well, since "judgments...characterize the nature of judgment" (OC 149), since "we use judgments as principles of judgment" (OC 124), you cannot learn the game independently of playing it; you cannot develop a capacity to judge if you have none to start with; you must grow up with it, as human beings always do (and most do, and some, perhaps, do not, get the hang of it: those who fail may be stupid, as Kant claims,[7] or impractical, as Aristotle says about Anaxagoras, or utterly monstrous in some sense, like those we call "psychotic," "sociopaths," or simply "inhumanly" abstract and cold). "From a child up I learnt to judge like this. *This is* judging. / This is how I learned to judge; *this* I got to know as judgment." (OC 128-9) Furthermore, insofar as one learns judgment "from a child up," insofar as it can be learned only from a set of specific judgments and not as an abstract method, truth and authority-relations come as a matter of course into the very essence of judging: "Must I not begin to trust somewhere? ...somewhere I must begin with not-doubting; and that is not, so to speak, hasty but excusable: it is part of judging" (OC 150). "A pupil and a teacher. The pupil will not let anything be explained to him, for he continually interrupts with doubts, for instance as to the existence of things, the meaning of words, etc. The teacher says 'Stop interrupting me and do as I tell you. So far your doubts don't make sense at all.'" (OC 310) "So this is it: I must recognize certain authorities in order to make judgments at all?" (OC 493)

The weight of the past rests heavily on the practice of judging, as it does, in the form of precedent, on Anglo-American common law, to which Wittgenstein returns again and again in *On Certainty* as a model for how we

---

7 (Kant, 1965), p.178 (A134=B173).

ought to conceive of knowledge.[8] "In a law-court," he says, correcting some mis-conceptions about the word "know," "...'I am certain' could replace 'I know' in every piece of testimony." (OC 8) Wild counterfactuals "wouldn't ever be taken into consideration there," he remarks pointedly (OC 335), implying that in philosophy we ought not to regard them as challenges to our knowledge either. He twice quotes, in English, the British legal phrase "certain beyond all reasonable doubt" (OC 416, 607), with obvious admiration for its pragmatic vagueness, uses "*der vernünftige Mensch*" in much the way British courts use "the reasonable man" as a standard for what assumptions to accept and what questions to take seriously,[9] and at one point asks whether "learned judges" would consider reasonable some of the things philosophers so consider (OC 453).[10]

From the law-court analogy we can trace the full implications of an epistemology based on judgment:

1) In the sense that judges are supposed to learn from precedents and follow them, and in the sense that a particular judge may fail or succeed at this, there can be a "way of judging." The way is indefinite, because the precedents, being particular, can take various and conflicting interpretations, but when a judge deviates radically from them, even if he gives a clever reading to justify his decision, others in the community will judge that he is wrong: either a higher judge will overturn the decision or the individuals making up the community will exercise their powers of judgment to condemn it. The correct use of judgment, the appropriate extrapolation of a way of judging, will be determined only by further judgment.

2) As there can be more than one set of precedents, there can be more than one way of judging. English law differs from American law, and an appropriate decision in a British law-court may be inappropriate in an American one. With regard to knowledge in general, Wittgenstein says explicitly, in the midst of his richest discussion of judgment, "Men have judged that a king can make rain," etc. (OC 132: see above). Of course, we may judge today that the king-worshippers were foolish, or that a culture supporting modern science is preferable to technologically more primitive ways of living, but that is analogous to judging American law to be superior to British or vice versa: we do not get away from the particularities, the traditionalism, or the risk of judgment.

3) As there can be more than one way of judging, there can be shifts in judgment. Western followers of science were king-worshippers themselves

8 OC 8, 335, 441, 485, 500, 557, 604, 607. Stephan Körner has told me in conversation that when he attended Wittgenstein's lectures as a young man, he found them remarkably similar to what he had learned when studying law, for which reason they struck him as both less difficult and less remarkable than they seemed to most of his peers.

9 OC 220, 254, 325, 334, 453. For a discussion of the "reasonable man" standard, see (Devlin, 1965), chapter 1.

10 See also OC 325, 500.

once, and many African and Asian cultures have adopted Western science. Clearly, the weight of the past does not so overwhelm judgment as to leave no room for change. Yet change radical enough to shift the very *way* of judging must at some point turn on a particular judgment, or set of judgments, that wildly defies or mis-interprets its precedents. Perhaps communities sometimes judge that there is a place for mis-judgment, or lets a mis-judgment go, failing to punish the judge(s) for deviation, or perhaps force—the force of circumstances or the peculiar might and position of a set of deviant judges—prevents a community from successfully suppressing a deviation from its way, and then, after a period of confusion, a new way of judging comes into being. "The mythology [of a culture] may change back into a state of flux, the river-bed of thoughts may shift." (OC 97) But we must keep this kind of radical change, comparable to an earthquake pushing a river into a new course, distinct from the constant small changes (rocks in the river, small mis-judgments that are accepted or overlooked) that occur within the normal flow of a way of judging, in accordance with the indefinite, the imprecisely bounded "nature" of judgment: "But I distinguish between the movement of the waters on the river-bed and the shift of the bed itself; though there is not a sharp division of the one from the other." (OC 97)

We will find these considerations about judging crucial, in chapters eight and nine, to the questions of what we can say about other ways of life, and of how our own might change.

4. It should now be quite clear that in speaking of interests as underlying our attachment to systems of beliefs, I in no way mean to reduce beliefs and arguments to expressions of emotion. If the interweaving of facts and desires did not do so already, the interplay of factors examined here would make it impossible to define our knowledge by a prior affective attitude towards the world. Instead, our interests and indeed desires are shaped by the same institutions and structures that bring us to believe a mesh of facts about the world. In consequence, we have no basis independent of our world-picture to criticize either what it says or the interests it serves.

For Wittgenstein, what we believe forms a mesh in which some beliefs are less questionable than others, but all are in principle contingent, and even the "substratum of all my enquiring and asserting" is of a piece with my enquiries and assertions. In addition, as OC 92, 132 and 209-11 show, he clearly thinks that this substratum or world-picture can vary from society to society. Note that he refuses to apply the words "true" and "false" to the world-picture itself, and we can extrapolate that he would also withhold those words from other people's world-pictures. Although it may appear otherwise, this position is not really in tension with our attempt to use "true" and "false" across incommensurable gaps, since we can agree that the terms apply appropriately to atomic sentences within a given world-picture but not to the pictures as a whole. Like tables and chairs, novels and codes of law, world-pictures are not the kind of thing that our language of truth fits. On the other hand, we cannot divorce the "essence" of a world-picture from all specific sentences. Some sentences belong strictly *within* a world-picture—they have a form and use clearly shaped by the world-picture, and happily take the appellations "true" or "false"—while others are so central to the picture that they shape the way it works as much as it shapes them. "Cigarette-smoking is harmful to your health" may easily be true or false, but not a formulation of the whole scientific method, or sentences like "there are material objects" and "our senses are not radically deceived." And such sentences as "the earth is round," or "the earth has existed for many centuries before my birth," may be called "true" or "false" insofar as they are plain empirical statements, but not insofar as they point the way towards skeptical possibilities, towards doubting our whole system of evidence.

I can now reformulate the account of truth in chapter 3: 1) "True" and "false" apply most comfortably to judgments for and against which we can easily give evidence (to all involved in the relevant conversation). 2) We recognize the dependence of our modes of giving evidence on certain fundamental judgments about the world, themselves contingent but used primarily as a measure of the truth of other judgments, and we are reluctant to give our words "true" and "false" the same force they ordinarily have in application to these central claims. We are not sure *what* force to give them, since we have trouble suspending the claims sufficiently to evaluate them. 3) When challenged on these fundamental judgments by people who intelligently disagree with them, we call the people "wrong," but we mean that we would like to get them to share our inherited background, to taste our training and social system, rather than that we think we should be able to convince them with our evidence.

Science, Ethics, and a Fifth Antinomy

> "...[I]n the combination of pure speculative with pure practical reason in one cognition, the latter has primacy...because every interest is ultimately practical, even that of speculative reason being only conditional and reaching perfection only in practical use." (Kant, *Critique of Practical Reason*)[11]

Sabina Lovibond, after arguing that science has no metaphysical priority over ethics, that the capacity for truth of statements in a realm of discourse depends on certain intellectual authority relations rather than a metaphysical success or failure to mesh with "the facts," finds herself having to save the phenomenon that in real conversation we allow much more room for disagreement about the nature of truth in ethical matters than in scientific ones. She accomplishes this

---

11 (Kant, 1956), p.126 (121).

by noting that "there are some 'language-games' in which it is not essential to secure a high degree of uniformity in the way people respond to a given situation," giving as an example the use of the predicate "fun": it is the person who tries to prove what is and is not fun, not the one who claims a first-person privilege in using the predicate, that fails to grasp the concept. As regards moral discourse, she says that "the reach of intellectual authority is relatively short," though "far from negligible." In consequence, her "moral realism merely denies [the *metaphysical*] distinction [between 'fact' and 'value']," and in no way commits itself "to denying that there are *phenomenological* distinctions between different language-games, in terms of the extent to which each is regulated by a 'pull toward objectivity.'"[12]

I find myself faced with a similar problem to Lovibond's, but, more uncomfortable than she is with naturalistic—hence external—explanations of our language-games, I offer a variation on her solution to it. Taking a cue from Kant, we may try to view the differences between our ethical and scientific thought the way we actually come across them in thought—provide a phenomenological foundation for the phenomenological differences, if you like. Very simply, then: a scientific discussion concerns matters well within our world-picture and takes place between people who share it, while an ethical discussion concerns the interests shaping the picture, may raise the question of whether we should hold this world-picture or some other, and may take place with people who do not share it.

When we discuss matters of science, we assume shared interests with our partners in dialogue. They are what we hold constant. Wittgenstein points out that "the same proposition may get treated at one time as something to test by experience, at another as a rule of testing" (OC 98). When we consider matters of science, our interests, their interweaving with training and institutions, and all other facts about our world-picture remain fixed, rules of testing, as if they were transcendental rather than empirical conditions. That is part of what we mean by "science"; once a discussion strays into questions about our interests and their relation to fact, it leaves science for philosophy, ethics, or intellectual history. Only a confusion of types of conversation might lead us to suppose that the interestedness of our world-picture can be brought to bear against the truth of a scientific claim, as if the interestedness of an entire world-picture were parallel to the particular cases, within the world-picture, in which the influence of desire can legitimately be used to discredit a set of beliefs. If I am right in my analysis, the very *possibility* of scientific truth depends on our having certain interests; in any case, interests not only differ profoundly from desires, but our world-picture alone gives us the context that allows us to show, in particular cases, that desires might compromise a truth-claim.

---

12 (Lovibond, 1983), pp. 66-8.

In contrast with science, ethical thought always puts interests into question. Sometimes this may take the form merely of holding them up against a certain desire or set of desires, showing how much less questionable they are, ultimately, than the desires conflicting with them, but sometimes we have to consider whether to revise the direction or priority of our interests. In the first case, we may be wondering whether we can excuse or justify a particular act of theft, adultery, deception, etc.; in the second, we may be sifting our intuitions on issues about which we have as yet either no ethical opinions or several, such as the rights and wrongs of abortion, or the value of an increased dependence on technology. We of course consider facts as well as interests in ethical discussions, but, even if we describe them exactly as we might in a scientific discussion, the context allows for questions about the fundamental aims and modes of evidence of science itself.

Ethical and scientific discussions are thus asymmetrical with respect to facts and interests. From the ethical point-of-view, science is, as it were, a handmaiden to our interests. Since we agree on its role in our lives, it can bracket out interests, and since we want it to produce results we will agree on, it *should* bracket out interests. Ethical discussions, on the other hand, always pertain to our entire conception of ourselves and our role in the world, and therefore cannot bracket out any part of our world-picture. Alfred Ayer has noted that in ethical debates we tend to dispute over the facts of a given case, rather than the underlying values,[13] and so we do, but facts come together with interpretations and fit into world-pictures. It would be ridiculous to try to characterize the Hindu practice of *sati*, or the current debate over abortion, without taking into account views about life after death, the existence and nature of a God or gods, or the purpose and essence of a human life. In the end, settling even such factual issues as when human life begins may thus depend as much on what interests one is willing to adopt as on what evidence one will accept. We cannot respect other people's ethical beliefs without respecting the factual beliefs that come along with them, which means that any program setting out to tolerate other cultures' values but not their claims to knowledge must fail. And since we have an interest in respecting other cultures' values (see chapter eight), we have reason to view their factual beliefs, on occasion, as somehow incomprehensible rather than just wrong. When we take up this view, we call the differences we have with the other culture "incommensurable."

Taken together with our earlier characterizations of truth, this account threatens to make all ethical disagreements incommensurable. If ethical disagreements always bring into question the whole of our world-picture, and discussions taking place at the borders of our world-picture challenge what we mean by "true" and "false," ethical discussions seem to lose that possibility of resolution rational argument holds out as its goal. I do not want to back off of

---

[13] (Ayer, 1952), pp. 110-11.

this implication too quickly, for it is indeed true that ethical incommensurability is more common than scientific incommensurability, and that taking up the ethical point-of-view is often a sure way of directing a conversation away from, instead of towards, resolution. Particular agents even within the same culture tend to disagree radically on ethical matters, and when they agree, they agree only about very specific acts: about *this particular* case of charity, theft, adultery, generosity. On the other hand, there are modes of evidence and argument in ethics as much as in science. Two people who agree on the nature of human life and the value of political freedom can profitably discuss whether making abortion illegal violates important civil ideals. What each seeks here is a clarification of his own interests, and in particular, a clarification of the distinction between his interests and his desires. Furthermore, two people who do *not* agree in their basic values, who differ importantly in their interests, may still find ethical conversation useful for the opportunity it offers for changing the interests of the other and exposing their own interests to the possibility of such change.

In ethical matters we thus deviate a little from the model of truth presented earlier. We are often, and always potentially, on the edge of our world-picture rather than within it when we consider ethical issues, and what we seek is either to confirm or to change our current interests. The paradigm use of the word "true" in ethics occurs when I show to my own or another's satisfaction that, for instance, a position on abortion or theft from large corporations meshes with our interests rather than just my or the other's egocentric and ephemeral desires. So much is clear, but how then can we appeal to truth in connection with a change in interests? It would seem that once an ethical claim has been shown to mesh or fail to mesh with our interests, we have nothing more to say about it, that there can be no further "external" check on our desires. Yet this is manifestly not the way we talk about ethics. I suggest that because we have in fact an interest in keeping our interests open to change (for reasons discussed in chapter three), we regard a claim that urges us to make such a change as now neither clearly true nor clearly false but *possibly* true, and definitely true or false once we have accepted or rejected the exhortation. "You should care more about religion, Henry," may indeed be false to Henry now, given that a full description of his interests (an appropriate deliberative projection) would show that he devotes just as much attention to religion as his interests would mandate, but if he comes to accept the admonisher's hierarchy of interests, he may say that the admonisher was right all along (note the difference between this and accepting the proposition "You would be happier [i.e., better satisfy your current interests] if you were more religious").[14] And while he considers the

---

14 I offer this as a way of beginning to explain how it make sense to provide and accept what Williams calls "external reasons." Clearly, that such reasons may be relevant to my ethical decisions is deeply tied to the possibility that I might convert away from my current hierarchy of interests; hence a fuller response to Williams must await the account of conversion that with which

advice, turns it over, tries it out, he may regard it as neither true nor false: this is the point where those words break down.

A caveat to what I have just said will show how it represents a revision of the model of truth presented earlier. As I have already indicated, the realm of the ethical is constituted not by a particular set of statements but by an attitude towards (all) statements, and strictly speaking incommensurability occurs only when we take up this attitude ("scientific" incommensurability then refers to what we might best call an ethical debate over the value of scientific evidence). Furthermore, there are some sentences—"prohibiting abortion is an unjustifiable violation of political freedom"—that can hardly be scientific, but almost any sentence can, in the appropriate circumstances, become an object of ethical dispute. The claim that man is closely related to the chimpanzee, for instance, is a mere matter of fact when discussing it with someone who shares the assumptions of evolutionary biology, but becomes a subject for and revelation of ethical differences when discussing it with someone who does not.

It follows that at the edge of our world-picture we hold scientific, as well as "purely ethical," claims true if and only if they mesh with our interests. I still want to claim, as I did before, that the appellations "true" and "false" fit most comfortably onto sentences well within our world-picture, where the rules for such usage are clear—except that I would now rather shift the focus away from atomic sentences and say that these appellations work best in the context of *discussions* within the world-picture. But at the edges of our ways of thinking, where we confront interests, training, institutions, etc. instead of grounds, "objectivity" comes to mean correspondence not with an empirical object but with our established interests—as opposed to our misleading and ephemeral desires. This does not mean that there are no differences at all between the staking out of our scientific and our "purely ethical" limits. The interests we appeal to when we justify science (in trusting and predicting sensory evidence, in satisfying biological needs and desires) are more widespread, perhaps more fundamental, than those that arise in most ethical discussions. We tend to think of these interests as universal among human beings, and therefore expect to encounter few incommensurable conflicts over them. Normally, when we meet people who do not accept, say, our medical practices, we assume they share the interests behind those practices and think we could persuade them to accept the practices themselves, while we make no such assumptions about our political, religious, or sexual practices. When we do run into incommensurable conflicts over scientific matters, the person we disagree with tends to have isolated a very small sphere of beliefs, often ones for which we have little direct and unambiguous data, from which he can dissent

---

this dissertation will end. John MacDowell gave a presentation responding to Williams via an account of conversion (as depending on something like de Sousa calls "seduction"—a view for which I have considerable sympathy) at the APA meeting in New York in December, 1987. Contrast Williams, "Internal and External Reasons," in (Williams, 1981).

without losing the benefits of the prediction and control (we believe, and he admits) we have attained over so many necessary and useful material objects. This, I think, is what happens with most educated people who deny evolution: they reason that its truth or falsehood need not bear on the technological success of science.

It should now be obvious that my use of "incommensurable" is more restricted than Kuhn's,[15] although I borrow the term from him. Incommensurability does not, as I understand it, arise paradigmatically in science, although—as in the dispute between Cardinal Bellarmine and Galileo—it might arise *over* science. Nor do I do want to say, with Paul Feyerabend, that there is nothing to choose between magic and science,[16] or, with Peter Winch, that we have methodological reasons not to consider the beliefs of other cultures false.[17] If we are talking within our world-picture, we can give lots of reasons for why we prefer science to magic; if we are talking at the edge of our world-picture, in the interest of clarifying our interests or coaxing others to share them, we find that in fact we opt for science over magic (most of us do, anyway); if we are talking beyond this point, to people whose interests we neither share nor take an interest in, nothing we can say, including that there is nothing to choose between our form of life and theirs, will make much sense. We can certainly never have *scientific* reasons for adopting the methods of another way of life in order to study it, since "science" refers us to a methodology which we at least regard as independent of ways of life. Science is a tool of our interests which demands that we suspend those interests; seeking what we regard as objects of universal interest, we hold interests fixed in argument and abstract from them as much as possible in research.

Consequently, Bernard Williams is quite right when, implicitly responding to Winch, he insists that "anything that can be empirically explained...fall[s] *within* the world of our language [world-picture]," that there could be no "sociological...or zoological, or materialistic" explanation of our world-picture because the very notion of explanation belongs to that world-picture.[18] But he is not right that that notion belongs to our world-picture because nothing outside our world-picture makes sense, because it makes no sense to suppose that there could be a plurality of world-pictures from which thinking might take place. Rather, Williams draws the limits of empirical explanation correctly because the word "explanation" plays a role in our world-picture closely bound up with science, and when we do science we suspend the relevance of world-pictures and act as though there were indeed a single conception of the world grounding all other thought. We can reject this view, however, when we engage in

---

15 (Kuhn, 1962), especially pp. 2, 66, 93-4, 97-100, 109-12, 198ff.
16 (Feyerabend, 1975), pp. 298-9.
17 (Winch, 1958), p. 101.
18 (Williams, 1981), p.152.

thought-activities other than science—in, for instance, ethics or certain kinds of philosophy.

I am suggesting that there is some significant—unbridgeable, indeed perhaps "incommensurable"—difference between the scientific and ethical approaches of our own world-picture, that the right hand of thought, so to speak, does not know what the left hand is doing. But how is this possible? We can reflect scientifically on ethics and ethically on science, and, from a position we like to call "philosophical," we can reflect on both. Furthermore, when we come to a notion like "world-picture," we do not want to be told that for science there is one world-picture (or none)[19] while for ethics there are several: we want to know how many world-pictures there *are in fact*, and then to make our ethical decisions on that basis.

Despite my attempt to finesse such suggestions as this last by blurring our distinctions between fact and desire, one may worry legitimately whether I am playing on two different meanings of "world-picture," as Williams presumably would have us believe,[20] and, if I am not, how we can possibly acknowledge our world-picture both as the only basis for explanation when doing science and as one of many, ontically conditioned, views when not doing science. Kant, with his antinomies and the (related) sharp division he draws between practical and speculative reason, provides the model for how we can understand thought as both single and bifurcated. With regard specifically to the way world-pictures function as frameworks for explanation, I offer a fifth antinomy:

Fifth Conflict of Transcendental Ideas

Thesis

There must be some non-relative standard for truth, against which all other modes of establishing truth can ultimately be measured.

Proof

Let us assume that there is no such standard. Now it is part of the use of our very word "truth" that we evaluate every given statement for truth or falsehood by means of other, logically prior statements setting truth-conditions for it. If there is no transcendental ground for this process, all

Antithesis

Any judgment can be called "true" only relative to some prior framework establishing what is to count as truth.

Proof

Assume that there is some non-relative truth claim or set of claims P, by which all modes of explanation and justification can be evaluated—some transcendental standard for truth. Now we normally come to understand sentences as true by learning what it would be for them not to be true, by

[19] As both Williams and Donald Davidson have shown, the considerations that mitigate against relativizing truth-claims to world-pictures, schemes, etc. ultimately suggest not that there is only one world-picture, scheme, etc., but that the very notion of any such thing is unintelligible. See Williams, *op. cit.*, and Davidson, "On the Very Idea of a Conceptual Scheme," in (Davidson, 1984), but contrast this book, chapter six.

[20] *ibid*, especially 150-1, 153-6.

statements setting truth conditions must themselves be empirical But this leads to the following situation: P will be true iff it satisfies test y. We can state this in a new sentence (P1): "P is true iff it satisfies test y". P1 will itself be true iff it satisfies test y1. This state of affairs can be formulated in yet another sentence P2, which we must in turn subject to another empirical check... We thus reach an infinite regress. But truth-conditions, to be truth-conditions of a statement at all, must sufficiently determine the truth of that statement, which means that they cannot regress infinitely.
Nor is there any help to be found in the declaration that truth-conditions regress to a finite network of judgments serving as a framework for determining truth. For how would we evaluate this claim? Against what background judgments, what framework, could we declare the existence of finite, and possibly multiple, frameworks? Either such a declaration would have to be accepted by fiat, violating the condition that a true statement must have truth-conditions (be true "in virtue of something"),[21] or it will lead to an infinite regress of frameworks like the one we just saw for individual statements. The very supposition that there could be a multiplicity of finite frameworks for truth thus implies that there exists a position beyond all of them from which we can see them *as* different—and we can see why we stick with the one we have.

The proposition that there is no transcendental standard for truth, when we draw out its full implications, is therefore self-contradictory; and empirical evidence cannot be regarded as the sole kind of justification. We must assume that there is a set of claims determinant of what we mean by "truth" which is not itself determined by empirical conditions. This is transcendental philosophy, without which, even in the ordinary course of science, no determination can ever be complete.
[cf. *Critique of Pure Reason*, A444-6][22]

recognizing what condition they rule out. And we come to accept modes of explanation and justifications according to how well they fit in with this ordinary use of "truth," how well, that is, they direct us toward true sentences and away from false ones. We thus use the word "true" for sentences we might have considered false. But clearly we do not know what condition P rules out, because if there were any such condition, P would be contingent upon the failure of that condition to obtain, and we would accept P only relative to whatever lets us know that the condition in fact does not hold. But if P holds, or we accept P, utterly independently of the obtaining and failure to obtain of every condition of the world, then it cannot serve as a ground for explanation. For the empirical claims and modes of evidence it is supposed to ground must show that certain conditions rather than others obtain, and a principle that holds regardless of all conditions can hardly guide us toward making such distinctions. Hence P turns out to be empty, irrelevant to knowledge, meaningless when proposed as a foundation for knowledge.

In empirical knowledge alone, therefore, must we seek for the justification and explanation of events in the world. Transcendental principles independent of empirical facts are no doubt a liberation from flux and provincialism, but also from the guidance of all meaning. For it is not permissible to say that the laws of transcendental thought enter into the order exhibited in the course of nature and shape of empirical law. Any rules of transcendental philosophy would be either empty or simply empirical principles under a different name. Empirical knowledge and transcendental philosophy differ as do significance and meaninglessness. Empirical knowledge does indeed impose upon the understanding the exacting task of always seeking higher and higher level explanations of events, their

21 Recall Wiggins' account of truth, quoted in chapter one, at note 72.
22 (Kant, 1965) pp.409-11.

verifiability being always conditioned by a possibility of further questioning. But in compensation it holds out the promise of satisfying answers that we understand to questions we in fact ask. The illusion of transcendental philosophy, on the other hand, offers a point of rest to the enquiring understanding in the chain of explanations, conducting it to postulates without truth-conditions, supposedly carrying meaning all by themselves. Such claims are, however, blind, and abrogate those rules through which alone true explanation is possible (cf.A445-7)

Observations on the Fifth Antinomy

1) I begin by noting that this antinomy fits Kant's general description of an antinomy very well: a) it deals with a question human reason necessarily encounters (A422=B450), b) both thesis and antithesis are unavoidable, not artificial illusions (A422=B450), and c) it arises from an attempt to seek the unconditioned (A416=B444)—here the unconditioned (or "self-evident") explanation.

2) My presentation of the conflict between absolutist and relativist approaches to truth has much in common with Rorty's argument in "The World Well Lost," which he himself repeatedly calls an antinomy.[23] One reason I have not used Rorty's own mode of argument is that I wanted my antinomy to parallel Kant's third antinomy; indeed, I try to recall Kant's language in that passage. It seems to me the two arguments ought to resemble each other: just as Kant there discusses the possibility of an action independent of empirical determination, so I here discuss the possibility of a thought independent of empirical determination. The latter may in fact depend on the former.

3) The significance of posing this issue as an antinomy comes out when we remember what Kant does with antinomies. Kantian antinomies are neither problems for further study at the end of a textbook on metaphysics, nor Hegelian contradictions to be somehow overcome. Rather, they are permanently, indeed in principle, immune to what Kant calls "dogmatic solution" (A484=B512). They are, however, open to "critical solution," by which Kant means that we can determine 1) what wrongly asked questions inspire them, and 2) when, and to what extent, we can regard the theses and antitheses as true. Kant famously and controversially stresses the "wrong question" approach to the first two

---

23 (Rorty, 1982), pp. 9, 12, 14. There are also similar arguments to be found in the "dilemma" on relativism that Gordon Bearn presents in (Bearn, 1985a), Appendix III, and in Hilary Putnam's discussion of relativism in "Beyond Historicism," (Putnam, 1983).

antinomies but the "both true" approach to the last two. I think the two approaches actually cohere nicely. The wrong question in each case arises from reflecting beyond the bounds of reason from two different perspectives simultaneously. If we have reason to adopt either perspective, we can regard its view as the true one, since any claim is transcendentally justified if it serves as the necessary condition for some other belief whose truth is given. And if we have reason to adopt both perspectives, we can regard both views as true. For Kant, practical reason demands the thesis of the third antinomy, thereby making that thesis transcendentally true, while speculative reason requires the antithesis, making it also true. I would argue, as regards my fifth antinomy, that when we participate in our language-games of truth, especially in logic, mathematics, and science, from within the perspectives of those practices themselves, we require the thesis, while when we examine these ways of speaking from the "outside," from the perspective, say, of sociology or anthropology, we require the antithesis. For the ethical perspective (as for the philosophical one), we require both thesis and antithesis.[24] When deliberating, casting about for the best decision, we hold to the antithesis, since we seek not merely what is in fact true (as we do in science or mathematics) but what to count as truth, and in that search we want to be able to suspend belief in any given system or principle—we want to be able to look "behind" it, and behind every further framework, at least until we run out of interest or time. Then we decide, and in deciding we revert to the thesis, holding or hoping that the maxim of our action is *in fact*, is *truly*, the right one. (It may seem here, as it will in comment 5 below, that philosophy and ethical deliberation are very similar kinds of activity: not everyone has such a conception of philosophy, but those who do include Plato, Spinoza, Kant, and Kierkegaard.)

4) If correct, this antinomy poses problems that none of Kant's antinomies raised, for it threatens the very project of doing (transcendental) philosophy. From what perspective, after all, do we come up with the antinomy itself? That of the antithesis? Then it is itself true only relative to a particular set of background beliefs, not in general or absolutely. That of the thesis? Then it is itself absolutely true and the antithesis is mere show.

The insight that this antinomy *both* reveals a necessary characteristic of our thought *and* makes only dubious and difficult sense is, I think, the later Wittgenstein's great contribution to philosophy. Many before him have approached the problem of whether thought can be transcendental (and absolute) or must be empirical (and relative to categories provided by experience), but they have always opted either for the thesis or for the antithesis of our antinomy. Indeed, writers like Winch, on the one hand, and Williams

---

[24] In an earlier version of this discussion (in *Philosophia*, May, 1989), I said simply that ethics requires the antinomy's antithesis. The subtler version here is due in part to the astute criticisms of Henry Chang, Haverford class of 1989.

and Jonathan Lear,[25] on the other, have tried to make Wittgenstein himself out as, respectively, a relativist and a transcendental idealist, sometimes also seeing him as in part confused, or ambivalent between the two positions.[26] In fact, Wittgenstein explicitly and forcefully puts the two positions together:

> *Zettel* 430: ...Our language-game only works, of course, when a certain agreement prevails, but the concept of agreement does not enter into the language-game...
>
> RFM III, 65 & 72: Are the propositions of mathematics anthropological propositions saying how we men infer and calculate?—Is a statute book a work of anthropology telling how the people of this nation deal with a thief etc.?—Could it be said: "The judge looks up a book about anthropology and thereupon sentences the thief to a term of imprisonment"? Well, the judge does not USE the statute book as a manual of anthropology...
>
> It is clear that we can make use of a mathematical work for a study in anthropology. But then one thing is not clear:—whether we ought to say: "This writing shews us how operating with signs was done among these people," or: "This writing shews us what parts of mathematics these people had mastered."
>
> RFM III, 75: Calculating would lose its point, if *confusion* supervened. Just as the use of the word "green" and "blue" would lose its point. And yet it seems to be nonsense to say—that a proposition of arithmetic *asserts* that there will not be confusion...
>
> We cannot say...that use of the word "green" signifies that confusion will not supervene—because then the use of the word "confusion" would have in its turn to assert just the same thing about *this* word.
>
> RFM IV, 4: But might not experience determine us to reject the axiom [that a straight line is possible between any two points]?! Yes. And nevertheless it does not play the part of an empirical proposition.
>
> OC 98: But if someone were to say "So logic too is an empirical science" he would be wrong. Yet this is right: the same proposition may get treated at one time as something to test by experience, at another as a rule of testing.

It is this antinomy that explains the difficulty of Wittgenstein's later philosophy. For reasons I have noted above, he cannot *prove* that there is such an antinomy, nor state its implications for our thought in general, without violating the conditions of its possibility. Instead, therefore, he *displays* it, and its results, by moving back and forth, in an analysis of our linguistic practices, between perspectives requiring the thesis and perspectives requiring the antithesis. For

---

[25] (Winch, 1958), pp. 14-5, 19, 81, 87, 100, 114-5, (Lear, 1983), and (Williams, 1985), pp. 97-99, 102-4.

[26] See especially Williams, *op. cit.* Compare also (Harries, 1969).

instance, PI 185 belongs under the antithesis, as Wittgenstein carries on a naturalistic examination of what we do in language, while 186 and 187, in which he assesses the presuppositions built into our terms "know" and "mean," move back to the thesis. More deeply, he swings between the thesis and antithesis to probe what we mean by our laws of logic. Take "A=A." When in the grip of our thesis, we often rush to title this statement a paradigm of absolute truth. Wittgenstein questions not so much its truth as what it could possibly mean:

> RFM I, 132: Frege calls it 'a law about what men take for true' that 'It is impossible for human beings... to recognize an object as different from itself."—When I think of this as impossible for me, then I think of *trying* to do it. So I look at my lamp and say: "This lamp is different from itself." (But nothing stirs.) It is not that I see it is false, I can't do anything with it at all. (Except when the lamp shimmers in sunlight; then I can quite well use the sentence to express that.)

When we find a context within which the law of identity would make sense as a sentence, it expresses an empirical truth that could easily be false. Someone may perfectly well say, "I'm not myself today"; the law of identity was not meant to demand self-identity in *that* sense. In what sense does it demand self-identity, then? It seems we have to add something to the ordinary notion of self-identity to make it a necessary relationship, irrelevant to shimmering lamps and slightly unwell people. But what? And if we do add what it takes to make self-identity a necessary relationship, are we sure that the notion remains intelligible? Having twisted terms away from their ordinary usage, where can logic turn to guarantee that they retain meaning?

If Wittgenstein were simply an ordinary language philosopher, he might let the matter end here, ruling logical self-identity out of language as an illegitimate extension of ordinary use. The added subtlety and complexity of his thought comes out in that he does not rest satisfied with this approach, but continues to recognize the demands of the fifth antinomy's thesis. For all that we may find the laws of logic unclear in their point and application, they still belong to our language and thus still represent something important about our relations to the world and each other:

> RFM I, 131-33: The laws of logic are indeed the expression of 'thinking habits' but also of the habit of *thinking*. That is to say they can be said to shew: how human beings think, and also *what* human beings call "thinking"....[T]hey bring out, or shew, the essence, the technique, of thinking. They shew what thinking is and also shew kinds of thinking.

Wittgenstein approaches all the so-called "laws of thought" this way,[27] chasing down their meaning into empirical contexts, worrying them to yield up any

---

27 (Wittgenstein, 1964), especially I, 131-134, I-*III*, 12-20, III, 81, 87, IV, 56-60, V, 9-41, VII, 11-12, 15, 34-5, 38, 43.

transcendental claims they might want to assert, then suddenly releasing them with the acknowledgement that there remains, still resisting his investigations, something about them essential to human thought. (Laws of thought constitute merely his paradigm of absolute foundations for knowledge: he also wrestles with the fifth antinomy in his critique of rules, reflections on private versus social meaning, and remarks on induction, scepticism, and religious belief.)[28] We may be able to do the same with our ethical rules and principles: imaginatively push them to appear unstable and contingent, until we can rescue, from our very dissatisfaction with that contingency, a renewed sense of just how necessary they are for us.

Since Wittgenstein uses naturalism and ordinary practice as a ground of explanation for logic as much as he uses logic as a ground of justification for ordinary use, even sketchy readings of what he finally wants to say about language must remain suspect. The antinomy allows no account of the relation between empirical facts and transcendental grounds to constitute a final resting point, and Wittgenstein instead seeks a point at which *we are satisfied* to let the ambiguities rest. He pursues in this something much like Rawls' "reflective equilibrium,"[29] only for all thought, not just for ethics. The role of the contemporary philosopher, the Wittgensteinian heir to the teachers who used to be called philosophers,[30] is to establish ever anew a balance we can live with between our mass of intuitions, on the one hand, dependent on each other as well as on empirical facts and desires, and our attempts to establish a systematic order among these intuitions, on the other, an order the intuitions themselves seem to call for yet always greet with a certain discomfort. The philosopher must find some kind of equilibrium between the viewpoints of our absolutist thesis and relativist antithesis.

I see that search as proceeding roughly as follows: We begin by hardening some proposition into a rule, "a paradigm with which experience is compared and judged,"[31] an absolute principle (A) we are inclined to measure with rather than to measure. This principle may be a matter of logic, but it could equally well be a matter of science, ethics, or aesthetics. In the former case, we will end up reducing our absolute principle to a sentence in itself virtually empty but gesturing beyond itself to some mode of thought we cannot imagine any rational creature lacking. But if A is a scientific, ethical or aesthetic matter, we attempt to work out the context against which we accept it while amassing at the same time cases we do not feel it fits very well. Thus we might set up Newtonian physics on one side and then on the other side bring evidence it does

---

[28] In PI 143-242, and 243-432, OC, *passim*, (Wittgenstein, 1979), and "Lectures on Religious Belief," in (Wittgenstein, 1970).

[29] (Rawls, 1971), p.20.

[30] "One might say that the subject we are dealing with is one of the heirs of the subject which used to be called 'philosophy'," (Wittgenstein, 1958), p.28.

[31] Compare RFM VI, 22 and VII, 74.

not explain well and examine what arbitrary desires or opinions might have led us to our original acceptance of it. If the weight of contrary cases is great, and the background against which we originally accepted it does not match the background against which we would accept a theory of physics now, then we take the Newtonian theory down from its absolute position and pronounce it to have been only a marker for a deeper, more all-embracing principle that is truly absolute. We set up a new candidate for that principle in its place, and the process continues. Similarly, we might propose an ethical principle as absolute—for example, a categorical prohibition on theft. Then we consider cases where established property relations are themselves unjust, paint scenarios in which the abolition of property seems desirable, and reflect on what conditions might have made us take this prohibition as absolute in the first place. Eventually we may say, with our antithesis, that no prohibition on theft can be absolute, or, with our thesis, that while "theft" as originally intended is not an absolute wrong, the prohibition on theft, suitably reconceived, was a marker for a deeper ethical truth about property relations that *is* absolute. We set up another candidate in its place, and the process continues.

What motivates this process, on the one hand, is Bernard Williams favorite pre-supposition—the notion that we want to get closer and closer to describing a world "already there," while on the other hand it is the desire to keep change alive in our thought and practices, to knock down the "already there" as inadequate to a dynamic and mysterious world. At any one point in time, we reach equilibrium when we find the cases our fixed principles exclude unimportant and the background that convinces us of those principles acceptable. Then the trick is, as Wittgenstein says, not to ask any further questions, to recognize where we are as the bedrock that turns our spades (PI 217; see also OC 471 and Z 313-5).

5) Both thesis and antithesis point up the dependence of an explanation's success on a background of other explanations, and the antithesis allows us to seek such backgrounds for all explanations, even of principles that are supposed to ground explanation itself. This would allow for precisely the "sociological...or zoological, or materialistic" explanations of our world-picture that Williams seeks to rule out. By contrast, the thesis suggests that such explanations will neither, as their sceptical (or Marxist or deconstructionist) advocates might claim, undermine the *truth* of our world-picture, nor, as the proponents of the strong program in sociology[32] might wish, provide a more fundamental understanding of it.

We can make better sense of the notion that even our account of explanation needs a background notion of explanation by recognizing that different kinds of explanations tend to require different kinds of backgrounds. Consider an

---

[32] For instance, Barry Barnes and David Bloor, "Relativism, Rationalism and the Sociology of Knowledge," in RR (Hollis & Lukes, 1982), and (Bloor, 1983).

interpretation of a passage from the Bible or the American Constitution. A listener who regards those documents as having a "spirit" within which he wants to live may accept the reading as a good one if it meets his general criteria for a good (devout, fulfilled, just) life, even if the interpretation bears little connection to the actual words of the text. In literary criticism in general, however, the acceptability of a reading depends on how well it solves problems in the text, matches other, related passages, and meets our conception of the history of the text's composition and the psychology of its author. Since these criteria are multifold and irreducible to each other, there will be readings that meet one criterion rather or better than another, and there will consequently be readings of varying acceptability to various readers, instead of one conclusive interpretation against which to judge all others. We use an altogether different set of criteria, on the other hand, when we come to evaluate scientific explanation, and these criteria—simplicity, fertility, predictive power, ability to solve problems in other theories—are themselves multifold and irreducible to one another. In ethics there are yet other criteria, more like those in reverent Biblical and Constitutional interpretation than those of either literary criticism or science. And in philosophy there are different criteria for the acceptability of answers to different questions, leaning us here further toward, there further away from, an ethical, a literary, a scientific approach, as well as demanding that we meet general standards of simplicity, clarity, philosophical fertility, coherence with the tradition of past philosophy, etc.

These types of considerations come out prominently in the writings of those concerned to demonstrate and elucidate the "hermeneutic circle," but I do not want to call all thought hermeneutic, all answers only "satisfying," rather than conclusive. That would be an insufficiently radical application of hermeneutics, as the Fifth Antinomy shows. What background, after all, makes the hermeneutic circle a satisfactory account of the basis of thought? On its own terms, it cannot itself be absolute, unconditioned by the needs of specific problems and approaches; the need to point it out can arise only when we see the limitations of those of our practices that demand final, absolute answers. But then the condition of its possibility is precisely that we have practices in which we make absolutist demands. And we do have such practices, where we draw sharp boundaries "for a special purpose" (PI 69), where something is gained by an assimilation of expressions (PI 14), where a simplified model of a thing helps clarify at least a "circumscribed region" of it (cf. PI 2-3, 6)—where the regularity and simplification of what we call "science," in short, serves our needs. Of course, this is science "for a purpose," but we nonetheless *have* that purpose, and if we are to serve it we must take the absolute constructions of science as they are and not reduce them to the non-scientific aims that shape them.

Thus sociological accounts of science cannot shake our faith in scientific truth-claims, although they may explain many facts of historical experience, meet our belief that our thought is interested, and gratify our interest in our own interestedness. We hold these concerns fixed when we do our sociology of science, while we hold other things fixed (including the truth-seeking nature of scientific thought) when we do the science itself. Neither realm reaches a more fundamental level of explanation than the other, except according to its own conception of what explanation is. The scientist may explain what the sociologist says about him in terms of a mechanistic account of the sociologist as a biological creature, while the sociologist explains what the scientist is saying in terms of a history of biological explanations. When listening to one of them right after the other, we switch the grounds on which we evaluate their explanations. We do not give one of the sets of grounds priority, except "for a special purpose."

6) I can now state more clearly the way in which scientific and ethical conceptions of truth are incommensurable:

From the perspective of science, ethical claims fail of absolute truth because they appeal to our interests, and truth should be disinterested. Science purports to be able to give a disinterested account of our concern with interests, and hence of our ethics, by showing ethics to be a biological development that has evolved to preserve human life in community.[33] We accept this explanation, or variants of it, against the background of our belief in evolution, the problems and ungrounded assumptions within our ethics that it accounts for, and the various biological and historical facts it can convincingly integrate.

From the perspective of ethics, scientific claims fail of absolute truth because they do not take into account the interests that shape science, and truth must and always does address our interests. Ethics purports to be able to give an account of disinterestedness, and hence of science, in terms of the interests it serves, by explaining how the rise of the experimental method had to do with the concern of sixteenth and seventeenth century Protestants to root knowledge in what every individual can accept, and of later generations to direct human attention from other-worldly to this-worldly pleasure, from fatalism and nostalgia for past paradise to an optimistic faith in the progressive submission of nature to human will. We accept this explanation or variants of it, against the background of our belief in the hermeneutic circle and the social bases of knowledge, the problems and ungrounded assumptions within our science it accounts for, and the various introspective and historical facts it can convincingly integrate.

Note that the scientific and the ethical perspectives can each claim to be "broader" than the other: the former, because it answers questions about more phenomena than ethics does, the latter, because it answers more of the questions human beings ask than science does. It seems to me that the ethical perspective more properly captures what we (ordinarily) mean by "broad" in this respect,

33 See (Mackie, 1978).

more of what that concept means to the way we live. Despite the fact that science can explain ethics, if we hold both science and ethics together in one cognition, ethics takes primacy—"the interest ... of speculative reason being only conditional and reaching perfection only in practical use."[34]

7) If we are willing to let the differences between the scientific and ethical modes of thought stand thus, we have tools with which to assess Williams' debate with Richard Rorty over the absolute truth of science. I quote the relevant passage from Williams in full:

> ...Richard Rorty has written:
>
> It is less paradoxical...to stick to the classic notion of "better describing what was already there" for physics. This is not because of deep epistemological or metaphysical considerations, but simply because, when we tell our Whiggish stories about how our ancestors gradually crawled up the mountain on whose (possibly false) summit we stand, we need to keep some things constant throughout the story...Physics is the paradigm of "finding" simply because it is hard (at least in the West) to tell a story of changing universes against the background of an unchanging Moral law or poetic canon, but very easy to tell the reverse sort of story.
>
> There are two notable faults in such a description of scientific success and what that success means. One is its attitude to the fact that it is easy to tell one kind of story and hard to tell the other. *Why* is the picture of the world "already there," helping to control our descriptions of it, so compelling? This seems to require some explanation on Rorty's account, but it does not get one. If the reference to "the West" implies a cultural or anthropological explanation, it is totally unclear what it would be: totally unclear, indeed, what it could be, if it is not going itself to assume an already existing physical world in which human beings come into existence and develop their cultures.
>
> The point that an assumption of this kind is going to lie behind any explanations of what we do leads directly to the second fault in Rorty's account: it is self-defeating. If the story he tells were true, then there would be no perspective from which he could express it this way. If it is overwhelmingly convenient to say that science describes what is already there, and if there are no deep metaphysical issues here but only a question of what is convenient (it is "simply because" of this that we speak as we do), then what everyone should be saying, including Rorty, is that science describes a world already there. But Rorty urges us not to say that, and in doing so, in insisting, as *opposed to* that, on our talking of what it is convenient to say, he is trying to reoccupy the transcendental standpoint outside human speech and activity which is precisely what he wants us to renounce.[35]

To take Williams' objections to Rorty in order:

a) Williams invests the word "explanation" with a heavy scientific bias. His use of the term in general displays this bias,[36] and his use of it here in particular demands of Rorty an interest in anthropology and the development of cultures in the physical world that the latter simply need not have. *Why* does Rorty's

---

[34] See text to note 11, above.

[35] (Williams, 1985), pp.137-8. See also (Williams, 1983).

[36] See, for instance, (Williams, 1981), p.152, and (Williams, 1985), pp.139-40, 150.

claim about easy and hard stories "seem to require some explanation"? Perhaps Rorty, realizing that an anthropological or biological account of what we think would run the risk of vicious circularity, abandons scientific explanation at precisely this point, trusting instead to his reader's pre-theoretical intuitions about what we do here in the West (and what those Easterners do differently) as a background against which to judge the truth of his claims. Perhaps not, but Rorty need not tell us why he considers the picture of the world "already there" so compelling: he can present this judgment, hope we will agree, and let it go at that. That would not be a good way of doing ordinary science or history, but in examining the roots of our thought he is not doing ordinary science or history. He is either addressing a quite extra-ordinary scientific or historical problem—or doing something else altogether.

b) I would say he is doing something else altogether, but it is not transcendental philosophy. Why must Rorty reoccupy a transcendental standpoint to step outside scientific speech and activity? All he has to do is occupy a *different* standpoint from that of science. To pursue Rorty's mountain metaphor, one need not fly above the whole range to criticize what is happening on any particular peak; all one need do is stand on a different peak (if that—all one really needs is to see that there *are* other peaks on which different activities take place). That is, if to the scientist (including the scientific historian of cultures) it inevitably looks like one must hold physical laws fixed in any explanation, to say otherwise one must only drop the scientific perspective and adopt another one. Clearly, Rorty does not make his remarks from a scientific perspective, but that does not mean he has adopted a transcendental perspective. He would be doing that only if he claimed for his view of science the absolute truth he denies to science itself. If he said, as Williams seems to think he does, "It is absolutely true that there are many perspectives and our thought is molded only by one," then his view would indeed be self-defeating. But I think he is only saying, "*From here* it looks as if there are ways of thinking other than the scientific one, although I know it does not look like that to you (scientists and Western historians) over there." And where is "here"? I suggest the ethical perspective, which, as we have seen, views science with as much scepticism as science views it, and, unlike science, does not have to proclaim its own "absolute truth." Indeed, at the end of his book, Rorty almost explicitly declares that he has been writing from an ethical perspective:

> Normal scientific discourse can always be seen in two different ways—as the successful search for objective truth, or as one discourse among others, one among many projects we engage in. The former point of view falls in with the normal practice of normal science. There questions of moral choice or of edification do not arise...The latter point of view is one from which we ask such questions as "What is the point?," "What moral is to be drawn from our knowledge of how we,

> and the rest of nature, work?" or "What are we to do with ourselves now that we know the laws of our own behavior?"[37]

Here, as in "The World Well Lost," Rorty evinces an awareness that his very assertion of multiple perspectives can itself be criticized as perspectival, that he cannot provide conclusive proof for it, only assert it as one side of an antinomy. It just happens that that side is the appropriate one for the questions of the ethical perspective.

8) Finally, the Fifth Antinomy can be posed as a dilemma about using ordinary language for philosophy. On the one hand, if the meaning of a word is fixed by its use, no new argument or facts need ever give us reason to change our use, and we indeed have reason to ride roughshod over any such considerations in order to maintain that use. To someone who claims that the word "soul," say, or "reality" or "meaning" or "understanding," cannot refer to what we thought it referred to, we simply reply that either the word or what we thought has not been correctly interpreted. On the other hand, the dependence of meaning on use instead of abstract rules or objects of reference also seems to imply that we can change the meaning of a word whenever we like. To someone who tells us that we are mis-using certain words and therefore talking nonsense, we can reply that we are re-interpreting those words, using them in a new way or for a new purpose, and, if we constitute a significant body of language-users, there will be little he can say in response.

From this double-edged aspect of reliance on use comes both the tyranny of those ordinary language philosophers and Wittgensteinians who label their opponents' positions as nonsense because "we don't speak that way," and the nihilism of those Wittgensteinians who find everything possible to be a reason for overhauling our artistic, religious, sociological, ethical or philosophical discourse. Since the appeal, in either case, is to the vague, ambiguous, and in any case *socially* defined extension of "use," no individual philosopher can marshal conclusive arguments for taking one or the other of these sides in his approach either to a particular word or to philosophy as a whole. Hence the tendency of debates in and about ordinary language philosophy to degenerate into shouting matches: "the positivist grits his teeth when he hears an analysis given out as a logical one which is so painfully remote from formality, so obviously a question of how you happen to feel at the moment, so psychological; the philosopher who proceeds from everyday language stares back helplessly, asking, 'Don't you feel the difference? Listen: you *must* see it.'"[38]

In application to the words "understanding" and "difference," this problem can become acute. Crucial to the arguments of my antinomy is that one side claims we cannot understand the existence of "different" frameworks unless

---

37 (Rorty, 1979), pp.382-3.

38 (Cavell, 1969), p.90.

we posit a point beyond all frameworks from which they can be seen as different, while the other side claims that we cannot understand what it would mean for there to be such a point. I might also say: on the one hand, "understanding" depends on there not being a significant difference between us and what we understand, while on the other hand, understanding the word "difference" depends on realizing that there can be something significant that we fail to understand. The former position is close to Donald Davidson, while the latter I will want to urge against Davidson. This makes my argument appear simply to concern intuitions about the words "understanding" and "difference," but, if the Wittgensteinian perspective on language is correct, such intuitions, far from being trivial, arise out of, shape, and reflect deep philosophical issues. And one of Wittgenstein's own remarks excellently sums up the importance and antinomous relationship of our intuitions about these particular words:

> PI 531: We speak of understanding a sentence in the sense in which it can be replaced by another which says the same, but also in the sense in which it cannot be replaced by any other. (Any more than one musical theme can be replaced by another.)
>
> In the one case the thought in the sentence is something common to different sentences; in the other, something that is expressed only by these words in these positions. (Understanding a poem.)
>
> PI 532: Then has "understanding" two different meanings here?—I would rather say that these kinds of use of "understanding" make up its meaning, make up my *concept* of understanding.
>
> For I *want* to apply the word "understanding" to all this.

CHAPTER FIVE

ON SCIENTIFIC REALISM—A REPLY TO WILLIAMS

I discussed two of Williams' arguments against Rorty in the last chapter. Williams' third and best argument takes the form of a positive case for what he calls "the absolute conception of the world."[1] Williams introduces this idea in *Descartes: The Project of Pure Enquiry*, as a condition for there being any knowledge at all: "If knowledge is possible at all,...the absolute conception must be possible too."[2] The absolute conception contains both every representation of the world and the ways in which those representations take place, both what is seen from the various perspectives we have of the world and the nature of those perspectives themselves. As such, Williams intends it to capture what we mean by "the reality which is there 'anyway'"[3]—the supposed object of knowledge.

What this means, and why it is so important, remain far from clear. Williams goes some distance towards clarifying the absolute conception when he brings it into his rebuttal of Rorty. There he suggests that it forms a middle ground between two conceptions of "world" discussed by Rorty in "The World Well Lost." For Rorty, the world out there to which our descriptions should correspond can be either "just...the stars, the people, the tables, and the grass" that "the vast majority of our beliefs not currently in question are currently thought to be about" or "something *completely* unspecified and unspecifiable."[4] In the first case, our beliefs will of course correspond to the world because "the world" is defined precisely by what they do correspond to; in the second case, the notion is so vacuous that nothing could be "about it" in any intelligible—specifiable and corrigible—sense at all. When we try to hold both views at once, identifying "world" both with what we ordinarily discuss and with the unspecifiable whatever that is really out there, idealism and scepticism begin to look like enticing possibilities, and the correspondence theory of truth like a significant position: "It seems to me epistemology since Kant has shuttled back and forth between these two meanings of world...[and this equivocation] seems to me essential to the position of those philosophers who see 'realism' or 'the correspondence theory of truth as controversial or exciting theses.'"[5]

---

1 See (Williams, 1985), pp.135-40, (Williams, 1983), and (Williams, 1978), pp. 65-7, 211-2, 239, 245-9, 301-3.

2 (Williams, 1978), p.65.

3 *ibid.*

4 (Rorty, 1982), p.14.

5 *ibid*, pp.14-5.

Williams accepts Rorty's view of his two conceptions of world, but regards the choice between them as a false dilemma. "There is a third and more helpful possibility," he suggests, of defining the world that is "already there" in terms of "some but not all of our beliefs and theories" and specifically in terms of those "beliefs and features of our world picture that we can reasonably claim to represent the world in a way to the maximum degree independent of our perspective and its peculiarities."[6] What he wants to identify as the beliefs and features capable of this surprising task - surprising, because one wonders from what perspective he could possibly even begin to pick out features as more and less independent of our perspective and its peculiarities—turns out to involve a resuscitation of a most old-fashioned distinction: between primary and secondary qualities.[7] By including primary but not secondary qualities under the absolute conception, by replacing all irreducibly phenomenological/perspectival/subjective terms and concepts with their measurable/scientific (I avoid the word "objective") correlates, Williams thinks we may approach a conception of the world that A) will hold independently of the peculiarities of our perspective(s), B) can explain how it itself, and the various more perspectival views, are possible, and C) can explain why scientists can and perhaps must (at least in principle) eventually cease disagreeing, why they converge. These three features, for Williams, define what we mean by "reality that is anyway or already there."

The Peculiarities of our Perspective; Primary and Secondary Qualities

Where does Williams *get* his definition of reality? The convergence of science alone does not presuppose it: if we always face the world from perspectives alien to it, if there is no world independent of our perspectives, our disagreements could still evaporate or be resolved as long as the relevant perspectives are sufficiently similar to one another. Williams seems to think that the *rational* resolution of a disagreement presupposes that there is something on which to agree, but even if we grant that as regards each particular disagreement, we need not presuppose a single such something behind the resolution of all disagreements. All issues, including scientific ones, could turn out to be to some extent independent of one another and not resolvable together. "Could turn out to be," but in the case of science *do* not: in fact we do seek a single explanation of all phenomena when we do science. We try to reduce astronomy, biology, geology as much as possible to a single physico-chemical explanation. Williams thus captures a characteristic of the science we actually practice, but it remains an open question why that characteristic constitutes a philosophical ground for what science should or must be.

---

6 (Williams, 1985), pp.138-9.

7 See also (Williams, 1978), pp.237ff, and (McGinn, 1983).

We might now think that Williams is helping himself to an ordinary language or a Wittgensteinian approach to philosophy, and appealing to the common use of words like "reality," "objective," "absolute."[8] Of course, this is not how Williams writes. He speaks of the absolute conception as a necessary presupposition, corresponding, if true, to a metaphysical fact about the world; he is not at all inclined to begin his sentences with "We say:" or include the phrase "what we call" in them. On the other hand, as Williams interprets him,[9] Wittgenstein indeed shows that conventions rather than transcendental facts or rules ground language, but goes on to draw the consequence that we must therefore not violate our fundamental conventions, which entails, among other things, that we may not appeal to their conventionality as a justification for changing them. Once recognized as truly the ground for what we say, conventions drop out of what we say altogether: "[Philosophy] leaves everything as it is."[10] It follows that the conventionality of such words as "reality," "objective" and "absolute," need not make their meaning any less fixed, any more subject to re-interpretation by those who agree that Williams' intuitions do belong to that meaning, but would rather they did not. Williams might almost say that if what he has picked out does belong to the meaning of "reality," etc., it belongs to that meaning necessarily.

But this is to misconstrue Wittgenstein. When philosophy leaves everything as it is, it also leaves our ordinary superstitions and contradictions about "reality," etc. immune from the kind of transcendental systematization Williams tries to impose on them. Although recognizing use as the ultimate ground for our language does entail not thinking we can arbitrarily or willfully overturn any given usage, it opens the way at the same time to a certain vagueness in definitions and principles, to possibilities of change and variability that prevent transcendental arguments from going through. Williams has got hold of only one side of Wittgenstein's antinomy; the other side militates against what he is trying to do. While it would be good for many Wittgensteinians to remember that Wittgenstein did not give us license to re-convene the uses of our language whenever we feel like it, in presenting conventions as our ground he could not but allow us to peek around their fixity even as we recognize it. If "reality," "objective," "absolute" have one use that demands convergence and freedom from perspective, they also have other uses where this is not the case—in magic, superstition, religion, ethics, psycho-babble: precisely those places where we might want to deploy an absolutist definition—and use alone will not enable us to choose between the one type of case and the other.

The situation gets worse when we come to primary and secondary qualities. Even if we were to assent in general to Williams' argument for the absolute

---

8 Compare also (McGinn, 1983), pp.74-5.
9 "Wittgenstein and Idealism," in (Williams, 1981).
10 (Wittgenstein, 1958), §124.

conception, whatever he tries to fill it with can be accused of being a mere product of a particular perspective. This is certainly the case with primary qualities. While something like the distinction between primary and secondary qualities may indeed play a role *in* science, it will not do as a ground *for* science. That subjective properties like color can be eliminated from the cause-effect relationships we see around us is neither an *a priori* truth, nor a fact of the use of our language, nor self-evident, nor in any other way necessary; it is a simple empirical truth, and as such itself needs grounding in principles about what can and cannot count as empirical evidence.

In addition, primary qualities cannot be separated from secondary qualities, and that for reasons which threaten the absolutist enterprise in general. As Williams himself notes, we can have perceptual illusions about size and shape just as easily as about color and heat.[11] Apparent size and shape, however, while lacking a convenient one-word label, are just as much the secondary qualities corresponding to real size and shape as color is the secondary quality corresponding to wavelength. Once we recognize this, we can see that our road to all the primary qualities runs only via secondary qualities. Perceptual illusions can and do block our way not only to color and heat but to size and shape, and to measurements of size and shape, and thus to measurements of wavelength and caloric energy. This, not the claim that primary qualities are actually in the mind, is the heart of the Berkeleyan argument against making the distinction in the first place,[12] and it remains a good one. For if we retain the distinction while recognizing that all we ever perceive, even when doing science, are secondary qualities, we enter on the primrose path to idealism or scepticism. To avoid those unpleasant and perhaps incoherent positions, we must leave reality as whatever the "vast majority of our beliefs not currently in question are currently thought to be about,"[13] allowing the distinction between primary and secondary qualities to surface only as a distinction between concepts more and less useful for the current notion of reality in the current form of what we call "science."

Self-Explanation

What advantage does Williams think a view derives from being able to explain how it itself is possible? There are at least two possibilities of failing to do this, and I think Williams wrongly takes them as equally problematic. On the one hand, a view can make its own explicability seem remote or even impossible. According to Williams, Rorty is guilty of this, in presenting a transcendental critique of transcendental philosophy. On the other hand, a view can simply say nothing about its own accessibility, leaving that perhaps as an

[11] (Williams, 1978), p.238.
[12] Cf. (Berkeley, 1974), pp.233-40.
[13] (Williams, 1978), p.65.

unexplained area for further investigation, perhaps as an assumption it cannot prove but must presuppose, perhaps as a mystery utterly outside of its domain. The first case certainly counts as an argument against its perpetrator's acceptability; the second at most leaves an explanation somewhat unsatisfying, but most explanations are unsatisfying in some regard.

Moreover, Williams' absolute conception is neither the only approach to knowledge that can give an account of its own existence, nor even clearly successful in this endeavor. Williams says that "it is an important feature of modern science that it contributes to explaining how creatures with our origins and characteristics can understand a world with properties that this same science ascribes to the world."[14] But Augustine's conception of knowledge as divine illumination shows equally well how creatures originating in "the image of God" can understand a reality with the properties that his Platonic Christianity ascribes to reality. When discussing Augustine's intellectual descendant Descartes, Williams acknowledges this feature of the latter's version of the absolute conception, but dismisses the argument for God on which that version depends.[15] But are there more justifiable fundamental principles on which to hang Williams' absolute conception? He himself stays away from the tricky subject of whether there are any fundamental principles of science and what they might be, recommending the absolute conception used in science not by its foundations but because it manages to explain its own possibility. Considered in that light alone, however, it does not improve on the rival Christian version (or any of a number of other religious versions).

In addition, as I have already hinted, it is not at all clear that "the achievements of evolutionary biology and the neurological sciences"[16] do truly explain the development of scientific knowledge or understanding. "Knowledge" and "understanding," after all, characterize *beliefs*, and we have considerable reason to resist any reduction of beliefs to neurological states alone. If we identify the word "belief" with mere patterns of firing neurons, we lose our grip on the thought that those patterns are *about* anything outside themselves, or that they can be relied on to provide predictions about the world. The claim that our brains have been selected out for producing adaptively favorable neurological patterns becomes itself a neurological pattern, not an argument *that* the patterns that have been selected are reliable. If taken to its absolute limit, the mechanistic account of the mind may undermine knowledge rather than support it.

Finally, we may well prefer Rorty's vacuous conception of "the world" to Williams' nonvacuous one. Williams says that "the substance of the absolute conception...lies in the idea that it could nonvacuously explain how it itself,

---

14 (Williams, 1985), pp.139-40.
15 (Williams, 1978), chapter five and pp. 211-2, 240.
16 (Williams, 1985), p.139.

and the various perspectival views of the world, are possible."[17] In general, however, self-explanation is either vacuously circular, if successful, or self-contradictory, if unsuccessful, and in any case it is unnecessary. "Explanations come to an end somewhere," and since there is no such thing as self-evidence, we might as well make the somewhere a ground we take for granted without evidence. Beginning with a hopelessly perspectival set of beliefs and principles may just be an ineradicable feature of our thinking.

Convergence

That a gradual convergence of views is in fact the best description of the history of science, especially over its entire development from the pre-Socratics to the present day, is to start with a highly dubious proposition. A more limited claim for the rapid and ever-increasing convergence of views in science, and convergence of human beings *on* science as the best description of reality, since, say, the Second World War, might be more plausible, but that would greatly reduce the breadth of evidence for the more general proposition. For the moment none of this matters very much, however, because Williams makes clear that he relies only on the *possibility of* convergence, not on actual convergence, to make his case for scientific realism. "In a scientific inquiry there should ideally be convergence on an answer, where the best explanation of the convergence involves the idea that the answer represents how things are...[W]hether convergence will actually occur...is not what the argument is about."[18] It is a fact about scientific discourse that it demands convergence, and that fact seems to entail the assumption that scientific discourse is realist.

But, as I have already indicated, the expectation of convergence need not in the least entail realism. Small groups of people in life-threatening situations (say, ship-wrecked on an island) tend to agree about actions more than other communities do, while chess players agree about expertise in chess more than musicians do about expertise in music. In the first case, the condition of agreement is shared need or interest, and in the second the condition is the nature of the rules of the game - specifically, the fact that in chess a precisely defined and always determinable achievement counts as success. Very similar factors can explain convergence in science. As practised in the Western academy, science (hard science, at any rate, and that is the only place where we will find convergence) moves according to quite strictly defined rules, and, through technology, it serves needs and interests that all human beings share (in which service it aims at fairly clear and easily determinable marks of success).

In addition, the differences between science and ethics when it comes to convergence are not nearly as sharp as Williams wants to make them. He admits himself that we can and do expect a considerable amount of convergence on

[17] *ibid*, p.139.
[18] *ibid*, p.136.

specific ethical qualities (what he calls "thick concepts"), and qualifies his claim that "in the area of the ethical...there is no...coherent hope [of convergence]" with the phrase "at least at a high level of generality."[19] But at a suitably high level of generality - the nature of reality, the possibility of reducing all explanation to physico-chemical terms, the adequacy of a biological account of the human being - there is not much hope of convergence in science either. Scientific inquiry achieves convergence only on specific experiments, theories, and principles in daily use, in which respect it does not differ in kind from ordinary ("thick") ethical discourse. Scientists may agree on what counts as an "electron," a "dinosaur," or a successful piece of software, but when it comes to terms like "particle" or "matter," "life" or "intelligence," they are as much in the dark as any two agents arguing over "goodness" or the purpose of human existence.

This brings us to the hint of circularity in Williams' discussion of convergence. When he says that in scientific inquiry there should ideally be convergence, "...where the best explanation of the convergence involves [realism]," or that he is outlining "the possibility of a convergence characteristic of science, one that could meaningfully be [viewed realistically],"[20] the qualification in each case ("where...," "one...") is ambiguous. It could merely indicate, as I have been assuming so far, that because science converges we may adopt a realist stance towards it, but it could also be meant to describe the *kind* of convergence characteristic of science, to say that in science we can have realistic convergence while any convergence we find in ethics will have nothing to do with realism. (The context, if anything, supports the latter interpretation, since the clauses are otherwise quite unnecessary.) Then we would indeed have a distinction between the convergence of science and that of the ship-wrecked community or the chess players, but one achieved at the price of circularity. For then Williams would be arguing that we must pre-suppose realism to explain the convergence of science because science converges in a way that pre-supposes realism.

There are arguments other than Williams' for regarding the demand for convergence in science as a mark of realism, but their various merits and demerits would take us too far afield.[21] I would like, instead, to turn back from possible to actual convergence. Aside from Williams, writers attempting to put science on a firmer footing than ethics, to give it a universal or at least transcultural status, have relied heavily on the claims that all human beings are interested in "explanation, prediction and control" of their environment, that science has enabled them to achieve these goals better than any other mode of thought, and that people all over the world have therefore been converging on science as the best explanation of reality. Some point out that, for all the desire

[19] *ibid.*

[20] *ibid*, pp. 136, 139.

[21] But see (Bearn, 1985a), chapter three.

of relativistic philosophers to bring out radical differences of outlook between Westerners and, for instance, African or Amerindian tribes, most non-Western peoples have quickly and eagerly embraced Western science and technology upon encountering it. Especially for a position like mine, which takes actual use as crucial to meaning, it might seem reasonable to accept a theory that satisfies the goals of explanation, prediction and control as *de facto* constitutive of what all people mean by "reality."

There is a lot to this suggestion, and if I reject it, it is not for want of respect for the importance of the fact that non-Western peoples have widely adopted Western science and technology. But Arabs, black Africans, Indians, Japanese, and Australian aborigines, to take but a small sample of the peoples recently converted to our outlook, have not always adopted our science in the *way* we have, not to serve as many of their societies' goals, not for the same goals, not, of course, as a natural outgrowth of their own approach to the world, and not, on the other hand, as an alternative that entirely replaces (even the conflicting elements of) their own approach. These limitations on the sense in which they have accepted our science and technology in turn restrict our right to attribute to them an interest in "explanation, prediction and control" as *we* interpret those terms. The vagueness of the terms when they are generalized too broadly may cover over significant differences of belief and attitude.

Two excellent arguments for a *de facto* community of human thought on scientific matters can be found in Charles Taylor's essay "Rationality" and Robin Horton's "Tradition and Modernity Revisited."[22] To some extent, they proceed in opposite directions. Taylor wants to say that the technological successes of "our modern scientific culture" have for good reason commanded the attention of every other culture we have encountered, while Horton shows that our own scientific thought rests on a level of pre-scientific thought that we share with every culture we know. But they are fundamentally proving the same point: that all human beings share a set of interests and standards by which they can agree that our science is tremendously successful. The linch-pin of both arguments is the claim that human beings in fact share an interest in the "prediction and control" of physical nature.

Taylor claims that "[t]here is an inner connection between understanding the world and achieving technological control over it which rightly commands everyone's attention," because "[o]ur ordinary, pre-scientific understanding of the world around us is inseparable from an ability to make our way around in it, and deal with the things in it."[23] Furthermore, understanding *must* be so tied to practice, "given the kind of beings we are, embodied and active in the world."[24] It follows that any theory which increases our ability to "make our way around" the things in our environment will receive, by that token alone,

---

22 In RR, (Hollis & Lukes, 1982).

23 *ibid*, p.101.

24 *ibid.*

approval from the "ordinary, pre-scientific understanding" that both scientific ("theoretical," for Taylor) and nonscientific cultures share. And since such understanding is part of what we call "rationality," we must suppose that any being we can translate will share it. As a result, "the immense technological successes of...our modern scientific" culture have invariably "command[ed] the attention of atheoretical" cultures when the two have met.[25] More traditional (less theoretical) cultures may retain a connection we have lost, between understanding the universe and coming into attunement with it,[26] but through that loss we have achieved a greater pure understanding than anyone else.

The problem with this argument lies in the vagueness of the phrases "to make our way around in" and "to deal with the things in." What counts as "things," to begin with? Can magical forces, totems, witches, and gods not be considered things? If so, making our way around will not be well measured by our success in merely producing food and shelter and evading dangerous animals. And for those who believe in magical forces, there need be no important difference between the dangers of a lion or a bacillus and the dangers of an evil spell. For those who include afterlives in "the world," Western achievements may not aid successful navigation around it at all.

Then, as Taylor himself admits, while the dissociation of understanding and attunement has been very good for the former, it "arguably...has been disastrous for the latter goal."[27] As Taylor also implies,[28] it has almost certainly been disastrous for the understanding of our fellow man. Now, one very good reason why this might be so is that some kind of attunement with other human beings is *part* of understanding them. But that suggests a more general conclusion about understanding: it might be reasonable for another culture, particularly one that included some of the supernatural possibilities of the previous paragraph among the things of the world, to argue that Taylor is wrong to dissociate understanding anything from coming into attunement with it. Such a culture might prefer to call what he claims as the success of the West "manipulation of objects" rather than "understanding," and might hold that technological success without attunement may command the attention of our lower desires but never the approval of our whole mind. It could thus preserve Taylor's probably correct insight that all human beings want some control over what we may call "the physical objects" around them and that such control forms part of what we call "rationality," but at the same time subordinate this interest to a wider sense of understanding in which ever-increasing "technological application,"[29] is not at all the final goal. Without believing anything we would consider intrinsically irrational, such a culture could be quite

[25] *ibid*, p.104.
[26] *ibid*, p.103.
[27] *ibid*.
[28] *ibid*, note on p.103.
[29] *ibid*, pp. 102, 101.

willing to give up some of our technological successes in favor of a greater attunement with the world, and could label the kind of thought enabling them to strike this balance "understanding."

A similar kind of response can be given to Horton. Horton draws a distinction between "primary theory" and "secondary theory." The first of these he claims to be something we in fact share with every culture we have so far met, and something we must so share if we are to establish a bridgehead from which to translate any other culture's language.[30] It consists of "middle-sized, enduring, solid objects," connected in "a 'push-pull' conception of causality, in which spatial and temporal contiguity are seen as crucial to the transmission of change," related to one another spatially and temporally in terms of a few simple dichotomies (left/right, above/below, etc.) and one trichotomy (before/at the same time/after), and admitting two major distinctions among its objects: "between human beings and other objects; and..., among human beings, between self and others."[31] In contrast, secondary theory allows for "hidden" as well as "given," strange as well as familiar, entities and processes, describing them by means of analogies with the objects of primary theory, and using them to explain, predict and control those objects more fully than primary theory itself can. The great differences between cultures arise in the realm of secondary theory, but those differences can to a large extent be moderated by the "'common core' of rationality" embedded in primary theory. According to this common core, not only can secondary theories explain, predict and control the events of primary theory, but their adequacy is and must be measured by their success in such activities.

Again, we may justifiably feel perplexed about just what is to be explained, predicted and controlled, about just what, in Horton's terms, is to belong to primary theory. To return to a favorite example, what happens to witches? Suppose Smith claims acquaintance with witches, as middle-sized, enduring and solid denizens of his everyday world. We might say that he simply attributes a property from secondary theory (some kind of hidden, long-distance causal power) to certain of the primary objects we all call "persons." But here a tension arises between Horton's definition of primary theory and some of the notions which give that definition its appeal. One such notion is the idea that we all normally want to explain, predict and control the objects we ordinarily encounter; another is that we all have an interest and belief in the middle-sized, enduring and solid (perhaps also liquid, but not gaseous) objects of unaided perception. These two kinds of objects need not be identical, however—everydayness is not necessarily equivalent to perceptibility—and a question arises as to whether Horton's "secondary theory" should and will suit the former or the latter. In our example, Smith may say that he is immediately aware of

30 *ibid*, p.260.

31 *ibid*, p.228.

the witchhood of the people in question in the way that we might be immediately aware that someone is tall although she is not standing next to anyone, or strong although she is not at the moment demonstrating any strength. To strip such everyday relational properties from primary theory would reduce it to an extreme phenomenalist's view of perception, which has notorious problems in accounting for cognition and is in any case not what Horton wants. His very distinction between "push-pull" and "hidden" causality, however, making the latter supervenient on the former, brings him very close to the phenomenalist position. And without that distinction he will not be able to rule certain very ordinary but problematic items of other peoples' worlds out of their primary theory (items which *they*, if asked, would probably include in it).

Worse, there are some purported entities that neither fit well into primary theory nor get their validity from it. Take "spirits," in a culture that believes in an afterlife. As in the case of witches, people may claim to perceive spirits directly, as objects to be theorized about rather than parts of a theory, but for the moment we can lean hard on the fact that spirits, while perhaps middle-sized, are by no means solid and enduring. Horton would probably justify their place in secondary theory by showing how they are used in explaining misfortune, say, or in trying to predict and control the coming year's agricultural yield. I want to stress instead their use in guaranteeing the existence of, and perhaps attempting to control one's place in, an afterlife. Now afterlives cannot possibly belong to primary theory, and they remain of interest even when they explain no primary-theoretical events. If they provide the basis for a belief in spirits, therefore, that belief, like the notion of the afterlife itself, will have no fallibility conditions among the events of primary theory. Afterlives and spirits are not alone in this respect; as before, beliefs in the inherent value of one's culture's way of life (its mode of attunement with the world) can function in much the same way. We may thus run into entities and beliefs that do not fit comfortably into either primary or secondary theory.

So what is "explanation, prediction and control of events" to mean once we recognize differences in the ontology of "events" between us and other people? Like Taylor, Horton rightly emphasizes that other peoples are in fact much more interested in negotiating their way around physical objects than "Symbolist" and "Fideist" anthropologists would have us believe,[32] but, also like Taylor, he draws too readily the conclusion that they are *as* interested in physical objects as we are. He ignores the possibility that they might, for instance, draw what we would consider an arbitrary line between some of the products of our ways of thinking and others, accepting what they find useful while rejecting anything that seriously threatens their alternative ontology. Taylor says, "it is difficult to understand how an increase in scientific knowledge beyond pre-scientific common sense could fail to offer potential recipes for more effective

[32] *ibid*, pp.208ff. See also (Horton, 1976).

practice...[G]iven the kind of beings we are, embodied and active in the world, and given the way that scientific knowledge extends and supersedes our ordinary understanding of things, it is impossible to see how it could fail to yield further and more far-reaching recipes for action."[33] But it is neither impossible nor difficult to see that people might consider their pre-scientific common sense quite-adequate-thank-you-very-much for their particular mode of embodiment and action in the world, and take no interest in practices we would consider more "effective." Or they might take an interest in just some of our recipes for action, regarding the others as of less inherent value (or indeed of negative inherent value) for what they conceive as a good life. And if their explanation, prediction, and control intersects with what we call "explanation, prediction, and control" but both ignores some of the objects we care about and extends to some objects of which we take no account, the phrase will no longer pick out any clear common core by which we can assess our similarities and differences with them.

Now a critic of this position might hold that, with regard to "explanation" at least, we do wrong to define our terms by their objects alone. Even if the objects the tribalists want to explain differ from what we want to explain, we can both mean the same thing by "explanation." And according to the meaning of that term, our science has advantages over theirs, since we can give an account (in historical, anthropological, or biological terms) of how they have developed their mode of knowledge, while they cannot do the same for us. In particular, they will not be able to explain why we, following what they consider an improper road to knowledge, should arrive at what they acknowledge to be technological successes; we, on the other hand, can easily give naturalistic accounts of the ways in which they outdo us.[34]

But the tribalists may respond that they *can* give an account of our successes: We succeed in certain realms by dint of the favor of the gods, spirits, or whatever, granted perhaps in order to teach the tribespeople that they are not the sole beneficiaries, creatures or subjects of the gods, perhaps to punish the tribe for some sin, perhaps because the gods need unspiritual beings to provide the earthly needs of their chosen people (the tribe itself). Why the gods have arranged the roles of different societies in this way, the tribalists may leave as a mystery known to the gods alone. (As it happens, these stories in fact capture the responses to modern science of many traditionalists in contemporary Judaism, Islam, and Christianity.)

Our critic may not be satisfied, however, claiming that the appeal to mystery throws doubt on whether this should count as an explanation at all. Explanations, he may say, should leave as little shrouded in mystery as possible, and should never employ mystery as a means of avoiding further questions.

[33] *op. cit.*, p.101.

[34] See *ibid*, pp.103-4, and 239-49. Something like this line of reasoning presumably also lies behind Williams' conception of "explanation."

But at this point differences in ontology return to haunt us. After all, if we are concerned primarily with physical objects—inanimate and non-intentional by definition—we may want explanations to approach complete perspicuity as much as possible, while if our primary object set contains entities like "spirits" and "gods," it could be a *condition* of satisfactory explanations that they not explain too much. A complete account of an intentional (hence free-willed by postulate) agent may necessarily be a false account.[35] Moreover, the tribalist may reasonably maintain what we might call a Kierkegaardian view of explanation in general: a successful account is obliged precisely to display the limitations of the human condition, not try either to ignore them or to transcend them with attempts at omniscience. He may add that no explanation can possibly explain everything, that all explanations have to start somewhere, by which it follows that our failed attempts at complete perspicuity should have no superiority in any terms over the weaker accounts of his tribe, since they, more realistically, avow their own limitations.

---

[35] Compare (MacIntyre, 1981), p.91.

CHAPTER SIX

ON DISAGREEMENT AND TRUTH—A REPLY TO DAVIDSON

According to Donald Davidson, we cannot take even a first step towards interpretation without "knowing or assuming a great deal about the speaker's beliefs,"[1] and in particular we need to assume most of those beliefs to be true. "Charity is forced on us; whether we like it or not, if we want to understand others, we must count them right in most matters." (ITI 197) It follows from the very methodology of interpretation, therefore, that "we could not be in a position to judge that others had concepts or beliefs radically different from our own." (ITI 197)

How does this apply to Awali, our interlocutor in chapter two? Must we refrain from saying that Awali's concepts and beliefs are radically different from our own? In that case, either his beliefs are really much closer to our own than they seem but he has made some kind of error, or there is indeed an irresolvable disagreement between us but for some reason it does not deserve the title "radical." Now, I went through an exhaustive study of error precisely to show that that category does not apply to Awali, while if Davidson is using the word "radical" so that it does not apply to this kind of difference, he owes us an account of what he means by it.

As I have already indicated in the first chapter, I largely share Davidson's approach to truth and language. That a language must be understood and evaluated holistically rather than sentence by sentence, that there are no privileged classes of sentences serving as foundations for the whole, that we determine judgments of truth against the bulk of what we already hold true and not against uninterpreted evidence or a foundational class of sentences, are all principles I require for my own position. For Davidson, it follows from these principles that there can be no such thing as a radically different set of beliefs. I must therefore show either that he is wrong to draw this conclusion, or that what I mean by "radically different" is not what he means by it.[2]

I think I need to adopt both of these strategies in part, but it is not easy to be sure about this because Davidson himself is importantly vague about what he means. To begin with, he leaves unclear the amount and kind of agreement he demands. We must, he says, "*maximize* agreement" in interpreting the words and thought of others; we must find a way to interpret those words and thoughts so as to reveal beliefs "*largely* consistent and true by our own standards";

---

1 "On the Very Idea of a Conceptual Scheme," in (Davidson, 1984), p. 196. Quotations from this volume will be incorporated into the text by "ITI" and page number.

2 See, in this connection, p.152 below.

"disagreement and agreement alike are intelligible only against a background of *massive* agreement." (ITI 27, 137, my emphasis) No doubt these general claims are true—in a *general* way, but what specifically do they prohibit? And do the metaphors of large size refer to quality or quantity—must we share a certain large number of beliefs, only certain very important beliefs ("massive" in their foundational or quasi-foundational role—perhaps logical or mathematical beliefs), or some combination of a large number of beliefs and a set of centrally important ones? To some extent, it is of the essence of Davidson's project that he cannot be more specific. To isolate a set of specific beliefs on which we must agree would lead him towards the foundationalist view of truth that he considers untenable, and to establish clear boundaries on what has to be and what does not have to be regarded as true would violate his holistic methodology.

On the other hand, there exist specific cases of conceptual conflict that would seem to betray "massive disagreement" under practically any interpretation of those terms. Suppose that we meet people who fail, in the ways described in chapter two, to fit such categories as "mistaken," "psychotic," "socially conditioned," etc., and that after all attempts at explaining the differences between us, we wind up inexplicably disagreeing with them on whether the earth is round, whether magical visions are more real than ordinary sense-experience, or whether astrology is the best means of predicting human events. Davidson might point out that we need to share a lot with these people to know that we disagree with them about these matters, and to know that we cannot resolve the disagreement by pointing out their intellectual limitations. I agree with this, but would argue that if we can still find ourselves with matters of such import—matters not merely of fact but of ways of ascertaining fact, of modes of evidence—unresolved and unresolvable between us, we have as massive a disagreement as we could ever desire or fear.

Yet I may still be talking at cross-purposes with Davidson, since he never professes himself to be concerned with the resolvability of disagreements. He says explicitly that he is not trying to eliminate differences of opinion, and perhaps even important and irresolvable disagreements like the ones I have proposed, can come under the heading of a difference of opinion. But if it is not their resolvability, exactly what is it about disagreements that can threaten the interpretive project?

Davidson takes care to allow for "modest examples [of conceptual contrast]" (ITI 184), for "breakdowns in translation when they are local enough," (ITI 192), for "sharers of a scheme to differ on details" (ITI 194). He says that his method "is not designed to eliminate disagreement nor can it" (ITI 196). On the other hand, he believes that "the attempt to give a solid meaning to the idea of conceptual relativism...fares no better when based on partial failure of translation than when based on total failure" (ITI 197). By a partial failure of translation, he means that "some range [of sentences in one language] could be translated [into the other] and some range could not" (ITI 185). In contrast, the local breakdowns in translation to which he refers on p.192 concern "simple predicates whose extensions are matched by no simple predicates, or even by any predicates at all" in cases where two languages share "an ontology,...with concepts that individuate the same objects." Here, no range of *sentences* fails of translation. For instance, there are differences between us and the Eskimos arising from their several words for snow, and between us and those South Sea Islanders lacking any word for snow, but in both situations the differences can be excellently expressed in the *sentences* of both languages.

Davidson rules out the possibility of an untranslatable range of sentences on the basis of his principle of charity. "[I]f all we know is what sentences a speaker holds true, and we cannot assume that his language is our own," he says,"then we cannot take even a first step towards interpretation without knowing or assuming a great deal about the speaker's beliefs...Charity is forced on us." (ITI 196-7) For this reason, he claims that we make "maximum sense" of even our differences with others by interpreting what they say so as to "optimize agreement," that "we improve the clarity and bite of declarations of difference...by enlarging the basis of shared...language or of shared opinion." (ITI 197) But there is a great gap between demanding charity as a first condition of radical interpretation, where all we know is "what sentences a speaker holds true," and trying to make "maximum sense" of what others say by employing charity throughout interpretation. In the first case, charity is indeed forced on us; in the second, it is an option. Of course, we cannot even recognize a range of sentences as such without assuming the general community of beliefs that we used to begin the process of interpretation, but recognizing something as a sentence does not entail fully understanding it or knowing why the speaker utters or believes it. To this extent, we may find a range of sentences untranslatable. It is quite true that "no general principle can force us" to interpret others as thinking differently from us rather than merely confused or wrong, and that I can always make *maximum* sense of what others say by assuming that they believe exactly what I do, but sometimes this striving for complete clarity seems misguided. We may deeply *not* want to make maximum sense of the other—we may want instead to see her as significantly different[3]—and no general principle can force us, either, to interpret the other as confused rather than untranslatable.

Now concerning Awali we want to know two things: first, could such a thing happen—could we ever reach such a severe disagreement and still have reason to trust our translations of the other? And second, if we can reach such a situation, can we give any sense to the notion that our disagreement is over the nature of truth, rather than over the truth of a proposition? Is there any sense at all to saying that what Awali believes may yet be true, that we cannot call

---

3 For ethical reasons of the kind I explore in chapter eight, especially section *x*.

him "wrong"? When Davidson makes room for disagreements on "details" and "differences of opinion," it is not clear whether he is allowing for this possibility. If two people differ in opinion, they may regard the matter of their opinions as independent of truth (as in a matter of taste), or they may each feel the other is wrong but lack evidence to settle the question. But a difference on a matter of truth that is *in principle* unsettleable does not fit either of these descriptions exactly. Given his Tarskian account of truth as inextricably bound up with translation, Davidson may well not feel that there can be a difference of this sort, and if he does not hold such a strong view, he at least gives no account of what it might mean for a difference to be in principle unsettleable.

Part of our problem here lies in applying Davidson's theory of interpretation to specific cases. His main concern is with, and his main arguments derive from, the interpretation of a linguistic whole. He may not even intend to demand that we interpret every single utterance strictly and solely in accordance with the principle of charity. He himself sets up, as necessary and sufficient conditions to ensure communication, the reconciliation of charity with "the formal conditions for a theory." (ITI 197) The latter may refer merely to something as uninformative as consistency and the avoidance of circularity, but a hint on the previous page allows us to fill it in tentatively with "considerations of simplicity, hunches about the effects of social conditioning, and...our common-sense, or scientific, knowledge of error." The question is, can charity taken together with even these qualifications account for all specific utterances that on first acquaintance seem wildly inconsonant with the beliefs and modes of evidence we normally take for granted?

Let us return to Awali's talk about his oracle as an example. A) On a loose version of Davidson's theory, we can simply describe enough of the beliefs we share with Awali to show roughly what he means by an oracle, what he takes to be the justifications for his claims about it, and what role those claims play in the rest of his thought, and then acknowledge that a gap exists between this information and an account of why he accepts claims and modes of justification we take to be, respectively, wrong and ridiculous. While identifying Awali's desires and beliefs on the whole, therefore, we would take Davidson's allowance for disagreement and local breakdown as permission to fail to locate the specific concatenation of desires and beliefs that would enable us to identify Awali's claims about his oracle either as unsuspected truth or as explicable error. B) On a stricter reading of Davidson, we would have to locate a specific desire and belief for every utterance, including what Awali says about the oracle. This entails saying, if we want to disagree with Awali, that he either has beliefs uninformed by truths of which we are aware, or has desires causing him to accept beliefs he himself would otherwise recognize as false, or does not mean precisely what he seems to mean when he talks about the oracle. But as we have seen in the second chapter, each and all of these alternatives may fail. Davidson's anti-foundationalism demands that his method of interpretation always issue, ultimately, in empirical statements like these, yet it is a feature of empirical statements that they must be able to fall in the face of contrary evidence. (Of course, we can interpret and re-interpret almost any evidence to meet conclusions we want it to show, but such a procedure violates the canons defining what counts as good evidence.)

Either way we look at it, Davidson's interpretive method runs into trouble in specific cases. On strategy A, it leaves an important gap; on strategy B, it winds up making implausible demands that threaten its own empirical grounding. Which strategy Davidson himself favors it is hard to say, for reasons I have already discussed, although he does hint at a preference for B in passages like the following: "To take an example, how clear are we that the ancients—some ancients—believed that the earth was flat? *This* earth? Well, this earth of ours is part of the solar system, a system partly identified by the fact that it is a gaggle of large, cool, solid bodies circling around a very large, hot star. If someone believes *none* of this about the earth, is it certain that it is the earth that he is thinking about? An answer is not called for...." (ITI 168) Of course, Davidson is too cautious to demand a decision in a case like this, but he does show a leaning towards re-interpreting utterances even in specific cases rather than merely admitting to large differences in belief for which radical interpretation cannot account. Again, one of his main targets in "On the Very Idea of a Conceptual Scheme" is Thomas Kuhn, who has made some unfortunate remarks about scientists sometimes living in different worlds from one another,[4] but who is primarily concerned to make the rather mild point that many shifts in the history of scientific thought cannot be explained solely by the adaptation of beliefs to changes in the available evidence. The attack on Kuhn implies that even such clearly irresolvable disputes as that between Galileo and Cardinal Bellarmine should be sufficiently amenable to charitable interpretation that everyone, even the parties involved, could in principle see the other as fundamentally either in agreement with himself or in explicable error.

I understand Davidson to be pursuing three main lines of argument in support of his position: 1) Belief, desire and action belong inextricably together, which means that to interpret one (here, the act of uttering) we must already have a firm grasp on the other two, 2) In order even to locate the object of a given belief, one must assume or demonstrate the believer to hold many other true beliefs about that object, and 3) Translation into a familiar tongue is our best key to what truth is, to how the word "truth" is used. My strategy in the rest of this chapter is to present an alternative mode of interpretation to the method of charity, then defend it against each of these positions in turn. I separate the lines of argument, here and in the following, only for convenience: in fact they, and my responses to them, support and depend on each other in

4 (Kuhn, 1962), pp. 118, 150.

numerous ways. As the discussion so far should have indicated, I am not sure whether what I have to say is a complement to Davidson's theory or a critique of it. Of what I have called strategy A, it is a complement; of strategy B, it is a critique. In either case, I now turn away from theories of interpretation and towards a theory of misinterpretation.

How to Misunderstand People

> ...[O]ne human being can be a complete enigma to another. We learn this when we come into a strange country with entirely strange traditions; and, what is more, even given a mastery of the country's language. We do not *understand* the people...We cannot find our feet with them. (Wittgenstein, PI, p. 223)

I begin by dropping the terms "interpretation" and "translation" in favor of "understanding," which I take to be broader. In particular, the latter embraces both the goal of such things as translation or scientific theory-building, and a more general "sense" for such things as how others feel or what a piece of music means. Recall the quotation from Wittgenstein at the end of chapter four:

> We speak of understanding a sentence in the sense in which it can be replaced by another which says the same, but also in the sense in which it cannot be replaced by any other. (Any more than one musical theme can be replaced by another.) ... Then has "understanding" two different meanings here?—I would rather say that these kinds of use of "understanding" make up its meaning, make up my *concept* of understanding. (PI 531-2)

I want first to clarify the differences between these two forms of "understanding," then show how, despite and through their contrast, they may define the term together.

Davidson's method of interpretation, as applied to specific cases, captures the first kind of understanding. According to Davidson, we understand a sentence only when we can fit it into what else we know. We understand a sentence only when we understand a language, and we understand a language only when we can make sense of the speaker's thoughts, actions and words as a whole. We can make such sense, in turn, only by applying the principle of charity, assuming that on the whole the speaker believes truths or errs in readily explicable ways. I shall call this holistic picture "interpretive understanding," since it entails fitting any particular claim into an interpreted whole. It fits what we do when we learn a foreign language, when we construct an anthropological or linguistic theory about another group, or when we try to understand a scientific or mathematical claim in our home language. If we apply it in all cases, we will never arrive at a situation in which someone confronts us with a radically new kind of truth claim or mode of evidence, since whenever we approach that point we can and must revise our translations to make the apparently threatening sentence conform better with our expectations.

Davidson permits fairly radical revisions of translation to satisfy this principle. When a Saturnian—whose language, by hypothesis, is translatable into English—says that he is translating a language of which we can make no sense, Davidson maintains "it would occur to us to wonder whether our translations of Saturnian were correct" (ITI 186). But such a denial of the homophonic reading of another's words, after we had already reached a fairly rich level of mutual translatability, would probably *not* occur to most of us.

In any case, quite apart from interpretive understanding, I may say I understand someone when I produce paraphrases of and responses to what she says that she agrees are paraphrases or appropriate responses, regardless of whether I can make full sense of what she means. I call this second kind of understanding "understanding by means of expressions of assent," or, for reasons that will become clear shortly, "phenomenological understanding." The difference between it and interpretive understanding comes out sharply in the following kind of case: a speaker declares and refuses to back away from a proposition we find ridiculous or inconsistent with other things we know she believes or think she ought to believe (given, among other things, our knowledge of her behavior in general). Each time we give a plausible interpretation of what she says, she insists that that's not what she meant, and each time we ask her if she really means some version of the to-us-ridiculous proposition we heard the first time, she assents. And she speaks good English, is intelligent, not joking, and sane. Now the strict Davidsonian, at some point like this, will have to resort to denying that our translations of the other's expressions of assent are correct, and avow total lack of understanding, but I think this is to misconstrue the situation. I am not completely in the dark with my counterpart here, I do understand at least her words and expressions of assent, and she will be justly annoyed if I suddenly pretend to total incomprehension.

I base my claim to understand, in this situation, on a framework of trust in the speaker as a possible source of truth, rather than on my own standards for what could possibly count as truth. Some say this is the heart of dialogue: that the participants, trusting each other as potential sources of a truth they may not now quite understand, primarily try to keep up with what is being said sufficiently to maintain the mutual acknowledgement of a sincere attempt at understanding.[5] Yet, if this is a type of understanding, it by definition does not fit into an interpretive whole. I feel unable to deny somehow understanding the speaker, in this case, not because I anticipate any way of resolving my problems with her statement, but because I know enough about *her* to trust her to be meaning something, even if I do not know exactly what it is.

---

5 See, for instance, (Buber 1971), and (Schutz, 1967).

In this sense "understanding by means of expressions of assent" corresponds to a familiar phenomenological fact about conversations: we often carry on conversations (respond appropriately and interestingly to others' words, receive such responses to our own) without making full sense of what is going on. In such a situation we may expect to put together what has been said in a way that makes more sense once we leave the conversation and go home, we may assume that the other party is for the moment confused, or we may assume that we are the confused ones and have missed something. I think Davidson assumes that such circumstances will ultimately disappear from or become irrelevant to the project of understanding, that they are extraneous to the real business, while I want to give them the central role that I think is their due. Of course, to produce the paraphrases and responses that allow the conversation to continue at all, we need to have at least vaguely in mind what might count as the kernel of truth in the other's remarks, which makes it look as if we are continually drawing nearer to a state of sharing all significant beliefs with the other. What matters most may be not that we approximate such an ideal, however, but that we continually, and inevitably or at least ultimately, fall short. Instead of coming closer and closer to sharing the other's beliefs, we may be merely building up a body of descriptions for beliefs we finally cannot share—learning a new language, if you like.[6]

Phenomenological understanding alone, as I describe it here, is a disjointed, discomfiting process, in which we make sudden sense of here a sentence, there a sentence, by connecting them with something familiar, but then wonder how the sentences fit together. In connection with it, I think of my first acquaintance with such elusive writers as Joyce, Kafka, Hegel, or Wittgenstein, or of conversations with Western-educated Hindus about why they find some ceremony in their religion particularly ennobling or revealing. In the latter case, my conversational partner might make a comparison, say with baptism or Jewish ritual immersion, which seemed to clarify matters—until I remembered that I was not sure what baptism and immersion "mean." In the case of a difficult poem or piece of fiction, I may begin to approach it by recognizing an image, a similarity with another text, or by saying, "This reminds me of how *I* felt in such-and-such a situation...," but again such comparisons often shed as much obscurity on the familiar object as they shed light on the unfamiliar one. We tend to feel we understand something new when we experience this alienation of baptism, immersion, image, text or situation; and we tend in these cases to find the recognition of obscurity a *part* of the new understanding.

But phenomenological understanding usually comes together with interpretive understanding instead of fracturing our world in such a disturbing way. We trust (some? many? most?) speakers enough to translate most of what they say homophonically, but only once we have provided enough of a context

---

6 More on this below, p.127.

for their words to establish that they are speaking a language at all. After that, we sometimes accept what they say even when it sounds strange or confused, and we sometimes re-interpret it instead, feeling "they can't mean *that*." More deeply, each of the two kinds of understanding can legitimately claim to ground the other. For without some interpretive understanding we would not know how to translate what we want to paraphrase, nor what to count as an expression of assent, nor whether the other is assenting to the adequacy of our paraphrase or to something else we are doing, while without phenomenological understanding, we would never acquire a language or set of standards of our own against which to measure the beliefs and words of others.

This latter point Davidson seems to miss. He gives a theory of understanding that matches what we do when we already have one language and want to understand a new one, but he does not and cannot say anything about what it is to acquire a first language. In this respect, those who see Davidson as somehow extending Wittgenstein overlook a central feature of the latter's work. Wittgenstein says about Augustine that he "describes the learning of human language as if the child came into a strange country and did not understand the language of the country; that is, as if it already had a language, only not this one" (PI 32). His own *Philosophical Investigations*, by contrast, focuses on how language is possible at all, and he again and again illustrates this question by way of the learning-processes each of us goes through for our first language.[7] What mystery turns the demonstration and behavioral training we receive at the hands of our parents and teachers into a set of *standards* for meaning and truth? Lacking any criteria or principles of justification, what ground do we have for accepting anything *as* a criterion or principle of justification? Of course, part of Wittgenstein's answer to this is to separate genealogical from logical accounts of justification: how I come to judge of truth and falsehood has nothing, logically, to do with what counts as true and false. But even if establishing the nature of truth and falsehood lies beyond my control, I must have standards on which to choose which criteria, which truth-claims, which theories of translation and justification, to use when judging of truth and falsehood, and those standards can only acquire sense for me out of a necessarily sense*less* prior training.

That there is something special about one's birth into language has been noted by, among others, Quine.[8] That there are two quite different modes of understanding, one of which requires interpretation against a given set of standards, while the other seems criterionless, inexplicable, and, in many senses, primal, appears in the writings of such diverse thinkers as Charles Taylor, Robin Horton, and Nelson Goodman. When Taylor distinguishes between "common sense" and "theory," and Horton between "primary" and "secondary" theory,

---

7 For instance, PI 5, 6, 9, 32, 35, 73, 143, 157, 185, 244, 257, and 361.

8 See (Quine 1960), p.59.

for Horton, the first of each pair is, like phenomenological understanding, a primal human approach to the world that can be neither further explained nor further justified, while the second, like interpretive understanding, receives explanation and justification from the first and to that extent cannot ground it. Goodman speaks of rightness in induction and categorization as being determined on the one hand by "inertia" (an unfortunately mechanistic term for what Goodman elsewhere describes as "entrenchment") and on the other by "initiative" or "novelty." Echoing the traditional language for re-birth if not for birth, Goodman describes the presentation of "new aspects of reality" as "revelation," and sees it as essential to the process of categorization, since entrenched predicates alone cannot fully account for "novel organizations that make...newly important connections and distinctions."[9]

I can now make clearer what I mean by incommensurable groups. A group's beliefs are to some greater or lesser extent incommensurable with ours if we can understand them well enough to know we do not understand them, and that means, in the terms I have now developed, that we can achieve interpretive *or* phenomenological understanding of the relevant belief claims but not both. That is, we may get to the point where we say, "Well, they say they believe x," and win their assent but not understand how they believe it, or we say "They can't believe x, so they must mean y when they say x," and find this claim more sensible but be unable to win their assent to it. (X itself, let us suppose, is empirically or prudentially false ("we go to the moon every night," "our oracle works better than your physicist"), and they have the experience, desires, and mental capability to know that.)

Now I speak of a *group's* beliefs because, as we have seen, we need to see a quite radically different *way of life* to understand a different belief as different rather than merely erroneous. We saw in chapter four that for us to regard a belief as incommensurable with our own, rather than simply wrong, it must have fit within a framework of justification, and that means, minimally, that it fits within a chain of argument that regresees to a socially established canon of evidence and argument. If the believer in question is not simply to be taken as mad, her belief must cohere with the beliefs of those from whom the person learns and with whom she comes in contact, with a set of her and their desires, with institutions passing on and entrenching these desires, with, in short, a coherent alternative set or hierarchy of interests. And even in that case we might still have other evidence to indicate that the other society is so seriously oppressed, so psychologically disturbed, or simply so ignorant, that we are willing to stick with the judgment of our interpretive understanding, but when we lack such evidence I think we will feel most comfortable admitting that the project of understanding has indeed, if in part, broken down. (But again, we

9 (Goodman, 1978), p. 128.

are never *forced* to do this.) In this way, our concept of understanding allows for the possibility of acknowledging the existence of beliefs and concepts that we cannot understand.

I am thus not denying that we experience a certain vertigo in conversations that seem to rely primarily on phenomenological understanding, precisely insofar as we fail to interpret what the other is saying as a whole. I do not deny that in that respect we fail to understand her, and I do not deny that a lot of interpretive stage-setting must take place before we can ever get to trusting another as an intelligible speaker at all. What I want to insist on is that both kinds of understanding must come together, such that we cannot claim comprehension when we have interpretive without phenomenological understanding any more than vice versa.

There is, of course, *some* slack between interpretive and phenomenological understanding. When a person insists that she loves her father while all the evidence points to her hating him, we can have confidence that she really means that she hates him, whatever she says about that interpretation. But the slack also works in the other direction: if we find someone's defense of astrology, say, insuperably baffling, we cannot on that account aver that her very words have ceased to make sense to us. To say that we have no understanding at all when we lack the interpretive kind is to prioritize the latter unjustifiably, and it is that error of which I accuse Davidson's claim that we can always accommodate differences with another by adjusting our translations.

I am indeed saying here that sometimes we understand people just well enough to know that we do not understand them, but if this seems paradoxical it is, I think, a paradox built into our notions of truth and understanding. We "*want* to apply the word 'understanding' to all this"—and if the fifth antinomy is correct, it betrays a similar ambiguity in the notion we call "truth." Whether our use of the terms "understanding" and "truth" imposes a paradox on the world or whether we are invited to that use by the world itself is a moot question. Not so moot is whether I have actually identified our notion of truth, or indeed any notion of truth that can be made intelligible. In the face of Davidson's powerful reading of Tarski, this may seem doubtful. Nor is it clear just where one can lessen one's grip on the Principle of Charity sufficiently to allow for the kind of mis-understanding I have described. To these questions I now turn.

Beliefs and Other Attitudes

A simple point first, on which I do not want to put too much weight. As Davidson himself recognizes, the process of interpretation cannot take belief in isolation from the other propositional attitudes. "A more full-blooded theory," he admits, "would look to other attitudes towards sentences as well as [that of accepting as true], such as wishing true, wondering whether true, intending to make true, and so on." (ITI 195-6)[10] But how is the radical interpreter supposed to tell which attitude the speaker is adopting? Perhaps she could assume that speakers *generally* adopt one attitude—say, accepting as true—but there is no reason *ab initio* to make such an assumption. And of course the interpretation of the sentence will differ widely depending on the speaker's attitude. X's utterance of P when it is raining near X could express a wish that the proposition "It is sunny" were true just as easily as an acceptance that the proposition "It is raining" is true.

This raises deep problems when we try to apply the principle of charity to beliefs and desires simultaneously. In a footnote to a recent essay, Davidson says that he "now think[s] it is essential, in doing radical interpretation, to include the desires of the speaker from the start so that the springs of action and intention, namely both belief and desire, are related to meaning."[11] Suppose now the native utters "gavagai" when a lion comes by, while at the same time grinning with every sign of pleasure and making as if to go up to the lion. From the utterance alone in these circumstances, charity tells us to assume that "gavagai" means "lion" and the native believes that this is a lion, but from the (apparent) desire evinced, charity tells us to assume that the native does not know what a lion is or has beliefs about them quite different from ours. Using charity on their desires, we may have to infer that they have quite a strange set of beliefs; using charity on their beliefs, we may have to infer that they have quite a strange set of desires. Nothing that I can see guarantees that we should be able to attain a satisfactory interpretation of both at once. The interlocking of desire and belief in interpretation only reinforces the connection of beliefs with interests we saw in the third chapter. And if we cannot guarantee that an interpretation will bring both the desires and the beliefs of others into satisfactory alignment with our own, this interlocking suggests that we may need to see some sets of propositional attitudes as radically different from—incommensurable with—our own.

A problem like this can run, moreover, throughout the course of interpretation. Does the native *believe* that spirits exist or *desire* that spirits exist, believe the oracle or desire that the oracle be right, believe that the life of her tribe is good and satisfying to her or desire to see it that way? Again, charity only forces us to admit that she has either some very strange beliefs or some very strange desires.[12] Of course we *may* find we can interpret the native such that neither her beliefs nor her desires seem strange, but the point is that we shall not *necessarily* find such a happy solution, and in cases where we fail, Davidson's theory has nothing to say.

---

[10] I am indebted to Sarah Buss for pointing out the relevance of this aspect of Davidson to my argument.

[11] (Davidson, 1983), p.433, note 7.

[12] Some may think strange desires are less of a problem, but Amélie Rorty, among others, has argued persuasively that charity is as essential to an explanation of desire as to an explanation of belief: (Rorty, 1980), pp.104ff.

Locating Beliefs

Davidson's clearest argument against massive disagreements is that we cannot determine what a belief or sentence is about without attributing to the speaker many other true beliefs about that subject matter. He presents this position in many places:

> ...[A] belief is identified by its location in a pattern of beliefs; it is this pattern that determines the subject matter of the belief, what the belief is about...It isn't that any one false belief necessarily destroys our ability to identify further beliefs, but that the intelligibility of such identifications must depend on a background of largely unmentioned and unquestioned true beliefs. To put it another way: the more things a believer is right about, the sharper his errors are. Too much mistake simply blurs the focus. ("Thought and Talk," ITI 168)

> Beliefs are identified and described only within a dense pattern of beliefs. I can believe a cloud is passing before the sun, but only because I believe there is a sun, that clouds are made of water vapor, that water can exist in liquid or gaseous form; and so on, without end. No particular list of further beliefs is required to give substance to my belief that a cloud is passing before the sun; but some appropriate set of related beliefs must be there. If I suppose that you believe a cloud is passing before the sun, I suppose you have the right sort of pattern of beliefs to support that one belief and these beliefs I assume you to have must, to do their supporting work, be enough like my belief to justify the description of your belief as a belief that a cloud is passing before the sun. ("The Method of Truth in Metaphysics," ITI 200)

> Just as too much attributed error risks depriving the subject of his subject matter, so too much actual error robs a person of things to go wrong about. (*ibid*)

On the whole, this seems most plausible. For someone even to say "wrong"—or "radically different"—things about the sun, she must hold enough true and familiar beliefs about the sun for us to recognize that it is the sun about which we differ. On this ground alone, I share much of Davidson's holistic approach to interpretation; I see incommensurability as possible only after a great deal of mutual translation has taken place. But the need to locate subject matter via true beliefs does not give Davidson as much as he sometimes thinks it does. Take, for instance, the passage, already quoted, in which he tries to shake our confidence that "the ancients—some ancients—believed that the earth was flat":

> *This* earth? Well, this earth of ours is part of the solar system, a system partly identified by the fact that it is a gaggle of large, cool, solid bodies circling around a very large, hot star. If someone believes *none* of this about the earth, is it certain that it is the earth that he is thinking about? (ITI 168)

Well, yes, it is certain. Davidson himself seems to acknowledge what an unfortunate example he has chosen, by following his series of questions with

"An answer is not called for." I don't know exactly how much more it would take to shake this particular intuition, but Davidson's own attempt makes rather a different point than he intends: that it takes a lot *fewer* true beliefs to identify the objects of discussion than we (some of us, at any rate) might at first think. After reading a lot of Davidson, and perhaps of Wittgenstein or Quine, we might be tempted to think that someone must believe all this stuff about our solar system to have any beliefs at all about the earth, but a little reflection on our pretheoretical intuitions and ordinary usage will tell us otherwise. To identify the earth as an object of belief we need only some general conception of it as the body of continents and oceans on which human beings live. Indeed, only with such a conception can we make good sense of the history of our knowledge of the earth, of how the beliefs of "the ancients" were gradually transmuted into (and at times came into conflict with) the modern view of the object of those beliefs.

I can make this point more sharply by contrasting Davidson's position with the causal theory of reference. Davidson recognizes, particularly in "Reality Without Reference" (ITI 215-25), that his views are in a certain tension with those of Kripke and Putnam, and he argues that his holistic approach to meaning fits in better with our intuitions about truth than the alternative route to those intuitions via reference. I, as I have already indicated, generally side with him on this issue. But, being less interested than he is in pursuing a thoroughgoing holism, less worried about paradox and ambiguity, and more concerned to preserve intuitions and ordinary uses, I would also acknowledge that in certain cases the causal theory expresses our intuitions about usage much better than holism. Nowhere is this more striking than when we come to objects that have interested all human beings in similar ways but about which a tremendous amount of scientific work marks the difference between our conception of those objects and that of our ancestors. In the case of such things as the sun, the moon, the earth, human beings, the most familiar animals and plants, and perhaps most other natural kinds, it makes sense to describe the use of the words denoting them in terms of an original labelling, not quite identical with ostension, in which a name became tied to a vaguely and inaccurately understood object. The nature of that object may have become much clearer and identified much differently over the centuries, but making sense of this process requires holding the meaning of the label fairly independent of any description of that nature, allowing the label to pick out the object solely by means of historical descent from the original identification. I will let this mild appeal to the causal account of reference sit together in uneasy tension with Davidson's holism, as I have let incommensurability sit with general agreement, or phenomenological with interpretive understanding. The ambiguity of truth, as something that must lie both beyond us (outside of our descriptions) and within our reach (determined by our descriptions) comes out again here. From the need to locate the subject matter of beliefs, Davidson will not necessarily get enough true beliefs to refute the possibility of a radical difference over the nature of the world.

Before moving on to his next line of argument, let us note that Davidson also uses the "dense pattern of beliefs" for a more subtle kind of identification: of an utterance as a sentence and a sentence as a belief in the first place. "The system of beliefs ... identifies a thought by locating it in a logical and epistemic space." (ITI 157) This partly just follows from his position on identifying the subject matter, since an utterance can only be an assertion or represent a belief if it has some subject matter,[13] but he also argues for it by pointing out that (what we call) assertions and beliefs must be capable of explanation and justification in terms of other assertions and beliefs. "Thoughts, like propositions, have logical relations [and] the identity of a thought cannot be divorced from its place in the logical network of other thoughts."[14] Furthermore, "nothing...could count as evidence that some form of activity could not be interpreted in our language that was not at the same time evidence that that form of activity was not speech behavior." (ITI 185)

Again, this position leaves open the possibility of a large chunk of beliefs being different from our own—each one false, in our terms, but the chunk large enough that they support each other against our contrary arguments and evidence. Colin McGinn says, about this aspect of Davidson,

> There is much plausibility to the idea that the content of belief...is determined by its relations, logical and causal, with other attitudes; so that the primary bearers of object-directedness are not beliefs strictly considered but batches of interrelated beliefs. It may even be admitted that there is no possessing one belief about an object without possessing further beliefs about it, and without a clear limit. But it does not *follow* from this holistic conception of belief...that any of the beliefs...thus interrelated are *true.*[15]

Contrary to what McGinn might expect, however, Davidson agrees:

> It may seem that the argument so far shows only that good interpretation breeds concurrence, while leaving quite open the question whether what is agreed upon is true. And certainly agreement, no matter how widespread, does not guarantee truth. This observation misses the point of the argument, however. The basic claim is that much community of belief is needed to provide a basis for communication or understanding; the extended claim should then be that objective error can occur only in a setting of largely true belief...[Imagine] an omniscient interpreter[:] he attributes beliefs to others, and interprets their speech on the basis of his own

13 While an attributer of belief to someone need not "produce a description of the object that the believer would accept, nevertheless [the attribution of belief] impl[ies] that there is some such description." In (Davidson, 1982), p. 320.

14 *ibid*, p.321.

15 (McGinn, 1977), p. 525.

> beliefs, just as the rest of us do. Since he does this as the rest of us do, he perforce finds as much agreement as is needed to make sense of his attributions and interpretations; and in this case, of course, what is agreed is by hypothesis true. But now it is plain why massive error about the world is...unintelligible, for to suppose it intelligible is to suppose there could be an interpreter (the omniscient one) who correctly interpreted someone else as being massively mistaken, and this we have shown to be impossible. (ITI 200-201)

This he has shown, if he has, not by means of the argument that specific errors need location in a setting of largely true belief. "The question whether what is agreed upon is true" depends rather on the claim—presented here via the hypothesis of the omniscient interpreter—that we cannot make intelligible even the *notion* of a truth radically different from the one issuing in the bulk of the familiar sentences we take to be true. And this constitutes the central issue between my position and Davidson's.

Truth and Translation

Davidson stresses over and over again that the point of Tarski's work on truth is not that T-sentences themselves are true, but that an adequate theory of truth for a language must entail all the T-sentences of that language. This simple and powerful insight Davidson calls "our best intuition as to how the concept of truth is used" (ITI 195), and he proposes to draw from it a deep connection between truth and the possibility of translation. Given the interdependence of meanings and beliefs, he suggests, we can interpret both without assuming one only by taking the utterances a person holds true as basic, and construing those utterances as expressive of the truths that hold, in our opinion, at the time of the utterance (ITI 27, 135-7, 152, 195-6). Only such a theory will avoid begging either the question of what the speaker means or the question of what she believes. Only such a theory, moreover, properly understands the way we derive our notion of belief, for "the concept of belief...take[s] up the slack between objective truth and the held true, and we come to understand it just in this connection." (ITI 170) Belief, meaning and truth are thus all notions that "necessarily emerge in the context of interpretation." (ITI 169)

Davidson sees his project as "invert[ing] Tarski's: we want to achieve an understanding of meaning or translation by assuming a prior grasp of the concept of truth." (ITI 150) This is not to say that the notion of truth need be easier or logically prior to the notion of translation, for Davidson also holds that we understand truth only by assuming a prior grasp of the concept of translation. Truth and translation, he believes, are inextricably bound up with one another. It follows from this view that we cannot make sense of a notion of truth that fails to validate the translation of supposedly true sentences into familiar sentences we already take to be true. The notion of a truth completely different from our own—one that issues in sentences that we would largely not believe or not understand, or one that does not issue in sentences at all—is therefore unintelligible. This view comes back in many forms when Davidson addresses versions of conceptual relativism: 1) We cannot both recognize someone as believing a set of true sentences and fail to translate (most) of those sentences into sentences we believe ourselves (ITI 137, 196), 2) We cannot conceive of a theory neutral reality, independent of our familiar means of individuation and organization (ITI 192-3), and 3) We can conceive neither of a non-linguistic way of grasping reality that we might attribute to animals,[16] nor of a super-linguistic way of grasping reality that we might attribute to God (the omniscient interpreter in the passage quoted above).

Translation into a familiar tongue does indeed seem to be our *best* intuition as to how the concept of truth is used, but it is not our only such intuition. While the foregoing attack on complete incommensurability has strong grounds, therefore, they do not go far enough to rule out the partial incommensurability we have been considering. Do not, that is, if we can pin down some other intuition about truth, a notoriously elusive concept. I propose to begin with a weaker suggestion, that we have some intuitions about *belief* that Davidson seems to have overlooked, and work from there to what he rightly sees as the related issues about truth.

• *Semi-Propositional Beliefs*

Davidson, like practically every other writer on the subject, takes for granted that belief is a propositional attitude;[17] when we have a belief, what we believe is a proposition. Now, a proposition, by definition, must be either true or false. Furthermore, unlike a mere sentence, it must represent its subject matter clearly and unambiguously. As soon as we see belief as a propositional attitude, therefore, we are already locked into a fairly tight connection between ascribing a belief, being able to interpret it as fully and definitely as possible, and being able to give truth-conditions for it. We can drive a wedge between belief and our familiar ways of assessing truth only if we can wean belief away from propositions.

In an article entitled "Apparently Irrational Beliefs," Dan Sperber tries to do just that. "The phrase 'propositional attitude' is misleading," he says, since "it obscures the fact that we can have such 'attitudes' to objects other than propositions in the strict sense...Propositions, as opposed to sentences or utterances, cannot be ambiguous and hence true in some interpretations and false in others. Yet some of our so-called beliefs have several possible interpretations and we can hold them without committing ourselves to any of

---

[16] See "Thought and Talk" in (Davidson, 1984), and (Davidson, 1982).

[17] Ruth Marcus complains about this widespread assumption in the course of proposing an alternative (that the object of belief is a "possible state of affairs"). See (Marcus, 1983).

their interpretations."[18] Sperber introduces Bob, who, upon hearing on the news, "Stagflation has recently become the main problem of Western economies," comes to believe that sentence without being quite sure what "stagflation" means. The object of his belief will not be just an utterance, since he "is capable of stating his belief by paraphrasing [the] utterance rather than merely quoting it[, and since he]...believes many of its implications (e.g. that Western economies have a new important problem)." (RR 168) On the other hand, he does not exactly believe the proposition beneath the journalist's sentence either, since the incompletely understood word prevents him from being able to identify his belief with any single proposition. "Suppose, for instance, that Bob thinks that 'stagflation' means either *a stagnant inflation* or *a combination of inflation and stagnation*; then the utterance 'stagflation has recently become the main problem of Western economies' has two possible propositional interpretations for Bob, one of which, he will assume, is the proper one..." (RR 169) A "conceptual representation that fails to identify one and only one proposition," Sperber calls "a semi-propositional representation." This phrase is meant to include not only cases like Bob's belief, which presumably has a proper interpretation (the one employing the correct meaning of "stagflation"), but also cases in which there is no "proper" interpretation. Either because the original utterance was to some extent unintelligible—the speaker from whom the believer picked it up having uttered "something which he himself does not understand so well, and of the content of which he too has a semi-propositional representation" (RR 170)—or because it was deliberately obscure or ambiguous, as is the case with many religious and poetic utterances, there may be no reason to favor the interpretation of it in terms of one proposition rather than another.

Sperber now allows "semi-propositional content" (RR 175) only to what he calls "representational beliefs." Unlike "factual beliefs," representational beliefs involve conscious "commitment to a representation" *of* a fact, rather than to a fact directly. While "holding a factual belief is [only] rational when it is consistent with, and warranted by [all] other factual beliefs of the subject [with closely related content,]" much weaker conditions may make it rational to hold a representational belief, especially one of semi-propositional content. In particular, "what may make it rational to hold a representational belief of semi-propositional content is evidence on its source." (RR 173) If I have reason to trust the person I am reading or listening to, to regard the person as honest, and wiser, better informed or more thoughtful than myself, I may have reason to believe what she says even if I do not completely understand it:[19]

---

[18] Dan Sperber, "Apparently Irrational Beliefs," in (Hollis & Lukes, 1982), pp. 167-8. References to this article will be incorporated into the text by "RR" and page number.

[19] Compare the role of trust in phenomenological understanding, above.

> [R]ather than believing factually that the proper interpretation of R is true, the subject may, with similar results believe (factually or representationally) that:
>
> R is what we were taught by wise people.
> R is a dogma in our Church.
> R is a holy mystery.
> R is deemed to be true.
> Marx (Freud, Wittgenstein...) convincingly argued for R.
> Only heathens (fascists, people from the other side of the mountain...) would deny R.
>
> Accepting any of these claims has little to do with the content of R and yet it would be enough to make the subject express R in an assertive form, invoke it freely, object to its being questioned, explore its possible interpretations, in short behave as a 'believer'. (RR 173)

And in certain situations these representational beliefs can play important roles in our lives. Sperber discusses many of the contexts into which I introduced phenomenological understanding. On the one hand he suggests that "a semi-propositional representation can serve as a step towards full comprehension," and calls this "a common experience of childhood, when so many lexical meanings are not fixed in our minds[, which] recurs throughout life in learning situations." (RR 170) Then he says that "the teaching of a Zen master, the philosophy of Kierkegaard, and, generally, poetic texts are cases" in which the semi-propositional spur to searching through a range of possible interpretations "may be of greater value than any one of these interpretations in particular." (RR 170-1) Finally he notes that it is part of the content of the mysteries of the Catholic church (as of many other religions) that their "meaning (i.e., [their] proper propositional interpretation) is beyond human grasp" (RR 175).

It may thus be rationally justifiable to hold some semi-propositional beliefs, but only factual beliefs, for Sperber, can constitute *knowledge*. (RR 171) Of course, representational beliefs of the fully propositional kind can be rationally held as if they were factual if they cohere with and are warranted by other factual beliefs (RR 172). But the representation providing the source of the representational belief will never suffice to establish the belief as knowledge, and a representational belief that is semi-propositional, hence incapable of being checked with the facts, cannot be even a candidate for knowledge. In this way we can maintain a strictly absolutist conception of knowledge, while allowing that people may rationally hold some beliefs incommensurable with our own. "[T]he very fact that, when assumed to be factual,...beliefs [radically different] from our own appear irrational is reason enough to assume...that they are representational beliefs with a semi-propositional content, thereby avoiding the costs of relativism." (RR 175) As representational beliefs, they are no longer irrational, but, since they are checked only against the reliability of their source rather than against the facts, they are no longer directly aimed at truth either.

Only at this point do I want to take issue with Sperber. His polemical use of the word "fact," implying that there exist clear and easily graspable external entities or events to which knowledge should correspond, suggests a return to such problematic theories of truth and meaning as verificationism, and without such theories there is no reason to consider the beliefs he calls "representational" any less candidates for truth than those he calls "factual". We may want to say that someone in Bob's situation would recognize himself as proposing two (or more) rival claims to truth, rather than one single claim, and that the representational belief is only a first stab at a more fundamental factual belief. But this notion that representational beliefs may only be midwives to the real candidates for truth disappears when we come to such things as the Kierkegaardian or Catholic mysteries. There obscurity, and resistance to any translation into a clear "proposition," is an essential part of the thing believed, while the believer holds such beliefs more fundamentally true, more fundamental *to* truth, than any claim Sperber would call "factual."

Suppose a person holds astronomical, geological, physical, biological, and historical beliefs largely or entirely on the basis of what an oracle, or her Scripture teacher, has told her. For Sperber, these would all be representational beliefs since they include awareness not "only of a fact [but]...of a commitment to a representation [as well]." (RR 171) What, then, are this person's factual beliefs? Claims about everyday life (what Charles Taylor would call "prescientific common sense" and Robin Horton "primary theory")? But these—"Worms spontaneously generate from food left in the sun," "Fish is good for the brain," "Cigarette-smoking is good for the health"—may be received from the same authorities that provided the more general beliefs, or they may be derived from or checked against those general beliefs. How about the immense number of beliefs we all derive from our own observations, of the form "There is an apple tree next to the Jones' farm," or "Horses are larger than pigs"? But we cannot interpret even these beliefs properly except insofar as they are brought together with their implications and with other beliefs—and in this wider context we may find that our friend with the oracle means "source of poisonous fruit" by "apple tree" and considers horses spirits from the netherworld. This does not prevent us from taking her observational beliefs as factual, but it does get rid of the possibility that she might check her commonsensical or scientific beliefs against her observational ones. She will therefore hold very few, if any, of the beliefs shaping what she considers her knowledge of the world on what Sperber considers rational grounds (consistency with and entailment by other factual beliefs of closely related content [RR 172]).

So what? Perhaps we have simply found a person who either rationally holds many representational beliefs and very few factual ones or irrationally holds representational beliefs as factual. Why should the possibility of such a person threaten us? There is no proof here that standards for knowledge can vary from culture to culture, only that there might be people without knowledge.

But the woman in my example can rationally challenge Sperber's definition of "fact." What does Sperber want her to check her representational beliefs against, other than her oracle? The testimony of her senses? Empirical events, as construed by our scientists? Surely one needs some reason to take those sources as fact, reality, etc., and the tribeswoman may prefer to count her oracle as the ultimate fact or expert on facts. Perhaps her oracle supplies her with a (semi-propositional) definition of "reality" different from our own. If so, she may have as good reason to accept representational beliefs as knowledge as we have to so regard the ones we call "factual."

In addition, and relatedly, not only the woman in my example but all of us rely primarily on representational beliefs. Of course, our sources are usually scientists, who we take to be direct conveyors of fact, but even those of us who *do* science check very few of their beliefs against direct observation rather than against the words of various authorities. And if some do engage in a thorough observational test of one or two particulars, it takes place against the background of a tremendous number of representational beliefs defining what counts as a good experiment, what general theories should make us review our results, and what other facts in the world these particulars must align themselves with. We may have a conception of the modern, Western world according to which our *society*, or at least our community of scientists, tests theories against the facts, but, as Sperber's analysis of them itself demonstrates, beliefs are always held by an individual subject, for whom a potentially factual claim may be representational (she just heard it somewhere) and a potentially representational belief may be factual (she checked it, while others believe it merely by hearsay). If, then, all the individuals of our society hold primarily or solely representational beliefs, there is no-one and nothing to tell any of us what our facts really are and which of our beliefs we really have good reason to count as knowledge. Instead, as individuals we check most of our beliefs against other representational beliefs that we *take* to be factual and we ultimately count certain representational beliefs as knowledge. It is individuals who constitute a society, moreover, even a society of scientists. Thus if anyone at all has a rational claim to knowledge—and for the word to retain its meaning most of us must have such a claim—she comes to it by dint of what Sperber calls "representational" rather than what he calls "factual" beliefs. But in that case coherence with other beliefs, rather than with the facts, is the criterion for knowledge, and semi-propositional representations can have as good a claim as propositional ones to that status. Even if I do not fully understand what my authority tells me, I may still have sufficient justification to count it as true.

• *Truth as Obscure, Perceived by Individuals, and Disclosed by Authorities*

I move from here to some intuitions about truth which have very little indeed to do with translation into a familiar tongue. Consider, first, that every individual in her lifetime in fact and perhaps necessarily falls far short of learning all truths known to human beings. Each of us has a severely limited access to truths, a weak sense of what the set of all (known) truths might look like, and cannot be quite sure whether (what it would mean if) "the Truth" can be adequately defined by the set of all truths. Second, each of us is primarily concerned about the truth insofar as it affects how we should live. Were it possible to choose between knowing what "truth" means but not knowing (in truth) how we should lead our lives, and knowing how to live but not knowing exactly what "truth" means, most of us would probably plunk for the latter. Indeed, one could reasonably argue that we can take no interest in, perhaps make no sense of, any choice, including this one, except against the background of an interest in how to live. There is therefore at least a possibility that we might be willing to live with—indeed, regard as *true*—certain sentences, including certain theories of truth, that we are at some time, in some part, in some manner aware are not exactly correct. As interested agents first and foremost, we might accept what an "objective observer" would consider debased truth, if it illuminated those truths we most need or want to know.

Paradox looms here (we surely want to know "truly" which truths we need to know and that seems to presuppose that we take the objective observer's viewpoint), but paradox is my third alternative intuition about truth. Whether G.E. Moore was right or not to make the parallel point about "good," it seems clear that in the case of "truth" we find it possible and necessary to ask "But is it true?" about any definition of truth, even one purporting to state a necessary equivalence. This applies, *inter alia*, to Tarski's theory and Davidson's use of it. If we accept Davidson's characterization of Tarski's work as our best intuition into how the concept of truth is used, we do so because we consider that characterization *true*, not because it merely meets its own conditions. (The latter is a consideration, but only because we regard self-consistency as a mark of truth.) The acceptance of any theory of truth (and *a fortiori* any truth claim) must occur against the background of a prior notion of truth, here assumed rather than defined—hence here, at least, obscure. If we want to examine this background notion, we will have to take some other conception of truth for granted, hence throw it, in turn, into obscurity. Light will not dawn for us at once over the whole of what we mean by "truth."[20]

We now have the materials with which to retell an old myth dear to the heart of relativists about truth. Suppose, for a moment, that we might personify Truth, or at least identify it with a personal God's plan for the world He has created.

---

[20] OC 141: "Light dawns gradually over the whole."

Suppose, further, that this Truth or God has the following relationship with Its human subjects: It reveals to each of a number of groups of them (or perhaps to each of them individually) what It wants them to do during their stay on earth, with the stipulation that they may know nothing further about Its nature, Its final plan for the whole world, or the role in that plan of other people. One group may be told to sacrifice calves in an idolless temple, another to bring vegetarian offerings to sculpted divinities, a third to turn inward and direct their hearts to "love" or "faith," a fourth to preach atheism and practice deeds of charity and civil justice. Should all of these people meet again in another world, each can presumably claim to have known truly what she was to do on earth, while none could rightly claim to have known the task of human beings in general.

Of course, so far, while our characters have little use for absolute, universal propositions about the nature of human action, we are not entangled in relativism. "I/we should do x" need not be taken as conflicting with "You should do y." But suppose that the God's revelations of how to act include different accounts of what the world is like, perhaps in order to make better sense of the prescriptions he gives. Just as a different divinity associates with each Homeric hero according to that hero's particular virtues and vices, so this God appears, and makes Its world appear, to each of Its subjects according to what It asks that subject to do. (The variations may show up only in small ways—in, say, the tendency of events in some individuals' lives to coincide or fail to coincide with prayers, astrological predictions, magic, etc.—so that the various subjects can still feel that they on the whole share one world.) Finally, suppose that the God tells each group, or at least some groups, to preach its way of life to the others. The people will then make not only different, but conflicting truth claims: "The world contains x but not y" / "The world contains y but not x," and "Not only I/we but you should do x rather than y" / "Not only I/we but you should do y rather than x." If they meet in another world, they might feel that they disagreed because they were all in part wrong. Yet if they find that the tasks they performed were in fact ones they truly had to perform, and that the beliefs they had about the world and the nature of human action were necessary to such performance, they may instead agree that on the whole their beliefs, even about the world and human action, were closer to the truth than any other beliefs they could have held, even if the alternatives would have avoided literal inaccuracy. They may feel that the nature of the world is best captured by descriptions fitting what we have to do in it.

It is important that we have had to imagine a God to tell these stories. Only against the background of an absolute truth that merely *appears* differently to different people—and which mandates the importance of these differences by making human knowledge appear to us as subordinate to human action—does a relativist myth make sense. With this in mind, an appropriate motto for our myth is Lessing's remark, "*Sage jeder, was ihm Wahrheit dünkt, und die*

Wahrheit selbst sei Gott empfohlen."[21] For these words, for his equally famous comment about choosing the striving for truth over the truth itself,[22] and for the extraordinarily rich notion of tolerance he laid out in *Nathan the Wise,* Lessing may fairly be taken as the founder of modern relativism.[23]

Lessing was also an important influence on Kierkegaard, who quotes the remark about the striving for truth as a heading for a section of his *Concluding Unscientific Postscript,* and Kierkegaard is the first to work out, forcefully and thoroughly, the three intuitions about truth I have begun to set up against or alongside Davidson's elaboration of Tarski. For Kierkegaard, the most fundamental fact about the human condition is our finitude—in potential knowledge, action, and ability to plan action. We can recognize our limitations, however, only against the possibility of a truth and way of living beyond them (else in what sense would they be limitations?), and this means recognizing that we live to some extent outside the Truth: in "Untruth," "Error," "Sin." To this traditional Christian position (to be found in the line of argument for God that runs from Augustine through Anselm to Descartes, among other places), Kierkegaard adds that we perceive our condition only insofar as we are individuals, from which perspective our limitations (death, for one) are obvious and there is no temptation to imagine we could overcome them, and that the conception of the Infinite against which we project our finitude is necessarily obscure to us, to the point of being paradoxical.

Kierkegaard's famous tag, "truth is subjectivity," does not mean, as it is sometimes taken to mean, that *all* truth depends on the individual subject,[24] or that *any* truth depends on the whims or imaginings of the individual subject, but that the truth that matters can only consist in how individual subjects appropriate "objective" facts, and philosophical reflections, for the way they live their lives.[25] The truth of action—what Kant called "practical" as opposed to "speculative" reason—must be subjective. This, however, is the truth most

21 Quoted in (Arendt, 1968), pp.233-4.

22 "If God were to hold all truth in his right hand, and in his left hand only the eternal pursuit of truth, with the condition that I should be constantly and forever mistaken, and were to say to me, 'Choose!', I would fall with humility at his left and cry, 'Father, give! The pure truth is surely for You alone.'" *Werke*, Maltzahn's edition, Vol. X, p.53, translation mine, quoted in (Kierkegaard, 1968), p.97 and note.

23 Compare also chapter eight, section A-x.

24 "... in the strict scientific disciplines ... objectivity is a requisite." (Kierkegaard, 1968), p.42.

25 "*The objective accent falls on WHAT is said,*" he writes, "*the subjective accent on HOW it is said.*" (Kierkegaard, 1968), p.181, his italics. Although he does not want to emphasize this aspect of the matter, that he considers "what" is said to be an important part of truth and communication, preliminary to the kind of subjective appropriation essential to ethics and religious belief, comes out clearly in the following passage, (keeping in mind that he identifies direct communication with objective truth, indirect with subjective): "As soon as the truth, the essential truth, may be assumed to be known by everyone, the [truth] becomes appropriation and inwardness, and here only an indirect form is applicable. *The position of an apostle is different, for he has to preach an unknown truth, whence a direct form of communication may in his case have provisional validity.*" (p.217, my italics). For the full discussion of his position, see pp.169-224, especially 174, 181, 206.

important to us (again, Kant would agree: indeed, only matters of action *can* be important, since importance is a category that makes sense only when making choices), and it is for that reason that we must see ourselves as so essentially finite. The limitations that we face as individuals—in time, foreknowledge, and ability to control our wills and environment—make trivial the possibility that mankind as a whole might transcend error and ignorance. Kierkegaard here sets himself against Hegel, who posited a fully revealed truth, albeit a dialectical one, as our ultimate goal. Insofar as we are ethical beings, says Kierkegaard, we do not care what mankind might be able to know or do, and we are all ethical beings and ethical beings first and foremost.

Although Kierkegaard's Absolute Paradox lies behind this too, the most forceful statement of our intuition about the obscurity of truth is to be found in Heidegger. Like Kierkegaard, Heidegger links truth and action ("He who truly knows what is, knows what he wills to do in the midst of what is"), and draws the necessary obscurity of truth as a consequence: "[e]very decision...bases itself on something not mastered, something concealed, confusing; else it would never be a decision."[26] From here, however, he takes an additional, important step. Not only as far as truth concerns action, but in any use or definition of truth, something obscure must lie behind every experience of clarity and understanding. Heidegger calls the tradition that sees truth in correspondence "our familiar and therefore outworn nature of truth in the sense of correctness," and complains that if verifying the correctness of a proposition always presupposes that "one really should go back to something that is already evident," the very notion of truth as correctness "still requires a further presupposition, that we ourselves happen to make, heaven knows how or why." (OWA 52) Rather, he suggests, a certain kind of "unconcealedness" (revelation, disclosure) must take place before we can accept, or even make sense of, the notion of correspondence:

> Not only must that in *conformity* with which a cognition orders itself be already in some way unconcealed....With all our correct representations we would get nowhere, we could not even presuppose that there already is manifest something to which we can conform ourselves, unless the unconcealedness of beings had already exposed us to, placed us in that lighted realm in which every being stands for us and from which it withdraws (OWA 52)

As the last phrase indicates, it is intrinsic to this revelation that it be accompanied by a certain obscurity, and as the poetic mode of presentation indicates, the revelation itself can only be vaguely, mythically described, not delineated clearly, nor defended.

---

[26] "The Origin of the Work of Art," in (Heidegger, 1971). References to this essay will be incorporated into the text by "OWA" and page number.

Let us take this as a cue to describe Heidegger's own myth of truth. (As we shall see, it is importantly reminiscent of the story I put in Lessing's mouth.) If stated simply—which Heidegger goes to extraordinary lengths to prevent us from doing—that myth might run as follows: The "world" embraces all that is open, clear, revealed to us, all that we know or should know, and all the ways in which things affect, inform, guide our decisions: "the world is the *self-disclosing openness* of the broad paths of [our] simple and essential decisions..." (OWA 4) "The world is the *clearing of* the paths of the essential guiding directions with which all decision complies." (OWA 55) Specifically, the closed that the world cannot endure is the earth, defined as that which lies beyond all human reach, grounding our world while limiting and threatening it. The world comprises the familiar, the ordinary (OWA 66, 76); the earth, the unfamiliar, the extraordinary. The earth conceals but shelters, defies understanding and decisions but provides their foundation and scope; the world responds to and grows out of the earth, but simultaneously tries to deny the essentially closed and "self-closing" nature of the earth by opening it up. A curious conflict arises, in which world and earth not only must struggle with one another but can achieve their true natures only through such struggle. "World and earth are always intrinsically and essentially in conflict, belligerent by nature." (OWA 55) Earth "shows itself [to us, as what it really is,] only when it remains undisclosed and unexplained" (OWA 47), but we come to that show only when we try to disclose and explain it. World would not exist—*we* would not be decision-makers and knowers (construing "knowing" as directed toward decision and hence in part guided by it)—if it (we) did not have to contend with earth.

> The earth cannot dispense with the Open of the world if it itself is to appear as earth in the liberated surge of its self-seclusion. The world, again, cannot soar out of the earth's sight if, as the governing breadth and path of all essential destiny, it is to ground itself on a resolute foundation. (OWA 49)

And in the midst of this contention truth happens. Heidegger avoids saying what truth "is," because from the point of view of the individual making a decision, truth cannot be static, and no static definition of it will meet her needs. Because earth is essentially unfamiliar and obscure, no general theory, or even myth about it (including this one), can adequately capture what it means. Because earth is matter for decision, no theory at all, and no single revelation of it, can capture what it means *to us*. Instead, a "space" or "clearing"—an "Open"—appears again and again in the conflict between world and earth, again and again forcing "the opponents, lighting-clearing and concealing, [to] move apart" (OWA 61), and in and by that Open we see, again and anew, our limitations at the present moment, and the decisions we must and can take at the present moment in the light of these limitations. The Open both provides the scene for the battle between world and earth and constitutes that battle. Without a scene by which we can see that we must struggle with what lies beyond us, there will be no struggle at all (the potential struggle will be concealed, hence a part of the earth), but once there is a scene of a battle, it follows that there must also be a battle. Since we can neither see the battle (set the scene) before it happens, nor participate in it until we see it, the Open must open itself (OWA 60-61). When it does, beings are "unconcealed" or "disclosed," and Heidegger pointedly notes that the Greeks used the word *aletheia*, which he translates as "unconcealedness" or "disclosure," for "truth." (OWA 36)[27]

Truth is "the primal conflict in which...the Open is won," "the opposition of clearing and concealing." (OWA 60-61) It is not "unconcealedness" alone, if that is to mean something that makes beings clear, that makes them accessible to our understanding (as happens, say, when we partake of Augustine's "divine illumination," or the related *lumen naturale*, or Descartes' "clear and distinct perceptions"), but the process of making some things clear while recognizing others as lying in obscurity. Since clarity and obscurity belong together necessarily, understanding the clear without recognizing the obscure is a failure to grasp the full truth even of the clear. Moreover, we do not recognize the obscure merely by labelling it as "obscure" and leaving it alone; there would be nothing we would have to call "obscure" if certain facts (our own deaths, our finite memories and imaginations, our imperfectly controllable desires) and ideas (the concept of truth, for instance) did not affect us even while they remain beyond us. We recognize the earth by acknowledging its conjoint importance and obscurity to us, by trying to penetrate it, failing, and attending to that failure. But this acknowledgment does not entail positing a permanently obscure realm of objects or events—that would be to have a theory of the earth, or, as Davidson would put it, to apply our concepts (of "objects," "events," "realm") where there is no possibility of translation into familiar terms. Instead, we recognize the obscure earth as *potentially clear*, as comprised of that which could become disclosed in another Open, "in which every being stands for us and from which it withdraws." (OWA 52) Earth must be capable of becoming world and world of falling back into earth, else there would be no conflict. In part, this happens simply because world comprises what is familiar to our thinking and deciding,

---

27 As Karsten Harries has pointed out to me, Heidegger later withdrew this claim as a translation of *aletheia*. See "The End of Philosophy and the Task of Thinking," in (Heidegger, 1977), pp. 389-90. Even here, however, he holds that "unconcealment," if not equivalent to "the natural concept of truth" or the term for that natural concept in Greek thought, is somehow essential to, prior to, perhaps a pre-supposition for, truth. That may be enough for my purposes. In addition, had Heidegger been willing to look outside what he seemed to consider the Greco-German tradition, I think he could have found a notion of truth itself as something other than and prior to correspondence, in, for instance, Biblical Hebrew, where *emet* means both "truth" and "faithfulness," and speakers are judged as truthful in accordance with their trustworthiness rather than their accuracy.

earth what is unfamiliar, and the very familiarity of the familiar tends eventually to obscure what is important about it, while our mere interest in discovery, as well as the shock of failing to achieve a project because of something we have forgotten or ignored, eventually brings the unfamiliar to light. In any case, truth can never be a single event—or an eternal one, even an eternal conflict—but must happen "always in some particular way," in and through some particular ("some being...something that is": as opposed to the general, which belongs entirely to world), and must "become historical" (OWA 78), that is, must occur in a different way for each "historical people." Only thus can we constantly see that we do not (cannot) see some of what matters to us; only thus can we be constantly reminded that we forget (must forget) some of what matters to us.

Let us linger a moment over the role of particularity and history in this picture. From Duns Scotus, who coined the term "haecceity" precisely for its impenetrable uniqueness, through Hegel, who first pointed out clearly that it can ultimately be neither described nor conceptualized,[28] philosophers have always taken the particular as the locus of the unexplainable. From general laws, after all, one can derive much about how something resembles other things of its type, but if a description of the type(s) it belongs to, the type of genesis it has had and the type of effects it can have, leaves anything out, no explanation of that residue will be possible. It is, moreover, unlikely, and impossible to prove, that any set of general laws will account for everything (we want to know) about *this* object, right here and right now. History in turn is mysterious because it depends on particulars, contingencies that no general laws ever adequately predict. It is also mysterious because it is what Heidegger calls a "task" (OWA 77): a decision or process of decision-making, hence something we (logically) cannot predict definitively.[29] These two reasons are linked, as it turns out, for if we were able to predict our futures definitively, the problem of the particular would be uninteresting at best. Suppose that we developed a set of physico-chemical laws allowing us to predict with certainty *all* the events in our environment, including (*per impossibile*) our own acts: we would probably no longer find any interesting sense in which we failed to explain all

[28] For Duns Scotus, see *The Oxford Commentary on the Four Books of the Sentences*, Book II, Distinction III, Questions 1, 4, and 6, in (Hyman & Walsh, 1978), pp. 582-9. For Hegel, see "Sense-Certainty," in (Hegel, 1977), pp. 5866. Heidegger explicitly sets his account against Hegel's concerns about particularity by insisting that the "openness of this Open, that is, truth, can be what it is, namely, *this* Openness, only if and as long as...[there is] some being,...something that is, in which the openness [can] take[...] its stand and attain[...] its constancy. In taking possession thus of the Open, the openness holds open the Open and sustains it. Setting and taking possession are here everywhere drawn from the Greek sense of *thesis*, which means a setting up in the unconcealed." (OWA 61) That with the term "thesis" he intends to evoke Hegel becomes clear in the Addendum: "...Hegel—correctly in terms of his position—interpreted the Greek *thesis* in the sense of the immediate positing of the object. Setting in this sense, therefore, is for him still untrue, because it is not yet mediated by antithesis and synthesis." (OWA 83).

[29] See (MacIntyre, 1981), pp.91-2, and (Beck, 1960), pp. 29-32.

particulars. We would, that is, not raise any further questions about the particular, and that might well mean that they would no longer be there to be raised. But there are theoretical problems with this project of prediction, rooted in the nature both of the physics we want to predict and of prediction itself—or rather of us, those who predict and accept predictions. And supposing (*per impossibile*?) that we could attain, if not certainty, at least a high enough level of accurate prediction to make our further questions about particular events disappear, more would be vitiated than Heidegger's approach to truth: we would also lose interest in science, in thought, and in decision. In any case, the important fact is that at this point we have neither completed such a project nor know whether it is possible; consequently, obscurity, and in particular the obscurity of the particular, continues to haunt us, and Heidegger's approach continues to grasp a prominent feature of our relationship to truth.

I can now summarize that approach as follows: truth consists in a conflict between the clear and the obscure, which must be disclosed repeatedly in clearings that are discrete, do not occur at our bidding, and matter to us only when we are willing, in honesty and acceptance of risk, to make our essential decisions. The fact that these revelations provide the basis for our decisions establishes them as a conception of truth. The particularity of the revelations makes the conception of truth essentially relativist. The fact that the revelations are not bidden by us, and involve a notion of obscurity so deep that they come to grips, via particulars, with the contradiction implicit in the very notion of a "notion of obscurity," suggests that this conception of truth may be the one we found lying behind us when we accepted Davidson's intuitions about translation. Heidegger would probably admit that Davidson excellently captures the truth we seek when we do science; on the other hand, science, he says, "is not an original happening of truth, but always the cultivation of a domain of truth already opened, specifically by apprehending and confirming that which shows itself to be possibly and necessarily correct within that field." (OWA 62) This seems to me right. In science we explore and test a realm, already essentially familiar, and there is no room for questions about whether we should be interested in this realm in the first place. We have already chosen it in "the original happening of truth" in which our history made this path of exploration a natural or worthy one for us. The significance of the obscure looms large only when our standard of correctness becomes a matter of decision (ethics), not when we pursue what we have already decided to regard as such a standard (science).

The fact that Heidegger's Open cannot be bidden dramatizes most vividly the comparison I have been drawing between these two conceptions of truth. If we cannot say in advance what will count as a disclosure of truth to us, if the Open constitutes both the matter of the conflict and its scene, both the matter of truth and the criteria for its being true, how do we know when a disclosure has happened? When Kierkegaard said that the Teacher must provide both a teaching (a truth) and the criteria for its being a teaching (being true), at least he had the grace to add that the Teacher was God, and that God could, even had to, transcend the (apparent?) laws of thought.[30] Heidegger attributes his paradox to no such divine source, but, as I have stressed by using the word "revelation" for what he calls "disclosure," he does seem to have theophany somewhere in the back of his mind.

In any case, his notion of truth is built on the model of the relationship we have to an authority. Not only does Being, which Heidegger for a long time placed at the heart of all disclosure, strongly resemble traditional conceptions of God—Heidegger inverts this comparison by regarding the notion of "God" as one of the many ways the West has tried to think Being[31]—but the very terms "disclosure" and "unconcealedness" imply that a *person* deliberately uncovers to us a thing that once was hidden. Heidegger rightly wants to keep *what* is disclosed importantly impersonal, and he employs works of art, not their creators, as model agents of disclosure, but he cannot get around the fact that the best way of putting what happens in the Open is that some thing—the work of art, the earth, the rift between world and earth—*speaks* to us.

Speaks, and in an important sense we cannot question. Of course, inasmuch as works of art are the agents of disclosure, and it is part of any thoughtful appreciation of a work of art for the audience to probe, explore, and challenge it in search of interpretations, Heidegger wants us to ask questions. He also praises questioning itself as "the thinking of Being [which] names Being in its question-worthiness" (OWA 62), saying of his own investigations into art that "[e]ach answer [concerning the nature of art] remains in force as an answer only as long as it is rooted in questioning." (OWA 71) But these are the questions one asks of a work of art when trying to appreciate it—reverent questions, questions designed to help one's understanding of what is being communicated, not to challenge that communication. Challenging questions have no place in response to a disclosure of the rift between world and earth, for a challenge implies that we have some more fundamental truth to set up against what we are learning, some (understood) ground against which to judge it, but the truth of the Open is of such a nature that if it is a truth at all it must ground everything else we do and believe. Challenging questions belong to our world, but the truth of the Open, by confronting our world with its earth, is meant precisely to put that world into question. Hence, one disclosure in the Open can be overturned only by another one. It is in this sense that "revelation," with its implication that we are passive audiences to someone else's act of communication, aptly characterizes the kind of relationship we have to the truth

---

30 (Kierkegaard, 1962), pp. 16-27, 65-7.

31 (Heidegger, 1969), pp. 60, 70-72. See also OWA 62—"Still another way in which truth comes to shine forth is the nearness of that which is not simply a being, but the being that is most of all"—and comment in (Langan, 1959), p.110.

Heidegger discusses, even though he does not mean either to invoke a divinity or to suggest that truth could appear for us without our participation as (interpreting) questioners and potential decision-makers.

Now consider what happens when we listen to an authority. Perhaps the authority utters sentences we do not fully understand, but which we believe anyway. What might that mean? Well, we understand the sentences well enough to paraphrase them somewhat and to draw out some of their implications, but a word, or a juxtaposition of words, or a use of words continually eludes us—we take up a semi-propositional attitude towards it. Suppose now that the implications the authority wants to draw include certain clear prescriptions for action. We can understand the prescriptions themselves fully, and can either draw them as implications ourselves, or at least see how they might be derived (the authority, we might say, uses an enthymeme, and we can imagine several plausible premises to fill the gap). As a result, we act on the prescriptions. In this case, since the original sentences help to explain our reasons for acting, we have every reason to call them objects of belief.

In just such a way can we use "beliefs" to designate the vague and indeterminate sentences with which Heidegger permits us to react to an Open, with the Open itself serving as the relevant authority. If the notion of semi-propositional attitudes makes room for sentences and beliefs that Davidson would not allow us, those sentences and beliefs become real truth-claims only when we accept the notion of the disclosure in the Open as a truth to which they (and they alone) can rightfully lay claim.

For ethical rather than epistemological reasons, however, we may well be a little worried by all this talk about authorities. If I am right about what Heidegger is doing, and if he is successful in that project, he has replaced God with a secular source of unquestionable authority. As was the case with God, this authority needs lesser human authorities to interpret it, for we will not and cannot all and always be present to its full light. And, indeed, Heidegger has been accused of setting himself up as a kind of oracle: "he adopts the stance of a prophet and lays claim to mystic insight and inspiration as the sole support of his dictates."[32] Regarding human beings as authorities of this kind is something from which most of us rightly shy away, and such ethical concerns prevent us from being able to embrace Heidegger's vision absolutely. Fortunately, as Heidegger implicitly acknowledges in the very notion of living in a "world," disclosure in the Open cannot possibly be our only intuition about truth. I want to keep it as one of two, balanced antinomously against Davidson's account of coherence with truths we already understand and accept. Both in our everyday lives and when we perceive the inadequacy of those everyday lives, we need a more familiar and fully grasped truth than Heidegger's.

---

32 (Versenyi, 1965), p.162.

On the other hand, as we have already seen, all of our thinking depends crucially on accepting some claims as authoritative, some teachers as authorities. To recall a quotation from chapter one, Sabina Lovibond criticizes the correspondence theory as a complete theory of truth by pointing to "our lack of access to any distinction between those of our beliefs which are *actually true*, and those which are merely *held true by us*," and noting that "[n]o such distinction can survive our conscious recognition that some human authority has to *decide* the claim of any proposition to be regarded as true."[33] We saw above how we necessarily treat our parents and teachers as authorities when learning our first language. Lovibond draws on this in a discussion of Quine's "pull towards objectivity." Quine uses that phrase to describe how the process of teaching leads us away from the "subjectively simplest laws of association" with which we initially classify objects, towards "a perspective on the world which is accessible alike to ourselves and to others."[34] Lovibond moves from here to the stronger claim that authority-relations constitute not only an empirical part of the psychological history of the learning process, but a logical part of what counts as learning and judging:

> ...it seems clear that to be in a position to exert the 'pull toward objectivity' is necessarily to be in a position of *authority* over those upon whom it is exerted. (Wittgenstein asks at OC §493: 'So is this it: I must recognize certain authorities in order to make judgements at all?' This is very much to the present point, if we take it as being of the essence of a 'judgement' that it be answerable to truth.)
>
> It is this relationship of intellectual authority between teacher and learner which explains Wittgenstein's admonition (OC §206) to the person who questions something which, for us, counts as a certainty: 'I can't give you any grounds, but if you learn more, you too will think the same.' 'If you *learn* more': not 'if I shine bright lights into your eyes.' The latter, indeed, might also be true; yet it would not, as the other does, display the special status of the speaker—his status as a subscriber to that 'totality of judgements' which has to be made plausible to anyone destined to participate in the going form of life. This status is what makes it correct for the speaker to identify the process by which the other person comes to 'think the same' as a process of *learning*...[35]

Finally, the possibility of authoritative disclosures of truth, paradoxically, increases our freedom. Only the possibility that we may hear from an authority outside of ourselves and mysterious allows us to suppose that we need not be locked in by the implications of the truths we already believe. For science this sense of being "locked in" might be illusory, or at worst not something to worry about, but for ethics a Davidsonian model of truth as that which translates into accepted sentences of a familiar tongue is extremely constricting. Heidegger allows us to posit that there might be a "radically new beginning" (in the words

---

[33] (Lovibond, 1983), p.37.
[34] *ibid*, pp 58,.63.
[35] *ibid*, pp.59,62.

of his student, Hannah Arendt) in our affairs and our beliefs about our affairs, a change of view not determined by either the events or the criteria in our past. From John Scotus Eriugena and Meister Eckhart's notion of man as a *causa sui*, reflecting God in the possession precisely of a capacity for unforeseeable (self)-creation, through the Renaissance and Enlightenment humanists who justified their eclecticism with a devout, if somewhat confused doctrine of relativism, to Kierkegaard's presentation of the criterionless choice as rooted in a divine Paradox, thinkers favoring an extreme reading of the notion of man's infinite possibilities have always connected those possibilities to an authoritative source of truth obscure in its very essence.[36]

Heidegger's version of authoritative mystery, and its illustrious ancestors, will be crucial to the discussion in chapter nine of how an ethics defined by cultural norms can yet make room for radical criticism of those norms. In addition, it will provide a way, as we may already begin to see now, to make sense of conversion to and from ethical beliefs, which arose in chapter one as a problem for Williams' position. When we convert, or imagine the possibility of our own conversion, when we want to say, or imagine we might want to say, that we are coming as if born again to a new first language,[37] we suppose that we might have a new relation of world to earth disclosed to us, that what seems obscure to us now could threaten what seems clear, that an authority we believe on the basis of more or less than a set of good reasons might lead us to reshape the foundations of all our reasons. It would be wrong to say that we rest ethical truth in the earth and therefore allow it independence of reason; rather, we rest it in the *relation* between world and earth, in the relation between phenomenological and interpretive understanding, holding indeed to a framework of reasons (world) in our everyday life but allowing the possibility of a rift between that everyday life and its inadequately understood ground (earth) to maintain towards those reasons the constant threat of a radical change. We are never *forced* to appeal to disclosure to explain a belief or action. As we cannot challenge the truth of a disclosure with other "evidence," so we cannot justify it; it merely makes sense of the phenomenology of conversion from one world-view to another in the eyes of the convert and of those who want to leave open, for themselves and for others, the possibility of conversion.

Unlike Winch,[38] therefore, I am not saying that cases arise within the practice of social science in which we must posit the existence of a radical difference between cultures, or a disclosive truth to explain that difference. I do not speak of disagreements about any specific kind of fact, but of cases where a disagreement about a fact may grow into or out of a vast disagreement about

---

36 I am indebted for this insight to Dermot Moran, in a 1987 seminar on medieval philosophy at Yale.

37 Or that we are engaged in what Goodman calls "initiative," Rorty "hermeneutics," and Kuhn "revolution."

38 (Winch, 1958).

modes of establishing fact. The disagreement is then "incommensurable" because no common measure can resolve it. It is "radical" because it goes to the roots of what we believe, of how we establish truth. Unlike a superficial difference, it does not disappear when we uncover more fundamental beliefs and bring them to bear on the original claims. It is a failure of understanding because at some point, while we still understand the other's sentences sufficiently to see them as sentences, we do not understand *why* she holds them. We do not understand what justification the sentences have, in what context to interpret them; we have phenomenological understanding (of the sentences as sentences) without interpretive understanding (of the sentences as propositions).

We can never be forced to take this line because no evidence could ever force us to accept as a candidate for truth a claim that might undermine all that we consider evidence. For this reason, I agree with Davidson that it is unintelligible to suppose we might allow for incommensurability when we are doing logic. Precisely what it means to be doing logic is that we seek principles determining all measure. I do not recommend acknowledging the possibility of radical difference when we do science either, beçause it is built into the practice we call "science" to seek empirical explanations of phenomena on the presupposition that our principles of empirical explanation are in fact true. But when we do ethics, only the dual conception of truth, by which we can hold on to the notion that our ethical beliefs are in fact true while allowing for the (possible) truth of other, conflicting ethical beliefs, can account for the way we understand such phenomena as conversion, intercultural conflict, and the internal criticism of our own values.

On the other hand, in pursuit of the notion that ethical and factual sentences not only are both claimants of truth but belong together and affect each other to the extent that the one may legitimately be a reason for altering one's view of the other, I do want to say that we may decide on what we want to *count as* "science" in the process of what I have been calling "disclosure." Disclosure can occur on many levels, and in the sense that Heidegger uses it—to encourage individuals constantly and repeatedly to base their decisions on what they find they learn in the presence of works of art—it rarely leads us to change our views on specific scientific evidence. Whether or not to count spirit, afterlives, etc. as real, however, or to plunk for the essential equality of human intellects, comes up as a question every time an Open opens itself amongst us, and from such questions comes the possibility that we may, as individuals, groups, or a society, opt to (re-)join African tribes, Hinduism, Orthodox Christianity or Judaism, or any other way of life that combines modes of weighing facts different from the secular Western one with a different purpose for living. That we do not do so (usually), is a matter of our accepting our earth as ours wherever others may stand, seeing the fundamentals of our lives as ultimately the way we want them to be, not of a proof by convergence, the nature of theory, or the nature of translation that our way of life grasps truth somehow more adequately than any other. It is importantly for *ethical* reasons, that is, that we in the West remain loyal to science.

We (here and elsewhere) capture the nature of truth best in an antinomy embracing both Davidsonian and Heideggerian intuitions. We suppose our ownmodes of evidence correct, but must be able at least to imagine giving them up. We cannot even make sense of any other way of thinking until we suppose it enough like our own to be able to translate it, but then we are willing to run into radical disagreements—knots of failure to understand, to have a basis for agreement—because we cannot and do not want to imagine what it would be for our truth claims not only to be correct but to define the whole nature of truth. But when we act on the supposition of a larger and hence obscure truth, we make not a scientific but an ethical decision (sometimes an ethical decision that concerns science). We posit the larger truth even in speculative reason, but make use of it only in the interest of practical reason. As Kant did with his antinomies, I intend mine to establish a mere possibility for us when theorizing about the world, which we suppose actual when acting in it. Exactly how we suppose this possibility as actual, exactly what instantiates it, forms the subject of the next chapter.

CHAPTER SEVEN

FROM "WORLD-PICTURES" TO "CULTURES"

To arrive at any true cultural relativism from the position developed so far, I need to translate "world-pictures" into "cultures"; I have to show how to give the Wittgensteinian metaphor *Weltbild* appropriate concrete instances. Writers on world-pictures normally either use that term as if its instances were obvious, or assume they can move directly from it to "culture." But a world-picture is a set of ideas, of interwoven sentences and beliefs, while a culture is a set of institutions and practices, in which ideas may comprise only a part. For Wittgenstein, the word "world-picture" on the one hand represents the complex of judgments necessary for any particular judgment to make sense, and on the other hand characterizes how beliefs are tied to the "form of life" of a group. The latter part of his view might seem to provide an opening in which to introduce culture, except that we have no reason to suppose that the group whose practices ground a world-picture corresponds in the least with what we would ordinarily recognize as a "culture." Wittgenstein's group might be larger than a culture—it might be able to include several different linguistic, religious, or political groups, as does, say, "Western Europe." Or it might be smaller, coinciding only with religious or political subcultures, like the Southern Baptists or the Libertarians. And if it seems as though all these larger and smaller divisions could also be called "cultures," that merely brings us to the second problem we will face in this chapter: that the word "culture" is too vague and ideologically charged to serve, without elaborate and careful definition, as an answer to the question about instantiation. It invites the twin errors of keeping "world-picture" and "culture" quite distinct while leaping unwarrantedly to the conclusion that they will match up, and identifying the latter tautologously with the former, so that we have no way to pick out concrete instances of either.

In beginning a response to these problems, I want to remind the reader that this book proceeds from the point-of-view of an individual ethical agent and insists, with Kant, that that standpoint differs from one of mere speculation, even speculation about ethics. The agent was concerned, when confronted with strict cultural relativism in the first chapter, about what had happened to her familiar practices of advice, rebuke and co-operation with others, and about what story she could tell herself about why she should not adopt the practices of other groups whenever she felt like it. My account, in succeeding chapters, of how her ethical claims could claim truth, and could do so while appealing to a socially limited, not a universal, framework of argument, should have assured her that advice, rebuke, and co-operation can flourish within groups, and that the members of certain groups can know that they want to continue to belong even when they run out of arguments for that commitment, but she presumably still needs to ask, "which groups?" If she wants to justify, order, and make her decisions according to the norms of the group to which she is committed, she needs to pick out that group and learn how to determine its norms.

Now, there are at least two other perspectives from which someone might seek a definition of culture. One is that of the scientist collecting data for a theory of human interaction, or of a historian or philosopher of culture. Such a person does not need a final, settled definition of the term, merely a rough guide, sufficient to motivate and give some direction to speculation and the gathering of evidence. A final categorization will take place once the evidence is in or the theory built. Moreover, the scientist and historian are interested in a definition primarily insofar as it enables them to predict human behavior in the future.

A second perspective shares this interest, but has a markedly lesser ability to tolerate vagueness and ambiguity. This is the perspective of the institutional representative, who may be an elected official or a school administrator, a bank manager or union leader, a curator or social worker, and her problems may range from settling disputes over hiring or property to accommodating bilingualism or religious differences in a school or arts program. She has to make *decisions* about cultures—whether to act or lobby on behalf of funding for a group's claim to deserve a school, a social center, or a state, whether to allow an individual the right, on the grounds of cultural difference, to violate the norms of her state, business, school, etc., whether to resolve a given conflict between groups or individuals in terms of cultural difference, and, if so, whether the relevant disputants should be separated or made to live together—and she will often need, in advance of her decisions, some firm line on what to count as a culture, so that her decisions will have the justice of clarity and consistency, so that she can resolve in advance as many difficulties as she can possibly anticipate, and so that her decisions will cohere with the other decisions of her institution and the society(ies) it serves.

Although politics is part of ethics, and the institutional representative clearly does think from an ethical point-of-view, it is not quite the point-of-view of the individual agent, with which I am here concerned. The individual also needs some sharp definition of "culture," but she needs a sharp line only on what to count as her *own* culture, not as culture in general. Furthermore, she need not have much interest in predicting and controlling people's actions, and her actions and decisions need not cohere with those of any other part of her society. For these reasons, all the well worked-out definitions and empirical evidence in the world is of no use to her if they pretend to show that her beliefs and attitudes are expressed by a group product which she does not recognize as expressing her at all. One criterion of a definition of culture being adequate for her is that she be able to say, "*That* is my culture!" of some application of the definition.

On the other hand, the agent herself will probably take some interest in what one might call the "external" view of what constitutes her culture. I argued in chapter three that our interests are fact—or world—guided, which here implies that one's identification with a culture is a matter about which one can go wrong. We all know of cases in which individuals insist that they have nothing Italian about them when all their tastes, habits and friends are Italian, or that they are Englishmen when they are only Anglophiles, and if we resemble these individuals we would like to know about it. Part of the rebuke and advice we give each other is rebuke and advice on whether one of us is fooling herself about her cultural identification. And this practice may in part be in the interest of the rebuker and advisor, who, as a self-aware Italian or Anglophile herself, may want company and co-operation in her projects or plight.

In addition, the distinction between defining "culture" in general and defining one's own culture is not one to which we can adhere strictly. For if the agent wants to pick out what truly counts as her own culture, she must have some interest in what that word and category means independently of her employment of it. She may well consider the scientists' and politicians' attempts to define the term faulty or skewed, but what they say, and especially the reasons and ordinary uses they adduce in support of what they say, must at least limit the general field in which she registers her dissent. We may come to a disagreement, between two agents or between an agent and the institutions among which she lives, on whether a given person is correct, in picking out her culture, to regard her family as more important than her schooling, or her nation as more important than her religion,[1] but the disagreements cannot range much more widely than this if we are to have a culturally-dependent theory of ethics at all.

My strategy in approaching this issue will be to move from a review of general considerations and definitions of "culture" to a discussion of why, for a combination of empirical and methodological reasons, we might want to consider religion, nationality or language as the prime markers for picking out a culture, and to conclude with a discussion of how it need not matter if we

---

1 Note that there at least two ways the agent herself can err, in constructing such a hierarchy: she can either misunderstand the nature or role of the relevant institutions (for instance, she may assume that nationality is unimportant because she fails to realize that what her pastor says in church has more to do with a nationalist than a strictly religious program), or she can repress, or fail fully to understand, the impact of those institutions on her own, specific development (for instance, in her case family may be much more or less important than it is to the average member of her society). That is, the empirical question of which institutions are most important to a particular agent has itself both an external (here, sociological) aspect and a subjective (here, psychological) one.

cannot come up with a definitive hierarchy among these criteria. I will be drawing on diverse sources, from the theory of world-pictures developed in chapters two through six to the history of nationalism and considerations about the way children are actually educated in ethics. "Culture" is a highly specialized word within our own tradition and language, but it is also the empirical means by which we identify ways of judging as complete and distinct wholes. The method of this chapter, like the subject matter, will therefore have to lie somewhere in between the theoretical speculation I have pursued thus far and the examination of specific traditions to follow in the last two chapters.

General Considerations

Let us start by considering what we might adopt as the concrete version of a world-picture if we did not opt for what we familiarly consider a culture. Since world-pictures are sets of ideas, one obvious (idealist) move might be to suggest that individuals act, and justify their actions, according to the norms embedded in ideologies, or philosophical texts, perhaps in the work of their favorite philosopher. At the other (materialist) extreme, one might want to derive norms purely from the behavior of the society with which the individual comes into daily contact.

To see what these options amount to, let me spell them out a little. People who want to "follow" the ideas of a certain philosophy might join a Marxist or Objectivist club, or a society for readers of Aristotle, which in turn makes its decisions about most matters, and advises its members to make their decisions, according to what the official mentor has to say on the subject. The members would presumably agree on a set method of interpretation as authoritative: majority vote, the word of those whom a majority agree are "experts," opening the text to a random page and having a random member expound it,[2] etc. Are they really following Marx, Rand, or Aristotle by these means? There are problems of whether they will get at what the philosophers in question "really" intended, but these problems arise for any method of interpretation, of any speaker or group of speakers. If we want to follow the norms of Memphis, Tennessee, do we determine those norms by appealing to a majority of the town's inhabitants, a set of supposed "experts," or some random sample? Even if we want to follow the values of our neighbor, Ms. Jones, it is not obvious whether we should appeal to her words, a selection of her words, or expert or majoritarian opinion among her listeners, in order to determine what she means.

A greater problem with this suggestion is that it traces norms to an oddly late starting-point. The social group seems something of an obstruction—if the individual wants to pick something as her favorite philosophy, presumably

---

2 Having a child open the Bible to a random verse was a traditional method of divination in Talmudic times: see, for instance, Babylonian Talmud, *Gittin* 56a.

she does so because it coincides with and expresses well some of what she already believes, and in that case she is not going to want to accept other people's interpretations of this philosophy. Indeed, we should not regard the particular philosophy as the *source* of her norms at all: the ethical beliefs that really shape her, that express her most deeply rooted interests and conception of the world, must surely have come earlier if she is to have reached the stage of having a favorite philosophy. The notion of a world-picture as the ground we find difficult to question, the underpinning of beliefs and questions, the determinant/expression of our longest-term interests, is not likely to match up with a philosophy chosen by a person who already has considerable education and a set of self-conscious goals.

Which brings us to the motivation for the opposite extreme. If a favorite philosophy comes too late, is too far from the given, the social group constituted by our face-to-face contacts seems as much a given as we could hope to find.[3] It also makes sense that such a group determines many of our beliefs. Certainly the contacts with our parents, teachers and close friends in our younger years are the source of much of the way we think and act, and throughout our lives we adjust our beliefs and attitudes, to some extent, in order to win the approval and meet the expectations of those whom we daily encounter.

But now ideas have been pushed too far out of the picture. Our parents and teachers speak from and for newspapers, canonical texts, and oral traditions. They thus immediately represent a larger society and its body of ideas to us. In addition, we do not merely *hear* what they say; we interpret it, reflect on it, and try to put the pieces we get at different times and from different people into some kind of harmony. Eventually we feel capable of saying that a particular face-to-face contact has misunderstood our shared social norms, and do not feel that the sum of all the people we meet face-to-face, even a weighted sum stressing the position of our parents and teachers, adequately matches what we conceive of as "our society." Among other things, the social group consisting of our face-to-face contacts is too transitory to serve the role, that I earlier attributed to society, of "establishing" desires, defining and refining interests. We cannot expect these individual human beings to have themselves performed the requisite long-term testing of desires against each other and the facts, nor, in most cases, do they alone form a group among whom the agent must spend her whole life, and to which she must therefore adjust. More probably, she sees the set of her face-to-face contacts as embedded in some larger, more enduring group, which she regards as the ultimate source of her, and their, beliefs and attitudes.

The problems with these two suggestions bring out what we must require of any attempt to instantiate world-pictures. To put it generally, the instances

[3] One well-known definition of culture holds that "the distinctive culture-bearing group" for an individual is constituted by those with whom he or she comes into face-to-face contact: (Kroeber & Kluckhorn, 1952), pp.130-4.

have to be social groups that are at least in part held together and defined by a set of ideas. Specifically, the theory I have developed of how such ideas work directs us toward a group that 1) shapes most of the materials that go into our childhood education, and 2) constitutes a more or less self-sufficient community, maintaining a more or less constant identity over time-spans substantially longer than that of an individual life. Only such a group can provide our most fundamental ideas, and only such a group can define and refine our interests. But with these requirements we come very close to standard definitions of "culture."

The modern, anthropological use of the term "culture" is said to have been invented by Gustav Klemm and introduced into English by EB Tylor, in his 1871 book, *Primitive Culture*. Tylor's definition of the word, in the first sentence of the book, served as the only definition in use for the next 30 years, and has dominated most discussions of the word ever since: "Culture...is that complex whole which includes knowledge, belief, art, morals, law, custom and any other capabilities and habits acquired by man as a member of society."[4] In the twentieth century, there have been fierce tussles over the word, and, according to Kroeber and Kluckhorn's *Culture: A Critical Review of Concepts and Definitions*, still the controlling text on the subject,[5] over a hundred and sixty definitions were proposed for it between 1920 and 1950. Unfortunately, many of them share Tylor's inclination to assemble a lot of different things without explaining why they belong together, and to leave the term "society" without a clear referent. But most of them have two properties of supreme importance for our purposes: they insist that cultures embrace the ideas as well as the institutions and practices of a society, and they speak of cultural products as being handed down from the past, as enduring in and taught as part of a tradition.[6] Two excellent examples are Sapir's 1921 comment that culture consists in "the socially inherited assemblage of practices and beliefs that determines the texture of our lives," and Clifford Geertz's 1966 definition of the term as "an historically transmitted pattern of meaning embodied in symbols, a system of inherited conceptions expressed in symbolic forms by means of which men communicate, perpetuate, and develop their knowledge and attitudes toward life."[7]

On the other hand, the definitions are so varied and in so much conflict with one another that some lack even these properties. Many talk about artifacts and patterns of behavior to the exclusion of ideas (Wissler, 1933: "the sum

---

4 Quoted and discussed in (Kroeber & Kluckhorn, 1952), pp.9,43.

5 Every reference work I consulted, from the 1968 *International Encyclopedia of the Social Sciences* through (Voget,1975), (see also the Encyclopedia articles and histories of ethnology in the Bibiliography), cited Kroeber and Kluckhorn as the definitive text on the word "culture," and most discussions of the word seemed clearly to be based on their work.

6 See, for instance, (Kroeber & Kluckhorn, 1952), pp. 46-7, 50, 55, 56, 65, 70, 86.

7 *ibid*, p.46 and "Religion as a Cultural System," in (Geertz, 1973), p.89.

total of the possessions and the patterned ways of behavior which have become part of the heritage of a group"),[8] and some allow for or explicitly include the products of highly transitory groups. When writers, like many functionalists, want to let the word cover "everything...artificial, useful and social"[9] that meets our biological or socio-economic needs, they leave little room for a distinction between the activities and beliefs of a group of a people who happen to wind up on a desert island and the more fundamental activities and beliefs of the societies in which such desert islanders grew up. Kluckhorn and Kelly, in 1945, push this problem to its limits when they recommend "speak[ing] of the culture of cliques and of relatively impermanent social units such as, for example, members of summer camps."[10] They prefer to restrict only the term "society" to more permanent and distinctive groups, and social scientists normally use "society" to isolate groups by strictly geographical, political or economic criteria—precisely to *avoid* appealing to ideas.

In short, the question of what kind of group will exemplify the holders of a world-picture re-appears within the history of defining the word "culture." I can here use the word in Tylor's, Sapir's and Geertz's sense, because that is probably its dominant meaning,[11] but we must keep in mind that we are not dealing with a clear, well-defined, generally agreed-on word. If we were, I could simply show that "culture" matches what I meant by "world-picture," and then look to empirical research to tell us what specific groups can be said to have a culture, and what factors determine the nature and limits of cultures. Instead, I am adhering *a priori* to one out of several senses of the term, but the adoption of that sense does not itself settle or make obvious what about culture might count as the concrete instantiation of world-pictures.

To make this a little clearer: once we hold that cultures instantiate world-pictures, we still have to work out what aspects of a culture to take as salient. Are cultures defined primarily by a religion, a language, political beliefs or structures (nationhood), or geographical isolation?[12] The anthropologist may not have to deal with such issues, since the groups with which she works usually display all of these criteria at once, but for the agent, especially in the modern world, precisely this is the crucial question. Agents in the modern world are all "hard cases" for the anthropologist, people whose religion tells them one

---

8 (Kroeber & Kluckhorn, 1952), p.47.

9 *ibid*, pp. 55, 72.

10 *ibid*, p.129.

11 Such important writers on the subject as Kroeber, Leslie White, and at times Kluckhorn himself, have used it that way: *ibid*, pp.58, 69-70,145 and (White, 1974).

12 There is also the problem, which will see cropping up repeatedly in this discussion (especially when we come to nationalism), of how to determine where one culture, however defined, ends and another begins: "A fully individuable culture is at best a rare thing. Cultures, subcultures, fragments of cultures, constantly meet one another and exchange and modify practices and attitudes. Social practices...never come forward with a certificate saying that they belong[...to one, rather than another, specific culture]." (Williams, 1985), p.158.

thing, educational background another, and state a third. If they indeed turn to these different groups and group products for ethical guidance, they need a decision-procedure for picking one over the others—in some cases, in most cases, or in all cases. We cannot answer this need by turning to empirical studies of culture, because the definition of the concept at which those studies aim is so unsettled and controversial that any investigator's conclusions will be far more determined by her opinion of what she is looking for than by the evidence she uncovers. How else to find such a decision-procedure, or to evade the need for it, is the problem we need to explore.

Definitions of "Culture": Language and Texts

The most common means of distinguishing cultures is by language. Indeed, before the word "culture" came to designate the ways of life of different peoples, those, like Herder, who felt that such ways of life played an important role in shaping thought, appealed to language as the hallmark and source of differences in thought.[13] Even Biblical and Classical Greek sources often identify the social allegiances of an individual according to what language he or she speaks.

Many of the enumerative definitions that Kroeber and Kluckhorn present include language in their list of cultural products. Clark Wissler, in 1920, puts language together with marriage and art in his examples of the "social activities" with which he wants to identify culture.[14] Ernst Cassirer equates culture with "language, myth, art, religion, [and] science."[15] More to our point, since lists give no priority to language among cultural products, is DM Taylor's description of language as "the vehicle of culture," and CF Voegelin's claim that "it is relatively easy to...define linguistics without reference to culture...; it is much more difficult to...define culture...without reference to language."[16] By contrast, H. Hoijer notes that people "sharing substantially the same culture" may speak different languages, while "peoples whose languages are related may have very different cultures."[17] And Franz Boas points out that while cultures shape languages, it is highly unlikely that "morphological traits of [a] language" will have any significant impact on the nature of its speakers' culture.[18]

From the point of view of the account of truth and world-pictures I have given so far, there is good *prima facie* reason to favor language as the prime mark of culture. A world-picture is after all a set of shared beliefs and interests, and people are more likely to develop shared beliefs and interests when they

---

[13] On Herder, see (Kedourie, 1961), pp. 58, 62. On his contemporaries, Gallatin and W. von Humboldt, see (Haddon, 1934), p.96.

[14] (Kroeber & Kluckhorn, 1952), p.43.

[15] (Cassirer, 1944), pp.22-3.

[16] (Kroeber & Kluckhorn, 1952), pp. 123, 122.

[17] *ibid*, p.120.

[18] *ibid*, p.115.

speak the same language, since then they can advise and rebuke one another, practise means of child-rearing with each other, co-operate in projects, and engage in reflective discussions. Of course, one can also do all these things with people whose language one knows only partially or via a translator, but in that case close contact will be more difficult and less frequent, and one would be likely to wind up sharing only broad, general patterns, rather than the specifics that shape so much of our activity.

On the other hand, we should not dismiss too readily the possibility of a culture among people with freely intertranslatable languages, nor assume too readily that shared language guarantees shared culture. The Jews, who for the past 2000 years have tended to share only a poorly spoken second tongue (Rabbinic Hebrew), not a native one, have still managed in that period to share more beliefs and goals with one another than with the societies among which they have lived. Furthermore, although linguistic difference remains very important to the various groups in India and Indonesia, the possession of shared second languages (Hindi and English in the first case, "Bahasa Indonesia" in the second), plus the desire of almost all the inhabitants to live in an independent and relatively powerful political unit, has led those groups to seek and in part to find a common culture. The various linguistic groups in Belgium and Switzerland have worked towards a similar goal for much longer, and with considerable success.

That linguistic unity is not a sufficient condition for harmony of interests is demonstrated most graphically by religious differences, from the fervent but peaceful disagreements among fundamentalists, mainstream Christians and Jews, and secularists in the United States, to the violent conflicts of Northern Ireland. Here, as in the complementary case of the unity among Diaspora Jews, the possession, and use in education, of certain texts, and certain traditions of interpreting those texts, plays a larger role than the mere language in which the texts are read and taught. Diaspora Jews are held together by their educational emphasis on the Hebrew Bible, the Talmud, and the medieval rabbinic commentaries, Catholics by the Latin Bible, the Church fathers, and certain medieval philosophers, Southern Baptists by the English Bible and a tradition of preaching, and secular Americans by the Constitution, the writings of its authors and their philosophical contemporaries, and the tradition of science and philosophy of science in the modern academy. In the last two examples, I have included preaching and academic teaching as a mode of producing shared texts: insofar as ideas can be conveyed in verbal expressions so similar to one another that one preacher or professor or congregant or student can predict fairly exactly what will be said in another church or school, "texts" need not be strictly limited to the written word. We can in this way allow that even non-literate societies may pass down texts, in the form of oral traditions of proverbs, stories, codes of law, etc.

With this broader use of the word "text," we may comfortably move to it as a more precise version of the cultural determinant I first tried to grasp as "language." By means of texts, and not merely by a language, do groups pass down interests and ideas; ethical rules, ideals and models, especially, come down in legal, exhortatory and imaginative literature. Groups that try to maintain a shared culture in spite of linguistic difference, moreover, or that want to separate themselves from the community with which they share a language, generally combine and dissent by means of an attachment to some text or set of texts. The unifying texts for the Belgians may be a body of positive law, while the separatist Ibos may share stories of past glory and recent oppression, but insofar as these groups become and remain a people at all they must pass some tales down to their children.

There remain the questions of how people develop separating or unifying attachments to texts at all, of whether I am not unreasonably privileging historical myths, records and memories over the histories that inspire such creations, and of what kinds of shared texts have most influence in establishing and shaping a cultural group. The first two questions, while intriguing in themselves, do not concern us much here. How groups come to be, how people come both to share interests and to build institutions together, are matters for the scientist or institutional representative, not the agent, to worry about. The agent primarily wants to find out which group she belongs to, and for that she needs to know how to identify groups, how to identify membership in groups, and perhaps how to dissent from a group or change from one to another. She does not need to know how groups come into existence, change, or split up, except insofar as that affects the question of identity.

It follows that the question of the relative influence of different texts and kinds of texts remains of great importance to us. We surely do not want to say that any shared history, for instance, establishes a separate culture. If all and only the people of Astoria, Queens discuss and recall some crime or scandal in their neighborhood, that does not turn them into a culture. Nor need every political division and sub-division in the world (Biafrans, Nigerians, Tamils, Indians, Iraqis, Arabs) reflect a single, or complete, cultural group. Instead, some texts tend to have an insignificant effect on the shaping of beliefs and ideals, while others are overwhelmingly important, and the relative strength of different kinds of texts varies from occasion to occasion. Thus on one occasion an epic, on another a religious writing, on a third a code of law, and on a fourth a set of quotations from a powerful leader, will have decisive impact on the formation of a culture. In addition, individuals tend to be shaped by several different texts and traditions of texts, and peoples tend correspondingly to overlap in various ways. An agent may be pulled in one direction by a Sunday school that raised her on the King James Bible, in another direction by a family that reveres the tradition of liberalism associated with the Bill of

Rights, and in a third direction by teachers and peers with a fondness for Romantic and Existentialist European literature. At least three sets of texts, at least three cultures, can in this way converge in a single individual.

These considerations do not make texts, and the single language in which a given text is usually conveyed, useless as a distinguishing mark of culture, but it does mean that we do not entirely solve the problem of identification by pointing to this mark. Cultures usually center around a few shared texts; languages are usually identified with certain texts, and texts with certain languages; hence shared language coupled with shared texts remains an excellent means of picking out most cultural groups in the world, as well as most of their members. But there are some hard cases in which this mark identifies too many or too few groups, and many hard cases, especially in the diverse and highly interactive communities of the West, in which it sifts out three or four groups with which an individual may identify but says nothing about how to select further among these three or four. For that further selection, we need to look more closely at the content of the various kinds of texts. I will keep the discussion relatively simple by restricting it to the two kinds of texts that today most commonly lay claim to constituting the decisive cultural determination: religious writings, and the writings and speeches of nationalism.

Definitions of "Culture": Religion

"Hath a nation changed its gods, which yet are no gods?" (Jeremiah 2:11)

For the world of the Hebrew Bible, religion was the hallmark of nationhood or peoplehood. Even when the Bible condemns the gods of other peoples as false and evil, it yet acknowledges that those peoples define themselves by their relationship to their gods. The word "god" here serves as a synecdoche for religion, and a religion here comprises a set of rituals, a sacred text, ethical precepts and civil laws—almost exactly what I have been calling a "culture." Of course, religions derived the authority with which they regulated practice not from some accepted theory of cultural determinism, but from the superhuman power, wisdom or benevolence of the gods in whose name they claimed to speak. For all that, the religious peoples of the Biblical world make a good model of a cultural relativism that has no problem with intra-cultural heterogeneity: should there be any conflict among local laws, practices, texts, etc., among what we would call the vestiges of external influences on the culture, the priests or "divinely-appointed" rulers can settle which norm or ideal is to take precedence in each particular case. And by appealing to the divine as their authority, these leaders rule out the possibility, for a believing populace, of any rational basis for dissent from their decisions.

Such, at any rate, is roughly the model for those in the modern world who would like religion to be once again the final determinant of culture. The sacred text, for these people, takes obvious priority over other texts as a source of norms, and sacred interpreters (priests, rabbis, mullahs) take similarly obvious priority over other interpreters. The problem, of course, is that nothing in the argument for the importance of culture makes either the existence or the ethical role of a divine being at all obvious. Since religious institutions do tend to provide socially-based ethical systems with a clear-cut decision procedure, it might be tempting to regard religion as the prime mover of culture anyway, were it not that for many modern individuals, and for many modern social groups, religion, far from providing the heart of culture, belongs merely to its remote past.

Furthermore, religions are not quite as monolithic as they like to appear. Within ancient Israel, priests, prophets, and kings, and later, priests and rabbis, struggled with one another for dominance in interpreting the law. And, throughout its history, even the supremely monolithic Catholic church has been unable to gain complete control over dissenting priests and communities who (quietly or openly) follow them. In the modern world, religions trying to come to grips with the power of scientific thought have had to appeal beyond their coterie of active supporters for aid in constructing self-understandings that can win legitimacy in the larger culture. Hence there are debates within the most devout Christian, Jewish, and Muslim circles over how properly to read the sacred texts. *A fortiori*, the relative importance of non-sacred texts, and non-sacred interpreters, remains an open question within these religious communities, and they are less inclined than they have ever been to agree unequivocally on who should count as a religious leader, or to accept the words of such leaders unhesitatingly.

DEFINITIONS OF "CULTURE": NATIONALISM

Nationalism has arisen in large part as a secular version of the project I have just ascribed to religion—the establishment of institutions that express, define and enforce culturally based ethical beliefs. By "nationalism" I do not mean the mere sense of patriotism or chauvinism with which that word is colloquially identified, but the doctrine, first developed at the end of the eighteenth century and still dominating the political scene today, that every nation in the world deserves a state (exactly one state) and every state has legitimacy insofar as it reflects the wishes of a nation (exactly one nation). As we shall see, "nation" not coincidentally means about as much and as little as "culture," and nationalism, unlike religion, self-consciously tries to provide a decision-procedure for culturally based ethics. We have found that after we attach "culture" to texts we still need to decide whether to pick out the relevant texts on the basis of shared language, history or religion (or any of a number of other criteria, such as race). Nationalism attempts to settle this question once and for all, and to impose its answer on each individual, at least within the group it selects, by means of a political structure and a body of positive law.

How this solution is supposed to work, and in what respects it fails, comes out clearly in the history of the nationalist doctrine. In the terms of a familiar distinction in jurisprudence, the history of nationalism follows a progression from "found" to "made" nations. For Herder and his contemporaries, nations were to be found in the natural divisions of the human race, ordained by God and endowed each with its own character, the purity and inviolability of which its citizens had a duty to preserve. Herder's "national soul" corresponds to the Leibnizean monad[19]—"singular, wonderful, inexplicable, ineradicable," an "energizing principle" of cultures,[20] which maintains the identity of a culture through all its changes and interactions. The national soul deserves independence for the same reason that individual souls deserve freedom: because the only morally healthy condition for a soul (mind, spirit, mental entity), according to the weird marriage of Kant's ethics and Romantic expressivism that dominated post-Kantian philosophy,[21] is one in which it develops according to its own, "internal" laws. Thus Herder, who wanted all nations to live in freedom; thus Fichte, who was passionately dedicated to specifically German unity and independence; and thus Schleiermacher, who attributed to each nation a different historical task.[22]

When these thinkers descended from their mystical visions to real historical or political projects, they had to find concrete determinations for their "natural divisions of the human race." For the most part they opted for language as the distinguishing characteristic of these divisions, but that brought its own problems. Language was viewed as the concrete expression of mental life, the means by which "man becomes conscious of his personality,"[23] and it was more likely to serve as a repository for group experiences than the individualist mental structures Kant had identified as "categories." On the other hand, as was already known, languages tend to borrow from one another, even to form curious hybrids. Then, many people learn more than one language, and may wind up speaking or writing in a language other than their native one. Fichte tried to prove that the presence of foreign words obscures a native speaker's own grasp on what she means,[24] and others embarked on a search, via such studies of folk speech and literature as the work of the brothers Grimm, for the original, primitive languages of the world, hoping that these would reveal the true

---

19 (Herder, 1963), p.xvii. See also (Cassirer, 1951), pp.230-3, (Ergang, 1966), p.86, and (Koepping, 1983), pp.38-9.

20 Ergang, Koepping, *loc. cit.*

21 See discussion in (Taylor, 1979), pp.1-14.

22 (Kedourie, 1961), p.58, (Kohn, 1965), p.36, and (Schmidt, 1956).

23 (Kedourie, 1961), p.62.

24 *ibid*, p.64.

nations.[25] As nationalism developed through the nineteenth century, language moved from its pride of place as *the* distinguishing mark to a position as one of a set of criteria, which also included race, history and religion. The interdependence of this set helped to determine, among other things, which languages were to count as pure and proper expressions of a nation, and which speakers of a language were to count as appropriate shapers and representatives of its use. For Charles Maurras, for instance, no Jew could properly speak French.[26]

If the fall from a simple, linguistic criterion into a morass of overlapping and conflicting ones looks familiar from our discussion of culture, that is because the theories of nations and of cultures arose at much the same time and for similar and closely interwoven reasons. In Germany, where both theories have their roots, the word *Volk* was often used for either "nation" or "culture," and both *Cultur* and *Nation* were seen—by Kant and Fichte, respectively—as a context for the full flowering of (individual) freedom.[27] Herder, moreover, is claimed as a major precursor by both nationalists and anthropologists. His search for the essence of each culture (*Volksgeist*) inspired the search of Adolf Bastian, the generally acknowledged founder of cultural anthropology, for essential "folk thoughts" (*Völkergedanken*);[28] his notion of each ethnic group as almost a Leibnizean monad, unique and irreducible, is echoed not only in Bastian[29] but in anthropological work as recent as Ruth Benedict's *Patterns of Culture*: "[a culture] is not merely the sum of all its parts, but the result of an unique arrangement and interrelation of the parts that has brought about a new

[25] *ibid*, pp.67-8, (Leaf, 1979), p.83, and (Koepping, 1983), p.43.

[26] (Kedourie, 1961), p.72.

[27] For Fichte, see (Kedourie, 1961), pp. 64-70, and for Kant see (Kant, 1951), pp. 105, 201-2, and especially 281. (Kroeber & Kluckhorn, 1952), pp.23-4, inexplicably, overlook this richest source of what "culture" might mean to Kant.) Fichte, it should be noted, took an interest in both *Nation* and *Cultur*: While the work Kedourie discusses is called *Reden an die Deutsche Nation*, (Kroeber & Kluckhorn, 1952), p.24, quote a passage from another work holding that *Cultur* is "*die Übung aller Kräfte auf den Zweck der völligen Freiheit*," (although, like Kant, Fichte means by *Cultur* something more like "the cultivation of the mind" than what anthropologists would mean). Herder uses the term *Volk* (as in *Volkslieder*, a word he coined - (Bluestein, 1963), p.119; see also text to chapter eight, note 187), as well as *Volksgeist*, for something that can probably mean either "culture" or "nation" (in the latter he was followed by Hegel: see (Avineri, 1972), p.16 and (Taylor, 1979) pp. 86-7, 96-100.

[28] On the connection of Bastian to Herder, see (Koepping, 1983), pp.83-6. On Bastian's seminal importance to the development of cultural anthropology, see, (in addition to Koepping, *passim*), (Haddon, 1934), p.64, (Penniman, 1965), pp. 111ff, 219, 238, and (Lowie, 1937), pp. 29ff, 71-3, 105. Lowie (73) reports that Franz Boas was "intimately associated with" Bastian's work, and Penniman that Boas "first introduced the concept of 'pattern' in the description of cultures," so the philosophical history of the notion that cultures form unique and irreductible wholes can be traced in quite a direct line, from Herder, to Bastian, to Boas and his many American students (including Kroeber, Mead, Lowie, and Benedict - a quotation from the latter of whom makes clear the connection of the word "pattern" to the Leibnizean monad: see text to note 32, below). Boas was also the first ethnographer to insist on learning the language of the peoples he studied, rather than relying on translators or pidgin English (Lowie, 1937), 132, thus taking seriously the methodological implications of his theoretical principles.

[29] *ibid*, pp. 43, 83.

entity."[30] On the other hand, the project of nationalism helped, as I noted above, to inspire much comparative linguistics and study of folk literature (indeed, the very word "folklore" and the establishment of societies for its collection came about in this way).[31] Finally, in a symbiosis that has provoked discomfort and self-examination right through the 1970s, anthropologists have been associated throughout their history with the service of those European powers who simultaneously represent one expression of nationalism and have attempted to contain or squelch other such expressions.[32]

It should not surprise us, then, that the indeterminacy we encountered in the concept of "culture" reappears in the concept of "nation." Every nationalist movement has found itself beset by sub—and super-nationalisms: groups, such as the Armenians, the Kurds, the German Czechs or the Muslim Indians, that defy the linguistic, historical or religious unity of a nation, and groups, such as the Pan-Slavs or Pan-Arabs, that would dissolve the nation into a larger whole. Among contemporary Third World states, says Clifford Geertz, "nationalisms within nationalisms" constitute a major threat to the "national identity in whose name the revolution was made."[33] He points out that most "Tamils, Karens, Brahmins, Malays, Sikhs, Ibos, Muslims, Chinese, Nilotes, Bengalis or Ashantis found it a good deal easier to grasp the idea that they were

---

30 Quoted in (Penniman, 1965), p.214.

31 See (Haddon, 1934), p.110, and (Bluestein, 1963).

32 Haddon (in 1934) writes happily of the close relationship between anthropologists and "Colonial Governments," and of the latters' recognition that one needs to understand "the native point-of-view" and "as far as possible, ...build upon what is best and most stable in the native polity" (p.141) He says that the possibility that anthropologists can provide advisory roles in colonial administrations indicates that there is a "great future of immediate practical utility for anthropologists" (p.142). Penniman (1965) notes that James Hunt, the founder of the Anthropological Society (a break-away from the Ethnological Society) in mid-nineteenth century America, was a champion of the cause of the American South and a "firm believer in taking anthropology into politics" (pp.90-1), that Otto Ammon and HS Chamberlain used anthropological arguments derived from Weisman and CL Morgan to show the superiority of the Teutonic race and the advisability of avoiding interclass (and presumably interracial) marriages (p.96), and that James Frazer, more than any other single person, made the European world "aware of the interest and value of studying the peoples of their empires," to the extent that a background in anthropology became desirable or even necessary for those who had any part in the administration of colonies (p.142). He also remarks that "[e]very teacher of anthropology has but to think of his own pupils who are district officers, missionaries, or special investigators all over the world" (p.252). Lowie gives us an idea of the motivations of Gustav Klemm, the coiner (in 1843) of *Cultur* in its anthropological sense, when he says that Klemm hoped and expected "priestly dominion" to be supplanted by "nations" (pp.11-2). He also notes that Henry Maine, the extremely influential author of *Ancient Law* (1861), served in the Indian colonial government (p.49). In reaction to this discomfiting history, Dell Hymes edited a collection in 1972, entitled *Reinventing Anthropology*, devoted to the proposition that "if anthropology did not exist, [it would not] have to be invented[, and] if it were reinvented, [it] would [not] be the anthropology we have now" (p.3). The anthropology we have now, he says (citing Lévi-Strauss), "cannot perhaps escape its history as an expression of a certain period in the discovery, then domination, of the rest of the world by European and North American societies" (p.5).

33 Geertz, "After the Revolution: The Fate of Nationalism in the New States," in (Geertz, 1973), p.237.

not Englishmen than that they were Indians, Burmese, Malayans, Ghanaians, Pakistanis, Nigerians or Sudanese."[34] As Geertz's list of ethnic groups indicates, part of the problem lies in the fact that nations, like cultures, seem unable to decide whether they ought to be religiously, linguistically, racially or historically based. The conflicts between Pan-Arabism and Pan-Islam, between Hindu, Muslim or Sikh "fanatics" and the idea of India, or among Malays, Indians and Chinese in today's Malaysia, demonstrate most dramatically the absence of a definitive criterion for nationhood.

One might suppose, as Herder presumably would have, that this problem could be solved by granting a state to every self-declared national group. Given the economic and military need, however, for a state to attain a certain minimal size, one stark statistic will deal the death-blow to this hope: while up to the sixteenth century the longest list of the world's peoples contained 177 separate groups, an early twentieth century estimate yielded 650 "primitive societies," and a 1931 estimate offered us "12,000 tribes, language-groups, nations, clans and other social divisions."[35] Twelve thousand nation-states is a prospect that would probably give pause even to Herder's contemporaries.

Hence the move, within nationalist movements as well as theoretical studies, to a view of nations as "made" rather than "found." As the revolution approached in most of the Third World, says Geertz, it was assumed that "the nationalists would make the state and the state would make the nation."[36] By appealing to loose and selective readings of the traditions of the dominant ethnic group(s), while instituting a common language and a common body of law, the new states tried to mold their disparate peoples into a political unity, somewhat distinct in its character and history from other such unities in the world, and therefore worthy of the title "nation." Nationalism in this sense "consists in defining, or trying to define, a collective subject to whom the actions of the state can be internally connected, in creating, or trying to create, an experiential 'we' from whose will the activities of government seem spontaneously to flow."[37]

Like found nationalism, made nationalism draws on an analogy between the socio-cultural group and the individual human being. Geertz's remark above about the collective subject bears an uncanny resemblance to Bernard Williams' definition of an individual agent's integrity: "his actions and his decisions ... flow from the projects and attitudes with which he is most closely identified."[38] Geertz makes this comparison explicit in a later article:

---

[34] *ibid*, p.239.
[35] (Hodgen, 1964), pp.211-2.
[36] Geertz, *op. cit.*, p.240.
[37] *ibid.*
[38] Williams, in (Smart and Williams, 1973), pp.116-7.

> [a state's] acts must seem continuous with the selves of those whose state it pretends it is...This is not a mere question of consensus. A man does not have to agree with his government's acts to see himself as embodied in them any more than he has to approve of his own acts to acknowledge that he has, alas, himself performed them. It is a question of immediacy, of experiencing what the state 'does' as proceeding naturally from a familiar and intelligible 'we.'[39]

Unlike the found nationalist, however, what the made nationalist finds fascinating about individual human beings is not their uniqueness, but their indeterminacy and (concomitant) capacity for self-creation. Here the made nationalist can take Hegel as a forebear, although in the context of his own time Hegel belonged in the anti-nationalist camp.[40] The very first definition of "personality" in the *Philosophy of Right* compares individuals and nations but warns that neither one has any personality until it achieves self-knowledge.[41] This is a theme that runs throughout the work. Nations constitute the "ethical substance" of a state, but not until a state has shaped it does that substance attain "a universal and universally valid embodiment in laws, i.e., in determinate thoughts," and the "recognition from others" that comes with such a determinate form.[42] For Hegel, a nation is not naturally or divinely ordained as a "division of the human race" from the beginning of historical time; instead, it develops from "a family, a horde, a clan, a multitude, etc." towards a specific and unified "mind" which it achieves only in the state.[43] By means of a political structure and a body of positive laws, the state forms an explicit and rational order out of the chaotic, non-rational, and conflicting traditions of the families, hordes, clans, etc. that make it up. This account retains hints of a one-nation-one-state view, in its appeal to pre-existing, identifiable, if vague and chaotic, ethical substances, but the decisive move in the creation of a nation is clearly the establishment of the state, and we can easily see that establishment as a way of grafting a decision-procedure onto the competing ethical claims of the various candidates for the status of "culture." That is, in Hegel's picture—and the one favored by many, if not all, modern nationalist states—we settle the conflicts between social norms via positive law (enforced, political, state law, as opposed to "moral" or "natural" law): by fiat, in effect, and that fiat, that body of enforced law, forges a unified social group out of the originally conflicting ones.

---

39 "The Politics of Meaning," in (Geertz, 1973), p.317.

40 See (Kedourie, 1961), note on p.36, (Taylor, 1979), p.117, (Avineri, 1972), pp. 35, 45-6, 69, 115, 240-1, (Hegel, 1971), pp.272-3 ("...it is the one sole aim of the state that a nation should *not* come to existence, to power and action,...[insofar as it is] a shapeless, wild, blind force...,"—which, of course, is precisely the respect in which a Romantic nationalist would want nations to come to power), and (Hegel, 1952), citations in notes 43-45 below and his note on pp.168-9.

41 (Hegel, 1952), p.37 (§35).

42 *ibid*, p.218 (§349).

43 *ibid.*

The advantage of this approach is that it does in fact, in many cases and for many purposes, settle disputes over what should determine a culture. The disadvantage is that positive law seems a most inappropriate medium for the final determination of ethical norms. States inevitably have jurisdiction over more than one reasonable candidate for a cultural group, in this world of 12,000 such groups, and laws tend to be made by means of a compromise among "special interests," which include but are not limited to cultures, rather than as an expression of any one of these group's norms. Furthermore, even in a democracy, legislators but imperfectly represent their constituencies, and an intelligent and benevolent dictator will but imperfectly understand her people's values and how best to implement them. As a result, while positive law does tend to embody serious moral thinking, aware of the importance of the issues with which it deals and sensitive to the values of the people it is to rule, it always constitutes at best a stab at a definitive set of ethical norms. It is usually, and (we believe) should always be, corrigible, and to keep it that way we need to maintain a distinction between culture and nation, or between nation and state, precisely so that we can use our culture/nation to correct our state. We want to keep our legal stab at expressing our values open to later, better attempts to express those values, or attempts at expressing a change in those values, and, if the law is widely inconsonant with its constituencies' norms, we want there to be an ethical option of dissenting from or even disobeying such law: hence the ethical traditions of civil disobedience and revolution. Moreover, precisely because positive law intrinsically entails the use of force, and force may be an ineffective, inappropriate or dangerous way of winning people around to an ethical position, practically every legal system ignores vast areas of ethical life. For all these reasons, while positive law often provides valuable ethical guidance, and forms *an* expression and determinant of most systems having reason to call themselves a "culture," the agent need not, and probably will not want to, regard it as the overriding, the final, arbiter of her culture's ethical beliefs.

An alternative account of made nationhood appeals to education, instead of positive law, as the primary function of the state. In a 1983 book entitled *Nations and Nationalism*, Ernest Gellner argues that our technological age has made it necessary for any "viable political unit" to have an educational pyramid supporting universities at which people can be trained to handle the complexities of contemporary management and engineering.[44] The possibility of such a pyramid, together with the difficulties of our technology itself, in turn requires the existence of an accepted mode of "explicit and reasonably precise communication"[45] among the population which the political unit is to serve. Not a peculiarity of nationalist ideologies, therefore, but the very nature of our

---

44 (Gellner, 1983), p.34.
45 *ibid*, p.33.

times demands that our states establish a certain homogeneity over a population of some minimal size (large enough to support the pyramid). Nationalist ideology merely reflects this need and inspires groups with the passion to try to turn their own language and culture into the dominant one within a given political unit.[46]

Gellner defines the state by a monopoly of legitimate education rather than the traditional monopoly of legitimate violence, and thereby provides a way out of some of the problems we saw when positive law became an ethical decision-procedure. Schools use a wider range of means of persuasion than law does, and can therefore deal with a wider range of issues. Teachers can represent more aspects of a community than can legislators and judges, because they are free to speak as a plurality while law must have a single voice.

But with this return to plurality we lose the decisiveness of positive law, and to Gellner's credit, he does not intend to set up the nation or the state as a moral arbiter. The state performs a pragmatic role, and its unitary education is geared to that role. Some attitudes and norms are bound to come with the scientific instruction it provides, but these may continue to vary from and conflict with one another, and they need not obliterate the norms a child learns from her parents, her religious institutions, her friends, and the books she reads. If a nation is made in Gellner's way, it will carry out programs in pursuit of certain well-defined aims all people tend to agree on (health and physical comfort, for example), not define and refine an entire conception of how to live.

All versions of nationalism, even Gellner's, *can* offer closure to a culturally based ethical theory. We *can* consider what we learn in our schools, as we *can* consider positive law, to be the final word on our ethical norms. "The nation," writes Rupert Emerson, "is today the largest community which, when the chips are down, effectively commands men's loyalty, overriding the claims both of the lesser communities within it and those which cut across it or potentially enfold it within a still greater society ... In this sense the nation can be called a 'terminal community' with the implication that it is for present purposes the effective end of the road for man as a social animal, the endpoint of making solidarity between men."[47] If we want to count one of our social groups as ethically overriding, we have better reason to identify that group as our nation than as any other group, and if want a final word on how to interpret our nation's ethical beliefs, we can most reasonably take positive law or the words of our teachers and textbooks as that final word. But if taking the law or what we learn in school as the last word on ethics seems ridiculous, since neither of these institutions is designed, even in principle, to embody, wholly and precisely, the beliefs of the society(ies) it serves, then perhaps we should question whether we need a cultural decision-procedure in ethics at all. Without such a

46 *ibid*, pp. 39, 46.
47 (Emerson, 1960), pp.95-6.

requirement, we could allow some vagueness and ambiguity in our identification of an ethically foundational community: our agents could admit that they have been raised by several communities at once, and accept that sometimes this may lead them to have conflicting norms on particular issues. In the final section of this chapter, I shall argue that an ethical theory can permit such tension without abandoning either usefulness or truth, and that we can therefore opt, as is plausible, for a pluralistic rather than a monistic model for a culturally based ethic, a model in which cultures overlap and even conflict within many of the individuals they inform.

Moral Dilemmas: A Model for a Plurality of Definitions

I, the author of this book, am, among other things, a Jew, an American, a child of immigrants from Germany, and a nominal British citizen. I have strong attachments to norms derived from the mostly Christian writings in which I was educated, from the political Liberalism common among my friends and relatives, from the Romanticism of the operas my parents love, from the rich law and ritual of the Jewish tradition, and from the elegance and elitism of the British society and literature which I relished as a child. On the whole, these cultures share a great deal with one another (not unreasonably, since their histories have overlapped for many years), but sometimes they conflict, producing in me mixed emotions—as when, looking in India at monuments to the British Empire, I was filled simultaneously with Romantic pride and Liberal shame—or even mixed directives—as when my "Christian" inclinations towards valuing absolute love lead me to believe I should immediately and entirely forgive someone, while my Jewish inclinations towards tempering mercy with justice tell me that unconditional forgiveness is not always respect. On the account this section will recommend, such conflicts need not interfere with my general sense that I am guided by my cultures in my actions, and I therefore need not finally decide which of the cultures is to predominate. My list of cultures, while long, is not indefinitely long; the cultures on the whole cohere; and on the whole I do have a pretty clear sense of which takes precedence over which (Liberal over Romantic, Jewish over Christian, to a lesser extent American over British). That there are hard cases where two of my cultures claim me almost equally means that my ethic is not complete, that my set of action-guiding principles does not guide all my actions. It does not mean that my ethic is incoherent, useless, or undefined.

This account fits what the contemporary literature likes to call "the moral facts." Most people, at least in cultures that have mingled freely with other cultures, can tell a similar story to my own. Most still feel that they are a product of a definite list and mix of cultures. Most have a pretty firm sense of which among their (sets of) norms generally take precedence over which others. And most feel that they encounter hard cases in which they do not know quite what to do, and, in particular, which of their cultures and sets of cultural norms to favor. Indeed, ethical theories claiming completeness by that very fact display a certain implausibility: it seems one of the essential features of ethical life that we run into situations where there is no clear right decision, and where we may not determine what to count even as the *best* decision, if we ever do, until after we have had to take some action in the midst of confusion.

Under the title "moral dilemmas," this subject has received a lot of attention lately. Bernard Williams suggested the inevitability of moral dilemmas in the 1960s, and held that they prove the falsehood of ethical realism.[48] Today most of the leading writers on the topic deny the incompatibility of dilemmas with ethical realism,[49] but agree that dilemmas are indeed inevitable.[50] The reasons they give for this vary. Ruth Marcus and Samuel Guttenplan both trace dilemmas to the limitations of our knowledge, while Philippa Foot sees them as the result of our having an irreducible plurality of virtues and values.[51] Closest to my own position is Alasdair MacIntyre's view that moral dilemmas arise out of our culture's peculiar heritage of a set of incompatible fragments from earlier moral world-views,[52] although I speak of overlapping cultures rather than fragments of culture, and do not restrict this condition to post-Enlightenment Western civilization.

The source of dilemmas is less interesting to me, however, than what kind of a threat they pose to a candidate for a moral system or theory. Do they constitute inconsistencies which we must resolve by means of some fixed decision-procedure, or can we tolerate them and therefore dispense with the various implausible decision-procedures surveyed above? I take it that cultural dilemmas form a subset of moral dilemmas—even within a single culture's norms, dilemmas may arise; indeed, as Marcus has pointed out, dilemmas can arise between actions mandated by a single norm[53]—and that whatever is true for moral dilemmas in general will be true *a fortiori* for specifically cultural ones. The very existence of moral dilemmas to which culture is irrelevant shows that the dilemmas to which our cultural theory leads us are not in themselves a reason to prefer some more traditional ethical theory. On the contrary, they provide a reason in favor of our approach over, for instance, a hard-line Kantianism or utilitarianism that demands a definite answer in every situation.

With this in mind, let us take a cue from Marcus' position on moral dilemmas. Marcus argues that we can define a set of rules as consistent as long

---

48 "Consistency and Realism," in (Williams, 1973), pp.204-5.

49 See Marcus, Foot, and Gowans in (Gowans, 1987), and (Guttenplan, 1979-80).

50 But see Earl Conee, "Against Moral Dilemmas," in (Gowans, 1987).

51 Marcus, "Moral Dilemmas and Consistency," in (Gowans, 1987), p.196, (Guttenplan, 1979-80), pp.75-6, and Foot, "Moral Realism and Moral Dilemma," in (Gowans, 1987), p.268.

52 (MacIntyre, 1981), chapter two.

53 Marcus, *op. cit.*, p.192.

as "there is some possible world in which they are all obeyable in all circumstances in *that* world."[54] As an example she gives the rules for "a silly two-person card game," in which higher cards trump lower ones and black trumps red.[55] Such a game is consistent in that there need not be any situation in which high reds are faced off with low blacks; sometimes, if not always, the game can be played to a conclusion. Inconsistency will only apply to a set of rules inconsistent in *all* possible circumstances, in which case the rules provide "*no* guide to action under any circumstance."[56] According to Marcus, our ethical rules are not inconsistent in this sense, only, like the card game, incomplete: they do not provide a guide to action in every circumstance. Moreover, they are much *more* complete than the card game, and their conflicts inspire us to reflect on them, change them, and reflect on and change those of our institutions helping to create circumstances conducive to moral dilemma.

Upholding a culturally based theory of ethics without being able to determine finally what counts as culture, and what counts as a given agent's culture, yields a set of rules and norms that are incomplete but not inconsistent, in Marcus' terms. The question is not whether there are circumstances in which an agent's various cultures conflict, but whether those situations arise so often as to make our approach practically useless ("silly," like the card game), or rarely enough as to mesh with our ordinary expectations of dilemma in moral life. If cultural conflicts made a cultural account provide significantly less guidance to action than a more traditional alternative, we would have not only pragmatic reason to prefer the alternative, but, given the bond I have insisted on between moral truth and the guidance of action, reason to regard the alternative as closer to the truth. A second question is whether I can offer any parallel to Marcus' suggestion that moral dilemma is a motivation for re-arranging one's actions "in such a way that, if one ought to do x and one ought to do y, then one can do both x and y."[57]

I think the account I have recommended can meet both these challenges. The standard alternatives to the cultural approach to ethics, namely a Kantian or utilitarian theory, demand an answer in too many circumstances and give one in too few. With their single, abstract principles, they present our moral world as if its situations were always capable of solution, while being unable to generate enough specific norms to handle almost any of them. The cultural approach gives us a plethora of specific, action-guiding norms, while ensuring, via the requirement that the norms derive from an interlocking set of beliefs responsible to a society's interests and practices, that those norms on the whole converge on non-dilemmatic directives. Furthermore, as we have seen, the groups with an ethical claim on us do not form an indefinite list. There are

---

54 *ibid*, p.194.
55 *ibid*, p.195.
56 *ibid.*
57 *ibid*, p.200.

severe constraints on what we allow to constitute a moral world-view at all. Minimally, such a view must be 1) articulated in some set of phrases and sentences, 2) capable of informing some educational system, and 3) capable of guiding the activities and discussions of a recognizable social body. When looking for a culture, therefore, agents will turn to traditions of literature and proverbs, religious practices and political institutions, from which most of them can reasonably pick out not more than three or four significantly different groups that might have a strong influence on them. From this much pluralism, individuals are unlikely to be overwhelmed by dilemmas.

The second challenge is more interesting, and it leads us in directions Marcus mentions but wants to resist. Marcus concedes that the fact that agents eventually do choose between their various norms and options is sometimes taken to be "a way in which, given good will, an agent can make explicit the rules under which he acts. It is the way an agent discovers a priority principle under which he orders his actions."[58] She goes on to question this suggestion, however, by means of an example in which one person (EM Forster) would choose his friends over his country while another would choose his country over his friends, but neither thinks the other's position *morally* inferior to his own. Instead, she wants to say, the difference between them is a matter of attitudes (towards friendship and intimacy, on the one hand, loyalty to country and principle on the other), of "the kind of persons they [wish] to be and the kind of lives they [wish] to lead." She does not make clear why these should not be taken as moral considerations, but presumably because in these matters one does not see a "reason for generalizing [one's] own choice to all."[59] I use the word "moral" in a much broader sense, and in that sense considerations about what kind of person one wishes to be and what kind of life one wishes to lead are *pre-eminently* moral considerations.

This leaves us with the very interesting possibility that one may define one's self and way of life *by* the choices that one makes. The agent may discover her own priorities, as well as reveal them to others, by looking at the choices she has made. As applied to my cultural theory, this view suggests that one way the individual agent settles the priority of the various cultures claiming her is by making choices, especially sets or series of choices, aligning her with one culture (or one subset of her cultures) more than with others, or interpreting and re-interpreting the claims of her various cultures so as to make the choices they mandate increasingly compatible. A welcome consequence of this suggestion is that the agent defines her cultural alignment more clearly and more thoughtfully as her life progresses. In this way, she comes to face fewer and fewer cultural dilemmas, although perhaps at no point do they disappear. In this way, also, especially insofar as she harmonizes and re-interprets what she

---

58 *ibid*, p.201.
59 *ibid*.

perceives of her competing cultures, does she arrange her life more and more "in such a way that if [she] ought to do x and...ought to do y, then [she] can do both x and y."

We are left with a picture in which culturally based ethics need not be threatened by the plurality of cultural identifications with which most people find themselves. In case the picture seems a little too neat, I want to add three caveats. The first concerns my rejection, in this chapter, of various candidates for a decision-procedure that would settle the conflicting claims of "cultures" once and for all. I have suggested in this section that the individual agent (perhaps unlike the scientist or institutional representative) does not need such a procedure, but nothing in my theory of world-pictures rules a decision-procedure out as morally or epistemologically unacceptable. The grounds on which I recommend the rejection of claims by religious or nationalist groups to provide such closure are quite independent of my earlier theory: because religious and nationalist groups do not (in fact) themselves avoid internal disagreement, because their means for settling issues seem irrelevant to what we generally consider ethical deliberation as well as to many of our specific ethical norms, and because, for most moderns, at least in the West, religion and nation do not embrace all that we consider our ethically relevant culture. For a group in which religious or nationalist authorities tend to agree amongst themselves, and in which religious or nationalist decisions are of a piece with the members' mode of ethical deliberation, or for an individual who wants to have, and believes she should have, an ethical decision-procedure, or who regards her religion or nation as the sum total of her culture, nothing I have said against the claims of these groups need hold.

Second, I have here ignored the possibility of conversion to a culture in which one was not raised. I do not want to rule that possibility out, of course, and I will consider it in chapter nine, but the discussion here concerns those who are trying to decide among groups and sets of beliefs which already have a claim on them. Unlike the possibility of conversion, this issue inevitably and necessarily arises for all ethical agents. How to understand such decisions is a pre-condition for having any culturally based ethic at all, while conversion has more to do with the specific ethical demand that cultural influence not be allowed to turn into cultural determinism, that a possibility of freedom from the given cultural norms be preserved.

Finally, Marcus' own understanding of how we progressively minimize the dilemmas we face involves an attempt to modify and reconcile our institutions, not merely to come to some kind of re-definition of one's self. The parallel to this, as regards cultural dilemmas, is that we have an impulse not merely to reconcile ourselves to our cultures, but to reconcile the cultures themselves. When in the grip of the notion that our ethical beliefs are *true*, we find the contradictions between the claims of different cultures an offense. Ideally, if ethical claims can be true or false, should not the true ones be consistent, and be perceived as consistent? I suggest that this question motivates the process of cross-cultural judgment and understanding, the process by which each culture—in differing ways—tries to transcend its social and historical limitations. Alasdair MacIntyre suggests, in discussing Sophoclean tragedy, that "[t]here *is* an objective moral order, but our perceptions of it are such that we cannot bring moral truths into complete harmony with each other."[60] People posit an absolute order for ethical claims and ways of life even though that order may in itself be ineffable, and when cultures meet they are often inspired, or forced, to pursue it. I turn in the next chapter to the forms that pursuit has taken in the West.

---

60 (MacIntyre, 1981), p.134.

CHAPTER EIGHT

THE DREAM OF UNIVERSAL RIGHT

Exploration of Universalist Traditions

The tradition of Western ethics itself posits an ethical ideal beyond itself, a universal ethic beyond traditions. That ultimately there is a universal moral order, a just and decent absolute beneath even the most conflicting perceptions of morality, is perhaps an essential dream of every ethic; it certainly belongs deeply to the Western one. The dream may be unattainable, even impossible to formulate adequately, but it remains important to us *as* a dream in any case. Our attempts to grasp and reconcile its various, sometimes conflicting meanings have played a crucial role in shaping both our self-definition, and our perceptions of, and relations with, other cultures.

I shall proceed in this chapter by way of a series of explorations of bits and pieces of our tradition I take to be significant for the understanding of universalism, in influential texts on such subjects as natural law, human rights, the state of nature, and cultural pluralism. Each of these subjects is vast, material for a book or even library and not a mere chapter. My intention is thus not to be comprehensive, but to begin a probe of what I think are five major motivations for cross-cultural judgment as they appear in the Western ethic: a desire for international peace, a desire to help friends visiting or living in foreign places, charity—a concern for the lives and minimal well-being of all people, respect—a concern for the freedom of all people, and perspectivalism—an interest in there being other outlooks from which ours can be criticized and inspired. These motivations do not all entail universalism, which is one of my persistent points in the ensuing stories. My other main point is that they in part conflict, producing a radical split within our tradition, between humanitarianism, which bases itself on charity and is concerned for what people seem (to us) to need, and cultural pluralism, which bases itself on respect and is concerned for what people say (to us) they need. To be more precise, where we ever got the idea that what our British, American and French revolutions called "rights" were universally desirable, on the one hand, and that "ethnocentrism" and cultural chauvinism were cardinal sins, on the other, are philosophical questions we ought to find most perplexing.

That we do find them perplexing is evidenced all over our contemporary world of letters, but it is not so clear that those writing on the subject have worked out exactly what bothers them. Ethnocentrism, for instance, is widely decried, but no-one says just what is wrong with it. The respectable, and ethically sensitive, anthropologist Colin Turnbull writes that crying out "how primitive...how savage...how disgusting" about the despicable practices of the Ik is "typical of the kind of ethno- and ego-centrism from which we never quite escape, however much we try."[1] Why we should want to escape from such a reasonable reaction, and why it should be analogous to the chronic selfishness we call "ego-centrism," he does not say. His colleague Clifford Geertz offers us, more self-consciously, the following stunning citation from a Danish explorer named Helms, on widow-burning in nineteenth century Bali:

> Following the large [tower] of the dead king, came three minor and less gorgeous ones, each containing a young women about to become a sacrifice....[T]he victims of this cruel superstition showed no sign of fear at the terrible doom now so near ... The courage which sustained them in a position so awful was indeed extraordinary, but it was born of the hope of happiness in a future world. From being bondswomen here, they believed they were to become the favourite wives and queens of their late master in another world. They were assured that readiness to follow him to a future world, with cheerfulness and amid pomp and splendour, would please the unseen powers, and induce the great god Siva to admit them without delay to Swerga Surya, the heaven of Indra.
>
> Round the deluded women stood their relatives and friends. Even these did not view the ghastly preparations with dismay, or try to save their unhappy daughters and sisters from the terrible death awaiting them. Their duty was not to save but to act as executioners; for they were entrusted with the last horrible preparations, and finally sent the victims to their doom....
>
> ... With firm and measured steps the victims trod the fatal plank; three times they brought their hands together over their heads, on each of which a small dove was placed, and then, with body erect, they leaped into the flaming sea below, while the doves flew up, symbolizing the escaping spirits.
>
> Two of the women showed, even at the very last, no sign of fear; they looked at each other, to see whether both were prepared, and then, without stopping, took the plunge. The third appeared to hesitate, and to take the leap with less resolution; she faltered for a moment, and then followed, all three disappearing without uttering a sound.
>
> This terrible spectacle did not appear to produce any emotion upon the vast crowd, and the scene closed with barbaric music and firing of guns. It was a sight never to be forgotten by those who witnessed it, and brought to one's heart a strange feeling of thankfulness that one belonged to a civilization which, with all its faults, is merciful, and tends more and more to emancipate women from deception and cruelty. To the British rule it is due that this foul plague of suttee is extirpated in India, and doubtless the Dutch have, ere now, done as much for Bali. Works like these are the credentials by which the Western civilization makes good its right to conquer and humanize barbarous races and to replace ancient civilizations.[2]

In response to this passage, Geertz writes:

> In a twist any true connoisseur of the modern earnestness led in beyond its depth must surely savor, Helms...turns [this ritual], via an outcry against the oppression

---

1 (Turnbull, 1972), p.11.
2 (Geertz, 1983), pp.38-9.

> of women, into an argument for imperialism. It is in extirpating such foul plagues...as this that the West earns its credentials to conquer and transform the East. The English in India, the Dutch in Indonesia...are on the side of mercy and emancipation, against deception and cruelty. In the space of a few paragraphs, we get some of the most thoroughly entrenched tropes of the liberal imagination (an imagination, I'd best confess, I more or less share)—the cultural integrity of 'simpler' peoples, the sacredness of human life, the equality of the sexes, and the coercive character of imperial rule—struck off against one another in a way that can only leave us at least unsettled. To have moved from the magic garden of the dreaming Orient to the white man's burden, Gauguin's world to Kipling's, so rapidly and with such fine logic is but the last imbalancing blow the text delivers. It is not only the Balinese and Helms who seem morally elusive when we finish this remarkable account. So, unless we are willing to settle for a few embroidery mottoes of the eating-people-is-wrong variety, do we.[3]

Notice that, while he confesses to feeling "unsettled" and thrown off balance, Geertz is willing to assume that Helms represents "the modern earnestness led in beyond its depth," and to imply that even here we should continue to regard imperialism as coercive and Kipling as merely an apologist—that we face more a conflict of our values than a sudden insight into why our predecessors justified imperialism in the first place. But these criticisms are a little harsh, for on the whole Geertz strikes exactly the right note. We indeed feel confused, seem "morally elusive" to ourselves, upon reading Helms' account. Today both our attitude towards "simpler" peoples and our attitudes towards human rights have become "entrenched tropes" rather than items of hot dispute and serious reflection; so we have nothing much to say when these tropes get thrown into conflict with one another. (I would add that, by contrast, the nineteenth century Helms has a lot to say—in both the best and the worst sense of that expression—and cite this as an historical example of the familiar receding, by dint of its very familiarity, from the Open of our consciousness.) Certainly, a blanket condemnation of ethnocentrism seems an inadequate response.

On the other hand, there are humanitarians who make one long for blanket condemnations of ethnocentrism. Consider the following letter to *Harper's*, after it ran a careful and thoughtful piece suggesting that Iran's regime in the mid-1980s was not as severe as it had been in the early days of the revolution:

> So John Simpson notes "the role of women in Iran is quite complex." *Chadors* are shorter nowadays, and a few women drive cars and wear makeup. Terrific. Mussolini made the trains run on time, and Hitler reduced unemployment.
>
> Simpson's portrait of Tehran today fits the white-male-journalist tradition that devotes a few paragraphs to half the population—women—then concludes things aren't so bad. Maybe not, for men.
>
> But Iranian women—without access to birth control, abortion, or equal rights—are the unwitting progenitors of the population explosion that Simpson mentions in passing. And the young men dying in a ridiculous and futile war are their sons.

3 *ibid*, pp.43-4.

> One wonders what a woman's view of life in Tehran would be....I suspect a woman's view might include a bit more anger and outrage—and more real truth than Simpson's puff piece.[4]

Presumably this reader's left-liberal clichés about "white-male-journalists" and the like go along with a general support for national self-determination. One wonders how, given the horrors of life in practically every Asian and African state. David Luban, whom I will discuss below, is at least consistent, by making clear that he finds talk of nations and sovereignty utterly irrelevant when it comes to matters of human rights, while Bernard Williams pokes some fun at the very idea that a culture has *per se* a right to survival, or against interference:

> Today all confrontations between cultures must be real confrontations, and the existence of exotic traditional societies presents quite different, and difficult, issues of whether the rest of the world can or should use power to preserve them, like endangered species; anthropological and other field workers find themselves in the role of game wardens.[5]

I think that anthropologists often do wind up looking like game wardens, but we shall see some reasons for them to embrace such a role. At this point, we have found nothing beyond the existence among Westerners of a state of confusion. Why we might presume against interference with cultures, and why we might override that presumption to protect important human rights, we have still to explore.

i. Natural Law

As a universalist ethical system, natural law always turns out to be either implausibly strong or so thin as to fail to provide any action-guiding norms. Either it somehow comes to incorporate notions of human nature peculiar to our specific community, and justifies us in making preposterous demands of the sort that all people ought to be monogamous, democratic, Christian, and properly dressed. Or it is restricted to the minimal conditions for any way of human life to flourish, but then, when we try to use it to ground our own ethic, we quickly lose our justification for all principles except such platitudes as "don't murder" and "keep your promises." In addition, the notions which natural law has claimed as its sources—universal "human nature," "reason," "intuition," "contract," "purpose," etc[6]—are seriously, if not irredeemably, confused. Does it follow that we need to discard natural law altogether, in law and ethics? Not at all.

---

4 Elaine Hopkins, "Letter to the Editor," *Harper's*, March, 1988.

5 (Williams, 1985), p.163.

6 There is a good discussion of putative grounds for natural law in JR Pennock, "Rights, Natural Rights, and Human Rights—A General View," (Pennock & Chapman, 1981), especially pp.10-12.

AP d'Entrèves has shown that natural law, throughout most of its history, served primarily as a weapon against legal positivism or realism, not as a ground for universalist moral theories. Originally a device by which Roman courts settled disputes under non-Roman law codes, its content was read off, first, from Rome's experience with neighboring cultures, and then, in the Middle Ages, from the Roman codes and the Scriptures. As a mode of interpretation, it pushed Roman jurists to seek consistency and common sense in both their own and their neigbors' legal systems; as a theory, in the Middle Ages, it declared that positive law ought not be the highest or final arbiter of right in a community. We have seen in the last chapter, however, that there is ample room to launch such a position without making any appeal to universal principles. A law permitting slavery may be condemned against a literary, or a religious, tradition valuing human equality. The ethics of a community are expressed in and shaped by many institutions in addition to the law. Indeed, we might say that the ethic of our community is rooted in, and expresses, our "nature" as members of that community, our specific nature, our nature—what comes naturally to us—as Westerners or Muslims or Malays. Or we might call our communal standards "natural law" because they arise more or less spontaneously with the forming of any community, as part of the "natural" human tendency to form communities, in contrast to the positive laws we establish and enforce in various self-conscious, highly artificial, and easily changeable ways.

The problem with this picture is that in one of its incarnations, as the source of what we today call "human rights," natural law does indeed make universalistic claims. In the form of the seventeenth and eighteenth century doctrine of "natural rights," natural law served primarily to protect individuals against the growing power of the modern state.[7] There is no need for universal principles to make sense of this polemic: condemning absolute power, and its attendant evils, is perfectly possible entirely within our Western, or even English and French and American, ethical traditions, and it is equally possible within those traditions to make a case for the need to keep a certain realm of the individual's actions free from political interference. But the Enlightenment doctrine of natural rights gave birth to what we now call "human rights," and we do tend to couch talk of these rights, at least, in universalist terms.

Now even this usage may simply betray a mistake. According to Michael Oakeshott, "the hard-won rights of Englishmen in common law crossed the Channel to become the Rights of Man of the Enlightenment."[8] The French looked over at the English, we might say, thought they would like to have the same kind of state, and tried to persuade their countrymen of its feasibility and appropriateness for them by claiming that English political ideas were actually of universal import. Yet this historical account also seems to miss something:

---

7 (d'Entrèves, 1970), chapter four and (Lauterpacht, 1945), chapter three.

8 DM MacKinnon, "Natural Law," in (Butterfield & M. Wight, 1966), pp.82-3.

we feel it is *true* that all human beings are entitled to claim certain things against their states—above all, life, and freedom from degradation.

But how much theory does such a claim demand of us? Earnest attempts to make recognition and protection of human rights a universal demand upon states, rather than merely a part of certain European constitutions, have arisen only after, and in part as a response to, the Nazi regime.[9] The horror of the death camps forms the starting point for many an argument that it is morally intolerable not to have some standard against which such practices can be condemned, whenever and wherever they occur. We can reasonably construe this as a reaction precisely to *such* practices. It is not necessary to assemble the whole apparatus of human rights or natural law theory in order to condemn the Nazis, and indeed attempts at establishing universal recognition for any human rights outside of the right against genocide have been notable for their failure.[10] We may regard the Nazis' methodical program of mass degradation and murder as "obviously" wrong (see section iii). Or we might say that in the case of the Nazis the affront to our specific norms is so deep that if we were to tolerate such behavior, we could not maintain our belief that we ourselves have respect and charity for all human beings: that tolerance in this case would destroy our values as much as intolerance might in other cases. Or we might say that in this case our moral intuitions in favor of tolerating other social systems are simply overridden by our moral intuitions in favor of helping other individual human beings. None of these positions requires that we see our intuitions as deriving from the "nature" of any or all human beings.

Even in its role as a ground for cross-cultural judgment, then, natural law has only recently in its history made a serious claim to apply universally, and it only succeeds in persuading us of that claim in very limited cases, and for reasons that need not help its cause elsewhere. This is not surprising. In its heyday, as a medieval political doctrine, natural law was primarily intended for use within the *Respublica Christiana*, among the heirs to Scriptural, Gospel, and Roman law; it did not tend even as much as the original Roman conception to apply to "outsiders." In principle it did so apply, of course, but that principle only became relevant with the Crusades and the discovery of the Amerindians,

---

9 See (Röling, 1960), p.114. Lauterpacht, who was writing in 1944, begins with Churchill's claim that one of the purposes of the war was "the enthronement of the rights of man," and makes clear that his aim in the book is to insist that this pledge be carried out.

10 In a later book, (Lauterpacht, 1951), pp. 400ff, Lauterpacht discusses the "Universal Declaration of Human Rights" that was actually passed after the war, indicating that it is disappointingly weak and excessively biased towards European and capitalist notions of "right" (given its Eurocentrism, it seems to have been passed by the General Assembly only because it was also unenforceable). Consider the empty and hypocritical way in which it has in fact been used, and the plethora of silly claims that have succeeded in wrapping themselves in the "human rights" banner. Consider also how difficult it was for Jimmy Carter to define just which human rights concerns were serious enough to override other foreign policy interests and commitments (why stick with the Shah, even for a day? why condemn Vietnam for its invasion of Cambodia?), and how easy and reasonable it seemed for his successor to abandon the policy.

and there the doctrine of "invincible ignorance" came in to block the application. As soon, that is, as it became conceivable that the canon lawyers might actually have to treat the natural law as a universal moral principle, enforcing it as they enforced local laws and morals, they developed intricate and powerful ways to distance themselves from their official universalism. Ethical discussion, recognized even these subscribers to a most universalist religious system, must take place as much as possible within the structures and stores of a community of practice.

ii. Francesco de Vitoria

Francesco de Vitoria, a Dominican priest of the sixteenth century who is sometimes considered the true founder of international law,[11] maintains that while we have no right to punish nations for breaches of the natural law (such as theft, fornication, adultery, or homosexuality), we can intervene in their affairs in cases of human sacrifice or cannibalism—"not," he says, "because cannibalism or human sacrifice is against the natural law, but because it injures the innocent."[12] But protecting the innocent from death we would normally consider a prime example of an enforcement of natural law. If it is more fundamental than that, on what basis is it justified? What method of proof is the wise and tolerant priest intending to use, when he draws limits to his toleration?

Vitoria claims, in *On the Indians*, that irrational creatures cannot have dominion,[13] for which he offers the argument that dominion is a right and irrational creatures cannot have a right because they cannot suffer a wrong. Now this seems rather weak, since it is obvious neither that irrational creatures can have no rights nor that they can suffer no wrong,[14] and the latter is certainly no *more* obvious than the former. So Vitoria offers a "proof" for the assumption that irrational creatures cannot suffer a wrong: "he who kept off a wolf or a lion from its prey would not do it a wrong, nor would he who shut a window to prevent the sun from shining in do the sun a wrong. [Else]...he who took away the grass from a stag would commit theft, for he would be taking what belongs to another against the owner's will." And with this he seems satisfied.

As a proof, it is remarkably shoddy work. No step seems to take us further than the last; the argument proceeds instead on the *assumption* that irrational creatures do not have rights, in a series of circles rather than a derivation from a more fundamental principle, or a demonstration that the opposite assumption leads to a contradiction. We have no sense, from this passage, of how Vitoria

11 See Antonio Truyol Serra, commentary on p.53, in (Serra, 1946), James Brown Scott, Editor's Introduction to (Vitoria, 1917), p.5, and (Scott, 1928), especially pp. 37-8, 89.

12 Quoted in (Hamilton, 1963), p.124.

13 (Vitoria, 1917), §20.

14 For an argument that irrational creatures do have rights, see Michael Tooley, "Abortion and Infanticide," in (Cohen *et al*, 1974).

considers rights to be grounded, nor of what he thinks is the general connection between rationality and having a place in the moral order. Yet he shows elsewhere that he is capable of constructing superb and subtle arguments.[15] What, then, is going on here?

I think Vitoria wants us to accept his remarks on stealing from animals as *obvious*, and take their obviousness as a starting point for argument at least as fundamental as any principle of natural law. It is *common sense* that one cannot steal from a cow or hurt the sun; the very ludicrousness of these examples, and the amusement they inspire, testify to their offense to (what we take as) the obvious. We are close, here, to the method of "ordinary language," and, earlier, "common sense" philosophy: foundations need not be logical truths (in *that* sense "self-evident"), transcendental principles, divine proclamations, or the testimony of the senses, but what we in fact most fundamentally take for granted. (And what is that? We may raise many questions about how that can be misjudged, but the defender of common sense will see such questions as just another philosopher's trick, another indulgence in excessive subtlety: it is usually obvious what is obvious.)

If I seem to be drawing too much from one paragraph of poor argument, consider Vitoria's direct appeal to ordinary language a few paragraphs later:

> And although this seems to be a dispute about a name, it is assuredly a highly improper and unusual mode of speech to attribute dominion to things irrational. For we do not ordinarily say that a man has dominion save over that which is placed within his control. For when we have not dominion, we speak thus: '"It is not within my control," "It is not in my power."[16]

Consider, also, Vitoria's discussion, in the introduction to these lectures, of what is fit material for ethical deliberation:

> ...there can be no moral investigation about [matters] which are certainly and notoriously lawful and seemly, or, on the other hand, about those which are certainly and notoriously unlawful and unseemly. For no one can properly raise a question whether we ought to live a temperate and brave and upright life or a wicked and base life, nor whether we ought to commit adultery and perjury, or cherish our parents, and other matters of this kind. Certainly such discussion would not be Christian.[17]

Basing himself on Aristotle's claim that there is no deliberation over the impossible and the necessary (*Ethics* III, 2), Vitoria extends this category to include acts "notoriously" right and wrong. In all three passages we have

---

[15] See, for instance, "seventh" through "nineteenth" (concerning exactly when and why heretics lose their right to property) in (Vitoria, 1917), pp.123-5.

[16] (Vitoria, 1917), p.125.

[17] *ibid*, pp.116-7.

examined, the commonly taken for granted serves as a legitimate, and in the last case the only legitimate, basis for philosophical discussion about ethics.

But what is wrong with discussing adultery and perjury is not that such acts appear obviously wrong to all mankind (Vitoria elsewhere says precisely the opposite), but that they appear obviously wrong to *Christians*. In these cases deliberation and debate would so much shake the ethical foundations of the community in which it took place that it could have no resolution, and would encourage only nihilism. Vitoria is comfortable with the usual style of ethical reflection in his time, in which one moved easily between argument and citations of authority, even though he is dealing with issues concerning people who could not be expected to accept his authorities. Even though he is talking about Amerindians, even though he acknowledges and even insists on their right to be sceptical of Christian teachings,[18] he quotes *Mark* to show that Christians have a right to preach the Gospel universally, and he quotes *I Peter* and *I Timothy* to show that the Indians have an obligation to "receive strangers and foreigners."[19] Clearly his intention is not to convince the Indians themselves of this. Rather, he is telling his Christian audience[20] what *they* can expect or demand of the Indians. "Obviousness" for Vitoria, as for some of the more self-conscious ordinary language philosophers,[21] consists in what is obvious to a community, not what may or may not be obvious to all mankind.

And to his community—as to ours—it is obvious that one should defend innocent human life, and it is obvious that the practices of human sacrifice and cannibalism, however they may be defended or even accepted by the victims, are gross attacks on innocent human life. On the other hand, while Vitoria's listeners would themselves find adultery, theft, bestiality, etc. obviously wrong, they need not find it obvious that *other* peoples would consider them (obviously) wrong, nor that others participating in them either would be innocent, or, if innocent, would suffer injury in a respect as essential as that of life. Thus Vitoria, an arch-opponent of the notion that we can force other peoples to live up to the natural law, drops his strictures against such moral imposition in certain cases not on the basis of a general theory of the natural, but because these exceptions, and these only, seem clearly necessary to him, to the extent that disallowing them would make his own position obviously wrong. A triumph, we might say, of moral intuitions over moral theory.

I would like to bring us up short, at this point, to reflect on the presuppositions of the foregoing discussion, since it serves as a good example of what I mean by "reading our moral tradition" in order to clarify our current

---

18 *ibid*, p.143.

19 *ibid*, p.154.

20 Which includes such luminaries as his Emperor, Charles V: (Hamilton, 1963), p.114 and note 1 on same page.

21 I am thinking in particular of Stanley Cavell.

moral thinking. It serves as a good example precisely because the interpretation of Vitoria as an ordinary language philosopher, and of ordinary language philosophers as akin to the medieval writers who used authorities as a source of evidence, may well seem strained. Suppose I am wrong, then. Suppose Vitoria has a more elaborate theory of innocence somewhere, or cites authorities for religious or political reasons only, or is simply confused. In that case my reading may still be taken as a clarification of our contemporary moral intuitions. For if Vitoria is confused, then his desperate attempt to salvage a right to save people from sacrifice and cannibalism shows that that intuition antedates the secularization and circumscription of ethics of the past two or three centuries, that the extra-ordinary priority we feel should be placed on respect for innocent life was as much and as extra-ordinary a priority for a man who had a much sterner conception of what made life worth living. If I am the confused one, on the other hand, my attempt to read him in this way still shows the extra-ordinary importance of this intuition to *me*, and should that reading have appeal to my readers, even or especially to those who think it ultimately fails, that appeal shows the importance of this intuition to *them*. Similarly, any arguments I have used in the course of this reading, whether they are Vitoria's own or not, will serve, if they so much as appeal to my readers, as partial modes of defense, as rhetoric of persuasion, for the rightness of the intuition I am trying to establish. Whatever Vitoria may be doing by citing authorities, I, in citing him, am staking a claim to what our community in fact takes as foundationally obvious, to the long-held, historically influenced, and variously established, pre-suppositions of our ethical discussion.

iii. "Gross Violations" of Human Rights

It is both poetically and logically fitting to move from a discussion of "obviousness" in Vitoria to the tendency of theoreticians of international law to maintain that humanitarian intervention is only justified when a government commits not merely wrongs but *obvious* wrongs against its own people. The *Vindiciae Contra Tyrannos* allows for one nation to aid indigenous resistance in another nation against "obvious tyranny";[22] Grotius believes sovereigns may intervene against other states in the case of "gross violations of the law of nature and of nations," "manifest and enormous oppressions" against the well-being of subjects;[23] Vattel allows for resistance and intervention "when it is a case of clear and glaring wrongs";[24] and Oppenheim's classical formulation of the right to humanitarian intervention speaks of acts that "shock the conscience of mankind."[25] Grotius, Vattel and Oppenheim, we should note, on the whole

22 Quoted in EC Stowell, "Intervention in International Law," in (Laqueur & Rubin, 1979), p.173.

23 (Grotius, 1901), pp. 247, 249.

24 Quoted in (Lauterpacht, 1945), p.45.

25 Quoted (among many other places) in Ian Brownlie, "Humanitarian Intervention," in (Moore, 1974), p.225.

rather oppose intervention of any kind, and have indeed helped to formulate the notions of state sovereignty and national self-determination that guide international thinking today. Like them, Michael Walzer in our own time has argued forcefully for the rights of people to determine their political structures and destinies out of the "common life" they have made for themselves, and like them he allows an exception when "the dominant forces within a state are engaged in *massive* violation of human rights," when a violation of human rights is "*so terrible* that it makes talk of community or self-determination or 'arduous struggle' seem cynical and irrelevant."[26] A general principle owing much to Vitoria's scepticism about our right to enforce even a universal standard is trumped in cases supposed to be so extreme as to constitute obvious exceptions.

What unites these sources most remarkably is their miserliness with examples or explications of what to count as "obvious," "gross," "clear," or "massive" wrong-doing. Presumably they prefer to appeal to a vague sense of what might produce a palpable effect on the "conscience" shared by all mankind because enunciating a universal principle of right would cut against the independence of communal deliberations. I would like to suggest that, as we saw with Vitoria, what is obvious also depends on communal traditions, rather than on some kind of moral perception all human beings might be supposed to share. The very similarity in rhetoric, the recurrence of an unexplained, vague, adjectival appeal to some sort of "moral sense," indicates that a tradition guides our thinkers themselves, while the few examples of obvious wrongs they do give indicate that *only* a tradition, not a sense, can tell us what we in fact find shocking.

To begin with, take Vattel's elaboration of "clear and glaring wrongs": "when a prince for no apparent reason attempts to take away our life, or deprive us of things without which life would be miserable,...who will question the right to resist him?"[27] We may well feel that, while the second category is too vague to be a minimal condition of universal right, the first at least is a paradigm such condition. But what counts as "no apparent reason"? Can heresy, in an Islamic state, count as sufficiently apparent reason? Reactionary politics, in a socialist state? Attempted overthrow of a democratic government? One could show any of these to be utterly destructive of the quality of life in their respective communities... Similarly, when Walzer elaborates his "terrible" violations of human rights as "cases of enslavement or massacre," we may wonder whether the reduction of peasants to abject and desperate emperor-worshippers under Haile Selassie, or the official and often tyrannical nationalization of means of production by many Communist states, should count as enslavement, and just

[26] Michael Walzer, "The Rights of Political Communities," in (Beitz *et al*, 1985), pp. 181, 192 (my emphases).

[27] Note 40, *loc. cit.*

how many killings, and with what justification or lack of justification, constitute a massacre.

On the other hand, it may seem repulsive even to raise these last questions, because we know exactly what Walzer is referring to: the enslavement and deaths in Hitler's concentration camps. We may also know what Vattel has in mind—political oppression by absolute rulers in the sixteenth and seventeenth centuries—and we certainly know that Vitoria was specifically concerned with human sacrifice and cannibalism. When we ourselves, today, want to accept the notion that certain acts (should) "shock the conscience of mankind," we probably also think of Hitler, and perhaps of human sacrifice and cannibalism. But all this bears out the point that we determine what is obvious against the background of our own community's experience; we take as paradigm cases of obvious wrong the examples to which our tradition of thinking about the subject has responded. From there, perhaps, we judge whether new cases are relevantly similar to the cases of Hitler or human sacrifice or cannibalism. We are hard put to formulate a general principle to determine these cases, however, and the principles we do formulate suffer from a vagueness that opens them to easy distortion at the hands of people with political reasons for such abuse. Thus Hitler's appeal to the tradition of humanitarian intervention to justify his annexation of the Sudetenland; Khrushchev's, when the Soviet Union invaded Hungary in 1956; and Brezhnev's, as the basis of the 1968 invasion of Czechoslovakia. Thus, on the other hand, Carter's unwillingness to accept Vietnam's stated reasons for invading Pol Pot's Cambodia, and the OAU's discomfort with recognizing clear and glaring wrong in Amin's Uganda.[28]

I am not saying, by any means, that there is anything right with massacre and enslavement, or even that they are other than obviously wrong, but that what "obvious" means in this context needs refinement. We sharpen our understanding of it by looking carefully at the tradition of its use, by examining the particulars that have inspired this tradition, and by emphasizing judgment rather than the formulation of principles. I do not think that it is any riskier to ask people to judge whether an act is relevantly similar to Hitler's killings than to ask them whether it falls under a proper definition of "unjustified killing" or "massacre." Indeed, a stress on (concrete) judgment rather than (abstract) definition might help *avoid* the preposterousness of calling Dubcek's Czechoslovakia a humanitarian offense or turning a blind eye to Amin's Uganda. At any rate, granting that there are acts which we both condemn to the point of trying to stop them, and want all people to condemn at least to the point of letting someone else stop them, need not lead us into the mystical and murky realm of a "sense" for the obviously wrong. Such appeals to sentiment have tended to be so vague that they can justify anything and nothing.

[28] On the Sudetenland, see Brownlie, pp.220-1. On Hungary and Czechoslovakia, see (Franck & Rodley, 1973), pp.277-8. On Carter and Vietnam, the OAU and Tanzania's invasion of Uganda, see David Luban, "Just War and Human Rights," in (Beitz *et al*, 1985), pp.205-6.

iv. *Invincible Ignorance: A Model for Incommensurability*

To the claim that we should not hold people to our moral judgments if they in principle do not accept those judgments, a common reaction is to suspect the "in principle," to suggest that no good line can be drawn between being unable to persuade in principle and in fact, and to note that in many cases—with children, insane people, and many criminals—we coerce even where we fail to persuade. And where we coerce, so the argument runs, there we certainly make moral judgments, unless the coercion has a purely pragmatic justification (which is not generally the case with children, insane people, and criminals).

That we do in fact have a tradition of letting our moral judgments have a lesser grip on those we cannot persuade of them can be shown by looking at the doctrine of "invincible ignorance" in medieval and Renaissance Christianity. "Invincible ignorance" refers to a lack of knowledge that the person in question has done everything in her power to overcome—which may be nothing, if no means to overcome the ignorance are available to her. According to venerable church tradition, dating back as far as Aquinas, invincible ignorance serves as a complete excuse for all wrongdoing, including offenses against the natural law and failure to accept Christianity. The former is the more interesting case to us, for it might seem that invincible ignorance of the natural law would be impossible. If natural law is by definition the participation of all human beings, Christian or not, in eternal law, how can anyone plead ignorance of it? Yet Aquinas, the very thinker who defined and gave central emphasis to the notion of natural law, allows for invincible ignorance of it—not, indeed, of its primary principles, but at least of the secondary principles drawn from it.[29]

Aquinas may well get the idea that ignorance cancels out moral responsibility from Aristotle, but the relevant sense of ignorance in Aristotle is quite different. Aristotle says that "a man may be [excused by virtue of] ignoran[ce] of who he is, what he is doing, what or whom he is acting on, and sometimes also what (e.g., what instrument) he is doing it with, and to what end (e.g., he may think his act will conduce to someone's safety), and how he is doing it (e.g., whether gently or violently)."[30] His examples make clear that he does not intend ignorance of the proper kind of moral ends and means to be included under the ignorance that excuses, and he says explicitly that "it is not mistaken purpose that causes involuntary action (it leads rather to wickedness), nor ignorance of the universal (for *that* men are *blamed*)."[31] Aristotle is looking for a general conception of the authorship of acts to which to tie the possibility of blame and praise, more or less akin to our conception of responsibility in

---

29 Aquinas provides at least a strong hint of this position in I-II, Question 94, Article 4 (Aquinas, 1953), pp. 49-50. His faithful follower Vitoria makes it explicit in (Vitoria, 1917), pp.146-7.

30 *Ethics* 1111a3-7.

31 *ibid*, 1110b23.

civil law, rather than for anything as already invested in the moral stance as what we call "culpability." And while he might deem a mentally deficient or deranged person not properly the author of some event if he or she cannot grasp the norms by which that situation should be guided, his general account of agency has nothing much to say about people of ordinary intelligence who do not know, or do not accept, the moral norms we hold to "around here."

So Aquinas adds a new twist to the ethical role of ignorance by making room for people who, without being either extraordinarily stupid or ordinarily mistaken, are yet understandably ignorant of some set of moral beliefs we hold to be true, unpersuaded of what we consider the right way to act. And as the doctrine passes down, through Innocent III's decretal letter *quod super his*, and Innocent IV's and Paulus Vladimirius' commentary on and use of that letter, to Vitoria's *De Indiis* and Grotius' *De Iure Pace ac Belli*, the invincibly ignorant become increasingly identified with those the Church accepts as beyond its persuasive reach—the (some) Jews, the Saracens, and later the Amerindians.[32] Vitoria prohibits forcing the Indians to practice whatever "cannot evidently be proved to them by natural reasoning,"[33] and Grotius—following the Thomist line presumably because of its intrinsic appeal alone, since he is not a Catholic—tells us that "as...in matters of civil law, ignorance is deemed an excuse, so with respect to the law of nature, wherever infirmity of understanding forms an invincible obstruction to the knowledge of its rules, such infirmity may be allowed as a vindication."[34] How ignorance of the supposedly self-evident natural law might be possible he shows by analogy with ignorance in mathematics:

> ...[We must make] an accurate distinction between general principles [of the law of nature], such as the duty of living according to the dictates of reason, and those of a more particular though not less obvious meaning; as the duty of forbearing to take what belongs to another. To which many truths may be added though not quite so easy of apprehension: among which may be named the cruelty of that kind of punishment, which consists in revenge, delighting in the pain of another. This is a method of proof similar to that which occurs in mathematics, the process of which rises from self-evident truths to demonstrations, the latter of which, though not intelligible to all alike, upon due examination obtain assent.[35]

For "invincible ignorance," I want to substitute "incommensurable beliefs." Vitoria and Grotius may suppose that some peoples have a chronic "infirmity of understanding" or an exceptionally "bad and barbarous upbringing,"[36] but

---

32 This history is well discussed in Robert L. Benson, "Medieval Canonistic Origins of the Debate on the Lawfulness of the Spanish Conquest," in (Chiappelli, 1976), volume I. See also (Vitoria, 1917), p.142 and the citations in the next two notes.

33 (Vitoria, 1917), p.138.

34 (Grotius, 1901), p.248.

35 *ibid.*

36 *ibid* and (Vitoria, 1917), pp.127-8.

even they are not entirely comfortable with this notion,[37] and we have today rejected such theories on biological, anthropological, and ethical grounds. We are also sceptical of "nature" and "reason" as a sufficient basis for ethics. Hence where our medieval predecessors say that "natural reasoning" runs out, we may speak of "reasoning natural to us," reasoning beyond which we can see no further appeal, reasoning that displays and delimits our world-picture. As long as the people with whom we are dealing "are not of unsound mind," as long as they have, as Vitoria says the Indians do, "a certain method in their affairs,...definite marriage and magistrates, overlords, laws, workshops,...a system of exchange,"[38] we are not inclined to take rejection of our way of life as a sign of their stupidity; we are inclined instead to see them as simply unpersuadable by us. Not unpersuadable as children, or insane or stubbornly evil people are. Such people will either lack the "certain method in their affairs" or reveal their stubbornness in hostility, refusal to listen, surprisingly bad arguments, etc.—all the symptoms of what was once considered vincible ignorance.[39] But unpersuadable in principle, as some people were once considered ignorant in principle, because our arguments simply cannot reach them. And as invincible resistance to persuasion can hardly make people more culpable for what we consider wrong-doing than would their stupidity, we may rely on the tradition of invincible ignorance to teach ourselves that we have a long entrenched commitment to withholding force, and even moral condemnation, where the possibility of sharing moral beliefs fails.

v. *The Right to Evangelize*

One of the modes of cross-cultural judgment I would like to place in between toleration and force is traditionally represented by missionary activity, which has modern descendants in such forms as cultural exchange programs or the Peace Corps. Vitoria and Grotius, for interestingly different reasons, believe that while non-Christians have every right to maintain their unbelief, we retain a right to try to persuade them otherwise. "War is no argument for the truth of the Christian faith," but war is permissible where legitimate speakers for Christianity are hindered in their work.[40]

---

37 *ibid:* In the very passage in which he speaks of their "bad and barbarous upbringing," Vitoria is primarily concerned to argue that the Indians are "not of unsound mind," that they have "the use of reason," albeit only "according to their kind." See also pp.160-1, where he warns that any claim that the Indians do not have enough intelligence to manage their own affairs should "be put forward without dogmatism and subject also to the limitation that any...interposition be for the welfare and in the interests of the Indians and not merely for the profit of the Spaniards. For this is the respect in which all the danger to soul and salvation lies."

38 *ibid.*

39 "Authors distinguish between simply vincible ignorance, which exists when some, but insufficient, effort is made to be rid of it, and crass or supine ignorance, in which...very little effort, if any at all, is made to dispel it. Ignorance is said to be affected or a studied ignorance when it is directly voluntary; a person prefers to remain in ignorance so as to be free from a sense of obligation." (Nealy, 1967), vol. 7, p.357.

40 (Vitoria, 1917), pp.157-8.

Vitoria's justification for this claim works, again, only given that his audience is already Christian. "Christians have a right to preach and declare the Gospel in barbarian lands," he says,[41] but his prooftexts for this, *Mark* 16:15 and *II Timothy* 2: 9, would convince no barbarians. When he turns from prooftext to argument, he claims that a previously established right to travel and be received as guests *a fortiori* yields a right "to teach the truth to those willing to hear [it]," but that Christianity *is* the truth he does not even try to prove. He is concerned to remind his audience that they have a duty of charity to their pagan neighbors not to let them remain deprived of the benefits of salvation, although he implies that this duty reveals a complementary duty on the neighbors' part to listen, and to accept the teaching when it is properly presented:

> If the Indians, after being asked and admonished to hear the peaceful preachers of religion, refused, they would not be excused of mortal sin. The proof lies in the supposition that they have very grave errors for which they have no probable or demonstrable reasons. Therefore, if any one admonishes them to hear and deliberate upon religious matters, they are bound at least to hear and to enter into consultation. Further, it is needful for their salvation that they believe in Christ and be baptized (*St. Mark*, last ch.), "Whoso believeth," etc. But they can not believe unless they hear (*Romans*, ch. 10). Therefore they are bound to hear, otherwise if they are not bound to hear, they would, without their own fault, be outside the pale of salvation.[42]

None of this would convince the most credulous Indian, but it should help establish, to the Western invaders, that using force to protect Christian preachers is truly an obligation of charity.

Grotius' most significant departure from Vitoria, as regards forceful intervention on behalf of morality and religion, comes in his justification for the right to preach. Rather than basing himself on the truth of Christianity and demanding asymmetric rights for Christians vis-a-vis other religious groups, Grotius argues that Christians have a right to preach because their doctrine is peaceful, and conducive to moral, hence political, virtue, from which it follows that they do not threaten any established political order: "the doctrine of Christ, apart from all the corruptions by the inventions of men, contains nothing hurtful, but everything beneficial to society."[43] More generally, he writes that

> [no]...danger [can] be apprehended from the spreading of doctrines, calculated to inspire greater sanctity of manners, and the purest principles of obedience to lawful sovereigns. Philo has recorded a beautiful saying of Augustus, who observed that the assemblies of the Jews were not Bacchanalian revels, or meetings to disturb the public peace, but schools of virtue.[44]

41 *ibid*, p.156.

42 *ibid*, p.144.

43 (Grotius, 1901), p.253.

44 *ibid.*

By giving an example from Roman relations with Jewry, Grotius makes clear that he intends his criterion for toleration to hold for doctrines other than Christianity. Not so clear is whether this criterion can in fact be satisfactorily applied. Many a state regards heretical doctrines as in themselves destructive of its conception of virtue, and thereby threatening to the body politic as a place for the development of virtue: being Bahai is itself anti-Islamic, according to Iran's current rulers, and therefore incompatible with the flourishing of an Islamic republic. Whether it will satisfy all rulers or not, however, Grotius' intuition as to which doctrines ought to be tolerated fits our own better than Vitoria's does. If we take his work as directed primarily to "Westerners," and not to all mankind, we can accept it as a clarification of our own criteria for missionizing. Grotius not provides us not with an argument that Christianity or anything else is an absolutely correct ethical doctrine that all men ought to hear, but with an account, if there *is* any doctrine we would like to spread, of the terms on which we think we can demand a right to spread it, and the terms on which we think we should let others spread their beliefs.

vi. Humanitarian Intervention

Those advocating humanitarian intervention usually oppose themselves to doctrines of complete non-intervention. Richard Cobden, in 1858, most forcefully put the latter position:

> I am against any interference by the government of any one country in the affairs of another nation, even if it be confined to moral suasion. Nay, I go further, and disapprove of the formation of a society or organization of any kind in England for the purpose of interfering in the internal affairs of other countries. I have always declined to sanction anti-slavery organizations formed for the purpose of agitating the slavery question in the United States.[45]

More mildly, Michael Walzer argues for a presumption against military interference in other countries' politics except where the violation of human rights is "so terrible that it makes talk of...self-determination...seem cynical or irrelevant,"[46] and Thomas Franck and Nigel Rodley argue that international law (as opposed, perhaps, to international morality), should not make exceptions even for such cases.[47] Proponents of humanitarian intervention differ by holding interference of any kind on behalf of individual rights to be either always, or much more widely, legal and moral. The pros and cons of this position depend heavily on pragmatic considerations (the costs of invasion, the need to maintain a balance of power, the possibility that the intervening power will judge wrongly or dishonestly, the possibility that political humiliation or oppression will outweigh the benefits to the invaded), and where ethical

---

45 Quoted in (Vincent, 1974), p.46.
46 Walzer, in (Beitz *et al*, 1985), p.181.
47 (Franck & Rodley, 1973), especially pp.304-5.

questions come in, they mostly concern matters I address in section x. At this point I want to take a brief look not at the justification of the doctrine, but at the way theorists and politicians have actually used it.

I begin with the *Vindiciae Contra Tyrannos*, which couples humanitarian intervention closely with the right to help fellow Christians against persecution: "[interference is justified] in behalf of neighboring peoples who are oppressed on account of adherence to the true religion or by any obvious tyranny."[48] Vitoria similarly gives us a special title to help Christian converts in pagan countries, "based not only on religion, but on human friendship and alliance, inasmuch as the native converts to Christianity have become friends and allies of Christians."[49] Lingering in these writings is the medieval concept known as the *Respublica Christiana*, under which system Christians felt an obligation to other Christians everywhere, regardless of temporal lords. It has indeed been argued that international law developed under Grotius and his successors precisely in order to create "a surrogate for the religious community, which had been the foundation of political community in the medieval period."[50] For a long time, the international community that resulted, insofar as it existed at all, was merely a secularized version of the old religious community, explicitly "invoking Christianity as a basis of [its] unity" until the Ottoman Empire was admitted to the Concert of Europe in 1856.[51]

And in almost every one of the major cases in which humanitarian intervention was invoked in the nineteenth century, Christian powers were coming to the defense of their own against the wrongdoing of infidels. The first such case concerns the 1827 Greek struggle for independence against the Turks, which Wheaton, a standard source for international law, justifies as the "interference of the Christian powers of Europe in favour of the Greeks, who, after enduring ages of cruel oppression, had shaken off the Ottoman yoke."[52] Then, in 1860, the European powers won the reluctant consent of the Ottomans to defend the Lebanese Maronites against an attack by the Druze. Ian Brownlie, on the whole a staunch opponent of humanitarian intervention, considers this one of the few cases in in which it might have been legitimate, while Franck and Rodley point out that even here the situation was hardly clear-cut: the Maronites had been planning a similar onslaught on the Druze for months, encouraging their followers with the claim that "their endeavor to attain undisputed possession of the Lebanon would be warmly countenanced by the Powers of Christendom."[53] Finally, Russia intervened against Turkey in 1877-8 on the purported grounds of the "outrageous persecution" of the Christians

---

48 Note 38, *loc. cit.*
49 (Vitoria, 1917), p.158.
50 See (Hehir, 1974).
51 (Nardin, 1983), p.67.
52 Quoted in (Moore, 1974), p.234.
53 (Franck & Rodley, 1973), p.282.

in the Balkans, and was joined by others against the same foe in Macedonia in 1903. The only major exception to this pattern in the nineteenth century is the American invasion of Cuba in 1898, which Brownlie, at least, does not consider a real case of humanitarian intervention.[54] Quite as striking is the absence of even the mention of such intervention, by European and American leaders, during the pogroms against Jews in nineteenth century Russia.[55]

The history of its actual use would make no difference to the principle if there were at least a consistency as to when the world's leaders claim a right to intervention, but the invocation of the doctrine by so many powers on false or minor grounds (Germany on behalf of the Sudetenland, the Soviet Union on behalf of Hungary, the United States on behalf of Cuba in 1961 and the Dominican Republic in 1965), together with their loud silence during tremendous persecutions of Armenians, Jews, Biafrans, and Indonesian Communists (1965), has turned it into a mockery. As a piece of law and practice, it richly deserves that status, but what about as a moral ideal? Well, one might say that it remains an ideal but the vagaries of politics make it impossible to realize, or one may say that those vagaries rob the ideal of any moral (which at least in part means "action-guiding") status at all. Or, and this is the course I recommend, one may accept the fact that we only intervene to help our friends—and even then usually when the friends and their persecutors are within our geopolitical reach (hence India on behalf of East Pakistan [1971], Vietnam on behalf of the Cambodians [1979], and Tanzania on behalf of the Ugandans [1979])—and build that fact into the doctrine. We may read Vitoria's remarks about helping friends into the very meaning of "humanitarian intervention," into what it ought to mean, or can only mean.

There is even a traditional ethical justification for this reading. Moralists have long drawn a distinction between perfect and imperfect duties. Perfect duties are so-called because they can be completely fulfilled: we know when they devolve on us, to whom we owe them, and precisely what we owe. Thus keeping a promise or contract is normally a perfect duty, and we have a perfect duty, to each person, not to lie. Imperfect duties we owe to everyone and no-one, and can never completely fulfill. Charity is the best example, but one could add general benevolence or supporting others in distress. To the latter we may assimilate the concern for everyone's human rights. Now, just as supporting others in distress, for all its imperfection, devolves on us more in some situations than others—when we are the siblings, parents, children, lovers, friends, or teachers of the person in distress or the person causing distress, when the person is in particularly acute distress, when we are nearby, or are specially equipped to help (with CPR, legal skills, a gift for certain kinds of talk)—so our duty to defend the rights of others devolves on us more in some situations, and quite

---

54 Ian Brownlie, in (Moore, 1974), pp.220-1.
55 (Franck & Rodley, 1973), pp.290-1.

analogous ones, than others: when they are our allies or oppressed by our allies, when the violation is particularly egregious, and when we can help more easily than others can.

On this account, we need not be embarrassed to admit that the limitations on charity characteristic of the *Respublica Christiana* and the nineteenth century international community continues to some extent down to our own day. Since 1856 we may have stopped calling on "Christian" unity, but for a long while we did tie international law to the world of "civilized" states.[56] John Stuart Mill explicitly held that international law could not apply in our relations with "barbaric" peoples, because they would not understand it.[57] The phrase "law common to civilized states" served as a definition of international law into the twentieth century, and the Statute of the International Court of Justice still lists it "among the sources of international law it recognizes."[58] Since 1943, the phrase "peace-loving nations" has come to describe legitimate members of the international community,[59] but the self-righteous contexts in which it is used, and the odd implication that some nations are ruled solely by violent ("primitive"?) passions, give "peace-loving" an air of being a euphemism for "civilized." Contemporary lawyers argue that we should apply our standards even when dealing with the uncivilized,[60] and define "civilized" so that it becomes virtually identical with the acceptance of international legal norms. The very survival of the terminology, however, reveals that talk of human rights occurs more readily among, and applies more readily to, a limited, if large, group of people, than among and to everyone, everywhere, in every situation.

vii. Double Standards: From Ius Naturale *to* Ius Gentium

Jews draw a sharp distinction between the obligations incumbent on fellow Jews and the obligations incumbent on non-Jews. Fellow Jews must keep 613 commandments, from observing the Sabbath to giving charity, while non-Jews need only follow the "seven commandments of the children of Noah": to establish courts of justice, and to avoid blasphemy, idolatry, incest, murder, robbery and eating flesh cut from a living animal.[61] Muslims demand that non-Muslims who live in their lands 1) avow monotheism, 2) not harm a Muslim, or offend against Muslim practices or interests, 3) not intermarry with Muslims, and 4) not practice usury.[62] The imagined world ruler in Buddhist thought would demand of all human beings only the five moral precepts of the Buddhist layman: 1) to "slay no living thing," 2) not to "take that which has not been

---

56 See (Nardin, 1983), p. 67, (Röling, 1960), pp. 17-55, (Bull, 1977), p.39.

57 (Röling, 1960), pp.28-9.

58 (Bull, 1977), p.39. But Bull also indicates that in practice this piece of the Statute may no longer be invoked.

59 (Röling, 1960), p.45.

60 (Greenspan, 1959), pp. 30-31.

61 (Hertz, 1972), p.33 (on Genesis IX:7).

62 (Khadduri, 1955), pp.165-6.

given," 3) to act rightly "touching bodily desires," 4) to "speak no lie," and 5) to "drink no maddening drink."[63] And Max Gluckman reports that the Lozi tribe in Southern Africa distinguish between their specific laws and more general "laws of humankind."[64]

We may call each of these distinctions a "double standard," if we like, the people concerned demanding and expecting less of those outside their communities than they do of themselves. Double standards can of course bring contempt for the outsiders, but by limiting a group's demands enough that outsiders can reasonably accept them without renouncing their own way of life, such divisions can also make co-existence between cultures easier than do single sets of principles. Our Western interest in the essential equality of all individuals inclines us to reject double standards as hypocritical or demeaning, but we then wind up having either to impose our entire ethic on unwilling peoples or to refrain from enforcing any ethical principles, and ethically justifying any use of force. Yet we too have worthy traditions of "double standards," notably the distinction between the natural law supposedly underlying all ethics and that part of the natural law shared by all nations—the *ius gentium*.[65] What constitutes the *ius gentium* is unclear, although from Vitoria on it seems to have included a respect for property and contract, some principles of war and peace, and some minimal "human rights," but it could include all principles that we find peoples actually sharing, all principles we consider necessary for peace, and/or all principles we cannot bring ourselves to refrain from enforcing. Along such lines, Peter Berger, in an article called "Are Human Rights Universal?", has suggested that we regard as universal rights to life and against terror, enslavement, mass expulsion, and the separation of families, not the "specifically Western values of [civil] liberty and [economic] equality."[66] The advantage of couching our demands for others in an explicit double standard is that we can recognize them as, like the oddly assorted demands of the Jews, Muslims, Buddhists, etc., at least in part an expression of ethical norms (intuitions) that are simply very important to us, not a rational consequence of some universally evident principle. The advantage of moving from a *ius naturale* to a *ius gentium* model of cross-cultural judgments is that we can place the need to seek actual consensus among peoples, however arbitrary, above the need to determine rational guidelines for action. We are more humble when we talk about a *ius gentium*, less prone to

---

[63] (Ghoshal, 1959), p.778.

[64] (Gluckman, 1967), p.207.

[65] It is said to be Vitoria who first separated off the *ius gentium* as a special law for the relations among groups of human beings. See (Serra, 1946), p.53, on Vitoria's substitution of *gentes* for *homines* in quoting Gaius definition of the *ius gentium*, and contrast the discussion of the *ius gentium* in Aquinas, I-II, Quesion 95, Article 4, and II-II, Question 97, Article 3, (Aquinas, 1953), pp. 62-4, 100-2.

[66] (Berger, 1979), pp.18-9.

the philosopher's error of assuming that one can ensure agreement with people by concocting arguments to which they "must" assent.

All the same, we probably cannot hold fast to a double standard that we consider purely arbitrary, and other peoples usually have some rationale for the distinctions they draw of this kind. Jews consider themselves to be a kingdom of priests,[67] hence to have, like priests, more obligations than other people; Muslims (like early theorists of the *ius gentium*) regard the laws concerning the acceptable non-Muslim (*dhimmi*) as largely provisional, designed to establish good enough diplomatic and economic relations with other peoples that the Muslim nation can flourish and spread its one, true message over the whole world.[68] We may want to justify our double standard with something like the Muslim pragmatism, or we may appeal to the distinction between those with whom we do and those with whom we do not share modes of evidence: we have one standard for people we can persuade and another, more minimal standard for those we cannot persuade.

viii. Consensus

In his article on human rights, Berger begins by indicating that he wants to make a case for "some universally valid standard of morality to which we can appeal" when judging other cultures, but goes on to argue for this by claiming that, as regards certain ethical matters, "we can call upon a *consensus* far wider than that of Western civilization."[69] He seems unaware that he has moved away from universality, perhaps because he assumes, as have many other writers (including Vitoria), that "universal consent is the voice of nature,"[70] that one can infer from the explicit consent of "nearly all nations"[71] to an implicit consensus of all nations. One cannot, however: inductive generalization does not apply to ethical beliefs, at least not as a reason why the exceptions to the generalization should change their mind. For we are establishing not an empirical fact—*that* we do only where there already exists agreement in interest and method—but a consensus, and consensus pre-supposes free choice, hence the possibility of dissent. Berger is therefore shifting his ground, but I welcome the shift, since consensus provides a richer and more appropriate basis for ethical appeals than do supposedly universal principles.

We saw in the previous section that many important ethical systems make provisions for a limited realm in which they expect that others can and will share

[67] Exodus XIX:6. See (Hertz, 1972) on this verse (pp.291-2), on Amos III:2 (p.153), and on Deuteronomy X:17 (p.789).

[68] (Khadduri, 1955), pp. 52, 162-6.

[69] (Berger, 1979), p.9. FSC Northrop makes a similar argument in (Northrop, 1952), chapter 14.

[70] Cicero, quoted in (Lauterpacht, 1950), p.99.

[71] Isidore of Seville, cited by Aquinas in discussing the *ius gentium* (I-II, Question 95, Article 4, Objection 1 [p.62]). Compare also Vitoria, on the binding force of the opinion of "the greater part of the whole world" (Vitoria, 1917), p.153.

their ethic. Berger makes the somewhat stronger claim that "all the major world cultures" uphold the ideal of having equal concern for the life and dignity of every human being. Buddhism, he tells us, "has as its highest moral tenet the 'respect for all sentient beings.'" The "Chinese [presumably Confucianist] tradition...holds, among other things, that government should be 'human-hearted' and that 'filial piety' is one of the highest human goods." And in Islam "every call to prayer...begins with an invocation of God..., whose nature is to be compassionate..., and who commands men to be compassionate also."[72] Hence we can condemn Cambodian atrocities in Buddhist terms, Maoist ones in "Chinese" terms, and Muslim "acts of cruelty"[73] in the name of Islam.

This general approach seems right, but I find the particular inferences again much too fast. From "respect for all sentient beings," "human-heartedness," or "compassion," there may yet be room for atrocities if 1) the victims are not considered sentient, human, or the kind of human deserving of or needing compassion, 2) death, torture, expulsion, or slavery is considered to be for the victims' good, a high mode of respect, or a form of compassionate treatment, or 3) death, torture, expulsion, or slavery is considered a regrettable necessity, an unavoidable violation of respect and compassion in the service of some higher or more final good. To argue against these moves in particular cases, we would need to know a lot more than Berger has told us about the Buddhist, Confucian, or Muslim traditions, as well as about how those traditions fare today among those we take to be their adherents.

But getting dragged into the detail of the other culture is exactly the advantage of Berger's approach. We then have to make our case from *inside*, where we can argue from a multitude of specific examples and argumentative strategies rather than from a set of principles too thin for significant inferences; where the more we argue the more we display, and probably develop, a substantial and not merely abstract respect for the other people; where our lack of familiarity opens us to a constant risk of refutation by the others and thereby removes from us the air, and perhaps the intention, of trying to impose something. Concretely, we need to study the other culture's language, religion, literature, political structure, and history, and that we wind up with such a need is in itself a reason to move from universalism to the active search for consensus.

I want to stress this point, as a mark in favor of the entire ethical approach I am advocating. As in science the entailment of a true and otherwise unexplained particular fact is a mark of a whole theory's value, so in ethics the entailment of a valuable and otherwise unjustifiable intuition gives us reason to adopt a general principle. If, therefore, a culturally based approach to ethics has as a consequence the necessity—not the easily overriden or ignored pragmatic value—of persuading other cultures in their own terms, and via

---

72 (Berger, 1979), pp.9-10.

73 *ibid.*

intense study of and immersion in those terms, it by that token alone has an advantage over universalism.

But what happens if (when) we utterly fail to persuade in the others' terms, if there simply is no place in Islam for compassion towards Muslim heretics, if we encounter a tribe that consistently and devoutly believes it has a right to eat foreigners? Well, we cannot expect philosophy to rule out all such cases or to provide comfortable answers to them; reflection misleads when it erases all actual difficulties. We *hope* to find a wide consensus on fundamental human respect, but we may even prefer that the consensus, where found, is truly willed, truly embedded in people's interests, and not merely a matter of common sense, an inherited human trait, or a conclusion entailed by reason. In such rare, extreme exceptions to this consensus as the Nazis, *I* would be willing to write off the people concerned as sick or evil, and use force to suppress them. If I were to meet the consistent and devout cannibals, on the other hand, I would probably first try to suggest to them that our way of life is more attractive than theirs, even to the extent of showing off our technological achievements. If I succeeded in enticing them to our ethic, at least I would know what I had done, that I had not merely argued but exhorted, and tried to bring about conversion. (If I wanted, I could then try to "make up" for such murky behavior by confessing to them, or encouraging them to do serious reflection, after they had converted, or I could simply accept a necessary but irremovable burden on my conscience.) Others might choose harsher tactics with the cannibals or less harsh ones with the Nazis—I move to the first person here because the possibility of facing the end of universal consensus on such fundamental matters also brings us to the edge of our local consensus about actions and beliefs—but what no-one could honestly do is simply make use of universally acceptable modes of persuasion in the service of a universally valid truth. Again, the recognition that consensus on fundamentals may not always hold, and of the moral ambiguity that awaits us where it fails, are consequences of the culturally based moral view that I think recommend it over universalism. They are consequences that recommend Berger's shift from principles to consensus and push us to take that shift more seriously than he does, to acknowledge that we seek thicker consensus than he has mentioned, and that the very embarkation on a search for it pre-supposes that we may not succeed.

ix. Peace

One clear object of inter-cultural (inter-national) judgments is the establishment of peace, and that aim not only diverges from, but may conflict with the establishment of a universal morality. This has not always been obvious. Leibniz devoted much of his life to reconciling the churches and determining universal principles of justice, as a basis for "la Paix perpetuelle en Europe."[74]

---

[74] (Schrecker, 1946), p.496.

Grotius dedicated his treatise on international law to peace between the churches as well as the nations, and Kant felt that "perpetual peace" would come only if all nations observed certain principles of justice, including the institution of republican governments.[75]

But peace is made between enemies, not friends,[76] and it may entail the submersion or compromise of some beliefs dear to the reconciling parties. We *may* make peace by resolving disagreement, but we may also make peace by agreeing to disagree, and we can live in peace even without agreeing to disagree as long as our differences are not matters we must fight for. By contrast, insistence on seeing our ethic as universal has frequently made peace impossible—sometimes rightly so, as in cases of gross human rights violations.

On the whole, the search for peace should therefore also incline us toward a double standard, a set of minimal conditions to which we can expect assent from others. It is probably the least universalist of our motivations for cross-cultural judgment. Writing in connection with the development of a philosophy for UNESCO, Richard McKeon noted that the purpose of the organization was to find ideas conducing towards "the maintenance of peace" and recommended that this be done "not by seeking principles on which action can be based, but by seeking agreement concerning actions based on different principles."[77] People might agree on common courses of action, he pointed out, while maintaining quite different reasons for those actions.[78] The founders of UNESCO, however, set its goal as "the intellectual and moral solidarity of mankind."[79] A vain hope, we might say, but even if it is not, and even if we grant its attractiveness, it is importantly a *different* hope from that of peace, and not at all, *pace* the founders of UNESCO, the only way to peace.

x. *Perspectivalism and Toleration*

Cultural relativism has served, as Eliseo Vivas puts it, "to defend nonliterates from the well-meaning, but often catastrophic, meddling of missionaries and the ruthless exploitation of imperialists,"[80] but do we need to condemn anything more than method here? Why should we have a *principle* of preserving, or even tolerating, the ways of life of other cultures?

Vivas describes well what is wrong with the way we (usually) have interfered with other cultures:

---

75 See (Schwarz, 1962).

76 Pierre Mendes-France, Philip Klutznick, and Nahum Goldman began their call for peace between Israel and her Arab neighbors, in the summer of 1982, with the words, "Peace need not be made between friends, but between enemies who have struggled and suffered."

77 (McKeon, 1948), pp.573-4, 578.

78 *ibid*, pp.575-6.

79 *ibid*, p.574.

80 (Vivas, 1961), p.65.

> Faced with the results of missionary meddling with the mores of a people, or with imperialistic exploit-ation, the anthropologist reacts, and his reaction is not only justified, but is indicative of the goodness of his heart. Here are peoples who ... have learned the hard way how to master nature for their own ends and are at least living a life of relative happiness and dignity in terms of their mores. A few years of meddling or of exploitation, and they become a pathetic lot. They lose their skills. Disorganization sets in. Their nakedness is covered—with ugly garments. They lose the urge to toil and they become beggars. In some cases they are destroyed not by somatic illnesses imported from the white world, but by something more insidious, moral illness, for somehow they lose their morale and their will to live. ... True, in some cases cannibalism is abolished by their exploiting masters, and in many cases modern medicine helps them. But what their "benefactors" do not, cannot, see is that [in the process the] ... people lose their identity and their dignity.[81]

Even if we overlook the slave trade, the theft of resources, the massacres and expulsions, and even if the practices we have changed are horrific or self-destructive, our meddling with other cultures, as powerful outsiders, leaves their members without the pride, and ability to guide themselves, that they would have if they had worked out of their own traditions. The result is demoralization, with former leaders impotent, parents humiliated in front of their children, and children growing up insecure and angry. From such conditions come, often and perhaps inevitably, social and economic deterioration.

It follows that we should beware even of well-intentioned help, and of challenging even practices like cannibalism, but it does not follow that any culture has in principle a right to our respect. We may frequently interfere on insufficient information, or in crude and insensitive ways, but in principle there is surely nothing so far to indicate that we ever ought to put the rights of cultures over the rights of individuals, or define the rights of individuals other than we ordinarily do in our own culture—to adequate food, shelter, health care, education, etc. If we should not cause social deterioration, and if meddling with pieces of a culture tends to do that, then perhaps we should take a more radically *anti*-cultural and *anti*-traditional approach. We might take away the children of a culture we dislike and raise them in our schools, or supply the members of the culture with a complete alternative education and set of values (a Christian one, perhaps, or a socialist one). Then the people may, in a generation or so, forget their past entirely and find their way happily around a replica of Western institutions, grounded in Western texts. Is it merely inconvenience that prevents us from trying to do this in Iran, say, or the developing nations of Africa?

As a formal doctrine, cultural relativism holds that it is in principle good for cultures to maintain their own ways, or at least that it is in principle wrong

---

81 *ibid*, p.66.

82 (Williams, 1985), p.159, and (Williams, 1981), chapter three.

for us to try to stop them. Bernard Williams is right that this is itself a universalist ethic,[82] rather than a mere corollary to an attack on ethical absolutism. He is wrong, however, to think that it has no support other than that attack. In fact it grows out of deep strands in our ethical tradition, of demands that we inculcate humility in ourselves as well as demands that we show others respect. (When we seek the well-being of all individuals, the good as we construe it ("what's good for them," as we say), then we are pursuing charity; we pursue universal charity, and sometimes we think we should universally pursue it. When we seek the freedom of all individuals, distancing ourselves from them enough to let them define what they construe as good (and for that they may (have to?) appeal to their culture), then we are pursuing respect; we pursue universal respect, and sometimes we think we should universally pursue it. But it does not always cohere with charity.)

The premises that properly come between relativism and universal toleration can best be found, I shall argue in this section, by looking at certain developments of Leibniz's ideas. Leibniz has been called the source of cultural pluralism in its modern form.[83] Henry Allison describes him as espousing "perspectivalism" and, through Lessing, founding "a relativistic...conception of religious truth."[84] We do not usually think of Leibniz's philosophy, as opposed to his political work, in terms of religious questions at all, much less cultural ones, but Allison shows convincingly how deeply Leibniz's religious views are rooted in his philosophy, and the step from religion to culture (as I have argued in chapter seven) is not a large one.

Let us begin with the meaning of "perspectivalism" in this context. Like Spinoza—and Cusanus, and many earlier figures, from Augustine to Eckhart and Maimonides—Leibniz takes the infinity of God and finitude of all other mental beings to entail that God is in some sense unknowable and the beings are to some extent confused. That finite monads are confused, that their finitude constitutes their confusion, that a way of putting this is to say they have a perspective and perspectival views are by that very characteristic inadequate, are all traditional beliefs. Leibniz adds that the monads are *essentially* perspectives, defined specifically by the limitations that distinguish them from God, but even this can be found in Spinoza.[85] Where he claims the tradition for his own is in drawing the conclusion, from the monads' irreducibility, that they cannot interact with, hence have direct or complete knowledge of, *each other*, and in taking the principle of sufficient reason to mean that they must all differ from one another. From windowlessness will come incommensurability between peoples; from variety will come the claim that

---

83 (Kallen, 1956), pp.48-51.

84 (Allison, 1966), pp. 130-1, viii.

85 See, for instance, Cor.Pr.10,II: "...the essence of man...must therefore (Pr.15, I) be...an affection or mode (Cor.Pr.25, I) which expresses the nature of God in a definite and determinate way." (Spinoza, 1982), p.69.

each people has something different to contribute to the world. But first we must move from monads to peoples, and from the fact of irreducible difference to why that fact might be valuable.

Leibniz himself opens up the possibility that monads might include entities other than individual souls. He describes the monad as a simple, a process of perception, a set of relations among all the things of the universe, and an expression of those relations[86]—but *as simple* it must be all these things at once. Hence its perception is irreducible (simple); its relations consist in perceiving, and its perceiving in having such relations; "perceiving" and "expressing" are identical; and the particular way the monad expresses/perceives the universe is unique and constitutes its uniqueness: "...[A]s the same city regarded from different sides appears entirely different,...so...there are a similar infinite number of universes which are, nevertheless, only the aspects of a single one as seen from the special point of view of each monad."[87]

From the expression of a set of relations it becomes much easier to move to culture than from the individual human soul. Holistic views of thought take sets of interlocking beliefs about (relations among things in) the world to be fundamental and irreducible, and some holistic views—certainly Kuhn's, Feyerabend's, Rorty's, and to a lesser extent my own—take these sets to differ irreducibly. All one needs to add in order to get cultural pluralism is that these interlocking beliefs are shaped by and shape, are expressed by and express, social institutions and relationships. Leibniz himself indicates that each religious sect functions like a monad, as "a confused expression of the ultimate truth,... consequently contain[ing] a relative truth,...[and as] merely one among a number of possible perspectives,...wrong [only] in denying the validity of opposing standpoints."[88] He also moves tentatively towards taking philosophical standpoints as monads, by trying to find a kernel of truth in every position with which he disagrees. "This tendency to find a measure of truth in diverse standpoints," says Allison, "serves, more than anything else, to distinguish his philosophy from that of such rationalists as Descartes, Spinoza, and Wolff, and...is grounded in his deepest philosophical insight—the universal harmony [of all perspectives]."[89] Lessing more fully carries out the modelling of religions on monads, Herder makes the shift to cultures, and both, like their successor Hegel, continue the work of seeking truth in all positions.

Now why might one monad need to respect another simply because the two are different? In the first place, I think Leibniz would see all monads as having

---

86 "Now this interconnection, relationship, or this adaptation of all things to each particular one, and of each one to all the rest, brings it about that every simple substance has relations which express all the others and that it is consequently a perpetual living mirror of the universe." Leibniz, "Monadology," in (Leibniz, 1974), §56. See also §§1,14.

87 *ibid*, §57.

88 Allison, 1966), p.130.

89 *ibid*, p.128.

a desire for knowledge, for truth. The very desire to exist (*conatus*) can be construed as a desire to know ("participate in"?) truth, in a monistic system, for which existence and truth must ultimately be identical, and an idealistic system, for which thinking entities are ultimately the only reality. In the second place, while Leibniz's principle of variety demands that each perspective differ from the others, his principle of sufficient reason demands that these differences be for the good, hence for the revelation of truth ("truth" and "good" must, once again, be identical). It follows that each perspective knows that the others contain truths it does not, and, by our first point, desires to know those truths. Finally, speculative and practical reason, philosophy and ethics, are but two faces of the same coin for Leibniz[90] (as for Spinoza), so the desire for truth should have an ethical counterpart. If we understand a desire for another perspective's truth as a desire to be taught by that perspective, we presuppose the existence and independent action of that perspective; if we understand the desire for another perspective's truth as the desire—in a world of eternal but windowless, entirely independent entities—simply to know what that other perspective represents, then that desire corresponds directly to the desire that the other perspective exist. In either case, the practical side of seeking truth seems to be respect.

With this, we have the materials to construct an argument from perspectivalism to toleration that neither denies the existence of an absolute truth nor contradicts itself by basing our need to respect others' differences on *their* conception of the good, or on a principle beyond all perspectives. According to this argument, we can continue to follow our own "internal principle," as Leibniz insists that every monad must.[91] We merely have to recognize that respect for others must, for each of us, be part of that internal principle. The argument runs as follows:

> 1) All human beings [and/or all cultures] are and represent limited perspectives on an absolute truth.
> 2) Each of these perspectives possesses some truth that the others lack and lacks some truth that they possess.
> 3) Each perspective, since it tries to express the whole, seeks the truths that it lacks
>
> ---
>
> Therefore, 4) each perspective must desire, minimally, the independent existence of the other ones.
> 5) The desire that something exist independently is respect.
>
> ---
>
> Therefore, 6) each perspective fundamentally must respect the others, and if it does not, it is to that extent confused.

---

90 See (Schrecker, 1946), p.489.
91 Monadology, §11. Compare also "Discourses," §XIII, also in (Leibniz, 1974).

This argument has two major problems: an equivocation over whether we actually learn truths from, or merely desire the existence of, other perspectives, and the question of why we ought to accept the metaphysics giving us premises one and two. The first problem appeared during the Enlightenment itself, and led to what appear to be two divergent traditions of toleration. The second reflects our unwillingness, in the twentieth century, to share Leibniz's faith in either pure rationality or a necessary being, especially as a basis for philosophy. I will say something briefly on the latter issue, then turn at greater length to the two traditions I have mentioned, suggesting that they succeed quite well in freeing themselves from their metaphysical origins.

Briefly, then: even if the metaphysical underpinnings fail, it may yet be part of the "inner principle" guiding the empirical "us" around here (the "Western monad") that we draw limits around our own knowledge and assume some significant truths to be in the possession of others. The very fact that Leibniz pursued his perspectivalist project, and so many after him took it up, supports such a hypothesis, as does the fact that his intuitions, if that is what they finally are, antedate the failures of colonialism to which Vivas attributes the impulse to relativism. It may be part of what I have called our "interests," at any rate of our fundamental ways of gathering and evaluating evidence, that we demand of ourselves humility and openness to what strangers might have to teach. Certainly the egalitarianism of the scientific method would indicate this, as would its hostility to "received ideas," its reliance on (uncertain, ungovernable) empirical evidence rather than (determinable, fixed) reason or intuition, and its encouragement of and development from plain curiosity.[92] And if, as Allison suggests, the success of perspectivalism in the eighteenth century was in part due to the devastating religious wars that preceded the period,[93] this historical conditioning does not cut against the doctrine's deep expression of our world-picture, for the peace that ended those wars can themselves be in part tied to the anti-traditionalism and uncertainty that brought forth science and became essential to it. What needs to be established is that consciousness of our own limitations and the possibility that others may have knowledge we lack is not merely an obvious empirical fact about ourselves, or an obviously useful rule of thumb, but somehow essential to our ways of knowing and acting. This I have already begun to do in the section on Heidegger in chapter six, and will continue in the discussions of Lessing and Herder below.

That we must split up perspectivalism into a negative and a positive tradition follows directly from the equivocation described above. The problem can be put in several other ways: 1) If the monads are windowless, how does each get the awareness that the others, or an absolute, so much as exist? If they are not windowless, in what sense can they be meaningfully called "irreducibly

[92] See the discussion of curiosity in (Harries, 1988).

[93] (Allison, 1966), p.2.

different"? Leibniz himself thought that we can know infinites "confusedly,...and know at least distinctly that they are such."[94] We can know "*that* the universe forms one thoroughgoing context, that it is the best of all possible worlds," although we are "incapable of grasping the details of this plan."[95] Presumably these facts are necessary pre-conditions for our own existence, and presumably we know through them our own finitude,[96] and that other finite perspectives must exist. Even this is not clear, as there is reason to wonder whether we know enough about the posited other beings to call them "perspectives," "monads," etc., but supposing that we grant everything so far, it remains entirely unclear how we could ever learn *from* the other perspectives. Why would Leibniz seek truth in other philosophical positions, or try to reconcile the churches? Allison claims that he combines a "recognition of the relative truth of each perspective or standpoint...with the belief in eventual progress to higher standpoints,"[97] but if, as Leibniz expressly says, "there is an *original imperfection in the creature* before sin, because the creature is limited in its essence,"[98] and if the creature can only follow out its essence, then there can be no progress beyond the truth already inherent in the creature's standpoint. Certainly there can be no progress at the behest of what the other standpoints have to say, although the fact of there being other standpoints might be an occasion for enlightening thought. Not necessarily a very interesting one, however, not itself more likely to enlighten than the fact of there being a God, or, to each monad, a manifold of appearances. What windowless others should be to us, or us to them, awaits further explanation.

2) If we are to follow our own internal principles, why should we take any account, in action, of the other monads at all? We cannot affect them anyway; we can certainly not destroy them;[99] and anything we learn by knowing of their existence (supposing 1, above, to be resolved), we derive from our own internal principle. So our desire for them to exist is no more than an acquiescence in the way God has structured the world, while in our action in general we should follow what we consider to be good regardless of any apparent effect it might have on others. A person whose principle is punching people in the nose—he is transfixed by the kernel of truth that it is good for curing hiccups—should punch everyone regardless of whether they want to be punched or not. Similarly, our desire for the truth in other perspectives should not prevent us from harming the representatives of those perspectives, if our definition of the good entails such harm. Of course, this might not be the case if we lose the faith that monads are eternally preserved by God, but without that faith the

---

94 Quoted in (Allison, 1966) p.129.
95 (Allison, 1966), p.129.
96 Compare Augustine, *On the Trinity*, chapter xv and Descartes, *Meditations*, III.
97 (Allison, 1966), p.133.
98 Quoted in (Allison, 1966), p.30.
99 See *Monadology*, §6,7,77.

assumption that they all contain truth will fall away as well. Either respect needs an argument independent of the various perspectives' truth, or their truth must be established on less metaphysical grounds.

I will suggest below that in *Nathan the Wise* Lessing develops the internal principle of respect, in the process nudging us somewhat away from Leibniz's metaphysics, while Herder abandons the windowlessness of the monad to open us to the possibility that his cultural monads might learn from one another. Together they elucidate the main forms that our traditions of ethical perspectivalism will take.

• *Negative Toleration: Lessing*

Nathan the Wise makes human confusion not only its theme but the structuring principle of its action. Those reading it for a relativist philosophy often miss this richness, by focusing exclusively on the parable of the three rings. In this story, recounted by the Jew Nathan to the Muslim Saladin under whose rule he lives, a father who is supposed to pass down a ring giving its wearer "grace with God and man" to his favorite son instead has two exact duplicates made, and, loving his sons equally, gives one to each. Through Nathan's own voice, Lessing first suggests that this situation itself resembles that of the three creeds (Judaism, Christianity, and Islam), for just as "the true ring was not proved or provable," so none of the creeds can establish that its historical—hence traditional, hence familial—foundation is more likely to be true than those of the others: "...history must be received in faith implicitly...[and surely we rest this faith] on them who from our childhood gave us proofs of love....How...shall I my fathers less believe than you your own?"[100] Then, when the brothers come to court, Lessing puts into the mouth of the judge an even more radical suggestion. "Your rings all three are false. The genuine ring perchance [your] father lost, and to replace it and hide the loss had three rings made for one," but if "each of you believe his ring the true one[,]...let each one strive most zealously to show a love untainted by self-care, each with his might vie with the rest to bring into the day the virtue of the jewel his finger wears...by gentleness, by spirit tractable, by kind deeds and true piety towards God."[101] Even if the ring be false, the brothers should act as if it were true, and that itself will replace the magic. "[T]he realization of the power of the genuine ring or the true religion," says Allison, "becomes not a gift but a task."[102]

That we accept our culture's ways on the basis of what our parents tell us, I am happy to accept (although I make no claims that *history* must be accepted on this basis); that we cannot finally prove the foundations of our way of life and thinking to be superior to other such foundations, I accept even more

---

100 *ibid*, Act III, Scene VII, in (Lessing, 1959), p.168.
101 *ibid*, (p.169).
102 (Allison, 1966), p.144.

readily; and I welcome the notion that the touchstone of a creed (culture) is how one lives in accordance with it. But Lessing has more than the three rings, and more than his views on history, to offer as a basis for regarding ourselves and others as in possession of less than a final and certain truth. Throughout the drama, his characters display an astonishing amount of ignorance and bad judgment. The Templar, especially—perhaps because he has never met Jews or lived among Muslims before[103]—misjudges first his own feelings for Recha, then Nathan's tolerance, then Nathan's good intentions, then what would be best for Nathan and himself, and finally Recha's feelings for him.[104] When he complains to the sultan that "everything in this strange world has many sides...[and it is] often hard to tell how they are reconciled," the latter responds that he is himself "a thing of many sides/Hard for me often to bring to harmony."[105] Here the "many sides" are clearly not Leibniz's transcendentally separate perspectives, but the different signals, motives and pieces of human behavior one encounters in ordinary experience, and the harmony is not Leibniz's God but a more humble emotional and intellectual equilibrium. Similarly, the war between Christians and Muslims in the background of the play may be inspired by metaphysical disagreement but has issued in most empirical disharmony—what Lessing calls the "blackest form" of the "[mad]...urge to have the better God, and to impose this better God as best on the whole world."[106]

In accordance with his taming of Leibniz's metaphysical concerns into facts of ordinary empirical life, Lessing is less optimistic than Leibniz about the possibility of making universal harmony real. Instead of reconciling the churches, he poses such reconciliation as "an ideal toward which the human race may strive, but which [it] can never completely realize."[107] Allison takes Lessing to be adopting Leibniz's optimism in that "[the]...conception of a benign providence, according to which everything is determined for the best, is one of the cardinal principles of Lessing's theory of the drama....The whole structure of [*Nathan the Wise*] is intended to exhibit the guiding hand of providence, leading all events by purely natural means to an inevitably happy issue."[108] This is indeed the case in the play, contrivedly and awkwardly so, and Lessing indeed makes such resolution a principle of dramatic fiction, but what Allison misses is that this is precisely a principle of *fiction*, not a belief

---

103 Act I, Scene II (p.119) makes clear at least that no Templar has ever been let live in Saladin's Jerusalem before ("...no captive Templar ever came into Jerusalem but to certain death; nor any such was ever granted freedom to walk Jerusalem streets"), and Act I, Scene IV (p.127) relates that this particular Templar "darkens not the door of any Jew."

104 Act I, Scene VI (pp.133-4), Act II, Scene V (pp.147-9), Act III, Scene X - Act IV, Scene IV (especially pp.178,187-9), Act V, Scene V (pp.207-8), and Act V, Scene VIII (pp.215-6).

105 Act IV, Scene IV (p.187).

106 Act II, Scene VI (p.148).

107 In (Allison, 1966), p.134.

108 *ibid*, p.146.

about the world. The poet should display reconciliation, Lessing says in the passage from the *Hamburg Dramaturgy* that Allison quotes, in order to intimate to us that just as in God "all things are resolved for the best, so also will it be here."[109] *In* God, not in this world, are things resolved, and in this world the best Lessing can say is that the poet should tell us they *will* be so. We can hope for such an end, and try to reach it, and the poet's job is to inspire us to such a task, but we have no proof, no philosophical or empirical assurance, that it will come about. In this light, we may take the artificiality of the plot in *Nathan the Wise* as deliberate. Lessing puts his vividly realistic characters, with their vividly realistic concerns and resigned comments about human beings having many conflicting sides, into a rigidly comedic format, forcing everyone at the end into one happy family in a way so outrageously unrealistic that it strongly implies the play is more a dream to be realized than a mirror of accomplished fact. Like Kant, Lessing turns Leibniz's principles from metaphysical realities to necessary hopes of human thinkers, but instead of arguing from metaphysical to transcendental philosophy, he leaves philosophy for fiction.

Before I can show how Lessing's practical (in the sense both of "pragmatic" and of "ethical") harnessing of Leibniz bears on contemporary relativism, I need to draw on Kant. Both the limitations of human knowledge and the importance of respect receive full philosophical attention only with Kant. Not only are we in common fact often ignorant, claims Kant, but we must act on an unprovable belief that freedom is possible, and an unprovable hope that universal harmony is possible. Respect for freedom—and consequently, according to some readings, for others' choices—thus becomes not merely one of the virtues we should pursue in our ignorance, along with Nathan's "gentleness, ... spirit tractable, ... kind deeds and true piety towards God," but the chief of all virtues, entailed by limitations on knowledge at the very foundation of ethics. This is not so distant from Lessing, who appeals to an essential limitation on the knowledge of the self (Saladin's "many-sidedness") and of the foundations of religion (its historicity, or, as I prefer to say, its dependence on tradition and authority), but Kant makes his claims more clearly and more powerfully, and it is from him that demands for us to respect cultural difference more directly take their inspiration.[110]

---

[109] Quoted in (Allison, 1966), note 85 on p.199.

[110] Among those citing Kant's "Copernican revolution" as the source of philosophical relativism (while always acknowledging that this was not Kant's own project) are (Goodman, 1978), pp. x, 6, (Rorty, 1982), and (Bloor, 1983), p.175 and notes 39 and 40 on p.206. Of course, simply turning the categories into a psychological or cultural fact not only requires an excessively naturalistic, and to my mind simplistic, reading of Kant, but has no tendency to promote any kind of *ethical* relativism. It can do so, however, when combined with a notion that each variety of categorization is a mode of "man's progressive self-liberation," so that the categories are a cultural phenomenon but culture is an expression of human freedom: this, I take it, is the position (Cassirer, 1944) intends to offer. (Quotation from p.228). See also (Bidney, 1949), especially pp.496-7, 536, 539).

The general form of those demands can be articulated as follows: 1) Each of us must respect the choices of others unless we are sure those choices are made unfreely (are in fact not choices) or in ignorance. 2) Each of us is in enough ignorance about the structures of others' wills (as Kant himself points out),[111] and about the empirical circumstances of others' choices (as Kant does not point out), that we rarely know when those choices are in fact unfree or based on ignorance. 3) Across cultures, or religions, the differences in what to count as knowledge are so fundamental, and irresolvable, that even in many cases where we might safely count a neighbor as unfree or ignorant we cannot do so for a member of another culture. The affirmation of these three positions together is often considered a version of relativism. Its opponents on the whole disagree only with 3), which they assimilate to 2). The interesting question then becomes, is there some larger than empirical gap between members of different cultures that would lead Kant's ethical philosophy—quite unrelativistic in intention—to demand relativistic suspensions of judgment?

This brings us to a debate between Michael Walzer and David Luban over humanitarian intervention. Walzer denies that foreigners are in a position to make judgments about such basic ethical problems in another nation as the adequacy of the union between people and government: "They don't know enough about its history, and they have no direct experience, and can form no concrete judgments, of the conflicts and harmonies, the historical choices and cultural affinities, the loyalties and resentments that underlie it."[112] To which Luban responds:

> ...why presume we are ignorant? We aren't, usually. There are, after all, experts, experienced travellers, expatriates, scholars, and spies; libraries have been written about the most remote cultures. Bafflingly, Walzer does not mention the obvious sources of information even to dismiss them. He seems to take as an *a priori* truth—it is part of the Romance of the Nation-State—that without "direct experience" a member of one culture cannot, ultimately, know what it's really like to be a member of another. But this is of a piece with "no man can really know what it's like to be a woman" or "you can't know what it's really like to be me": even granting their validity, we don't assume that such conditions preclude making true judgments about other people.[113]

To begin to cash out what Walzer may mean by "direct experience," I take a cue straight from Lessing. Lessing tells us not to judge other people's religions because that is tantamount to casting aspersions on their, and all of our, non-rational but essential ties to our parents. As I want to adapt this claim, it applies not to the passing down of history but to the passing down of interests and

---

111 (Kant, 1964), pp.74-5 (407).
112 Walzer, in (Beitz *et al*, 1985), p.220.
113 David Luban, "The Romance of the Nation-State," in (Beitz *et al*, 1985), p.241.

traditions, as well as simply to the process of *passing down* itself, dependent as it is on authority—both of which are crucial to the way we acquire bodies of knowledge and ways of thinking. Even if there are matters of fact at issue between groups, therefore, the differences in how the groups get at these matters may not allow of resolution, and in recognition of that fact we may need to pursue our own inherited ways and not cast aspersions on the heritage of others.

It follows that the true sharing of ethically relevant information between cultures may entail a sharing of interests, and that is what Walzer probably means by "direct experience" and "concrete judgments." Consider this in a very everyday sense: what happens when even a thoughtful traveller or expatriate recounts her experience? She comes, let us say, from El Salvador to the United States. She begins to speak here, and now the pain she remembers is less vivid, the pressures less frightening. On the other hand, she needs to make her story interesting and clear to her audience, hence to exaggerate a little here and there, and to leave out details. She forgets some details, and does not realize that others are important (the way heat affects people's decisions, perhaps, or how the joys of communal bread-baking—I'm making this up—keep families attached to the place). We, listening to her, are distracted, sceptical, even more distant from the events, even less aware of what details to stress, and interpret what we hear in terms of what *we* would do, with our interests and inherited beliefs, in such circumstances. From a large number of reports like this there may indeed *be enough information* to construct a reasonably accurate picture, but that does not mean that any individual, from here, knows enough about what is important to construct it. What concrete judgments about action make most sense to the Salvadorans themselves depends on what they want, day to day, out of their lives, on the body of judgments they have inherited, or made and lived with so far, and on a huge body of details the relative importance of which become clear only in terms of the other two factors. We are therefore generally as adrift, vis-a-vis other cultures, as the Templar in Jerusalem, liable with every judgment to go so far astray that the theoretical pre-supposition of mutual understanding becomes in fact a vanishing possibility. To experience "directly," we must share interests. To judge "concretely," we must share circumstances. Without both, there remains in principle a possibility of understanding other human beings, and that possibility makes clear that the argument here yields us only a presumption, to be overriden in clear and drastic cases (see section iii), but in general we should rather be aware of our ignorance, and plead it as an excuse for withholding judgment.

From Lessing, once more and finally, we learn the necessity of not assuming that one way of action is right and cuts across all cultures. That assumption could offer a slightly different response to position 3) above: whether or not there are differences across cultures in what to count as knowledge, there is one right way to act. I take this to be what Lessing calls "this madness, this pious urge to have the better God." From him, and, whether he would like such an inference or not, from Kant, we know that we have no proof for any such single right way, and in accord with that ignorance we may insist on a presumption in favor of withholding cross-cultural judgment.

• *Monads with Windows: Herder and His Successors*

The typical language of nationalism and cultural relativism—that groups of people have "souls" and deserve to express them freely—does not follow at all from what I have drawn from Lessing. The presumption against interfering with a culture or religion is only indirect: we need to respect the freedom of individuals, and individuals may express their freedom through the norms, and by affirming the value, of their culture. We do not get from this any reason for holding that the culture itself has or constitutes a soul worthy of our study, attention, or preservation. This, not so much because we can make nothing of "soul" as applied to culture—I have made that comparison myself, in discussing Leibniz—but because we have no reason, as yet, to take any interest in the nature or expression of other and distant souls. Even if we swallow hard and accept the excessive mysticism of using the phrase "different souls" to describe gaps in cross-cultural communication, we have no reason to think—indeed, we have reason *not* to think—that cultures we should tolerate, because we are unsure we understand them, have anything to say to us.

As Cassirer points out,[114] Herder, who practically invented the modern notion of culture, based his conception of it on Leibniz's monads, and it was also Herder who powerfully forged the demand that we in the West learn about how to live by looking at other cultures. To call a culture a monad is to call it unique, composed (at least in part, but irreducibly) of beliefs, and foundational for action. It is hard to over-emphasize the importance of this characterization for Herder's nationalist successors, down to the present day. Fichte, while still allowing for a distinction between individual and group freedom, insisted that "[o]nly when each people, left to itself, develops and forms itself in accordance with its own peculiar quality...does the manifestation of divinity appear in its true mirror."[115] His Danish contemporary, Bishop Grundtvig, spoke of peoples as having a "hidden but active life-force" (*conatus*?), while Bluntschli, in Switzerland, said that the "national spirit (*Volksgeist*) and...national will (*Volkeswille*)...[are] something more than the mere sum of the spirit and will of the individuals composing the nation."[116] The Frenchman Ernst Renan called the nation "a soul, a spiritual principle," while Mazzini declared that "God has divided the human race into masses ... evidently distinct; each with a separate

114 (Cassirer, 1951), pp. 230-3. See also (Koepping, 1983), pp.38-9, and (Ergang, 1966), p.86.
115 Quoted in (Shafer, 1955), p.19.
116 Quoted in *ibid*, pp.24-5.

tone of thought, and a separate part to fulfill."[117] As late as 1951, German Arciniegas, in an article on culture, declared it "the human right of every people to reveal its soul, to express itself freely."[118]

If there is a Leibnizean God, and He has divided the world up into distinct groups, then it may well be that each should "express" itself and live "freely," but then, as I have pointed out earlier, no human being need worry about the survival and freedom of these groups, for those matters will be metaphysically guaranteed—even if no member of the group continues to live (materially), or every member is in chains. The demand for political freedom, therefore, and for others to take an interest in the survival and self-expression of a given culture, must be based on something else. Using Lessing, I translated the distinctness of cultures into concrete terms providing a presumption in favor of cultures ruling themselves. Using Herder, but a side of Herder in some tension with his appeal to monads, I want now to explore why other cultures might interest us.

This side of Herder appears in his deep belief in the value of diversity, in his speculation that through the "wild confusion" of individuals opposing one another the world will achieve equilibrium and harmony (a face of truth, for a Leibnizean), in his interest in recording the history and collecting the folklore of many peoples, in the fact that his nationalist passions had the unique characteristic, for his time, of aiming at states for all peoples and not just, or primarily, for the Germans, and even in such a claim as that we "must enter the spirit of a nation before [we] can share even one of its thoughts or deeds."[119] For a strict nationalist, or for a Leibnizean theorist of group thought like Lessing, the implication here would be that it is difficult or even impossible to share another group's way of thinking. For Herder, the suggestion is that "the spirit of a nation" forms a necessary antechamber, but not a barrier, to cross-cultural understanding. His monads thus reward empirical study, and interact fruitfully in "wild confusion"; they are no longer windowless.

They cannot, therefore, any longer be Leibniz's metaphysical simples, but they can bear as much of a tamed, empirical resemblance to those substances as do Lessing's religions. Herder responded philosophically to Kant with something much like Wittgenstein's views, a century and a half later:[120] an emphasis on language above mental or ideal categories, a refusal to let philosophy escape the ordinary vagaries of language, and a tendency to doubt the possibility of making sense of any principles outside of some empirical context. It would be difficult and risky for me to lay out, or to lay too much weight on, Herder's metaphysics, but it seems that he regards cultures and

---

117 Quoted in *ibid*, pp. 26, 20.
118 (Arciniegas, 1951), p.33.
119 (Herder, 1961), p.181.
120 In the "Metacritique to the Critique of Pure Reason," discussed in (Harries, 1983), p.244.

individuals as *relatively* stable entities in the midst of an empirical, confusing, perhaps Heraclitean flux, led by God in no clear direction, at least from the individual's perspective, but presumably towards the Good.[121] Since they are empirical and only relatively stable, they must work to preserve each other, but they can also learn from each other, in the midst of the flux.

And it seems that each culture can only preserve its identity as an active rather than a passive part of the flux—actively seize its own internal principle, as it were—through stimulation by the national "spirit" at the heart of its community. The "spirit of the nation," for Herder, comes from the *Volk*, the primitive community providing the "energy and creative force" of any culture:[122]

> It will remain eternally true that if we have no *Volk*, we shall have no public, no nationality, no literature of our own which shall live and work in us. Unless our literature is founded on our *Volk*, we shall write eternally for closet sages and disgusting critics out of whose mouths and stomachs we shall get back what we have given.[123]

It is true that Herder here admonishes his own culture to return to its *Volk*, but his main point is that only a *Volk*, and not the institutions of "civilized" culture that attempt to rise above it, has the mysterious energy to give life to a literature and way of thought. Presumably this derives from the fact that only a *Volk* will have the basis in tradition and irreducible complexity of detail to have something to say about the concrete circumstances of action.

From a strict reading of Leibniz, we might think that every culture must be inspired by its own *Volk*, as Herder on the whole assumes, but he also put together the first collection of *Volkslieder* out of more than simply German songs, and, as we have seen, had leanings towards allowing his cultural monads

---

121 Koepping says that Herder took over the notion of "life-force" from Leibniz and posited it as the "energizing principle of living organisms, including cultures and societies, which all evolve and change through interaction, and are thus different, in their constant flux, from any mechanical assemblage." (pp.38-39) Compare also Herder, *op. cit.*, pp.187-8: "Do you see this river, flowing on, how it springs from a tiny source, swells, divides, joins up again, winds in and out, and cuts farther and deeper but, whatever, the intricacies of its course, still remains water...Might it not be the same with humankind? Or do you see that tree growing there, or that striving man? He must pass through different ages of life, between which are apparent resting-places, revolutions, changes, and each of which obviously constitutes a form of progress from the one before. Each age is different, but each has the center of its happiness within itself. The youth is not happier than the innocent contented child; nor is the peaceful old man unhapppier than the energetic man in his prime...[A]nd yet the striving never ceases. No-one lives in his own period only; he builds on what has gone before and lays a foundation for what comes after...The Egyptian could not have existed without the Oriental, nor the Greek without the Egyptian...History may not manifestly be revealed as the theatre of a directing purpose on earth...for we may not be able to espy its final end. But it may conceivably offer us glimpses of a divine theatre through the openings and ruins of individual scenes."

122 (Bluestein, 1963), p.123.

123 Quoted in (Bluestein, 1963), p.118.

to interact. At any rate, as his ideas pass down, in a direct line, to Walt Whitman and then to EM Forster, the emphasis comes to lie on being inspired by *some* primitive community, not on whether the primitive community happens to be one's own. Gene Bluestein has shown just how deeply Herder influenced Whitman, in beliefs about and interest in slang, folk culture, folk music, nationalism and internationalism.[124] Forster's tie to Whitman can be found in the very title of *A Passage to India*.[125] There is thus some historical reason to suppose that the traces of Herder in Forster's novels are not coincidental.

According to John Colmer, Forster was led to write by his travels, where he sought, as did many in his time, the *genius loci*, the "spirit of the place."[126] Since this "spirit" can be "incarnate[d] and interpret[ed]" by the inhabitants of the place,[127] there is considerable kinship between it and Herder's "spirit of the nation." And in four of Forster's five published novels, a central character or set of characters is inspired to live with greater "passion" or "heroism"[128] by an experience in a foreign land, in three cases a violent experience. Italy's violence inspires George Emerson and Lucy Honeychurch of *A Room With a View*, and Philip Herriton and Miss Abbott of *Where Angels Fear to Tread*; Germany more quietly gives new life to Helen Schlegel of *Howard's End*; and India, again violently (in psychological terms, at least), overturns the lives of Adela Quested and Mrs. Moore in *A Passage to India*. The Indian experience is the clearest, summed up by the superb image of an echo that seems to rob life, and particularly *English* life, of any point or meaning:

> There are some exquisite echoes in India; there is the whisper round the dome at Bijapur; there are the long, solid sentences that voyage through the air at Mandu, and return unbroken to their creator. The echo in a Marabar cave is not like these, it is entirely devoid of distinction. Whatever is said, the same monotonous noise replies, and quivers up and down the walls until it is absorbed into the roof. "Boum" is the sound as far as the human alphabet can express it, or "bou-oum," or "ou-boum,"—utterly dull. Hope, politeness, the blowing of a nose, the squeak of a boot, all produce "boum."
>
> ...the echo began in some indescribable way to undermine [Mrs. Moore's] hold on life. Coming at a moment when she chanced to be fatigued, it had managed to murmur, "Pathos, piety, courage—they exist, but are identical, and so is filth. Everything exists, nothing has value." If one had spoken vileness in that place, or quoted lofty poetry, the comment would have been the same—"ou-boum." ...Devils are of the North, and poems can be written about them, but no one could romanticize the Marabar because it robbed infinity and eternity of their vastness, the only quality that accommodates them to mankind.... [S]uddenly, at the edge

---

[124] (Bluestein, 1963), *passim.*

[125] On the connection to Whitman, see (Beer, 1962), p.147, and (Levine, 1971), p.157.

[126] (Colmer, 1975), p.267.

[127] *ibid.*

[128] (Forster, 1922), pp. 48, 67-77, 108-10, 144-5, 310, and (Forster, 1937), pp. 208-10, 216, 240-1, 246-50.

> of her mind, Religion appeared, poor little talkative Christianity, and she knew that all its divine words from "Let there be Light" to "It is finished" only amounted to "boum."[129]

Notice how many pieces of English life, from "talkative Christianity" (clearly not the harsh German, mystical Spanish, or luxurious Italian variety!) to the absurd, Wildean humor of juxtaposing "hope" with "politeness" and "the blowing of a nose," are here thrown against the Indian echo. Notice how Forster even tries to undermine the English romantic's expectations of Indian mystery: this is not one of your poetic hints at infinity. In *A Room With a View* and *Where Angels Fear to Tread*, the alien place contained murders, squalid and touching scenes of love and peasant life—everything "you might expect" of Italy. Here, India defeats even these English hopes. Only the fact of its alienness can change a life, and then only in the sense of making the people affected aware of the power and strangeness of the world, and the absurdity of their own conventions in that light, not in the sense of bringing about a new understanding of and reconciliation with the alien place itself. Mrs. Moore leaves the echo to scoff at marriage and at a rape trial: "all this rubbish about love, love in a church, love in a cave, as if there is the least difference, and I held up from my business over such trifles!"[130] The English teacher, Mr. Fielding, tries harder to understand India's obscurity, making friends with the novel's Muslim anti-hero Aziz, but he winds up leaving to marry in England, and the last lines of the book tell us that his friendship with Aziz must fail, and fail for ineffable reasons:

> "Why can't we be friends now?" said [Fielding]...."It's what I want. It's what you want."
>
> But the horses didn't want it—they swerved apart; the earth didn't want it, sending up rocks through which riders must pass single file; the temples, the tank, the jail, the palace, the birds, the carrion, the Guest House, that came into view as they issued from the gap and saw Mau beneath: they didn't want it, they said in their hundred voices, "No, not yet," and the sky said, "No, not there."[131]

Englishmen cannot come into direct relationship with the alien place, although it inspires them to a better life. They may now live more richly, but that life cannot be carried on in the place that enriched it.[132]

I have spent some time on Forster because he excellently represents the romanticization of the foreign, in which we want to preserve other cultures so that they can inspire our own. We have seen a source for this apparently

---

129 (Forster, 1952), pp. 147, 149-50.

130 *ibid*, p.202.

131 *ibid*, p.322.

132 This is also true in the earlier novels: English men and women are inspired by Italy and Germany, but they return home to live, and especially to marry. The one who does marry an Italian (Lilia in *Where Angels Fear to Tread*) learns nothing and dies quickly, in childbirth: she is not one of the inspired but part of the inspiration for others.

preposterous suggestion in Herder, where it has some quasi-philosophical support in the form of principles of activity and individuation roughly derived from Leibniz's account of the monad, but why would a contemporary writer think that another culture can give us energy or truth we cannot find by ourselves? That many of us do is clear. It is a commonplace among travellers, and in travel literature, that exposure to other groups shocks one into reflecting on one's own life,[133] and we can find Forster's sentiments in a thinker on quite the other end of British imperialism. "Let me make clear," writes the Indian poet Rabindranath Tagore, "that I am not distrustful of any civilization because it is foreign. On the contrary, I believe that encounter with such forces is necessary to preserve the vitality of our intellectual nature....European culture...has roused our intellectual life from the inertia of its old habits to an increasing awareness, resulting from the very contrast it offers to our mental traditions."[134] And Horace Kallen, defending "cultural pluralism" as a goal for United States policy, cites Justice William Douglas: "We have wanted a land where our people can be exposed to all the diverse creeds and cultures of the world."[135]

Is all this merely a version of the cliché that seeing other people's peculiarities helps us to discover our own? I don't think so, if only because each of these writers speaks, not primarily of learning some new fact in cross-cultural contact, but of acquiring a new "energy," "passion," "vitality," etc. Each speaks of this inspiration as coming not when people merely read about another culture, but only when they travel to it or live within it. The inspiration in question matters to individuals, comes from "direct experience," consists primarily in a revelation of the familiar we ignore or forget, and tends toward a change in action. It thus closely resembles what I described in chaper six as Heidegger's account of truth in art, and this comparison has indeed been made, by Lawrence Hinman, in an article recommending a hermeneutical approach to culture:

> ...the hermeneutical model of understanding suggests that mutual understanding between forms of life first becomes possible when one is willing to acknowledge one's own pre-suppositions as such and be open to the possibility that another form of life may reveal the limitations and inadequacies of those pre-suppositions in comparison with its own. The confrontation with another form of life seems for precisely this reason to present us with a unique opportunity to recognize and put our own pre-suppositions to the test, for it is precisely this contrast which throws into relief pre-suppositions which would otherwise be noticed only through the shadows they cast.[136]

---

[133] For sophisticated expressions of this idea see, for instance, (Chatwin, 1987), or consider Hannah Arendt's attempt to link Kant's notion of "enlarged thought" in the *Critique of Judgment* to the experience of tourism. (Arendt, 1982), pp.16, 43, 75-6).

[134] Quoted in (Northrop, 1952), p.74.

[135] (Kallen, 1956), p.187.

[136] (Hinman, 1983), p.349. See also (Koivisto, 1955): "When a member of culture A comes into contact with culture B, he comes to see his own culture 'in a new light.' What were formerly 'self-evident truths' are no longer so regarded." (p.56).

As ways of judging which aver, at least on one side of an antinomy, that the truth must lie beyond themselves, cultures need an "outside" to keep them self-critical. The energy spurred by confrontation with the unfamiliar is something we might very well expect to dissipate without the recurrent appearance of that unfamiliar. Only an "outside" lets us know that we are limited, and defined by those limitations; only an "outside" shapes us and recalls us to our "internal principle." Heidegger says this happens in the presence of the world/earth struggle worked in art, but it happens yet more radically, more fundamentally, in cultural encounters that shake up, for one or many of us, the very notion of art, the life we lead in its presence, and the discipline of Western academic thought. This is perhaps truer for the West than for any other of the world's cultures. The West is practically unique in regarding contact with other cultures as a good in itself. As a result of our very success in the pursuit of scientific truth, we fear that we are losing all sense of what the truth about how to live might be. Since Herrder, or even Leibniz, one response to that fear we have instituted is the hope that we might find that something of that truth by looking at, or immersing ourselves in, what others believe it to be.

This gives us a presumption in favor of promoting the diversity of cultures, but it does not, any more than the "respect out of ignorance" principle I derived from Lessing, give us more than a presumption in favor of preserving any given culture. We may need an "outside," but we do not need (certainly *may* not need) any given outside. From Heidegger's own arguments, we could reasonably defend a need for people to create and preserve *some* artworks, but not this or that artwork, or any set number or kind of them, or way by which they should be preserved.[137] For each work of art we have only a presumption in its favor, overrideable for many reasons, as long as the destruction of this work does not mean the end of all art. Similarly, we have an interest in there being *some* cultures besides our own, but only a presumption in favor of preserving any particular one that challenges us, a presumption that is overrideable in the name of other ethical concerns, at least as long as some alternative to our own way of life remains.

The two presumptions we have found—against destroying and in favor of preserving any given other culture—constitute, I think, the strongest case we could expect to make for the toleration of different cultures as different. Certainly we have intuitions against interfering with other ways of life or pronouncing our own the best or only way, but these intuitions are limited by humanitarian concerns for the individual participants in other cultures. We surely do not (any longer?) want to say that the preservation of cultures is an absolute end. Suffice it, then, that such preservation is a respectable and not a silly end, less sentimental or condescending than it might at first appear, and rooted in deep traditions we have about respect and about truth.

---

137 He himself allows temporary neglect as a form of preservation: OWA 67.

The Uses of Universalism

I would like to close by summing up the disparate purposes that universalist traditions serve in our culture. We have seen some purportedly universalist doctrines turn out not to be universalist after all. On the whole, this was true for natural law, which places itself in contrast more to positive law than to local morality, and for humanitarian intervention, which shows in practice that it better represents our (legitimate) interest in our friends and kin(d) than in all mankind. Then we have found that some of our interests do extend to all people, but in sometimes divergent ways. For simplicity's sake, I categorize these under the headings "charity," "respect" and "peace." "Charity" is meant to capture the aspect of human rights doctrine (and as such, *one* aspect of natural law) by which we see a concern for the most obvious needs of all human beings—primarily, an absence of murder and torture—as essential to our being able to maintain our own ethical self-respect. We cannot believe that any ethic, any way of life, is worthwhile at all if it allows us to tolerate the kind of degradation we associate with Nazi Germany, and this belief expresses itself in a "gut feeling" that revulsion at such behavior requires no rationale at all. "Respect" summarizes what we have probed in our sections on invincible ignorance, consensus, and perspectivalism. For various reasons of our own, we want people freely to express their own ethic, and we do not want to impose our ethical standards on those we cannot persuade of them; this sometimes conflicts with charity. "Peace" is an end that requires the good efforts of all people but that need not depend on everyone's sharing the same ethical standards for all action. Instead, it requires consensus merely on certain specific aims and practices, which may be more easily attained via a set of "double standards" than in the unending fight for human homogeneity.

Concerning the tensions among these various motives for universalism, I make three suggestions. First, it is helpful for us always to keep in mind that both our interest in caring for others *and* our interest in tolerating them come from our own tradition, from our own beliefs and history. We may then return to sources in that tradition for resolution of specific conflicts of interest. Just how far did this or that text or historical experience drive us toward respect or charity? Did its intention (if a text) or impact (if an experience) extend to the type of situation we face in this specific case, or should we turn here to a different influence, perhaps geared towards the other interest? We should practice these kinds of questions and interpretations, rather than ingenious derivations from abstract theories.

From here, the second point follows closely. Conflicts between interests do not occur as abstract arguments over respect versus charity, but in specific situations, and they therefore require a set of *judgments* rather than a theory. We are short today on universalist and anti-universalist judgments, not on theory, although texts to inform and occasions to inspire such judgments abound.

Perhaps we should think of ourselves as constituting a court of ethical common law, in which we do best to take each case of cross-cultural interaction on the model of cases and decisions that have gone before—precedents, and arguments for or reflections on those precedents. I made this suggestion already in section iii, where it was to apply to gross violations of human rights, but we can extend it to our other issues as well, from what kinds of evangelism and cultural interference are acceptable and unacceptable, to what to count as "argument" or "persuasion" and what as "indoctrination." The advantage of judgment over theory is that it allows us to acknowledge the richness of concrete decisions; the disadvantage seems to be that we risk not knowing what to do in a situation, or at least not having a clear guide in advance to which all participants can adjust their decisions. I believe this is a risk built into all action-directed (practical) thought, however, and approaches that appear to remove it turn out in fact to be illusory. Theoretical principles also fail to tell us unequivocally what to do in specific situations, by having either nothing or too much to say. And the success of common law courts should assure us that precedent can provide solutions and a standard for public guidance just as well as theory.

Finally, where we cannot say anything satisfactory in favor of caring instead of tolerating, or vice versa, we may still need to act and then we must act in silence. "Silence," that is, in the sense of no longer offering justification, of "ceasing" (as the etymology of the word would have it) to justify. We cannot avoid having such situations arise, and we should understand and accept the fact that silence is not always a way of giving up, but an inevitable consequence, at times, of the fact that justifications run out (neither I, nor my culture, can think of everything, especially in advance), while the need for decision—to act or refrain from acting—does not. Sometimes it is right to stop widows from burning, or to let them burn,[138] even if we cannot quite say why. Our traditions, and the development of a set of judgments, may help us ethically where a concentration on theory has hurt, but we will still sometimes know what to say only after we act, or not even then, or find then that we acted wrongly. Such are the risks in any ethic, at least any preserving the space of indeterminacy that allows for integrity.

---

138 RK Saxena has pointed out the delicate balance that the British had to observe in the nineteenth century, in order to suppress *sati* without inciting riots or otherwise grossly disrupting the political and social harmony of the communities in which it (rarely) took place: (Saxena, 1975).

CHAPTER NINE

INTEGRITY

Responding to JJC Smart's version of that doctrine, Bernard Williams has complained that utilitarianism can make no sense of the value of integrity. Integrity, he says, is "closely connected" with the idea that "each of us is specially responsible for what *he* does, rather than for what other people do."[1] Integrity may be called "one's moral identity,"[2] one's identification with certain projects and commitments "which in some cases [one] takes seriously at the deepest level, as what [one's] life is about."[3] For a person with integrity, actions "flow" from these projects and commitments; they are "the source of his actions."[4]

These words return us to the notion of the self for which I criticized Williams in the first chapter.[5] He seems, I said there, to lay undue stress on a self's living up to its own specific definition, while at the same time demanding that that definition be self-created. To the question, "why live up to your own definition?" he has no good answer, nor to the question, "why create this or that definition for yourself?" (Why adopt just *these* projects?) In providing foundations for ethics, integrity appeared to be a bad place to start. But the fact of our moral consciousness, the simple fact that we do set great store on having and living out a specific identity, Williams captures eloquently and truly.

Ethics can proceed from an account of the self, or of a formal condition of the self like freedom or consistency, and then try to justify specific values, norms of decision, etc., or it can begin by accepting the reality of virtues or values and then try to make room for a self. The advantage of the first approach is that it never loses sight of the audience needing to hear it—an individual decision-maker—but it runs the risk of never being able to derive any (non-selfish) values, or give any (non-selfish) reasons for adopting values. The second approach has no problem making sense of objective values, but can wind up distancing those values so far from the moral agent that either they seem completely arbitrary or the agent is told to renounce his self in the name of some kind of determinism. The cultural relativist, in particular, frequently seems to tell us either that our ethics are just an accompaniment of the fact that humans happen to breed cultures, or that we shouldn't worry about the fact that our culture tells us what to do because we can't help following it anyway. I want

1 Williams in (Smart & Williams, 1973), p.99.
2 *ibid*, pp.103-4.
3 *ibid*, p.116.
4 *ibid*, pp.111-2.
5 See p.15.

to avoid this trap, and shall therefore now try to show how individuals can embrace their culture's norms as their own. This may be none too easy, since my approach seems to share some of the unpleasant qualities Williams attributes to utilitarianism. He complains repeatedly about the utilitarian's tendency to tell people what they should do regardless of their individual feelings and beliefs, and sometimes he uses language that could apply equally well to any version of cultural determinism. The utilitarian, he says at one point, makes the agent "into a channel between the input of everyone's projects and an output of optimific decision."[6] Read "moral beliefs" for "projects," and "acceptable decision" for "optimific decision," and I appear to hold the same ridiculous position.

As may be apparent by now, I intend to get out of this situation by showing how integrity is built into our very language-games in ethics, and indeed I cite Williams because he provides an elegant example of how the language for integrity may work. Notice that he does not tell us exactly what the referent of the word is. Instead, he unworriedly uses the metaphors "source" and "flow" and "identity," with (justifiable) confidence that we will know just what he is getting at. This does not mean that integrity is a *mere* language-game, or that we merely happen to have such a language-game, but that language-games, here as elsewhere, can reflect deep facts about the way we live and must live, what we imagine and what we cannot imagine.

The language-games of integrity guide us, as Williams indicates, towards integrating our selves with our actions in as coherent a way as possible, but they are also closely bound to ways in which we talk about truth. Sissela Bok writes that "the word 'integrity' comes from the same roots which have formed 'intact' and 'untouched' [and] is used especially often in relation to truthfulness and fair dealing."[7] Being "untouched" implies being independent, in the sense that my cultural approach still needs to account for, and being "intact" implies being unified, in the sense that Williams discusses, but what do the independence and unity of a self have to do with truth? I suggest that, just as one can only determine the internal consistency of an object or system according to an external standard of what it "is supposed to be," so even the individual self can only determine its own internal coherence if it is trying to live up to some external measure, if it can take its ideals and the maxims of its actions as corresponding or failing to correspond with the truth about how to live. Writing about repentance, which he considers a restoration of "spiritual integrity,"[8]

---

6 (Smart & Williams, 1973), p.112.

7 (Bok, 1979), p.27. Compare also Hannah Arendt: "...when [the philosopher] enters the political realm and identifies himself with some partial interest and power formation, [he] compromises on the only quality that could have made his truth appear plausible, namely, his personal truthfulness, guaranteed by impartiality, integrity, independence." ("Truth and Politics," in [Arendt, 1977], p.250).

8 (Soloveitchik, 1984), p.51.

Rabbi Joseph Soloveitchik insists that the soul finds coherence only when it breaks apart from all social and cultural influences and comes into a direct relationship with God:

> Man cannot be considered upright and trustworthy if he is subject to the sways of public opinion, if he seeks to find favor with some, to please others and to be popular everywhere. When man repents, he has to settle one account only, and when he comes to confess he must have in mind only that he is standing "before God, blessed be He."[9]

The religious traditionalist says that one achieves one's own integrity only when confronting God; a less directly theological version of that claim might simply hold that one must at least take oneself to be tracking some absolute ideal. The paradox of integrity is that a self achieves independence and unity only when it attempts to follow an external standard, to come into correspondence with an ethical truth; the paradox of truth, as we have seen, is that it needs both to be independent of the thoughts and wishes of all individuals and to be something that individuals can recognize and choose to follow.

In ordinary usage, this marriage of integrity to truth comes out in the fact that we may use the word "integrity" to describe people whose ideals we do not share,[10] but not those who lack any ideals. The actions of the latter may have some consistency, but one we are loath to consider deliberate: we are more likely to believe that one who consistently "drifts" through life, or acts in a consistently childish, silly and/or egoistic way, has been determined by some unfortunate psychological condition than that he has chosen such a manner as an ideal for which to strive. And we are likely to consider one who "pursu[es] an ideal of sincerity," to use Harry Frankfurt's words, without recognizing that "as conscious beings, we exist only in response to other things, and we cannot know ourselves at all without knowing them," as thereby reducing sincerity itself to "bullshit."[11] Frankfurt insists that sincerity will make sense only in relation to an "objective reality," a truth about things to know and adhere to. There is no sincerity, and *a fortiori* no integrity, where it makes no difference what specific shape a self takes, what specific life-plan an individual follows.

In discussing ethical truth, I have thus been concerned with integrity indirectly from the very beginning of this book, and began to address the issue of the individual's adherence to a specific ethical perspective in chapter seven. To have integrity an individual needs a specific content, a sense that he cannot give up at least some of those commitments without "losing his soul," and a sense at the same time that he is free to accept or reject those commitments, that he has adopted this identity himself rather than having thoughtlessly, or

9 *ibid*, p.80.

10 Although we must be able to see their goals and standards *as* ideals at all: hence the inappropriateness of talking of a Nazi with integrity.

11 (Frankfurt, 1987), p.17.

unconsciously, had it inculcated in him. In chapter seven, I addressed the problem of how a self might come to identify with a specific culture, how it might answer the question, "why should *this* be my culture, rather than some other group or set of ideas?" Unlike naive cultural determinists, I tried to resist the temptation to see the self as a free-floating, independent organism that happens to be molded into one or another shape by the social environment in which it is raised. Instead, I took "culture" and "self" as interwoven, such that there was no self until an individual emerged from a process of human teaching, and there was no "culture," in the sense of the fullest social expression and shaper of human thought, independent of the choices of individuals. It followed that, to the ethical agent, culture will necessarily appear in multiple ways—as literature, as religion, as political entity; as this or that particular group—reflecting the different ways in which people are raised, choose to act, and choose, in turn, to raise their children.

In chapter eight I considered the ways in which individuals in our culture can remain faithful to it in the face of the recognition that other cultures do not always share its ethic, the sense in which we need not or cannot give up our culturally informed commitments, even when they come to look somewhat arbitrary. Williams, like Strawson (and Hume) before him,[12] tells us that "our moral relation to the world is partly given by [our moral] feelings, and by a sense of what we can or cannot 'live with.'"[13] Hence, "to come to regard those feelings...as happenings outside one's moral self, is to lose a sense of one's moral identity; to lose, in the most literal way, one's integrity."[14] Williams' target is again the utilitarian, but the toleration of activities in other cultures that outrage us could also require a suspension of moral feelings we are unable to live with. In direct response to that possibility, I spent much of the last chapter arguing that our inability to accept certain kinds of acts, to face ourselves afterwards if we allow them, is precisely the right source of justification for ceasing to tolerate, and that toleration itself, as a general attitude towards members of other groups, follows not from an abstract principle of relativism but from our own specific feelings and commitments.

What remains is to show to each individual why he might reasonably be said to have chosen, to hold as his "own," the cultural norms with which he finds himself, rather than merely to have "fallen into" them, to have wound up with a specific identity as a matter of determination or chance. I construe this question as turning on the matter of consent, and intend to answer it, indirectly again, by examining the language of that activity. In particular, I will emphasize the fact that while consenting to something need not require an explicit affirmation of consent, it does require that one have *an unexercised option of dissent*. That is, if we wish to say that the individuals of our culture consent to

---

12 See (Strawson, 1974), p.24.

13 (Smart & Williams, 1973), p.103.

14 *ibid*, pp.103-4.

its norms, we must posit, in theory and practice, a possibility of their dissenting, even if people rarely or never make use of that possibility. For which reason I approach the problem of integrity, in this chapter, by asking how dissent can occur in a culturally based ethic.

Political Dissent

> We all live and survive by a kind of *tacit consent*, which, however, it would be difficult to call voluntary. How can we will what is there anyhow? We might call it voluntary, though, when [a] child happens to be born into a community in which dissent is also a legal and *de facto* possibility once he has grown into a man. Dissent implies consent...; one who knows that he may dissent knows also that he somehow consents when he does not dissent.[15]

Simon Blackburn, arguing directly against a Wittgensteinian conception of moral truth, objects that it leaves "no room for [the notion]...that a man who dissents from the herd may yet be right."[16] "One of the essential possibilities for a moral thinker," he maintains, "is that of self-criticism, and of the thought that our own culture and way of life leads us to corrupted judgment." It is not easy to see how to construe this possibility "if objectivity is somehow 'based on' consonance in a form of life."[17] On the Wittgensteinian view, when two parts of the general consensus diverge on an issue, it seems that there is no right or wrong between them, and when one person differs from all the rest he is necessarily wrong.[18] Yet in actual practice "moral judgments are not based on consensus in such a way that they cannot be turned on that consensus, and find it lacking."[19] Rather, "if most of us came to find wanton violence admirable, that is not what is for wanton violence to become admirable: it is what it is for most of us to deteriorate, in a familiar and fearful way."[20] Blackburn recommends that we adopt instead a projectivist moral sentiment theory, like Hume's, in which self-criticism can be understood as the use of some of our dispositions to evaluate others. Just as one may dislike one's own cowardice or pride, so we may all condemn and try to alter our shared chauvinist, or aggressive, or obstinate tendencies, even though both the tendencies and the source of condemnation are dispositions.

This objection, while aimed at a crucial issue, does not give the consensus account enough credit. It is tempting to take the very short line of pointing out that disagreement with our consensus might be one of the things the consensus itself considers good: in liberal democracies, at least, we may say that we have a tradition of criticizing our traditions, an agreement that disagreement is

15 "Civil Disobedience," in (Arendt, 1972), p.88.
16 (Blackburn, 1981), p.171.
17 *ibid.*
18 *ibid*, pp.172-3.
19 *ibid*, p.174.
20 *ibid.*

healthy. But this way of putting things either leaves the legitimacy of disagreement a paradox or implies that we merely "agree to disagree." Agreeing to disagree does not at all meet Blackburn's concerns, and if the consensus view can allow more than that, the question is not what disagreement a particular consensus might happen to permit, but whether, and how, self-criticism can be construed as intrinsic to the structure of consensus in the way that self-revision is intrinsic to the structure of our dispositions.

Lovibond describes a consensus view that has such a possibility of self-reflection, arguing that forms of life tend to be "imperfectly coherent," that they "encompass...institutions which are dedicated to incompatible (or dubiously compatible) ends," from which "there can arise...competing habits of judging and reasoning...whose exponents can engage in mutual rational criticism."[21] "Rational dissent" is thus clearly possible, the dissenter normally belonging to a subgroup of the general consensus, which shares enough judgments with the larger group to engage in debate with that group, and to attempt, as the dispositionalist does within his set of emotions, to revise some parts of the agreement in judgment by using other parts of it: "The dissenting values, too, are grounded in the [shared] form of life whose partially alienated members draw upon them to articulate and justify their own alienated condition."[22] About the lone dissenter, the solitary person who refuses to "goose-step...along with"[23] even a subgroup of everyone else, Lovibond says that his belief in the *correctness* of his dissenting position "prefigures, through its implicit [cognitivism], a condition in which others will have come to share [his] values."[24] In other words, even the lone dissenter lays claim to elements of the shared form of life, and assumes that a sub-group of the community, followed eventually by the whole, can and will come to accept these elements as indeed the appropriate ones to stress.

Lovibond's description admirably captures the workings and self-understanding of much real moral practice, in contemporary society, from civil rights movements, to the position of many abortion activists (on both sides), to the views of those who hold vegetarianism, or an abhorrence of hunting, to be not merely a personal sentiment or preference but a goal for all people. In the United States, we have a society with some elitist and some egalitarian values and institutions, some practices reverent of religion, especially when it comes to sexuality and the definition of life, and some dedicated to the secular views of those same issues, some traditions aiming at a deeper compassion for all living beings than most people achieve, and some aiming at a rugged approach to the natural order in which, among other things, inter-species killing is accepted as a normal part of that order. These splits allow for opposing claims

---

21 (Lovibond, 1983), p.128.

22 *ibid.*

23 Blackburn, p.173.

24 (Lovibond, 1983), pp.163-4.

to right, some of which win over the whole (the civil rights movement), some of which remain in constant tension with one another (the abortion controversy), and some of which dig in to form a fairly stable polarization between majority and minority (hunters versus animal rights supporters). Not by chance, all these examples are political. I will argue in the next section that there is an important kind of moral dissent about which Lovibond has little to say. But let me first flesh out just how the consensus view can make room for political disagreements.

Hannah Arendt most forcefully and subtly demonstrates such a possibility. For Arendt, dissent forms an intrinsic part of the (ideal) political community, and the political community is the (ideal) place for moral norms to be expressed. The political for her is quintessentially a realm of discourse, in which important issues are debated and deeds occur as a kind of theater, to be criticized and reflected upon by the citizens as if they constituted an audience:

> The performing arts...have indeed a strong affinity with politics. Performing artists—dancers, play-actors, musicians, and the like—need an audience to show their virtuosity, just as acting men need the presence of others before whom they can appear; both need a publicly organized space for their "work," and both depend upon others for the performance itself....The Greek polis once was precisely that "form of government" which provided men with a space of appearances where they could act, with a kind of theater where freedom could appear.[25]

Arendt ties this theatrical conception of the political to a reading of Kant's *Critique of Judgment*, by which political discussion, much like the talk of art critics and audiences, centers around propositions one wants to share with others but cannot prove either by reason or by empirical evidence. The political debater therefore proceeds, like Kant's aesthetic debater, via an attempt to imagine himself in the position of others in his community, and, from those positions, to "woo their consent," or allow himself to be so wooed:

> I should like to draw upon the first part of Kant's *Critique of Judgment*, which, as "Critique of Esthetic Judgment," contains perhaps the greatest and most original aspect of Kant's political philosophy....Kant [there] insisted upon a...way of thinking, for which it would not be enough to be in agreement with one's own self, but which consisted of being able to "think in the place of everybody else" and which he therefore called an "enlarged mentality"...Taste judgments...are...held to be arbitrary because they do not compel in the sense in which demonstrable facts or truth proved by argument compel agreement. They share with political opinions that they are persuasive; the judging person—as Kant says quite beautifully—can only "woo the consent of everyone else" in the hope of coming to an agreement with him eventually. This "wooing" or persuading corresponds closely to...the convincing and persuading speech which [the Greeks] regarded as the typically political form of people talking with one another.[26]

---

25 (Arendt, 1968), p.154.

26 *ibid*, pp. 219, 220, 222.

It is in this discursive forum that Arendt believes freedom, the practical self-definition of the human being, most fully finds a home:

> The field where freedom has always been known, ... as a fact of everyday life, is the political realm.
>
> ... the actual content of political life [consists in] the joy and the gratification that arise out of being in company with our peers, out of acting together and appearing in public, out of inserting ourselves into the world by word and deed, thus acquiring and sustaining our personal identity and beginning something entirely new.[27]

On such a conception of the political, dissent is not only tolerable but essential, not only a part of "imperfectly coherent" communities but of all communities.[28] Politics is discussion, for Arendt, and discussion does not proceed without disagreement. The grounding of this arena for discussion in freedom, moreover, especially the freedom Arendt calls "beginning something entirely new," entails that disagreement will not only be endemic but will constantly take new forms, turn in surprising directions, turn on the ever different choices of ever new individuals, rather than coagulating into set blocs of majorities and minorities, warring or entrenched groups. Hence there can be lone dissent as well as group dissent, the only condition on this being that the lone dissenter, who as such remains a participant in the discussion, lay claim to the agreement of others (attempt to woo their consent)—as does the aesthetic iconoclast who declares an extraordinary object or style to be "beautiful." When Arendt comes to her profound and careful defense of civil disobedience as a part of the American tradition of politics, she stresses the fact that "the civil disobedient, though he is usually dissenting from the majority, [does act] in the name and for the sake of a group."[29]

It is only in the essay on civil disobedience, however, that she begins to give full recognition to the fact that not all moral action can be construed as political. We have seen above how Arendt in several earlier essays located freedom paradigmatically in the political realm. In "Civil Disobedience," she distinguishes disobedients importantly from conscientious objectors, whom she says are moral but not political actors because "conscience is unpolitical."[30] Conscience, taking place as and within "the soundless dialogue between me and myself" by which she characterizes thinking, tells me how to live as an

---

[27] *ibid*, pp. 146, 263.

[28] Note that this account fits what chapter seven says about the necessary splits within cultures, and within the definition of the term "culture." There too the divisions arise from the interrelation of individual effects upon a community and community determination of individuals. This interrelation is predicated, however, on the possibility of a more fundamental kind of individually chosen action than Arendt offers, a more fundamental kind of freedom. I consider that possibility in section B of this chapter.

[29] (Arendt, 1972), p.76.

[30] *ibid*, pp. 60, 62ff.

individual, perhaps as a philosopher,[31] but not as a citizen; indeed, if I bring it into the "marketplace" I thereby transform it into a mere opinion, which for it, as for "the philosopher's truth," amounts to a loss of the qualities that define its very form and role.

This account of conscience and of truth recalls the Heidegger of *Being and Time*, for whom discourse, especially among the "they," the "marketplace" (polis), both claims and diminishes truth, for whom the "call of conscience," the call to authenticity, comes in silence:

> Losing itself in the publicness and the idle talk of the "they," [Dasein] *fails to hear* its own self in listening to the they-self....If Dasein is to be able to get brought back from this lostness of failing to hear itself[,]...[t]his listening-away to the ["they"] must get broken off...and [the] listening-away gets broken by the call [that]...arouses another kind of hearing which...has a character in every way opposite....[T]he call must do its calling without any hubbub and unambiguously, leaving no room for curiousity [as idle talk always does]....*That which, by calling in this manner gives us to understand, is the conscience.*[32]

Arendt had introduced the notion of the silent dialogue between me and myself earlier, in "What is Freedom?" and "Truth and Politics,"[33] but there—and perhaps, to some extent, even here—she was uneasy about allowing it to be fully non-political. In "What is Freedom?" she writes that "the appearance of the problem of freedom [of the will] in Augustine's philosophy was...preceded by the conscious attempt to divorce the notion of freedom from politics, to arrive at a formulation through which one may be a slave in the world and still be free,"[34] and goes on to suggest that despite the "strong anti-political tendencies of early Christianity," a "Christian thinker," namely Augustine himself, was the first to come up with "the philosophical implications of the ancient political idea of freedom."[35] Augustine's freedom of the will turns out to be roughly conscience, while the "ancient political idea" yields what she wants to call "natality," but she reads natality into a most non-political section of Augustine (see below) while she derives conscience from a deliberate attempt by politically oppressed Romans to"reason [themselves] out of the [political] world."[36] Now the supposedly non-political conscience, besides having its roots in a reaction to a political situation, consists in a "dialogue," albeit a silent one, a form of thinking and arguing which would seem to go well with a conception of politics as discussion and civil disobedience as communication. At the same time, the supposedly political "radically new beginning" ("natality"), besides coming out of a piece of eschatological argument in

---

31 (Arendt, 1978), pp. 31, 122, 185, 190.
32 (Heidegger, 1962), pp.315-6.
33 (Arendt, 1968), pp. 157-8, 245.
34 *ibid*, p.147.
35 *ibid*, p.167.
36 *ibid*, p.157. Cf. also pp. 146-8, 245, 263.

Augustine, by definition does not and cannot belong to a tradition, hence should fit but poorly into an ongoing discussion of opinions in a community of shared history and ideas. In addition to these hints of paradox, consider the fact that Arendt locates both notions of freedom historically, and in canonical texts, rather than deriving them from necessary conditions of thought or action: she seems reluctant to let her own work fly free from tradition and ongoing discussion. It is hard to resist the conclusion that Arendt, possibly because of the stupidity and insensitivity she had witnessed in Heidegger's attempt, first to bring his lofty abstractions into politics, and then to divorce himself from that realm entirely, cannot bring herself to allow any fully non-political dimension to human life, at least until she uses the Heideggerian word "conscience" for internal freedom in the late essay "Civil Disobedience" and the equally late study *The Life of the Mind*.[37] At any rate, while I will begin considering the specifically non-political kind of dissent (freedom) with Arendt's notion of "natality," its curious ambiguities and vagueness will lead me to supplement it, and the history she gives for it, with a set of texts whose alienation from politics is more complete than she was ever able to countenance.

Radical Dissent

"It is in the nature of beginning that something new is started which cannot be expected from whatever may have happened before."[38] Thus does Arendt describe natality in *The Human Condition*, and she makes clear, here and elsewhere, that she regards it as the prime characteristic of human action. Alasdair MacIntyre also talks about the "radically new," and he also sees unpredictability as an essential feature of human action, although of the four sources he gives for unpredictability only one,[39] seems close to Arendt's concerns:

> It is at first sight a trivial truth that when I have not yet made up my mind which of two or more alternative and mutually exclusive courses of action to take I cannot predict which I shall take. Decisions contemplated but not yet made by me entail unpredictability of me by me in the relevant areas. But this truth seems trivial precisely because what I cannot predict of myself others may well be able to predict about me. ... [For] an adequately informed observer provided both with the relevant data about me and the relevant stock of generalizations concerning people of my type, my future, so it seems, may be representable as an entirely determinable set of stages. Yet a difficulty at once arises. For this observer who is able to predict what I cannot is of course unable to predict his own future in just the way that I am unable to predict mine; and one of the features which he will be unable to predict,

---

[37] I can find no reference to the word "conscience," at least as a technical term, in any of Arendt's writings prior to "Civil Disobedience." Nor does there seem to be any substantial discussion of Heidegger prior to *The Life of the Mind* ("Willing," pp.172-94).

[38] (Arendt, 1958), pp.177-8.

[39] And *not* the one he calls "radical newness."

> since it depends in substantial part upon decisions as yet unmade by him, is how far his actions will impact upon and change the decisions made by others. ... Now among those others is me. It follows that insofar as the observer cannot predict the impact of his future actions on my future decision-making, he cannot predict my future actions any more than he can his own; and this clearly holds for all agents and observers.[40]

The unpredictability here, however, lies most deeply in the agent's point-of-view, not the observer's, while for Arendt, determined as she is to make freedom political, the reverse is true: "Every act, seen not from the perspective of the agent but of the process in whose framework it occurs and whose automatism it interrupts, is a 'miracle'—that is, something which could not be expected."[41] But actions do not generally seem to interrupt the processes in which they occur. Indeed, it is a notorious problem for both "free will" and "originality" theorists that, as MacIntyre acknowledges, it always seems possible for an outsider to place a supposedly free act into a perfectly plausible causal chain beginning outside the agent, or to analyze a supposedly original creation into a chain of influences quite independent of the author.

The example with which Arendt likes to illustrate her idea of beginning—human birth—and the text to which she attributes it—"that a beginning might be, man was created," (*City of God* xii, 20) which concludes a discussion of why God would not condemn us to endless cycles of happiness and misery—only increase the oddity of her account. Human birth by no means constitutes an unprecedented event to any of us; it brings something into the world whose first appearance is usually its *most* predictable; and it is a result of a very familiar causal chain. Certainly, there may be a feeling of radical novelty for the parents, at least if this is their first child, and an imagined feeling of radical novelty for the adult version of the baby, reflecting back on what birth might have been like, but these feelings are illusions, reinforcing, if anything, the impression that novelty—originality, beginning, freedom, etc.—is itself an illusion. Arendt suggests that if Augustine had drawn out the full implications of the passage she cites, "he would have defined men, not, like the Greeks, as mortals, but as 'natals.'"[42] This is an implicit challenge to Heidegger (not the Greeks) and his Being-towards-death, but it is much more plausible to understand human projects and self-definition in terms of an anticipation of our deaths, which we face as adults and which can affect our choices, than as a development out of or response to birth.

Nor was Augustine, by any means, slack in drawing out the implications of his own words, if only because the passage ending in those words was concerned with the origin of the first man, not the birth of subsequent ones.

---

40 (MacIntyre, 1981), p.91 (see also 92).
41 (Arendt, 1968), p.169.
42 (Arendt, 1978), "Willing," p.109.

"Every man," interprets Arendt, "being created in the singular, is a new beginning by virtue of his birth,"[43] but Augustine was not talking about birth at all. The creation he refers to (Gen. 1:27 and 2:7) does not even involve birth; his emphasis is on the novelty of the creating act, not of what happened to be created; and it is God's creation, not man's, that forms the source and definition of novelty.

Had Arendt been less queasy about mysticism, especially antisocial mysticism, and even more especially antisocial mysticism that inspired Heidegger,[44] she might have found a better source for natality in the writings of Meister Eckhart. Augustine, after all, remains political in his very rejection of politics: he renounces the city of man only to seek a city of God. Eckhart, by contrast, like his successor Heidegger, is frustratingly oblivious to the possibility that social interaction of any kind could ever be of importance. But Eckhart, far more than Augustine, is the appropriate philosopher of birth and newness. In sermon after sermon, he hammers at the same one theme: that God is born in the soul, that the soul has no purpose except to allow God to be born into it, and that God has no function or activity other than to be born over and over:

> Why did God beome man? So that I might be born to be God—yes—identically God.
>
> [God] begets [his Son] in the soul just as he does in eternity...
>
> All of God's efforts are directed to reproducing himself. He gives [himself] to everything alike and yet they all behave differently, each seeking to reproduce himself.
>
> God desires urgently that you, the creature, get out of his way—as if his own blessedness depended on it. Ah, beloved people, why don't you let God be God in you?...You get completely out of his way and he will get out of yours—you give up to him and he will give up to you. When both [God and you] have forsaken self, what remains [between you] is an indivisible union. It is in this unity that the Father begets his Son in the secret spring of your nature.[45]

The originality of this position lies in the fact that for Eckhart the Incarnation is not (as Creation is for Augustine) a historical event, to which we may look as a model, or in which we may have some kind of symbolic "participation," or by which the world of our action is structured and informed, but an eternal characteristic, indeed the only and the defining characteristic, of God, the world, and ourselves—all of which are and must be identical. This thoroughgoing monism, derived perhaps from John Scotus Eriugena[46] and anticipating

---

[43] *ibid.*

[44] "[Arendt] told Mary McCarthy she was convinced that 'the so-called late Heidegger' was entirely influenced by the work of the German mystic, Meister Eckhart, and she knew well enough that universities are not designed for helping mystics return to earth from their philosophical flights." (Young-Bruehl, 1982), p.444.

[45] (Eckhart, 1941), pp. 194, 98, 190, 127.

[46] Dermot Moran suggested this, in a 1987 seminar on medieval philosophy at Yale.

Spinoza, comes too close to pantheism, self-worship, the denial of contingency, and the denial of sin, to be congenial to mainstream Christianity (hence Eckhart's trial for heresy), but it provides those who do take it up with powerful reasons to define human being by "birth." And "birth" for Eckhart means exactly what it does for Arendt: the unexpected, the undetermined, something that is not entailed by any idea or action and not anticipated by any feeling. In awaiting God's birth in us, he feels, we should withdraw to silence, strip ideas from our minds, withhold ourselves from any attitude except "releasement" (*Gelassenheit*):[47]

> ...where is [God's] word to be spoken?...[I]n the purest element of the soul, in the soul's most exalted place, in the core, yes, in the essence of the soul. The central silence is there, where no creature may enter, nor any idea, and there the soul neither thinks nor acts, nor entertains any idea, either of itself or of anything else.
>
> What should a man do to secure and deserve the occurrence and perfection of this birth in his soul? Should he co-operate by imagining and thinking about God, or should he keep quiet, be silent and at peace, so that God may speak and act through him? Should he do nothing but wait until God does act?...[Good and perfect] persons know that the best life and the loftiest is to be silent and to let God speak and act through one.[48]

It follows from this great concern with ceasing to anticipate that Eckhart had to repeat his message again and again, lest the last time he taught, the last way he phrased his thought or read it into the Bible, itself become the "idea" to which we cling instead of releasing ourselves to God's birth.

I could pass from the notion of "releasement," or of the overturning of habitual thoughts and ways of acting, directly to the later Heidegger, but I go instead via Kierkegaard, to bring to the fore a problem about ethics. The danger of Eckhart's vision is that it may lead to a contempt for the ethical, and indeed Eckhart has scant respect for "good works," in any ordinary sense:

> Praying, reading, singing, watching, fasting, and doing penance—all these virtuous practices were contrived to catch us and keep us away from strange, ungodly things. Thus, if one feels that the spirit of God is not at work in him, that he has departed inwardly from God, he will all the more feel the need to do virtuous deeds....But when a person has a true spiritual experience, he may boldly drop external disciplines, even those to which he is bound by vows, from which even a bishop may not release him.[49]

---

47 This is Reiner Schürmann's translation of *Gelassenheit*, which he uses in a book suggesting strong philosophical connections between Eckhart and the later Heidegger: (Schürmann, 1978).

48 (Eckhart, 1941), pp. 96, 98.

49 *ibid*, pp.115-6. M.O'C. Walshe reports some doubt as to the authenticity of this sermon, but he himself appears not to share this doubt. (Walshe, 1979), vol. I, p.36, note 1.) I am indebted to Professor Michael Sells (Religion, Haverford College) for pointing this out. He feels that my general point about Eckhart and ethics will go through, though he does not think it comes quite as unambiguously out of the text as I indicate.

Kierkegaard shares much of Eckhart's approach to religion, as we shall see, but he is alive to the ethical problems such inward turning may raise. Like Eckhart, Kierkegaard believes that only the relationship between self and God can be of interest to the religious individual; like Eckhart, he characterizes that relationship as outside ordinary ways of thinking and acting; and like Eckhart, most importantly, he believes God's revelation must establish its own locus in the mind. In connection with this last point, the following passage from Eckhart will find resonance in the core of both Kierkegaard's and Heidegger's thought:

> For God does not intend that man shall have a place reserved for *him* to work in, since true poverty of spirit requires that man shall be emptied of god and all his works, so that if God wants to act in the soul, he himself must be the place in which he acts—and that he would like to do. For if God once found a person as poor as this, he would take the responsibility of his own action and would himself be the *scene* of action....Thus we say that a man should be so poor that he is not and has not a place for God to act in. To reserve a place would be to maintain distinctions.[50]

The parallel poverty for Kierkegaard consists in lacking the conditions (criteria) for divine truth. If truth is not merely recollected but learned, he says, if, as the supposition of an external truth requires, we do not already possess all truth relevant to our lives, then

> ...the Teacher must bring [Truth] to [the learner]; and not only so, but he must give him the condition necessary for understanding it...But the one who gives the learner not only the truth, but also the condition necessary for understanding it, is more than teacher. All instruction depends upon the presence, in the last analysis, of the requisite condition; if this is lacking, no teacher can do anything. For otherwise he would find it necessary not only to transform the learner, but to recreate him before beginning to teach him. But this is something that no human being can do; if it is to be done, it must be done by the God himself.[51]

And as the word "recreate" indicates, Kierkegaard too favors the metaphor of (re-)birth for the realization of undetermined and unexpected novelty:

> In so far as the learner was in Error, and now receives the Truth and with it the condition for understanding it, a change takes place within him like the change from non-being to being. But this transition from non-being to being is the transition we call birth. Now one who exists cannot be born; nevertheless, the disciple is born. Let us call this transition the *New Birth*, in consequence of which the disciple enters the world quite as at the first birth, an individual human being knowing nothing as yet about the world into which he is born...[52]

But Kierkegaard does not take lightly the ethical implications of this position about birth. In *Fear and Trembling* he emphasizes action rather than truth, but

---

50 *ibid*, pp.230-1.
51 (Kierkegaard, 1962), pp.17-8.
52 *ibid*, p.23.

the paradox of a conditioned containing its own conditions appears anyway, in the form of a choice containing its own standards for choosing. Choices, like the acceptance of truth, are intrinsically something we perform on the basis of prior criteria, but this is a criterionless choice:

> ...one knight of faith can render no aid to [an]other. Either the individual becomes a knight of faith by assuming the burden of the paradox, or he never becomes one. In these regions partnership is unthinkable. Every more precise explication of what is to be understood by Isaac [that which must be offered, in faith, for sacrifice] the individual can give only to himself.[53]

A person who acts on faith cannot explain himself to others. Yet such explanation is the distinctive mark of the ethical, since Kierkegaard, following Kant, identifies the ethical with the universal—that which is both applicable and explicable to all human beings. The faithful individual has "an absolute relation to the absolute," that is, a God-determined relation to God, not a relation, even an absolute (God-determined) relation to the universal;[54] hence his position cannot be "mediated," which means both "justified" and "explained."[55] "Abraham cannot be mediated, and the same thing can be expressed also by saying that he cannot talk. So soon as I talk I express the universal, and if I do not do so, no one can understand me."[56] But it follows from this that Abraham's position, and the position of the faithful person in general, looks very much like that of one who has made no ethical choice (who lives in "the aesthetic," which is also unmediated),[57] and exactly like that of one fully committed to evil:

> The tragic hero who is the favorite of ethics is the purely human, and him I can understand, and all he does is in the light of the revealed. If I go further, then I stumble upon the paradox, either the divine or the demoniac, for silence is both. Silence is the snare of the demon, and the more one keeps silent, the more terrifying the demon becomes; but silence is also the mutual understanding between the Deity and the individual.
>
> The demoniacal has the same characteristic as the divine inasmuch as the individual can enter into an absolute relation to it. This is the analogy, the counterpart, to that paradox of which we are talking. It has therefore a certain resemblance which may deceive one.[58]

---

53 (Kierkegaard, 1974), p.82.

54 *ibid*, p.103.

55 Cf. *ibid*, p.82, on "universal categories," p.67, on "argumentation," and pp. 102-3, 122, on making oneself "intelligible."

56 *ibid*, p.70.

57 *ibid*, pp. 79, 92.

58 *ibid*, pp. 97, 106.

Now, Kierkegaard does think there are discernable differences between the demoniacal and the divine,[59] and that some, particularly "those who possess faith," may be able to set up "certain criteria"[60] informing us what conditions do *not* count as a relation to the paradox, but nothing can ever guarantee for us what conditions do so count. We may never uncover more than a *via negativa* to religious commitment. This comes out when the pseudonymous author of *Fear and Trembling*, who says he can only admire, not understand Abraham, tells us that the examples of silent heroes he has adduced "do none of them contain an analogy to Abraham," but only "at the moment of variation [from Abraham's case] indicate as it were the boundary of the unknown land."[61] He also tells us that "distress and anguish are the only legitimations [of the state of faith] that can be thought of, and they cannot be thought in general terms, for with that the paradox is annulled."[62] In other words, the knight of faith necessarily goes through distress and anguish, but not everyone going through distress and anguish is a knight of faith, and as soon as these emotions are set down "in general terms"—as criteria—people without faith will be inclined to induce such pain in themselves as a way to faith. In that case, however, the distress and anguish reflect self-determination rather than God-determination, which means that one abandons the paradox of choosing to let God determine one's choice, and falls into temptation instead.[63] "The ethical expression for what Abraham did is, that he would murder Isaac,"[64] and nothing Abraham can say, or we can say about Abraham, will render the religious transformation of that wrong intelligible:

> Abraham keeps silent—but he *cannot* speak. Therein lies the distress and anguish. For if I when I speak am unable to make myself intelligible, then I am not speaking—even though I were to talk uninterruptedly day and night. Such is the case with Abraham. He is able to utter everything, but one thing he cannot say, i.e. say it in such a way that another understands it, and so he is not speaking.[65]

Silence is the price of faith, although silence, precisely where faith makes itself most clearly known, is ethically unacceptable. What I call "radical dissent" in this chapter functions in exactly the same way, but the paradox I want to offer consists in inserting this silent act *into* ethics, in making ethics swallow the ethically unpalatable.

Before I explain this, however, let us turn to Heidegger. The echo of Eckhart's remark about God's creating the scene of His own appearance occurs

---

59 The demoniacal *can* talk, for one: see *ibid*, p.106.
60 *ibid*, p.67.
61 *ibid*, p.120.
62 *ibid*, p.122.
63 Cf. *ibid*, p.106, where the demoniacal merman does not "spare himself any torment."
64 *ibid*, p.41.
65 *ibid*, p.122.

in Heidegger's writing as the notion that the Open—the scene of "unconcealment" or revelation—opens itself:

> The openness of this Open, that is, truth, can be what it is ... only if and as long as it establishes itself within its Open. ... In taking possession...of the Open, the openness holds open the Open and sustains it. ... Clearing of openness and establishment in the Open belong together. They are the same single nature of the happening of truth.
>
> The work is...transported into the openness of being—an openness opened by itself. (OWA 61, 66)

As for Kierkegaard and Eckhart, this self-created creation signals the possibility of radical newness:

> The establishing of truth in the work is the bringing forth of a being such as never was before and will never come to be again.
>
> ...unconcealedness of what is has happened here, and...as this happening it happens here for the first time...(OWA 62, 65)[66]

With a perhaps unconscious allusion to the Kierkegaardian "leap of faith," Heidegger ties these reflections to the very nature of an origin: "To originate something by a leap, to bring something into being from out of the source of its nature in a founding leap—this is what the word origin (German *Ursprung*, literally, primal leap) means" (OWA 77-8).

The great importance of Heidegger, in this tradition about "beginnings," lies in that he alone is finally able to take it out of the realm of theology. He does this by way of what I take to be another allusion to Eckhart, and a brilliant twist on it. Eckhart himself writes as follows:

> ... the vision and experience of God is too much of a burden to the soul while it is in the body and so God withdraws intermittently ... What one grows to know and comes to love and remember, his soul follows after. Knowing this, our Lord hides himself from time to time, for the soul is an elemental form of the body, so that what once gains its attention holds it. If the soul were to know the goodness of God, as it is and without interruption, it would never turn away and therefore would never direct the body ... Since ... the divine goodness is alien to this life and incompatible with it, faithful God veils it or reveals it when he will, or when he knows it will be most useful and best for you that he do so.[67]

Heidegger adopts, as a powerful and oft-reiterated component of his thought, the notion that concealment belongs inevitably with unconcealment, but not as a contingency, or a consequence of the incommensurabilty of soul and body. That division goes awkwardly, in any case, with Eckhart's monism, but Heidegger does not need to enter into such theological niceties because he takes

---

66 in (Heidegger, 1971).

67 (Eckhart, 1941), p.110.

issue with a much more glaring problem in the Eckhart text: that familiarity breeds eternal attention and concern. Rather, what is familiar fades from true understanding and commitment by its very familiarity: "Truth is never gathered from objects that are present and ordinary." (OWA 71) The particulars of "this life" are therefore not alien to the vision of truth but essential to it, because only particulars can be ever new, ever unexpected, ever challenging to the familiar, ever a reminder that *we* are particular beings who can attend to some things only by allowing others to return to obscurity: "...self-concealing, concealment, *lethe*, belongs to *a-letheia* ["disclosure"], not just as an addition, not as shadow to light, but rather as the heart of *aletheia*."[68] This gets rid of Eckhart's "other-worldliness," in two senses of the term. It makes particularities (this-worldliness) crucial to revelation, and—thereby—releases revelation from dependence on an alien and immaterial God.[69]

If we look now at the particulars to which Heidegger attributes the possibility of opening, we can make a transition to how his ideas matter for a cultural account of ethics. Heidegger's list of revelatory particulars in the "Origin of the Work of Art" makes interesting and eclectic reading:

> One essential way in which truth establishes itself in the beings it has opened up is truth setting itself into [art-]work. Another way in which truth occurs is the act that founds a political state. Still another way in which truth comes to shine forth is the nearness of that which is not simply a being, but the being that is most of all. Still another way in which truth grounds itself is the essential sacrifice. Still another way in which truth becomes is the thinker's questioning, which, as the thinking of Being, names Being in its question-worthiness. (OWA 61-2)

And still another way truth happens is the appearance, development, and coming to self-consciousness of a culture. Like an artwork, moreover, which may be preserved or transformed by the criticism it receives and the subsequent artworks it inspires,[70] a culture may be preserved or transformed by the acts of the people it informs. Each act both belongs to the culture and may overthrow it, just as each artwork or critical foray both belongs to the Open of a previous artwork and may establish a new Open, and each question of Being both is rooted in prior questions and may make those questions lose their point. Hence there is room in each culture for the possibility that an act may open up a new Open, beginning a new culture or undermining the old. This is the possibility of radical dissent.

Let us now translate these ideas out of the Heideggerian vocabulary. Radical dissent consists in an act that, unlike political dissent, cannot find and should

---

68 (Heidegger, 1977), p.390.

69 My point here is not to deny that there is a God, but to insist that an ethical theory in the modern world—in the modern West at least—cannot depend on theology (or any sort of other-worldliness): it fails if only theists can believe it.

70 See OWA 67, on the role of "the preservers."

not seek grounding in a minority strain of the political whole, in one legitimate opinion within the debate constituting politics. It has, by contrast, *no grounding at all*, at least insofar as grounds are defined as ethical beliefs held in common by the group in which it takes place; it is, quite literally, criterionless. The radical dissenter may follow some quite gentle and appealing practice, like the Jain unwillingness, in respect for all life, to eat anything but fruits, or may attempt something obnoxious or horrifying, or may hold beliefs and practices that could take a political form—vegetarianism or conscientious objection or opposition to abortion or an extreme commitment to charity—but refuse to justify himself by our traditions and shared norms, or to use any group or spokesperson as a guide by which to adjust his choices. For this person, following the cultural norms around him would in fact be, at least in some respects, mere social determinism, and he declares his freedom by removing his way of living from the need to be justified in such terms.

The question remaining is not, "why tolerate such a claim to right action?" As long as the acts the person performs are themselves not abhorrent to our ethic, are ones both our bodies and our norms can live with, we have no reason not to tolerate them, even if we do not understand them or find their mode of justification obscure. The question we must ask is whether we can, and if we can whether we should, find some way of understanding these acts as true *dissent*, rather than idiocy, as having some ethical place although they fall outside of our normal modes of justification. I think we can and should, for the same reason we should make sense of the Kierkegaardian criterionless choice and the Heideggerian revelatory Open: that the particular culture which alone gives us a perspective at all–the particularity of which enlightens and guides us–is limited by that very particularity, and may be superseded by a new perspective.[71] To use Kierkegaard's language, the absolute truth we have to posit as grounding our ways of making ourselves intelligible, may require us, by its very transcendence of those ways, to suspend them, hence to act rightly but unintelligibly. And in the terms of my own position: the antinomy concerning absolute and relative truth requires us to hold out a possibility that our ways of (ethical) justification are only provisional, and that someone could

71 When I say "superseded," I intend to imply that we at least may regard the overturning of our limitations as an *improvement* on the perspective we had before. Heidegger, as Karsten Harries has pointed out to me, would not intend to imply this: for him, disclosure is a step that never moves "forwards," only sideways. As far as he is concerned, there is no ultimate or absolute truth to which we might consider ourselves to be approximating. I posit such a truth, on one side of an antinomy, and suppose that at least *some* disclosures might be a step forward, out of an Enlightenment interest that I presume we (around here) have in "progress": out of a sense that if we are not to move forward, there will be no sense in moving at all. But this means that we have what Kant would call a practical but not a speculative interest in seeing the overturning of our culture as a possible closer approximation to some absolute truth; we preserve the possibility of a disclosure that would transform our modes of evidence for ethical and not for scientific reasons. We lack, in principle, the means of proving any newly disclosed way of seeking truth to be itself "truer" than the last one.

therefore lay claim to (ethical) truth without adducing supporting statements that would justify or clarify his position to us. We posit such a possibility much as Kant posits the possibility of independence from causal determinism—to make here the truth, there the freedom in ethics intelligible to ourselves. And as there we never know whether any given act represents real freedom from physical causes,[72] so here we never know whether any given position actually represents truth independent of justification.

What, then, is the practical significance of supposing a possibility of radical dissent? Very little. To take the most extreme case, at the level of radical difference we may be unable to rule out Nazism as a possible ethic any more than we can any other way of life—we may be unable to distinguish between the demoniacal and the divin—but that does not mean we should not suppress or attack Nazism, condemn Nazis, even, in any ordinary sense, call the doctrine "absolutely wrong," "absolutely abhorrent," etc. What we have to realize is that in saying "Nazism may, in the radical sense, be right," or "there is a radical possibility that Nazism is right," we are not using "may" and "possibility" in anything like their usual sense. There are here two quite different language-games with the phrase "may be right." One voices a possibility within our ethic. In that case "You may be right" means "I don't know the circumstances of your act well enough," "I haven't thought enough about your practice or justifications," or (when speaking to a political dissenter) "I haven't considered your critique of the majority position thoroughly enough," and implies "When I learn more or think further, I may agree with you." The other language-game voices what Wittgenstein, and perhaps Stanley Cavell, would call a "philosophical" possibility, one that by its very nature reflects only a general fact about our modes of speaking and thinking (grammar), not a consideration one would take into account in making day-to-day decisions. In this case "You may be right" means "Any human being may be 'right,' without my understanding him," not "I need to consider your case further before I make a firm judgment."

Comparing ethics to art is once again helpful. "That may be an artwork," and "you may be an artist," also have a double meaning. They can mean, "I need to look, listen, read more carefully, learn more about your style, or the context in which you work, etc.", or they can mean, "Any human creation may turn out to be a work of art and any human being an artist; your work doesn't seem like art to me, and I don't think further attention will make me change my mind, but perhaps someday, some people will consider it art." (Compare also "Anything can happen," voiced once by an adventurer, another time by a philosopher.) From the dissenter's point-of-view, the practical significance of this radical "possibility" is that its price is silence. Those who dissent from both majority and minority strains in a culture's norms and modes of

72 (Kant, 1964), pp.74-5 (407).

justification cannot expect their neighbors to regard them as noble, or their beliefs as profound. If they do have such expectations, they are confusing their position with that of the political dissenter, and should either enter into the discursive fray—in which they may anticipate refutation, mockery, and the assumption, on the part of their fellow talkers, that anyone shown to be severely out of touch with the tradition will change his mind—or withdraw from it utterly, to the silence of unintelligibility.[73] They may of course appeal, as I have done in describing radical dissent, to the tradition exemplified by Eckhart, Kierkegaard and Heidegger, in order to show us that we know how revelation of truth could (at first, or to some) be unintelligible. But that tradition says only what the possibility of radical newness *might* look like, and *to* the individual experiencing it; it does not and cannot tell us whether any given case instantiates that possibility. Appeal to the tradition therefore cannot by itself win respect for the dissenter from us, although if he is indeed committed, silent, and sincerely apolitical, in the manner recommended by Eckhart, Kierkegaard and Heidegger, we may soften our contempt or condemnation with sympathy and the suspension of explicit judgment. The dissenter may not want to be fully apolitical, in recognition of the possibility that radical dissent can found a new community, but in that case he is expressly in conflict with our society and we have no reason to withhold judgment. In either case, the relation obtaining between this individual and us will take place in silence, although the silence may take the form of a noisy lack of communication rather than an absence of sound.

It is dangerous to give examples of a possibility that resists definition, but I will attempt one anyway, to make my account so far a little more concrete. Let us suppose, for the sake of this example, that while the law had its exceptions, procedural constraints in application, and lenient traditions of interpretation, a prohibition on adultery as deserving of death was in fact enforced and widely accepted among first-century Jews. In any particular case, condemnation might be conjoined with a strict process of judicial inquiry, and a feeling, among the condemners, of some discomfort or guilt about the fact

---

73 "The true knight of faith is always absolute isolation, the false knight is sectarian...The sectarian punchinello...has a private theatre, i.e. several good friends and comrades who represent the universal just about as well as the beadles in *The Golden Snuffbox* represent justice. The knight of faith, on the contrary, is...absolutely nothing but the individual, without connections or pretensions. This is the terrible thing which the sectarian manikin cannot endure. For instead of learning from this terror that he is not capable of performing the great deed and then plainly admitting it...the manikin thinks that by uniting with several other manikins he will be able to do it...The sectaries deafen one another by their noise and racket, hold the dread off by their shrieks, and such a hallooing company of sportsmen think they are storming heaven and think they are on the same path as the knight of faith who in the solitude of the universe never hears any human voice but walks alone with his dreadful responsibility." (Kierkegaard, 1974), pp.89-90. Examples of what may happen when people forget this requirement of an honest and deeply radical challenge to the ethic around them might include the tragedy of Jonestown, or of the MOVE house in Philadelphia.

that "so many go free while this one meets his fate," but no-one would have believed *in principle* that sinful people should not condemn others, that in particular they should not condemn adulterers, or that they should not, in a proven case, condemn an adulterer to death. So whatever exaggerations and misrepresentations of Jewish justice may inform the Gospel account, the general point that Jews would not (ordinarily or ever) have made *this*, Jesus', judgment in the case of the woman taken in adultery, will remain true.

Then Jesus may count as a radical dissenter, telling a story about unconditional love that no body of his countrymen had any way of understanding (as he would put it), or accepting (as they would put it). Only a ragged group of social outcasts followed him around, or so let us suppose, since the Gospel itself invites such an interpretation. Eventually these followers formed a new community, with a new, and significantly different, set of judgments (not just about adultery but about law and love generally), with daily practices that differed slightly but irreconcilably from those of other Jews, and with interests, behind the judgments and the practices, in a new hierarchy. Neither the truth nor the wisdom of Jesus' teachings alone created this new community, as we would have expected if it had simply "grown" out of the judgments of the old community. Instead, to these teachings were added a history—of the sacred events Passion and Resurrection, according to the Christian believer, of the rejection of Jesus' followers by the synagogues, according to the secular historian—and a social context (divinely ordained again, according to the believer; simply a consequence of the history, according to the non-believer). An average Jewish citizen at the time of the woman taken in adultery, or at the time the story of such a woman was circulated, even a "liberal," politically dissenting Jew, would therefore have had no reason to regard Jesus' words as part of the discussion in the Jewish community.

This is a model, if my account is anywhere near satisfactory, not of a Jesus who "corrects" the Jews, but of how something that looks simply like a mistake in judging, to the community in which the judgment originally appears, may reasonably be taken by a later community as a foundation and paradigm case of a new way of living and thinking. The two perspectives I have tried to maintain throughout this book come out here in the fact that a naturalist can describe these events as merely how a new society, and perhaps ethic, tends to develop, while a believer may equally well characterize them as a move toward—or, if Jewish, away from—the truth. The believer will surely adopt this second attitude, but need not feel he can *prove* his attitude correct, any more than the naturalist can prove his. There is simply a shift in judging, which each individual may, or may not, appropriate ethically in his decisions.

The wrinkle in this example is not so much that Jesus' followers regard him as divine, for a very similar story can be told about the Buddha or Mohammed, who are not so regarded, but that the dissenter in this case, as in the cases of the Buddha and Mohammed, winds up forming a new community rather than being accepted as a legitimate alien, a possible truth-seeker, by the old one. There will, however, be similar wrinkles in the stories of any candidate for radical dissenter famous enough to have attracted a following. Is Socrates such a dissenter, or St. Francis, or St. Theresa, or Eckhart, or other Christian mystics, or Jewish, Buddhist and Muslim hermits and strange sages, or Kierkegaard, or his Philistine knight of faith,[74] or Gandhi, or even Thoreau? We cannot say for sure, about any of these people, but the fact that we imagine them as candidates at all tells us how we imagine, and more importantly *that* we imagine, radical dissent as an ethical possibility—somehow, somewhere, even if we do not know exactly where or how.

Conversion

Bernard Williams makes two not entirely compatible remarks about conversion. At one point, he tells us that "there are no fixed boundaries on the continuum from rational thought to inspiration and conversion,"[75] while in another place he says that in the case of moving between "incommensurably exclusive" systems of belief there is "little room...for anything except conversion."[76] In the first case conversion seems but a short way down the reflective road from rational thought, while in the second case it appears more like a leap, a radical shift. The context of the second quotation, however, makes clear that there too Williams considers conversion part, if at the extreme end, of a continuum: "even conversion," he says of the incommensurable case, "had better be something which can be lived sanely,...[which means] 'retaining [one's] hold on reality'...[not] engaging in extensive self-deception, falling into paranoia, and such things."[77]

For the position I am defending, conversion does not belong on a continuum with rational thought. I prefer Kierkegaard's use of the term: "In consequence of receiving [the truth and] the condition [for truth], the course of [the disciple's] life has been given an opposite direction, so that he is now turned about. Let us call this change *Conversion*...."[78] And similarly, Stanley Cavell writes, "[c]onversion is a turning of our natural reactions; so it is symbolized as rebirth,"[79] a passage best read in connection with a paragraph about a page earlier:

> Some children learn that they are disgusting to those around them; and they learn to make themselves disgusting, to affect not merely their outer trappings but their skin and membrances, in order to elicit that familiar natural reaction to themselves;

---

74 *ibid*, pp.49-51.
75 "Internal and External Reasons," (Williams, 1981), p.110.
76 "Truth in Relativism," (Williams, 1981), p.139.
77 *ibid.*
78 (Kierkegaard, 1962), p.23.
79 (Cavell, 1979), p.125.

> as if only that now proves to them their identity or existence. But not everyone is fated to respond as a matter of course in the way the child desperately wishes, and desperately wishes not, to be responded to. Sometimes a stranger does not find the child disgusting when the child's parents do. Sometimes the stranger is a doctor and teaches the child something new in his acceptance of him. This is not accomplished by his growing *accustomed* to the disgusting creature. It is a *refusing* of foregone reaction; offering the other cheek. The response frees itself from conclusions.[80]

Conversion is the realization, or at least *a* realization, of new birth, natality, by which one turns, inexplicably and unjustifiably, to what one takes to be a new version or vision of the truth,[81] a new set of "interests" or "natural reactions," a new way of taking things for granted ("nature") and a new course of life. It belongs to ethical reflection as the antithesis that defines the limits of such reflection, not as itself a limit, an extreme, of such reflection as it normally takes place. In normal or ordinary reflection we consider and debate ethical principles and judgments accepted in (some part of) our society, and we direct the deliberation according to stories and modes of justification similarly familiar to us. It is a familiar fact *that* sometimes these norms and modes fail a person or situation, *that* some people opt, in such circumstances, for a more or less mystical rejection of their old ways and possibly an (equally mystical) acceptance of new ways or a new society, and that we, seeing such a moment of extra-ordinary change, may call it "conversion," but it is not and cannot be familiar to us *what* this conversion consists in. By definition the conversion takes place outside, radically outside, our familiar norms and ways of arguing. We may well, taking up the naturalistic perspective, attribute someone's conversion to his losing grip on reality, engaging in self-deception, etc., while the convert himself feels he has moved closer to reality and self-knowledge without being able to explain to us, trapped in the "old ways," how he has come to this new light on the real and the true. (Faith and dementia, says Kierkegaard, are as close as the divine and the demoniac.)[82] Or we may consider the conversion sane, sincere, and even healthy, while the convert, although he probably agrees, feels we are missing the main point. And if we are concerned with what is truly right rather than the well-being of this particular individual, we *are* missing the main point, for the strange or nutty shift may be the true conversion while the healthy re-orientation of manner and practice may not be a conversion at all. We cannot determine the true convert any more definitively than we can determine the true radical dissenter.

On the other hand, we can imagine the possibility of conversion well enough to rule out for ourselves, and to help others to rule out for themselves, obviously

---

80 *ibid*, pp.123-4.

81 I borrow "version or vision" from (Goodman, 1978), p.2.

82 (Kierkegaard, 1962), p.116.

false conversions.[83] Conversion is not a *mere* shift from culture to culture, like the mere shifts from career to career, love-relationship to love-relationship, or belief to belief, that occur in everyday life within our culture.[84] Nor is it a device to justify positions or actions once the normal channels of our culture have failed; in this sense, too, it does not belong on a continuum with those channels. Hence we can easily proclaim insincere my character Jones in chapter one,[85] who used the indefinability of conversion to elude our condemnation of his sexist behavior. We cannot so easily tell the woman in chador[86] she is insincere or self-deceiving, because it is not clear these terms of ours any longer have a grip on her. But if they do, our claim will have an effect, and if they do not, that in itself is a sign she has indeed converted (begun to convert?). To help ourselves, and to rebuke the merely hypocritical, we can describe the language-games by which we imagine the possibility of conversion. If one is seriously wondering to convert, or whether he has converted, he may ask, "Do I really feel 'called', by an absolute, to a new way of thinking and living? Do I really feel that the extra-ordinary has been thrust forward for me and the ordinary thrust down? Has a new light dawned over the whole of my past life and social context,[87] or am I merely (over-)reacting to a particular incident?" Such questions need not have easy or immediate answers, but they should make us feel silly and ashamed when we are clearly overdramatizing a situation, and they should make more and more sense, take more and more specific forms, and come up in more and more specific circumstances, if we are really converting.

If we think we are converting, but find we are not, or know that we cannot even imagine such a thing seriously, then we should find that we are, and how deeply we are, committed to our own culture. In fact, the passing of a crisis about conversion often leads the individual concerned to explore his own traditions in search of answers to whatever was troubling him. The possibility of dissent and conversion enables each of us to see our consent to our culture as having a real alternative, but precisely when we decide not to exercise that alternative, we may have less fear that our ordinary norms could just "slip away" from us. They will not "slip away" because we are not self-creating, self-sufficient and self-integrating beings onto which cultural norms simply get themselves stuck. Rather, integrity exists within cultures. The language-games by which an ethic or culture makes its specific judgments and defines its way of judging, expresses its toleration and rejection of alternatives to itself, and builds disagreement with and withdrawal from its own norms into those norms themselves, in these very ways constitute what we, as individuals, consider our own integrity.

---

83 Compare the negative criteria, above, for true radical dissent.

84 Any such ordinary change may of course bring on conversion, but then the new job, lover, or particular belief is only the occasion, not the substance, of the conversion.

85 pp.13-4.

86 pp.16ff.

87 OC 141: "Light dawns gradually over the whole." (See text to chapter six, note 20).

BIBLIOGRAPHY

Allison, Henry, *Lessing and the Enlightenment*, (Ann Arbor: University of Michigan Press, 1966).

Anyanwu, KC, "Cultural Philosophy as a Philosophy of Integration and Tolerance," *International Philosophical Quarterly* 25, (Sept. 1985).

Thomas Aquinas, *The Political Ideas of St. Thomas Aquinas*, ed. Dino Bigongiari, (New York: Hafner Press, 1953).

Arciniegas, German, "Culture—A Human Right," in *Freedom and Culture*, ed. UNESCO, intro. Julian Huxley, (New York: Columbia University Press, 1951).

Arendt, Hannah , *Crises of the Republic*, (New York: Harcourt Brace Jovanovich, 1972).

——, *Between Past and Future*, (New York: Penguin Books, 1977).

——, *The Life of the Mind*, vol.s 1 & 2, (New York: Harcourt Brace Jovanovich, 1978).

——, *Lectures on Kant's Political Philosophy*, ed. R. Beiner, (Chicago: University of Chicago Press, 1982).

Aristotle, *Nicomachean Ethics, in The Basic Works of Aristotle*, ed. Richard McKeon, (New York: Random House, 1941).

Arndt, C.O.,& Everett, S. (ed.s), *Education for a World Society*, (New York: Harper & Brothers, 1951).

Ayer, Alfred, *Language, Truth, and Logic*, 2nd edition, (New York: Dover, 1952).

Baudet, Henri, *Paradise on Earth*, trans. E. Wentholt, (New Haven: Yale University Press, 1965).

Bearn, Gordon, *Relativism and Realism: The Nature and Limits of Epistemic Relativity*, Ph.D Dissertation, Yale University, 1985a.

——, "Relativism as *Reductio*," *Mind* 1985b.

Beck, Lewis White , *A Commentary on Kant's Critique of Practical Reason*, (Chicago: University of Chicago Press, 1960).

Bedau, Hugo (ed.), *Civil Disobedience*, (New York: Pegasus, 1969).

Beitz, Charles (ed.), *International Ethics*, (Princeton: Princeton University Press, 1985).

Berger, Peter, "Are Human Rights Universal?", in *Human Rights and US Foreign Policy*, ed.s B. Rubin & E. Spiro, (Boulder: Westview Press, 1979).

Berkeley, George, *Three Dialogues Between Hylas and Philonous*, in *The Empiricists*, (Garden City, NY: Anchor Books, 1974).

Bidney, David, "On the Philosophy of Culture in the Social Sciences," *Journal of Philosophy* 39.

Bloom, Harold, *The Anxiety of Influence*, (New York: Oxford University Press, 1973a).

——, *A Map of Misreading*, (New York: Oxford University Press, 1973b).

Bloor, David, *Wittgenstein: A Social Theory of Knowledge*, (New York: Columbia University Press, 1983).

Bluestein, Gene, "The Advantages of Barbarism: Herder and Whitman's Nationalism," *Journal of the History of Ideas* 24, (1963).

Bok, Sissela, *Lying: Moral Choice in Public and Private Life*, (New York: Vintage Books, 1979).

Borges, Jorge Luis, "Kafka and His Precursors," in *Labyrinths*, ed. D. Yates & J. Irby, (New York: New Directions, 1964).

Brierly, JL, *The Law of Nations*, (Oxford: Clarendon Press, 1928).

Buber, Martin, *I and Thou*, trans. W. Kaufmann, (New York: Scribner, 1970).

Bull, Hedley, *The Anarchical Society*, (New York: Columbia University Press, 1977).

Burke, EM, "State of Pure Nature," (listed as "Pure Nature, State of"), *New Catholic Encyclopedia*, (New York: McGraw-Hill, 1967).

Butterfield, Herbert & Wight, Martin [ed.s], *Diplomatic Investigations*, (London: George Allen & Unwin, 1966).

Cassirer, Ernst, *Essay on Man*, (New Haven: Yale University Press, 1944).

——, *Rousseau, Kant, and Goethe*, trans. P Gutman, PO Kristeller, JH Randall,Jr., (Princeton: Princeton University Press, 1945).

——, *The Philosophy of the Enlightenment*, trans. FCA Koelln, J. Pettegrove, (Princeton: Princeton University Press, 1951).
Cavell, Stanley, *Must We Mean What We Say?*, (New York: Scribner, 1969).
——, *The Claim of Reason*, (New York: Oxford University Press, 1979).
Chatwin, Bruce, *Songlines*, (New York: Viking Books, 1987).
Chiappelli, Fredi (ed.), *First Images of America*, (Berkeley: University of California Press, 1976), vol I.
Cody, A., *A History of Old Testament Priesthood*, (Rome: Pontifical Biblical Institute, 1969).
Cohen, M, Nagel, T.,& Scanlon, T. (ed.s),*The Rights and Wrongs of Abortion*, (Princeton: Princeton University Press, 1974).
Colmer, John, *EM Forster: The Personal Voice*, (Boston: Routledge & Kegan Paul, 1975).
Cooper, David, "Moral Relativism," *Midwest Studies in Philosophy* 1978.
Davidson, Donald, *Essays on Actions and Events*, (Oxford: Clarendon Press, 1980).
——, "Rational Animals," *Dialectica* 36 (1982).
——, *Inquiries into Truth and Interpretation*, (Oxford: Clarendon Press, 1984).
De Sousa, Ronald, *The Rationality of Emotion*, (Cambridge: The MIT Press, 1987).
D'Entreves, AP, *Natural Law*, (London: Hutchinson & Co., 1970).
Devlin, Patrick, *The Enforcement of Morals*, (New York: Oxford University Press, 1965).
Dhami, Sadhu Singh, "The Impact of the British on India," *The Dalhousie Review* 22, (January, 1943).
Dudley, E., & Novak, M. (ed.s), *The Wild Man Within*, (Pittsburgh: University of Pittsburgh Press, 1972).
Durkheim, Émile, *Elementary Forms of the Religious Life*, trans. JW Swain, (New York: Free Press, 1915).
——, *On Institutional Analysis*, ed. & trans. M. Traugott, (Chicago: University of Chicago Press, 1978).
Eckhart, Meister, *Meister Eckhart: A Modern Translation*, trans. & ed. R.E. Blakney, (New York: Harper & Brothers, 1941).
Edel, A. & Edel, M., "The Confrontation of Anthropology and Ethics," *Monist* 47, (Summer, 1963).
Emerson, Rupert, *From Empire to Nation*, (Cambridge: Harvard University Press, 1967).
——, "Self-Determination," *American Journal of International Law* 65, (1971).
Engelmann, Paul, *Letters from Ludwig Wittgenstein, with a Memoir*, trans. L. Furtmueller, ed. BF McGuiness, (New York: Horizon Press, 1968).
Ergang, Robert, *Herder and the Foundations of German Nationalism*, (New York: Octagon Books, 1966).
Feyerabend, Paul, *Against Method*, (Atlantic Highlands, NJ: Humanities Press, 1975).
Foot, Philippa, *Virtues and Vices*, (Berkeley: University of California Press, 1978).
Forster, EM, *A Room With A View*, (New York: Alfred A. Knopf, 1923).
——, *Where Angels Fear To Tread*, (New York: Alfred A. Knopf, 1943).
——, *Howard's End*, (New York: Vintage Books, 1954).
——, *A Passage to India*, (San Diego: Harcourt, Brace, and Jovanovich, 1952).
——, *The Longest Journey*, (New York: Vintage Books, 1962).
Franck, T., & Rodley, N., "After Bangladesh: The Law of Humanitarian Intervention By Military Force," *American Journal of International Law* 67 (1973).
Frankfurt, Harry, "Freedom of the Will and the Concept of a Person," *Journal of Philosophy* 68 (1971).
——, "The Importance of What We Care About," *Synthese* 53, (1982).
——, "Reflections on Bullshit," *Harper's*, Feb., 1987, p.17 (re-printed from *Raritan*, Fall, 1986).
Freeman, Derek, *Margaret Mead and Samoa*, (Harmondsworth: Penguin Books, 1978).
Gadamer, H-G., *Truth and Method*, trans. Sheed & Ward Ltd., ed. G. Barden & J. Cumming, (New York: Seabury Press, 1975).
Gandhi, Mohandas, *Non-Violent Resistance*, (Ahmedabad: Navajivan Publishing House, 1951).
Gardner, Martin, "Beyond Cultural Relativism," *Ethics* 61, (Oct., 1950).
Gay, Peter, Introduction to 1963 re-printing of Cassirer, 1945.
——, Introduction to Ernst Cassirer, *The Question of Jean-Jacques Rousseau*, trans. & ed. P. Gay, (New York: Columbia University Press, 1954).

Geertz, Clifford,*The Interpretation of Cultures*, (New York: Basic Books, 1973).
——, *Local Knowledge: Further Essays in Interpretive Anthropology*, (New York: Basic Books, 1983).
Gellner, Ernest, *Nations and Nationalism*, (Oxford: Basil Blackwell, 1983).
Ghoshal, UN, *A History of Indian Political Ideas*, (Oxford: Oxford University Press, 1959).
Gluckman, Max, *The Judicial Process Among the Barotse of Northern Rhodesia*, (Manchester: Manchester University Press, 1967).
Golding, Martin P., "The Concept of Rights: A Historical Sketch," in *Bioethics and Human Rights*, ed. E. & B. Bandman, (Boston: Little, Brown, 1978).
Goodman, Nelson, *Ways of Worldmaking*, (Indianapolis: Hackett Publishing Co., 1978).
Gould, Steven Jay, *The Mismeasure of Man*, (New York: Norton, 1981).
Gowans, C. (ed.), *Moral Dilemmas*, (New York: Oxford University Press, 1987).
Greenspan, Morris, *The Modern Law of Land Warfare*, (Berkeley: University of California Press, 1959).
Grotius, Hugo, *The Law of War and Peace*, trans. Francis Kelsey, (Indianapolis: Bobbs-Merrill, 1925).
Guttenplan, Samuel, "Moral Realism and Moral Dilemmas," *Proceedings of the Aristotelian Society*, 1979-80.
Haddon, AC, *History of Anthropology*, (London: Watts, 1934).
Hallett, Garth, *A Companion to Wittgenstein's "Philosophical Investigations"*, (Ithaca: Cornell University Press, 1977).
Hamilton, Bernice, *Political Thought in Sixteenth Century Spain*, (Oxford: Clarendon Press, 1963).
Harman, Gilbert, & Krausz, "Moral Relativism Defended," *Philosophical Review* 84, (re-printed in Meiland, 1982).
——, "Relativistic Ethics: Morality as Politics," *Midwest Studies in Philosophy*, 1978.
Harries, Karsten, "Two Conflicting Interpretations of Language in Wittgenstein's Investigations," *Kant Studien*, 1969.
——, "Copernican Reflections and the Tasks of Metaphysics," *International Philosophical Quarterly* 23 (1983).
——, "Truth and Freedom," in *Edmund Husserl and the Phenomenological Tradition: Essays in Phenomenology*, ed. R. Sokolowski, (Washington, DC: Catholic University of America Press, 1988).
Hartung, Frank, "Cultural Relativity and Moral Judgments," *Philosophy of Science* 21, (April, 1954).
Hegel, GWF, *Philosophy of Right*, trans. TM Knox, (New York: Oxford University Press, 1967).
——, *Phenomenology of Spirit*, trans. AV Miller, (New York: Oxford University Press, 1977).
Hehir, J. Bryan, "The Ethics of Intervention," in *Human Rights and U.S. Foreign Policy*, ed. P.G. Brown & D. MacLean, (Lexington: DC Heath & Co., 1974).
Heidegger, Martin, *Being and Time*, trans. J. Macquarrie & E. Robinson, (New York: Harper & Row, 1962).
——, *Identity and Difference*, trans. Joan Stambaugh, (New York: Harper & Row, 1969).
——, *Poetry, Language, Thought*, trans. and intro. A. Hofstadter, (New York: Harper & Row, 1971).
——, "The End of Philosophy and the Task of Thinking," in *Basic Writings*, ed. DF Krell, (New York: Harper & Row, 1977).
Held, V.,Morgenbesser, S.,& Nagel, T. (ed.s), *Philosophy, Morality, and International Affairs*, (New York: Oxford University Press, 1974).
Herder, JG, *JG Herder on Social and Political Culture*, trans. & ed. FM Barnard, (Cambridge: Cambridge University Press, 1961).
——, *Reflections on the Philosophy of the History of Mankind*, trans. & ed. F. Manuel,(Chicago: University of Chicago Press, 1968).
Herskovits, Melville, *Man and His Works*, (New York: Alfred A. Knopf, 1952).
Hobbes, Thomas, *Leviathan*, (Harmondworth: Penguin Books, 1968).
Hodgen, Margaret T., *Early Anthropology in the Sixteenth and Seventeenth Centuries*, (Philadelphia: University of Pennsylvania Press, 1964).
Hollis, M.,& Lukes, S. (ed.s), *Rationality and Relativism*, (Cambridge: The MIT Press, 1982).

Holtzman, S.,& Leich, C, (ed.s), *Wittgenstein: To Follow a Rule*, (London: Routledge & Kegan Paul, 1981).
Honderich, T. (ed.), *Morality and Objectivity*, (London: Routledge & Kegan Paul, 1985).
Horton, Robin, "Professor Winch on Safari," *European Journal of Sociology* 17 (1976).
Hubbard, William, *Complicity and Conviction*, (Cambridge: MIT Press, 1980).
Hyman, Arthur, & Walsh, James (ed.s), *Philosophy in the Middle Ages*, (Indianapolis: Hackett, 1973),
Hymes, Dell, *Reinventing Anthropology*, (New York: Random House, 1972).
Janik, A.,& Toulmin, S. *Wittgenstein's Vienna* (New York: Simon & Schuster, 1973).
Jenks, C. Wilfred, *The Common Law of Mankind*, (London: Stevens & Sons, 1958).
Kallen, Horace, *Cultural Pluralism and The American Idea*, (Philadelphia: University of Pennsylvania Press, 1956).
Kant, Immanuel, *Critique of Judgment*, trans. JH Bernard, (New York: Hafner Press, 1951).
——, *Critique of Practical Reason*, trans. LW Beck, (Indianapolis: Bobbs-Merrill, 1956).
——, *Groundwork of the Metaphysic of Morals*, trans. HJ Paton, (New York: Harper & Row, 1964).
——, *Critique of Pure Reason*, trans. NK Smith, (New York: St. Martin's Press, 1965).
Kedourie, Elie, *Nationalism*, (New York: Fred Praeger, 1960, revised 1961).
Kenny, Anthony, *Wittgenstein*, (London: Penguin Books, 1973).
Khadduri, Majd, *War and Peace in the Law of Islam*, (Baltimore: Johns Hopkins Press, 1955).
Kierkegaard, Søren, *Philosophical Fragments*, trans. D. Swenson, H. Hong, (Princeton: Princeton University Press, 1962).
——, *Concluding Unscientific Postscript*, trans. David Swenson and Walter Lowrie, (Princeton: Princeton University Press, 1968).
——, *Fear and Trembling*, trans. W. Lowrie, (Princeton: Princeton University Press, 1974).
Koepping, Klaus-Peter, *Adolf Bastian and the Psychic Unity of Mankind*, (St. Lucia: University of Queensland Press, 1983).
Kohn, Hans, *Nationalism: Its Meaning and History*, (Princeton: D. Van Nostrand, 1965).
Koivisto, WA, "Moral Judgments and Value Conflict," *Philosophy of Science* 22, (January, 1955).
Kripke, Saul, *Wittgenstein on Rules and Private Language*, (Cambridge: Harvard University Press, 1982).
Kroeber, AL, *The Nature of Culture*, (Chicago: University of Chicago Press, 1952).
——, & Kluckhorn, C., *Culture: A Critical Review of Concepts and Definitions*, (Cambridge: Peabody Museum of American Archaeology and Ethnology, 1952).
——, & Parsons, T., "The Concepts of Culture and of Social System," *American Sociological Review*, October 1958.
Kuhn, Thomas, *The Structure of Scientific Revolutions*, (Chicago: University of Chicago Press, 1962).
Lacquer, Walter,& Rubin, B. (ed.s), *The Human Rights Reader*, (Philadelphia: Temple University Press, 1979).
Ladd, John, "The Issue of Relativism," *Monist* 47, (Summer, 1963).
Lahbabi, M.A., "Cultural Pluralism and Human Civilization," trans. Virginia H. Ringer, *The Personalist* 40, (July, 1959).
Lakin, R.D., "Morality in Anthropological Perspective," *Antioch Review* 21, (Winter 1961-2).
Langan, Thomas, *The Meaning of Heidegger*, (New York: Columbia University Press, 1959).
Lauterpacht, H., *An International Bill of the Rights of Man*, (New York: Columbia University Press, 1945).
——, *International Law and Human Rights*, (New York: FA Praeger, 1951).
Leaf, Murray, *Man, Mind, and Science*, (New York: Columbia University Press, 1979).
Lear, Jonathan, "Leaving the World Alone," *Journal of Philosophy*, 1982.
——, "Ethics, Mathematics and Relativism," *Mind*, 1983.
Leibniz, Gottfried, *Monadology* and *Discourses*, in *The Rationalists*, trans. G. Montgomery with revisions by AR Chandler, (Garden City: Anchor Books, 1974).
——, *The Political Writings of Leibniz*, ed. & trans. Patrick Riley, (Cambridge: Cambridge University Press, 1972).

Lessing, G.E., *Laocoön, Nathan the Wise, Minna von Barnhelm*, ed. WA Steel, (London: JM Dent & Sons, 1959).
Lewis, David, "Radical Interpretation," *Synthese* 27 (1974).
Locke, John, *Second Treatise on Government*, in *The Social Contract*, intro. E. Barker, (New York: Oxford University Press, 1960).
Long, A.A. (ed.), *Problems in Stoicism*, (London: The Athlone Press, 1971).
Lorimer, James, *The Institutes of the Law of Nations*, (Aalen: Scientia Verlag, 1980, (re-print of 1880 Edinburgh edition)).
Lovejoy, Arthur, *Essays in the History of Ideas*, (Baltimore: Johns Hopkins Press, 1948).
——, *The Great Chain of Being*, (Cambridge: Harvard University Press, 1964).
Lovibond, Sabina, *Realism and Imagination in Ethics*, (Oxford: Basil Blackwell, 1983).
Lowie, Robert A., *The History of Ethnological Theory*, (New York: Farrar & Rinehart, 1937).
Lukes, Steven, *Émile Durkheim: His Life and Work*, (New York: Harper & Row, 1972).
McGinn, Colin, "Charity, Interpretation, and Belief," *Journal of Philosophy* 74, (Sept., 1977).
——, *The Subjective View: Secondary Qualities and Indexical Thoughts*, (Oxford: Oxford University Press, 1983).
McGuinness, BF, *Wittgenstein and his Times*, (Oxford: Basil Blackwell, 1982).
MacIntyre, Alasdair, *After Virtue*, (Notre Dame: University of Notre Dame Press, 1981).
McKeon, Richard, "A Philosophy for UNESCO," *Philosophy and Phenomenological Research* 8 (1948).
——, "Conflicts of Values in a Community of Cultures," *Journal of Philosophy* 47, (April, 1950).
Mackie, John, "The Law of the Jungle - Moral Alternatives and Principles of Evolution," *Philosophy* 53, (1978).
Maimonides, Moses, *The Book of Knowledge* (vol. I of the *Mishneh Torah*), ed. & trans. M. Hyamson, (Jerusalem: Feldheim Publishers, 1981).
Mandelbaum, David, "Anthropology," in the *International Encyclopedia of the Social Sciences*, ed. D. Sills, (New York: Macmillan, 1968).
Marcus, Ruth Barcan, "Rationality and Believing the Impossible," *Journal of Philosophy* 80, (1983).
Marquez, Gabriel G., *One Hundred Years of Solitude*, trans. G. Rabassa, (London: Pan Books, 1978).
Mead, Margaret, *Coming of Age in Samoa*, (Harmondsworth: Penguin Books, 1943).
Meiland, J. & M. Krausz (ed.s), *Relativism: Cognitive and Moral* (Notre Dame: University of Notre Dame Press, 1982).
Midgley, EBF, *The Natural Law Tradition and the Theory of International Relations*, (New York: Harper & Row, 1975).
Miller, Kenneth, "John Stuart Mill's Theory of International Relations," *Journal of the History of Ideas* 22, (Oct.- Dec. 1961).
Montaigne, Michel de, *Essays*, trans. JM Cohen, (Harmondsworth: Penguin Books, 1958).
Moore, John N. (ed.), *Law and Civil War in the Modern World*, (Baltimore: Johns Hopkins University Press, 1974).
Mounce, H., "Understanding a Primitive Society," *Philosophy* 48, (1973).
Naipaul, VS, *Among the Believers: An Islamic Journey*, (New York: Vintage Books, 1981).
Nardin, Terry, *Law, Morality, and the Relations of States*, (Princeton: Princeton University Press, 1983).
Nawaz, MK, "The Concept of Human Rights in Islamic Law," *Howard Law Journal* Spring, 1965.
Nealy, F.D., "Ignorance (Moral Aspect)," *New Catholic Encyclopedia*, 1967.
Newton-Smith, W., "The Role of Interests in Science," in *Philosophy and Practice*, ed. A. Phillips Griffiths, (Cambridge: Cambridge University Press, 1985).
Northrop, FSC, "Concerning UNESCO's Basic Document on World Philosophy," *Philosophy East and West* I, (January, 1952).
——, *The Taming of the Nations*, (New York: Macmillan, 1952).
Numelin, Ragnar, *The Beginnings of Dipolomacy*, (New York: Philosophical Library, 1950).
Paelian, Garabed, "The Meaning of Culture," *Indian Philosophy and Culture* 10, (Sept. - Dec. 1965).
Pascal, Blaise, *Pensées: Thoughts on Religion and Other Subjects*, trans. WF Trotter, ed. HS & EB Thayer, (New York: Washington Square Press, 1965).

Penniman, TK, *A Hundred Years of Anthropology*, (London: Gerald Duckworth, third edition, 1965).

Pennock, J. & J. Chapman (ed.s), *Human Rights*, (New York: New York University Press, 1981).

Perry, David, "Cultural Relativism in Toulmin's *Reason in Ethics*," *The Personalist* 47, (July, 1966).

Pettman, Ralph (ed.), *Moral Claims in World Affairs*, (London: Croom Helm, 1979).

Pitcher, George (ed.), *Wittgenstein: The Philosophical Investigations*, (Notre Dame: University of Notre Dame, 1968).

Pitkin, Hanna, *Wittgenstein and Justice* (Berkeley: University of California Press, 1972).

Platt, John (ed.), *New Views of the Nature of Man*, (Chicago: University of Chicago Press, 1965).

Putnam, Hilary, *Realism and Reason*, (New York: Cambridge University Press, 1983).

Quine, W., *Word and Object*, (Cambridge: The MIT Press, 1960).

Rawls, John, *A Theory of Justice*, (Cambridge: Belknap Press of Harvard University Press, 1971).

Reichenbach, H., *Experience and Prediction*, (Chicago: University of Chicago Press, 1938).

Rorty, Amelie (ed.), *Explaining Emotions*, (Berkeley: University of California Press, 1980).

Rorty, Richard, *Philosophy and the Mirror of Nature*, (Princeton: Princeton University Press, 1979).

——, "The World Well Lost," in *Consequences of Pragmatism*, (Minneapolis: University of Minnesota Press, 1982).

Rosenne, Shabtai, "The Influence of Judaism on the Development of International Law," *Nederlands Tijdschrift voor Internationaal Recht*, April, 1958.

Röling, Bernard, *International Law in an Expanded World*, (Amsterdam: Djambatan N.V., 1960).

Rousseau, J-J., *First and Second Discourses*, ed. R. Masters, trans. R. & J. Masters, (New York: St. Martin's Press, 1964).

Sacks, Oliver, *The Man Who Mistook His Wife For A Hat*, (New York: Summit Books, 1985).

Sartre, Jean-Paul, "Bad Faith," in *Being and Nothingness*, trans. H. Barnes, (New York: Washington Square Press, 1956).

Saxena, RK, *Social Reforms: Infanticide and Sati*, (New Delhi: Trimurti Publications, 1975).

Schmidt, Paul T., "Some Criticisms of Cultural Relativism," *Journal of Philosophy* 52, (Dec., 1955).

Schmidt, R., "Cultural Nationalism in Herder," *Journal of the History of Ideas* 17, (June, 1956).

Schrecker, Paul, "Leibniz's Principles of International Justice," *Journal of the History of Ideas* 7, (Oct., 1946).

Schürmann, Reiner, *Meister Eckhart, Mystic and Philosopher*, translations with commentary, (Bloomington: Indiana University Press, 1978).

Scott, James Brown, *The Spanish Origin of International Law*, (Washington: School of Foreign Service, Georgetown University, 1928).

Schutz, Alfred, *The Phenomenology of the Social World*, trans. G. Walsh & F. Lehnert, (Evanston: Northwestern University Press, 1967).

Sen, A. & Williams, B. (eds.), *Utilitarianism and Beyond*, (New York: Cambridge University Press, 1982).

Serra, Antonio Truyol (ed.), *The Principles of Political and International Law in the Work of Francesco de Vitoria*, (Madrid: Ediciones Cultura Hispanica, 1946).

Shafer, Boyd, *Nationalism: Myth and Reality*, (New York: Harcourt, Brace, 1955).

Singer, Milton, "Culture," in the *International Encyclopedia of the Social Sciences*, ed. D. Sills, (New York: Macmillan, 1968).

Smart, JJ & Williams, B., *Utilitarianism: For and Against*, (Cambridge: Cambridge University Press, 1973).

Snare, F.E., "The Diversity of Morals," *Mind* 89, (July, 1980).

Soloveitchik, Joseph, *On Repentance*, trans. & ed. P. Peli, (New York: The Paulist Press, 1984).

Spinoza, Baruch, *Ethics*, trans. S. Shirley, ed. S. Feldman, (Indianapolis: Hackett Publishing, 1982).

Strauss, Leo, *Natural Right and History*, (Chicago: University of Chicago Press, 1953).

Strawson, PF, "Freedom and Resentment," in *Freedom and Resentment and Other Essays*,(London: Methuen, 1974).

Swinburne, Richard (ed.), *The Justification of Induction*, (London: Oxford University Press, 1974).

Taylor, Charles, *Hegel and Modern Society*, (New York: Cambridge University Press, 1979).

Turnbull, Colin, *The Mountain People*, (New York: Simon & Schuster, 1972).
Van Dyke, Vernon, "The Cultural Rights of Peoples," *Universal Human Rights* 2, (April-June, 1980).
Varley, HL, "Imperialism and Rudyard Kipling," *Journal of the History of Ideas* 14, (Jan., 1953).
Versenyi, Laszlo, *Heidegger, Being and Truth*, (New Haven: Yale University Press, 1965)
Verzijl, JHW, "Western European Influence on the Foundation of International Law," *International Relations* I, (Oct. 1955).
Vincent, RJ, *Non-intervention and International Order*, (Princeton: Princeton University Press, 1974).
Viswanatha, S.V., *International Law in Ancient India*, (Bombay: Longmans, Green & Co., 1925).
Vitoria, Francisco de, *De indis et De iure belli relectiones*, ed. E. Nys, trans. John Bate, (Washington: The Carnegie Institute of Washington, 1917).
Vivas, Eliseo, *The Moral Life and the Ethical Life*, (Chicago: University of Chicago Press, 1950).
——, "Reiteration and Second Thoughts on Cultural Relativism," in *Relativism and the Study of Man*, ed. Schock and Wiggins, (Princeton: Van Nostrand, 1961).
Voget, Fred, *A History of Ethnology*, (New York: Holt, Rinehart & Winston, 1975).
Wellman, Carl, "The Ethical Implications of Cultural Relativism," *Journal of Philosophy* 60, (March, 1963).
White, Leslie A., "Human Culture," in the *Encyclopedia Britannica*, 1974 edition.
Wicclair, Mark, "Rawls and the Principle of Non-Intervention," *John Rawls' Theory of Social Justice*, ed. G. Blocker & E. Smith, (Athens: Ohio University Press, 1980).
Wiggins, David, "Truth, Invention, and the Meaning of Life," *Proceedings of the British Academy*, 1976.
Williams, Bernard, *Morality: An Introduction to Ethics* (New York: Harper & Row, 1972).
——, *Problems of the Self*, (Cambridge: Cambridge University Press, 1973).
——, *Descartes: The Project of Pure Enquiry*, (Harmondsworth: Penguin Books, 1978).
——, "Auto-da-Fé," (Review of Rorty, 1982), *New York Review of Books*, April 28, 1983.
——, *Moral Luck*, (Cambridge: Cambridge University Press, 1981).
——, *Ethics and the Limits of Philosophy*, (Cambridge, Mass: Harvard University Press, 1985).
Williams, Raymond, *Culture and Society*, (New York: Columbia University Press, 1958).
——, "Culture and Civilization," in the *Encyclopedia of Philosophy*, ed. P. Edwards, (New York: Macmillan, 1967).
Winch, Peter, *The Idea of a Social Science and its Relation to Philosophy*, (London: Routledge & Kegan Paul, 1958).
——, "Understanding a Primitive Society," *American Philosophical Quarterly* 1 (1964).
Wittgenstein, Ludwig, *The Blue Book and The Brown Book* (New York: Harper & Row, 1958a).
——, *Philosophical Investigations*, trans. Anscombe, (New York: Macmillan, 1958b).
——, *Remarks on the Foundations of Mathematics*, ed. von Wright, R. Rhees, Anscombe, trans. Anscombe (Oxford: Basil Blackwell, 1964).
——, "Lecture on Ethics" and Addenda, in *Philosophical Review* 1965.
——, *Zettel*, ed. GEM Anscombe & GH v. Wright, trans. Anscombe, (Berkeley: University of California Press, 1967).
——, *Lectures and Conversations on Aesthetics, Psychology and Religious Belief*, from the notes of Yorick Smythies, Rush Rhees & James Taylor, ed. Cyril Barett, (Oxford: Basil Blackwell, 1970).
——, *On Certainty*, ed. GEM Anscombe & von Wright, trans. Denis Paul & Anscombe, (Oxford: Basil Blackwell, 1977).
——, *Remarks on Frazer's Golden Bough*, ed. Rhees, trans. AC Miles, (Atlantic Highlands, NJ: Humanities Press, Inc, 1979).
——, *Culture and Value*, ed. GH von Wright & H. Nyman, trans. Peter Winch, (Chicago: University of Chicago Press, 1980).
Wong, David B., *Moral Relativity*, (Berkeley: University of California Press, 1984).
Young-Bruehl, E., *For Love of the World: A Biography of Hannah Arendt*, (New Haven: Yale University Press, 1982).

Philosophy of History and Culture

This series presents original books broadly concerned with philosophical treatments of the ideas of history and culture, with historically and culturally embodied entities, and with methodologies and interpretive strategies pertinent to their explanation and understanding.

1. HERTZBERG, L. and J. PIETARINEN (eds.).
Perspectives on human conduct. 1988. ISBN 90 04 08937 3
2. DRAY, W.H.
On history and philosophers of history. 1989. ISBN 90 04 09000 2
3. ROTENSTREICH, N.
Alienation. The concept and its reception. 1989. ISBN 90 04 09001 0
4. ORUKA, H.O.
Sage philosophy. Indigenous thinkers and modern debate on African philosophy. 1990. ISBN 90 04 09283 8
5. MERCER, R.
Deep words. Miura Baien's system of natural philosophy. 1991. ISBN 90 04 09351 6
6. VAN DER DUSSEN, W.J. and L. RUBINOFF (eds.).
Objectivity, method and point of view. 1991. ISBN 90 04 09411 3
7. DASCAL, M. (ed.).
Cultural relativism and philosophy. North and Latin American perspectives. 1991. ISBN 90 04 09433 4
8. WHITE, F.C.
On Schopenhauer's Fourfold Root of the Principle of Sufficient Reason. 1992. ISBN 90 04 09543 8
9. ZEMACH, E.M.
Types. Essays in Metaphysics and Aesthetics. 1992. ISBN 90 04 09500 4
10. FLEISCHACKER, S.
Integrity and Moral Relativism. 1992. ISBN 90 04 09526 8